GENEROUS LIVES

GENEROUS LIVES

American Catholic Women Today

JANE REDMONT

WILLIAM MORROW AND COMPANY, INC.
NEW YORK

Grateful acknowledgment is made for permission to reprint portions of the following:

"Gather Us In" by Marty Haugen. Copyright © 1982 by GIA Publications, Inc., Chicago, Illinois. All rights reserved.

"For Strong Women" from *Circles on the Water* by Marge Piercy. Copyright © 1982 by Marge Piercy. Reprinted by permission of Alfred A. Knopf, Inc.

Library of Congress Cataloging-in-Publication Data

Redmont, Jane.
    Generous lives : American Catholic women today / Jane Redmont.
        p.   cm.
    ISBN 0-688-06707-7
    1. Women in the Catholic Church—United States.   2. Women,
Catholic—United States—Biography.   I. Title.
BX2347.8.W6R43   1992
282'.092'273—dc20
    [B]   92–7950
                                                                         CIP

Printed in the United States of America

First Edition

1   2   3   4   5   6   7   8   9   10

BOOK DESIGN BY BARBARA COHEN ARONICA

*To my sisters and brothers of the Paulist Center
Community
with love*

*and in memory of Anne Frank,
who taught me, very early, the fragile power of
the written word*

ACKNOWLEDGMENTS

This book owes its life to a multitude of friends, colleagues, and former strangers.

Above all, I want to thank the more than 110 American Catholic women who opened their homes and offices to me and agreed to be interviewed for this book. I thank them for their wisdom and eloquence and for trusting me to be faithful to what I saw and heard.

I thank my lucky stars for John Brockman, my agent, and Katinka Matson, his partner, whose literary acumen and powers of persuasion launched me on this journey. I am deeply grateful to Jim Landis, former publisher of William Morrow and Co. and editor-in-chief of Beech Tree Books, for taking a gamble on me, and to Jane Meara, my first editor at Morrow, for her warm encouragement, her unwavering confidence in my work, and unforgettable lunches at Manhattan's Park Bistro. Elisa Petrini, Jane's successor, jumped into the project with enthusiasm and nurtured me through the final year of writing, offering sound editorial advice and generous hours of comfort on the telephone as head of the neurosis-prevention squad. To have one fine editor is good fortune indeed; to have two in a row is as close to a miracle as one comes in the publishing business.

I owe special thanks to my hosts during my travels around the Lower 48: Barbara and Rafael Aldave, Deborah Blackmore (now Deborah Blackmore Abrams), Anne Burke and Mary Casey, Kate Connolly-Weinert (then Kate Connolly) of blessed memory, Arthur Dewey and Barbara Davis, Chris and Kay Harte, Janet and Ed Harte, Fred and Sarah Hofheinz, Mary Hunt and Diann Neu, Peter Klein, Luke and Marjorie Lamb, Andrew and Stephanie Monahan O'Brien, Mary Olivanti and Jim Simonson, Jacqueline and Ralph Olivanti, Lucy Seal, and my cousins Larry and Magdalena Shushan and Diana Tokaji and Robin Gaster. I thank Joanne Belanger and Greg Rakauskas, Jacqueline Bruhn, Elizabeth Earls, and Susan Thompson for caring for my home and my cat during these research trips.

To find the women of *Generous Lives*, I contacted almost every person I knew in the U.S. as well as some people I had never met. Friends, colleagues, friends of friends, relatives of colleagues, chance acquaintances, laypeople, sisters, clergy (even a bishop or two), Catholics and non-Catholics, women and men helped me to identify and contact the women I interviewed. The fact that I cannot name all these people—who probably number around two hundred—in no way lessens my gratitude to them. For those interviews which I conducted in my imperfect Spanish, I received able transcribing and translation assistance from Jane R. Lindley, Mary Rittinger, and Margie Ruiz.

I thank my parents, Joan and Bernard Redmont, for their support and love during this arduous process, and my brother, Dennis, for his early contribution to the buy-Jane-a-computer fund. Ian Howard kept the computer humming and its innards in coherent order; without him, I would probably be sitting on the floor at this very moment, pasting little pieces of paper together and tearing out my hair.

Writing a first book based on nationwide research with a limited budget and no institutional support (save the precious publisher's contract) is not conducive to sanity, solvency, or long vacations in the south of France. For nearly six years I was my own research assistant, field worker, secretary, office manager, copy editor, gofer, housekeeper, cook, and sole breadwinner. The work was often joyful and never boring. It was also strenuous. During the research and writing of *Generous Lives,* for which I left a full-time job in pastoral ministry, I worked as a freelance journalist, lecturer, and preacher, development consultant, and justice of the peace. I lost several friends to cancer and AIDS; my cat died; my computer broke down several times; I ran out of money and got into debt. I would not have survived with body and soul intact without my friends: They listened to me when I needed to ramble, tolerated my silences and distraction, prayed for me, took me out to dinner, put up with me in my worst moments, and assured me repeatedly that I would complete this project.

For his loving care, endless hospitality, and phone calls at all hours of the day and night, I thank and cherish Peter Klein, whose friendship of over two decades is one of the great delights of my life. Maureen Dallison Kemeza's gentle presence and sharp intellect made a precious contribution to my theological reflection and brought me comfort. Liz Rice-Smith was a priceless conversation partner; her passion for healing and justice and her psychological insight were crucial to the shaping of this work. Kerry Maloney helped me stay on track and laugh. Chandra Taylor Smith prayed, listened, commiserated, and cheered me on. Mary Hunt and Diann Neu were fountains of humor and hospitality. Daughters of several traditions—Baptist, Catholic, Episcopal, and United Church of Christ—these women are my beloved sisters and witnesses to the natural ecumenism that thrives among women in the ministry. Jack Finnegan, my old canon law teacher, former pastor, and friend, took time to muse with me about church structures, human foibles, and what it means to belong. Marie Augusta Neal, Sister of Notre Dame and sociologist, taught me years before this book was born to raise questions about who defines the situation; I will always be grateful to her for that lesson.

Joanne Bray, Rinda Burleigh, Pat Connolly, Michele DiPalo and Jeff Duboff, Gita Esmieu, Gail Garinger and Henry Dinger, Peggy Hutaff, Danielle Lévi Alvarès, Julia Lieblich, Bill Mayer, Maureen McMann, Bart Mitchell and Susan Siebert, Mariette and Marisa Murphy, Rosalind Picard, Ellen Reuter and Phil Haslanger, Jim and Ann Roosevelt, Tom Shaver, Pat Simon, and Dan Wakefield were there above and beyond the call of duty with spiritual and material comfort. Harvey Cox encouraged me from the start and enriched my thinking with his merry spirit and broad vision. Sara Hazel, Chris O'Rourke, and Margaret Studier graciously stepped in to help me with the final mountain of detail. My goddaughter, Lauren Elizabeth Dinger, helped me realize that I needed to take time off from my serious grown-up book to write a story about a princess and two dragons. David Toolan, fellow writer and kindred soul, gave me loving words at the right time.

The members of my writers' group—Reena Bernards, Debra Cash, Ann Claire Greiner, Bernardine Hayes, Gina Ogden, and Elena Stone—have been cherished companions. They have given me a wealth of insights from Jewish and Christian traditions and feminist scholarship, from their professional and activist backgrounds, and from their work in fiction, poetry, criticism, sociology, psychology, and journalism. I am proud to have them as colleagues and friends.

Two of my dearest friends, Judy Neal and Kate Connolly-Weinert, died during the writing of this book. Both were Catholic women. They were strong, loving, and wise. Their presence inhabits these pages. I give thanks for their generous lives.

I thank the women, men, and children of my local church, Boston's Paulist Center Community, to whom this book is dedicated. I thank them for driving me crazy with their cheerful "How's the book?" for six years, for their generosity in feeding the poor and welcoming the stranger, for their friendship, and for their prayers.

Finally, I owe a great debt to Caryl Rivers, who leaned across the table one day in the Boston University faculty dining room and said, "Why don't you write a book about Catholic women?" Thank you, Caryl, for getting me started.

Cambridge, Massachusetts

CONTENTS

Jesus was at Bethany in the house of Simon the leper; he was at dinner when a woman came in with an alabaster jar of very costly ointment, pure nard. She broke the jar and poured the ointment on his head. Some who were there said to one another indignantly, "Why this waste of ointment? Ointment like this could have been sold for three hundred denarii and the money given to the poor." And they were angry with her. But Jesus said, "Leave her alone. Why are you upsetting her? What she has done for me is one of the good works. You have the poor with you always, and you can be kind to them whenever you wish, but you will not always have me. She has done what was in her power to do; she has anointed my body beforehand for its burial. I tell you solemnly, wherever throughout all the world the Good News is proclaimed, what she has done will be told also, in memory of her.

—The Gospel According to Mark

What is needed is a patient unearthing, a purposeful listening, a multiplicity of voices speaking not just from the margins but from the depths, the starting place of healing.

—Elena Stone

Who defines the situation?

—Marie Augusta Neal, SND

GENEROUS LIVES

PROLOGUE

Now this is what I want: I want to hear your judgments. I am sick of the silence of women. I want to hear you speaking all the languages, offering your experience as your truth, as human truth, talking about working, about making, about unmaking, about eating, about cooking, about feeding, about taking in seed and giving out life, about killing, about feeling, about thinking; about what women do; about what men do; about war, about peace; about who presses the buttons and what buttons get pressed and whether pressing buttons is in the long run a fit occupation for human beings. There's a lot of things I want to hear you talk about.

—Ursula K. Le Guin

American Catholic women. When you read these words, what do you see? Do you see an old woman of Irish ancestry with pale, wrinkled skin, fingering her rosary beads in the back of a church? Do you see schoolgirls in uniform, a flock of plaid-skirted, well-behaved children of assorted sizes? Do you see a nun in a habit?

Do you see your neighbor, your coworker, your mayor, your mother, yourself?

Consider this: The Congresswoman rising to debate a bill on Capitol Hill is a Catholic woman; the cashier ringing the register at the supermarket counter is a Catholic woman; the homeless adolescent walking in the rain with a plastic bag over her head is a Catholic woman. The scientist in the nuclear physics lab and the peace activist chained to the fence of a nuclear weapons plant in nonviolent protest are Catholic women. At a demonstration outside a city clinic, dozens of women are carrying signs, both "pro-life" and "pro-choice"; there are Catholics on both sides.

American Catholic women are Vietnamese immigrants in California proudly displaying photographs of their sons in the uniform of the U.S. Marine Corps. They are Mexican-American college students studying marketing in San Antonio. They are German-American farmers in Wisconsin, wiping their foreheads in the August sun. They are African-American lawyers who live in the suburbs of Washington, D.C., and commute back to the city every Sunday to attend their home churches. They are Junior League members volunteering at the Indianapolis Children's Museum. They are women in jail for drug-dealing in Massachusetts.

Many of these women go to church on Sundays, read the Scriptures from the pulpit, distribute the bread and wine of communion at Mass at their local parish. Others refuse to set foot in church except perhaps for a wedding or a funeral. Still others have created their own worshiping communities; they meet in each other's homes, sit in a circle, sing, break bread, and speak new words over the blessing cup.

What does it mean to each of these women to be Catholic? To be a woman? To be an American? This book presents some of their answers. It examines how they vote, love, work, and pray. It is a book on "Catholic women in American society" more than "women in the Church," but it does ponder the reasons why many women remain active, grateful members of the Catholic church and why many others choose to leave, quietly or slamming the door. I have defined as "Catholic" women who are Roman Catholic by birth, upbringing, desire, choice, or affiliation. I am purposely inclusive. If I told only the story of Catholic women who fit a certain mold—only the happy ones, only the angry ones, only the women who go to church—I would not be telling the story of American Catholic women in its fullness, richness, and poignancy.

In 1986 and 1987, I traveled around the continental United States to interview Catholic women in cities and rural areas, in suburban towns and public housing developments. I also conducted update interviews on the phone with some women in late 1989 and early 1990, and a few interviews in 1991. In all, I spoke with and quote in the book over 110 women.* The youngest of these was seventeen at the time of the interview, the oldest ninety-two. Some were recent immigrants, others women whose families had been in the U.S. for generations. They were descendants of landowners and slaves, migrant workers and union leaders, business leaders and salesclerks.

I traveled from the urban Northeast to farms and suburbs in the Midwest and cities on the West Coast; from northern towns where Catholics descended from nineteenth-century immigrants are a majority of the population to stretches of the South where Catholics are in a minority of three or four percent. I visited communities at extreme ends of the country where the earliest Catholic settlers had come: south Texas, where the old Spanish missions still stand and the land was once a part of Mexico; Maryland, where English Catholics from the landed gentry sailed up the Potomac in the seventeenth century; and the Upper Peninsula of Michigan, where Jacques Marquette and his Jesuit companions crossed vast expanses of forest and lake by horseback and canoe.

I tried to encounter each woman as if she were myself in search of a listening heart, and to accord her the respect I would want to receive. Although I did interview a few friends and acquaintances, I actively sought out women whose experiences and cultures were distant from my own. Aware of my own biases, I tried to ask questions that were open-ended and allowed the woman I was interviewing to name the world in her own words.

My sample of Catholic women is not systematic, but it is representative. The diversity of ages, cultures, and life-styles reflects the diversity of the American Catholic female population, with a few exceptions; for instance, while I interviewed Latina women from several different cultures, I spent more time with Mexican-American women in the Southwest than with any other Hispanic group.

I found that the lines between religious or political liberals and conservatives were not as clearly drawn as the media or our own hasty descriptions of each other would have us believe. I met a woman who supported the building of weapons capable of destroying millions of human beings and who took in children unwanted by others to raise them as her own. I met a woman firmly opposed to the ordination of

---

*Some women asked to be given a pseudonym when speaking about specific issues or events in their lives; accordingly, a number of women are quoted under two different identities to protect their privacy. Most of the women agreed to be quoted by name. A few requested that their identities be concealed and that they be given pseudonyms throughout the book. Pseudonyms are indicated by quotation marks.

women in the Catholic church who was studying the Bible in a group led by an ordained Lutheran woman. I met a self-described conservative Republican who was adamantly pro-choice and a self-described liberal Democrat and feminist who believed abortion was murder and should be illegal in all cases.

These are living, complicated, changing human beings. Most of them are what we would call ordinary. They are not famous, though readers will recognize the names of a few well-known women here and there—public officials, writers, a college president. Catholic women today are prominent in politics, education, science, and the arts, and, despite the Church's traditional constraints upon women, in the religious world. They are everyday Americans, working to make ends meet, raising families, concerned about their personal growth as well as the needs of others and the life of their communities.

This book is not based on written questionnaires. It was shaped in kitchens, living rooms, offices, church buildings, coffee shops, and the out-of-doors. Sometimes children tugged at us while we spoke. Some of the women wept. Many of them laughed. Often I cried and laughed with them.

The words *American Catholic women* bring to mind recent controversies about religion and politics, sexuality and authority, academic freedom and Roman documents. Stepping behind the headlines, I found a complex and varied group of people, uncommonly generous, active, and strong. I write *Generous Lives* to honor the experience and wisdom of women who are American and Catholic. It is not meant to be the final word about them. I hope it will generate many conversations both public and private.

This is what I saw and heard.

ONE

MARLENE JONES

"We have so much to give."

Born in the 1940s, Marlene Jones has lived in the San Francisco Bay area for most of her life, but her family roots are in New Orleans, where both her parents were born and raised. We are sitting in the living room of Marlene's apartment in San Leandro, California, where she lives alone.

Jesus is the man who got me through my divorce. Because my pain could never be as great as his, and he survived it. Jesus cried, so I knew it was okay for me to cry. And he had a good time, and he drank wine, and when they ran out at Cana he made some, so I knew it was okay for me to have a good time and drink some wine too. He's so many things. He's my friend, he's my brother. He's the person I can tell things to and it'll never come back to me; I won't be criticized for it; I won't be judged. He's very safe.

God to me is an old black man with wrinkles in his face and white, white hair, a gentle smile and a soft-spoken voice, like a grand-father—like my grandfather: I used to be able to sit on his lap and he'd rock me to sleep. There are times when I can still feel my grand-father's arms around me. God is a friend when there are no friends. I talk to Him in my head, like He's always there. And He is always with me. Always. There's a warmth I feel sometimes when I'm praying, and I can't describe it other than it's very quiet and gentle. It's safe, and I know the Holy Spirit is with me.

I was in the fourth grade when my father and mother moved from West Oakland, which was predominantly black, to East Oakland, where we were the only blacks in the parish. People wouldn't sit next to us. People wouldn't talk to us. My father, being the staunch Catholic that he was, believed that "You don't go to church to serve man; you go to church to serve God. Therefore you will go to Mass on Sundays whether these people acknowledge you or not." So we did.

There was a school attached to the parish. My mother went to enroll us, and the Mother Superior, the principal, wouldn't come out to speak to her. So we didn't go to Catholic school from then on: My mother said she wasn't going to have us exposed to that kind of environment. It's only through the grace of God that all of us remained Catholic, believe me.

My mother was Methodist but went to Catholic school, married my father, and decided to become Catholic after we were [first] enrolled in Catholic school. We spent a lot of summers in New Orleans. It's my second home. I still go once or twice a year. The people are warm and concerned. It was in New Orleans that I had my first experience in a totally black environment. My aunt took me to a concert at Dillard University. I had never been in an environment of all black folks, and I felt something I'd never felt before. I felt that I belonged to something. I was about seventeen.

I have three sisters. As children we used to go to nine o'clock Mass, the children's Mass, and then we'd go to my grandmother's house and she would take us to her church, which at that time was forbidden; you weren't supposed to go into Protestant churches. But my mother, coming from a Protestant background, said, "It's okay, you won't go to hell, I promise you." So we got a taste of both. It was a very nice blend.

[My family] listened to a show on the radio called *The Rosary Hour.* All of us found a certain amount of solace through prayer, so we weren't really forced to do it. I remember praying by myself as a kid all the time: "Give me strength to get through whatever I have to do. . . . Help me in this test. . . . So what if these people don't speak to me, I know You love me, that's all that matters." [God to me was] very present.

For a lot of Catholics I've met, God was to be feared. To us He was always very loving and someone we could turn to when we had nobody else to talk to, and the Blessed Mother was right there by His side. We took that to heart. Even when I couldn't talk to my mother I knew the Blessed Mother understood and would hear my prayers because after all, she was the ultimate; she was the mother of Jesus himself, so she had to be the top banana. I still say my Rosary going to work in the morning.

I graduated from high school, went on to college, and after my second year I met a man and we ended up getting married, and that was the end of my education for a while. I had majored in sociology and minored in music. [I was married at] twenty-one and went to work immediately. Had no choice because at that time he didn't have a job. I had a baby. We stayed married for ten years. My son is now twenty-one.

[My husband and I divorced and I got] married again, [and] by this time I had kind of fallen away from the Church. My prayer life hadn't ceased, but I believed, because I didn't know any better, that I was excommunicated because I was divorced,* and therefore I was an outcast and the Church didn't want me. Even when I went to Mass I'd sit in the back of the church and I wouldn't receive the sacrament, and I felt hollow inside.

So I thought, "Well, I'll go to my husband's church," because he was a Baptist. When I went to his church I discovered that I missed my church even more. I couldn't be a good Baptist. I was Catholic. It was something that was innate. I ended up going back to my church and associating myself with a young priest; he and I talked for hours and hours and hours and hours, and finally my guilt began to become less guilt. He told me a story that I'll carry with me as long as I live. He said, "If Chuckie came to you and he had committed the worst sin in the world, and he was hungry and tired and just needed to be home, would you turn him away?" I said, "Of course not, that's my son. What kind of parent do you think I am?" And he said to me, "What makes you think you're a better parent than God?" And with that, I came back full speed ahead, never more to leave my church again. That was about 1978. To this day he and I remain friends.†

---

*Neither the 1917 Code of Canon Law nor canonical legislation for the American Church ever legislated the excommunication of divorced people. Canons of the Third Council of Baltimore in 1884 (which gave us the *Baltimore Catechism*) specified that divorced Catholics who remarried without an annulment were excommunicated. Other divorced Catholics (those who had not remarried or who had remarried after receiving a church annulment) were not. However, according to Rev. John T. Finnegan, Jr., past president of the Canon Law Society of America, from that date until the 1970s, the U.S. church practiced "creeping excommunication," in which the local tradition enforced by clergy became more strict than church law. Most divorced Catholics believed, or were made to believe, that they were excommunicated.

Excommunication for divorced and remarried people was lifted by Pope Paul VI in 1975. Under this legislation, Catholics who have divorced and remarried without a church annulment may not receive the Eucharist and other sacraments, but are entitled to pastoral care on the part of the church and full participation in parish life. Divorced Catholics who have not remarried, and divorced Catholics who have remarried after obtaining a church annulment, may continue to receive the sacraments, as was technically the case—but not usually the practice—before 1975.

These distinctions are unknown to some and lost on others, who experience the lack of access to the Eucharist as excommunication (the literal meaning of the word).

†Some divorced Catholics seek annulments of their marriages through the diocesan tribunal, which is known as the *external forum*. A church annulment enables a divorced Catholic to receive the sacraments, including a second marriage in the Church. In granting an annulment, the institutional church is not declaring that the marriage never took place, but that the marriage

As it turns out, my second marriage wasn't working. In retrospect, I know now that it couldn't work: It was a marriage for all the wrong reasons. I decided, with the assistance of the same priest, to get a divorce. I said to him, "Now what am I going to do? I can't be a Catholic divorced twice." And he said, "Yeah, you can." The Church doesn't recognize my second marriage. He said, "We're going to get you an annulment from your first husband, because that wasn't to be to begin with." I'm in the process of getting that annulment. It's not a good thing. I didn't walk up an aisle with a veil in front of my face thinking, "Well, if it doesn't work out, I'll just get a divorce." I was going to be married for the rest of my life. I have to almost prove to the Church that for whatever reason, I wasn't mature enough to be married, which I wasn't. It wasn't a good marriage; my first husband is an alcoholic; it hurts to have to talk about it. My first husband and I remain friends to this day because we have the tie that binds and that's our son. Now I have to open up those ugly old wounds. But I have no choice; if this is what I have to do, then I'm willing to do it. It's important to me because my church is important to me. There isn't a perfect institution in this world, and the Church is no different.

When I was married to my second husband I did very little [in the community]. The things I was involved in were things that he was involved in. For a while I really lost a little bit of my identity. But then I was invited by the bishop to be on the advisory board for the Pastoral Center for Black Catholics for the Diocese of Oakland, about five years ago. This board meets the needs of black Catholics that are not met on a parish level. A prime example was myself. There was no way in the world that I could go to my church and have my needs met. You can take that white, European church and do whatever you want with it, but when I want to say, "Thank you, Jesus," I can't do that in a white church. I had never heard gospel music in a Catholic church;

---

was never sacramental in the full Catholic understanding of "sacrament" because of one or the other partner's incapacity for full relationship or his or her lack of commitment to the permanency of marriage. It does not, contrary to popular belief, deny that there was a human marriage or have any bearing on the legitimacy of the children of this marriage. Still, "If you push this too far logically," says one canon law expert, "it has holes in it." Church law does provide another avenue known as the *internal forum*. It may be used as an alternative to the tribunal, in cases in which the divorced Catholics and the clergy determine that seeking an annulment would be either dehumanizing or discriminatory—for instance, in the case of persons whose level of literacy would prevent them from filling in lengthy forms, or whom the process of going through the tribunal would severely alienate from the Church. In the *internal forum*, the return to the sacraments follows the divorced person's ongoing conversation with the priest and consultation with his or her conscience.

I don't think I'd want a steady diet of it, but I certainly liked it. We had revivals, we'd have men's days of prayer, ladies' days of prayer, picnics where black folks could get together and share their faith, their love for each other, and maintain that camaraderie that will always be there.

Through the Pastoral Center, I organized a group for black divorced Catholics, because through my trials I discovered that there were black Catholics who, in 1985, 1986, still didn't know that you could go to Mass and go to communion on Sunday [if you were divorced]. They were living pre-Vatican II. It was as if they waited for the priests in the pulpits to say to them, "It's okay for you to do these things now." And how many priests are going to get up there and do that? They don't. Plus, the Office for Divorced Catholic Ministry is in Pleasant Hill; there are no black folks in Pleasant Hill. So I made an appointment with the bishop and I expressed my concern. I told him that it was only through my suffering that I realized that other people are suffering. I got a group together and we now have thirty [members] and that's where my heart is.

Sometimes we get hassled. But the important thing is the director of Divorced Catholic Ministry in the diocese is behind us a hundred percent, along with the bishop. I was asked by a white priest who is also on the advisory board to the bishop, "Why is it necessary that 'you people' have to have your own group?" There are reasons why people get together in their own groups—not to set themselves aside or apart from other people, but there are problems that are innate to black people like there are problems innate to other races and they want to deal with them on that level. To me it would be like airing my dirty laundry if I told somebody, "My husband left me for a white woman, and I can't deal with that." I don't want to express that in mixed company.

Most of the people in my group, including myself, had really, really heavy guilt trips laid on them by their families. They didn't ask you if you were hurting: "What are you going to do about church now? You can't go to communion anymore! What's going to happen?" Well, the truth of the matter is that you can go to communion, and nobody's going to stop you. You have to do what your heart leads you to do. I don't think any person can turn anybody away from the table of God. Most divorced Catholics I know are simply not waiting for somebody to say, "Okay, it's time, you may go to communion now." And thank God for it. We had people in our group who were [sitting around waiting.] There was one man who had been divorced for thirteen years who went to Mass every single Sunday, sat in the back of the church. Never remarried; there wasn't even a reason for him [not to go to communion.] He didn't even know [he could go]. I understand. I didn't go to communion. If this priest had not talked to me the way he talked to me I probably would be sitting in the back of the church now, too.

My parish is predominantly white. The people are very warm, very gracious, good people: that's what makes a parish. It's big—two thousand. I sing in the choir. My father belongs to the St. Vincent de Paul Society and he works diligently. My whole family's in the same parish. I moved out here when Chuckie was a baby, and that's the parish I was in, [so I stayed]. Believe it or not, they weren't nice at all, back then. Something happened; maybe God just smiled on them and softened their hearts.

I thought [Vatican II] was the best thing that ever happened. I didn't have a difficult time adjusting to it; maybe that's because of my Protestant mother. I used to think priests had consecrated hands: This man stood with his back to me and did something I could never understand, and it had to be good because I was there every Sunday and every Holy Day. All of a sudden one day I woke up, and I thought, "Maybe it's not so right and I don't understand all this and why does he have to turn his back on us, and why do they have to say Mass in a language that nobody understands? That is really dumb." That was before the changes. But I had no choice. Then [Vatican II] happened and I was grateful: I think God heard our prayers. I have friends who are priests who are really men. I have girlfriends who are nuns who are women; they're not somebody up there someplace that you don't even look at. Remember when nuns had to travel in pairs and had to be in before the sun went down, and you didn't dare see a nun eat? I didn't think they ate.

[Reconciliation]* has a place because it's a sacrament, but it has a very small place. I don't need to go to the priest to tell him my sins. I like to think I have a pipeline to God. I can do that for myself. I can pray and when I've done something wrong I can ask God for forgiveness. I don't need a middle person to do that for me. I'll go to Reconciliation maybe once a year, especially around Easter because that's that old thing,† but other than that I don't go.

---

*The changes in name reflect an evolution in the theological understanding of the sacrament—from Confession to Penance to Reconciliation—though Catholics tend to use all three names interchangeably.

†Prior to Vatican II, the requirement to receive communion at least once a year (the "Easter Duty") focused on confession as a necessary preparation for the Eucharist.

When we were kids if you ate meat on Friday that was a mortal sin and if you didn't get to Mass on Sunday that was a mortal sin. And then there were the venial sins. Sassing your mother was definitely a venial sin. I can remember going to confession and telling the priest that I didn't empty the garbage and I was really sorry for that and my mother was really irritated with me. I don't know if I can define sin. If a girl went out and got pregnant twenty-five years ago she had committed a sin. But is that really sinful? I don't think so. Maybe sin is going over to another country and blowing them up. Killing people is sinful. Poverty is sinful. Illiteracy in this country is sinful.

[What makes me angry] is people mistreating people. People lying to each other. The games people play. Husbands mistreating their wives. Wives mistreating their husbands. People mistreating their children. Children are precious. God gives us children and they're supposed to be loved and nurtured and that doesn't always happen. People shooting people. The U.S. going over to other countries doing things they have no business doing. Those things make me angry.

[The key issues for me] are nuclear armament—reducing it—and social issues: welfare, Aid to Dependent Children, jobs. We spend billions of dollars to kill each other and when it's all over nobody will be able to tell the story. That's dumb. That's real dumb. There are people sleeping in the streets and we spend millions of dollars to murder people. Why do people have to sleep on the streets? I heard on the news that there was a house in Oakland where people were sleeping; the house was boarded up and nobody lived in it, and they made those people move. I don't understand that. And we're sending money to the Contras when we need to feed our own. Sometimes I think we need to mind our own business a little bit more. My grandmother used to say, "Charity begins at home and spreads abroad."

Do you know what I do? I pray to people I have loved who have died. I know my grandparents are saints, and I pray to them. I had a friend who at forty-two died, a week before last, and I pray to Philip because I know he was a good Christian, and a loving friend. Sometimes I even feel their presence; I can still feel my grandfather's arms around me, just as I felt them when I was a child.

[For me Mary] is high on the totem pole. She's really high. Christ left her when he was twelve years old and teaching in the Temple. And she had to know how to deal with that. She had to allow him to go and be the person he came here to be. That's not easy for a mother. It wasn't easy to send my son to his father when I knew I couldn't provide the right environment here at home [with my second husband].

It wasn't easy for me to put my son on an airplane and send him to [college in] a place I'd never heard of before. She's the mother of all mothers. She's the queen of all queens.

[Catholicism means] tradition. There's vestments and beautiful music and pipe organs and grand pianos and bishops and archbishops and popes and cardinals and it's all those things that make Catholicism what it is. I don't know any Catholic who doesn't like to have a good time. And that to me is a good time. This diocese had its twenty-fifth jubilee, and the bishop was [dressed] in fuschia. I said to him, "Don't you look handsome in your beautiful fuschia." That's what it's all about. It's the tradition. It's saying the Rosary with your family, it's the special treatment you get when you make your First Communion or your confirmation.

All the ethnics had the food concession at this twenty-fifth, and I was slinging barbecue all day long; all I had time to do was to go in the bathroom and wash my face and put this cotton jumpsuit on [before the celebration]. All the people were dressed up because, after all, the bishop was going to be there, and I smelled like smoke. So I said to him, "Do you recognize this scent?" He said, "No, I don't think so," and I said, "It's called 'Eau de Barbecue.'" He laughed. He's a real dear.

I'm a Catholic because my father was a Catholic, because his father was a Catholic, because *his* father was a Catholic. I don't put anybody's religion down. I sometimes go to a Protestant church when I want to hear some really good gospel music and I want a fire-and-brimstone sermon. There is only one God; there are many paths to Him. And it makes no difference how you get there as long as you get there. I not only have a tradition in my family, I like that tradition. I like being a Catholic.

There's an aura about the papacy. I truly believe that St. Peter was the first pope and this man is walking in St. Peter's shoes and that's not a lightweight role. You've got to have somebody up there; there's got to be a leader. I respect that office. I just wish he'd change some of his views. Maybe in time.

I don't think I could be so outspoken and opinionated if it wasn't for the women's movement. It's nice to see women doing things in church. [Our parish has altar girls.] I like that a lot. One day they're going to realize that women can be priests. [If I could] see women in the pulpit, that would be the biggest change I'd want to see. I have [heard women preach]. It is a grand experience. They have so much to say and so much to give. We can learn so much from them. [And priests] should have the option [of getting married]. I think it's almost sinful to take that option away from a human being.

"Feminist" means some woman who has the confidence, the know-how, and sometimes the plain old gumption to stand up for what she believes in. I can speak my mind and not be sorry for it. I can tell them how they treat women. I've never thought of myself as a feminist, but if that makes me a feminist, so be it. Some would say black women have been feminists all their lives. We had to be strong. We had to be loving. We're still mothers. We had to stand up and speak our piece because our men couldn't. We had no choice.

I think the Church is outdated in its practices of birth control. Especially now with AIDS. What are you supposed to do, abstain? I'm human and I'm not going to do that. And I'm not going to have a baby either, at forty-three years old. I wouldn't make a very good mother at my age. [They should] open their eyes; wake up and smell the coffee. It's that simple.

My heart tells me that it's a crime to kill a baby and a fetus is a baby. My head tells me that it's my body and that if I want to do it it's my business. I don't think anybody can dictate that to anybody. The Church tries. But I have a problem with it. If abortions were illegal, poor folks would suffer, with the back-room abortions, women bleeding to death. If a woman wants an abortion she's going to have one, one way or another.

My son is at Langston University in Langston, Oklahoma. It's good for him. He had never been in a black environment, had no sense of who he was or where he was as a black male in America. His first semester he wrote me a letter I'll never forget; he said, "Mom, you will never believe this. The professors are black, the president of the college is black, all the students are black. And there are girls! There are black girls in this school!"

I have no doubt that Chuckie will be a good father and a good husband. He spent enough time around his mother and his aunts and his grandmother to know how to treat ladies. I think that's something women have to teach their sons. You just don't grow up knowing you have to sometimes send flowers or tell somebody they look nice or they smell nice. If a child doesn't learn that, he doesn't know that. Chuckie knows it. And hopefully he'll get a good wife who'll want babies. I look forward to baptisms and First Communions and Confirmations and all those things. The cycle goes on.

I would probably be devastated if I found out that my son was gay: I wouldn't have grandchildren; I wouldn't see a "normal family" and I place so much credence on that. But I certainly wouldn't toss my son to the wind. The reality is there are gay people all around us and if we are to be as Christ is, we have to love them too. I don't think Jesus would have turned anyone away who was gay. And I wouldn't either.

[I'm a] credit analyst. I'd rather be doing other things, but for right now, it's not a bad job. I have forty units to finish [at college]. I hope to finish in a year; my job will pay for it. My son's away at school, and my life is my own. I can do anything I want to do for the first time. One day I'd like to have a job I'd really like. But I especially want someone to share my life with. One day God's going to bless me with that. This time God will find a man because I'm not looking. He's going to take this man and place him in my life and I'll know that it will be right.

Right now I feel more successful than I've ever felt in my life, and it certainly doesn't have anything to do with anything monetary. I'm free. I've grown. If that's not success, I don't know what is.

Today it's good to be black and Catholic, because the Catholic Church is now recognizing our gift of blackness. That's important; we have so much to give. Hopefully they'll hear us. We don't want to take over. We don't want a separate church. I'm a cradle Catholic, and I want to be able to say, "I'm black and I'm Catholic" because both of them mean equally as much to me. I'm not embarrassed by either nor will I be intimidated.

Being an American, I'm free. Being a black American, I'm free. I'm free to worship in my church in the way that my parents and grandparents and great-grandparents did and as my son will and his children will. Maybe that could only happen in America, and for that I'm grateful; I'm thankful to Almighty God. I'm thankful that in America I can say, "This is what I'm going to do. If you don't give it to me I'm going to take it." I could only do that in America, to my knowledge: Say it, and take it, and don't turn around to see if anybody is coming behind you to get it. You say it and you take it and that's it. Hopefully we won't have to take it because it's ours anyway. But if we do, we will.

TWO

PLURALISTIC AMERICANS, POETIC ADULTS: CATHOLIC WOMEN TODAY

Religion is imagination before it's anything else. The Catholic imagination is different from the Protestant imagination. You know that: Flannery O'Connor is not John Updike.

—Andrew Greeley

We are not now and never have been a white, middle-class nation. And in our own perilous times it seems absolutely essential that all of us who write for the public about the definition of America must make it powerfully clear that our only humane future as a nation is located in a multi-cultural, multi-vocal, multi-racial territory.

—Vincent Harding

"We"—meaning by "we" a whole made up of body, brain and spirit, influenced by memory and tradition—must still differ in some respects from "you," whose body, brain and spirit have been so differently trained and are so differently influenced by memory and tradition. Though we see the same world, we see it through different eyes.

—Virginia Woolf

Marlene Jones's wisdom, embedded in the ordinary life, can transform our public conversations about religion, love, and the common good. Change often begins with the telling of stories.

The past two decades have produced a wave of books on the experience of women. They embrace the fields of psychology, literary criticism, sociology, history, religious studies, poetry, and political science. One of the best known, Carol Gilligan's work on women's psychological development and moral decision-making, speaks of the "different voice" of women.[1] This voice has not fully found its way into public conversations and institutions; it is thus absent from the policy discussions that shape our lives. Men and women, Gilligan writes, differ in their understanding of human relationships and in their mode of making moral decisions. Neither way of viewing the world is better than the other; what is detrimental is for one voice to be neglected, ignored, silenced, or devalued, and for the other to be presented as the voice of universal human experience.

Respect for the ordinary experience and wisdom of women was the recurring wish of the women I interviewed. This was especially true when they spoke about their church. Not all the women I met lamented the hierarchical nature of the Church, the exclusion of women from the ordained ministry, or the use of exclusively male language in worship, though well over half were displeased with one or more of these areas. But virtually all wondered aloud whether they are viewed as fully adult human beings in their religious family. "The respect just isn't there," said Cincinnati social worker Roberta Tenbrink, echoing Catholic women around the country. In this way, the women I interviewed were not unlike the diverse group of Catholic women consulted by the U.S. bishops in preparation for their forthcoming pastoral letter on women's concerns.[2] They expressed a range of opinions about feminism and the roles of women and men in church and society; the very word *feminism* was a source of some ambivalence among them, as it is for other Americans today. But all agreed that women had distinctive experience and wisdom to offer and asked that they be recognized.

One of the changes Catholic women most wanted to see in the Church was the opportunity for women to bring this wisdom into the public forum, whether the pulpit, the seminary classroom, or the policy-making bodies of the Church community. Many women longed for the powerful symbol of female leadership in the sacramental life of the Church, but even more of them wanted, quite simply, a public voice in the Church's corporate life. I asked Carmen Benavente de Orrego-Salas of Bloomington, Indiana, what she thought of the proposed bishops' pastoral on women's concerns. "It would be more appropriate if there were some women bishops," said Carmen, who does not consider herself a feminist.

Some women simply noted the lack of acknowledgment they had experienced and observed. "Men cannot move themselves too much without us women," said Rafaela Canelo, a nurse's aide and community worker in San Francisco. "We women in the Church do many things that are not recognized. Sometimes we work more than a deacon, more than a priest, and they don't realize it. They do not know how much time we are working in the community; they absolutely do not notice it. We are the deacons who walk in the street seeing the suffering of people. We women are continually working day and night and that work is not recognized. And the work that we do in a spontaneous way, with good will, without looking for recognition of any kind—we do this simply because it is our vocation, and because our feelings are sensitive in regard to suffering."

"If we look at what women have been doing in life, we see that a large part of it can be called 'active participation in the development of others,' " Jean Baker Miller, M.D., writes in *Toward a New Psychology of Women*.[3] As a matter of course, women "do for others," often unselfconsciously, as Rafaela Canelo points out. Among Catholic women raised with self-giving love as the Christian ideal, this movement toward others is doubly ingrained. Being a good Catholic and being a good woman have been synonymous with living a generous life. But women have often cared for others at the expense of caring for self. Many of the women I interviewed spoke of learning the difficult lessons of self-love and had begun to include neglect of self in their definitions of sin.

Rarely did this new perspective eliminate or even diminish the generous impulse. Catholic women are still, as in the past, "doing for others" in both their public and private lives. What they are beginning to do (fearing that they are selfish even as they do it) is to examine the ways in which they exercise their altruism and generosity, and to make more conscious choices about them: to care for others, but to take care of themselves. Marlene "lost a little bit of my identity," she said, when she was married to her second husband, giving up all community involvements but his. But when she began to recapture her own interests, they led her to found the support group for black divorced Catholics, a place where she could both nurture and be nurtured.

Marlene Jones and many of the other women who speak through this book share a common perspective with scholars of women's studies, labor historians, artists exploring forgotten cultures, and theologians who write from the perspective of the poor: The only way to understand and protect our common humanity is to encourage a fuller, richer chorus of voices. "We widen our circle," Vincent Harding writes, "not in a quest for modish 'diversity' but out of a deep hunger for authenticity."[4] What we need, in other words, is to learn to think in the plural.

The many and the one: This issue dogs today's Catholic Church in and outside the U.S. The American Catholic church today is theologically, liturgically, politically, culturally, and sexually diverse. Can the Church become catholic and remain Catholic? How, as a body, will it continue to deal with the pluralism in its midst?

During the writing of this book, diversity also became a major topic of public discussion in the United States, as it does in some form every time this country undergoes a major shift in the composition of its population. Debates about multiculturalism in education and the arts and editorials about the fragmentation of the American social and cultural fabric began to fill the newspapers. Does the center hold? they asked. The Catholic and American debates began to parallel each other. They became the constant background of this book.

Of the many voices in church and society, some have been loud, others muffled: Sooner or later, talk of pluralism leads to talk of power. Power is the ability to make and enforce decisions, but even more fundamentally, the capacity to define reality and have one's definition believed. Catharine McKinnon writes about the relationship between power and perceptions of reality: "Having power means, among other things, that when someone says, 'This is how it is,' it is taken as being that way. . . . Powerlessness means that when you say, 'This is how it is,' it is not taken as being that way."[5]

Filmmaker Henry Hampton uses a visual analogy to make the same point. "It all depends on point of view," writes Hampton, the producer of *Eyes on the Prize,* the television series about the civil rights movement and its aftermath. "Point of view, while rarely stated, tells you whose world it is and who controls it."[6] What life looks like depends on where you stand.

"Who defines the situation?" Sister Marie Augusta Neal, S.N.D., used to ask her sociology of religion students as a visiting professor at Harvard. Who decides what is important? Who decides what is true?

In the news business, who decides what is news? In public life, who makes policy? In couples, friendships, and families, who defines what constitutes love and loyalty? In the Church, who proclaims and comments on the message of the Gospel? Who leads the community in its public prayer? Who decides what the Church is and what defines a Catholic?

"This is how it is," Marlene and the other women said to me. "This is how we define the situation." This book deliberately moves their definitions of the situation—in the Church, in society, and in their private lives—"from margins to center," in the words of the biblical scholar Elisabeth Schüssler Fiorenza.[7]

Just as it would be a mistake to assume that men and women think alike or that the wisdom of one can be subsumed within the other, it may be equally dangerous to assume that all women—and all Catholic women—speak in one voice. More than their similarities, what struck me first about the women I interviewed was their diversity: the regional differences, the racial and cultural, ideological and religious differences. This made the appearance of common threads all the more remarkable.

American Catholic women cannot be defined, nor do they define themselves, simply in their relationship to the institutional Church. For some, Catholicism is a conscious and pervasive influence, for others not. Catholic women (and Catholic men) do not have a uniform relationship to their Catholicism. They affiliate and identify in a variety of ways. Joy Duffy, an executive secretary in the San Francisco office of a major accounting firm, said to me, "I've never thought of myself primarily as a Catholic woman; I identify as a woman hard at work." Joy was raised a Catholic, attends Mass on Sundays, and easily answers "Catholic" when asked about her religion, but "Catholic" is not her primary identity. For Marlene Jones, on the other hand, the adjective "Catholic" signifies a more active, intense, and communal reality.

Catholicism shaped the memories, the daily life, and the imagination of the women I met, but it was filtered through a variety of cultural forms, through the social and bodily experience of being female, through the prism of each woman's family background, and through her American identity. Marlene Jones is who she is not only because she is Catholic, but because she is African-American, because she was born in the 1940s and came of age in the 1960s, because of her educational, economic, and emotional histories, because she is a mother, because her roots are in New Orleans and her home is in the San Francisco Bay area.

Being a Catholic woman in the United States has as much to do with "American" and "woman" as it does with "Catholic." These three realities not only coexist but mingle: Sometimes it is hard to distinguish and sort them out. When Mary Wunnicke welcomed me into her Wisconsin farmhouse and set a place at the family table for me, was her generous hospitality a product of the Christian teaching on love of neighbor, of women's traditional priority of caring for others, or of the neighborly spirit of the American heartland? Hard to tell—probably all three.

American Catholics today number between fifty-four and seventy million, depending whose research one decides is authoritative and how one chooses to define a Catholic.[8] Andrew M. Greeley has pointed out in several of his works of sociology—most recently in *The Catholic Myth*[9]— that Catholics are now more highly educated and highly paid than their Protestant counterparts. By the mid-1980s, sixty-one percent of Catholics in this country were white-collar workers as opposed to fifty-five percent of Protestants. Greeley has documented in several of his books the "twin revolutions taking place within the American Catholic population—the change from counterreformation to ecumenical age and from immigrant to professional."[10] According to George Gallup, Jr., and Jim Castelli's *The American Catholic People*,[11] the percentage of Catholics with a college background (currently estimated at forty percent) has more than doubled in the last twenty years. Both Greeley's research and Gallup and Castelli's reveal the American Catholic people to be increasingly educated, tolerant, and supportive of women's rights.

Was there ever, even in the days when the shape of the liturgy and the words of common prayer were uniform, a single American Catholic culture? The novels of Mary Gordon have popularized the Irish Catholic immigrant urban culture of the Eastern seaboard, but they reflect only a part of the American Catholic experience. In the neighborhoods and outskirts of Boston, where I live, I pass a Roman Catholic church every few miles, sometimes every few blocks. As I drove from Virginia into North Carolina on one of my research trips, Fundamentalist Bible programs made their appearance every half inch on the car radio dial. Catholic churches were scarce. "This is the Bible Belt," twenty-three-year-old police officer "Jenna Santini" told me as she discussed her life in a southern city. "They don't understand why Catholics can drink, dance, and party." In the South, Catholics appear lax to other Christians, who view with suspicion their leisure habits and the fact that Catholics do not espouse a literalist approach to the Biblical text. In the North, on the other hand, Catholics are often perceived (or stereotyped) as conservatives by members of other faiths. "Every now and then," said Brigette Rouson of Washington, D.C., a twenty-nine-year old attorney, "somebody will say, 'Oh, you're Catholic—you're not supposed to drink, you're not supposed to curse, you're not supposed to smile, you're not supposed to have sex' "[12]

Life in the "Catholic ghettos" of New York, Philadelphia, and Boston is far from the experience of the women of Minnesota and Wisconsin with whom I spoke. (Both states have significant Catholic populations.) Recalling her pre–World War II Minnesota childhood, the writer and *Commonweal* columnist Abigail McCarthy said, "The Catholic church was the One True Church and there was always a certain upset when someone married a non-Catholic." Yet midwestern Catholics, "except for the Chicago Irish, came from rural parishes and had a life that was more like their Protestant neighbors. There's no way you can be separate in a village of five hundred. My little town had two thousand people. Nobody was on top so nobody could be below. There was a kind of practical ecumenism. We went to each other's church socials; we used the gymnasium in the public school because we didn't have one in the Catholic school. All our Protestant friends came to Midnight Mass because that was the best show in town. I don't think this is part of the experience in the eastern enclaves." "There is no Catholic ghetto in rural America," thirty-eight-year-old Ellen Reuter said to me, remembering her childhood in a small Wisconsin town. "The real distinctions were between town and country. That mattered more than whether you were Lutheran or Catholic."

In the Northwest, Catholics are in the minority—but so are members of other faiths. In Washington and Oregon, a significant percentage of the population[13] reports no affiliation to a religious group. "So it's not taken for granted as it is in the Northeast that most people belong to a church," Mary Boys once said to me. A Sister of the Holy Names and professor of theology at Boston College, she grew up in Seattle, Washington. "In our neighborhood, people across the street were Mormon, Assembly of God, Catholic, and a number weren't churchgoers." She added: "The other thing that strikes me about Catholicism [in Boston] is that the institutional church has been a political player to a degree that it simply couldn't be in the Northwest. You'd never find a Monsignor O'Brien Highway in Seattle."

Whatever their relationship to the surrounding regional culture, all American Catholics have been affected by the reforms of the Second Vatican Council. Announced in 1959 by Pope John XXIII and brought to completion in 1965 by John's successor, Paul VI, the Council did not define any new dogmas of the Catholic Church. Instead, this gathering of the world's bishops spoke to the Church—and, for the first time in history, to the world at large—about the character of the Church itself, its inner life, and its mission in the world.

One of the most significant changes brought about by the Council was the transformation of the understanding of the relationship between church and world. The language of the Church, both locally and in official documents, began to change. Drawing on biblical and early Christian sources, the Council documents spoke of the Church not as a bastion under siege, but as a presence in the world; not as a stronghold, but as a sacrament; not as a purveyor of Latin culture, but as a teacher and student of the message of Jesus Christ among the varied peoples of the earth. This redefinition of the relationship between church and world has affected Catholic understandings of mission, religious education, social justice, ministry, theology, and the relationship between culture and religion.

Alongside the shift in relationship between church and world came a shift in Catholic self-understanding. Marlene was not alone in welcoming the sea change of Vatican II. Vatican II, the women said, helped them to be adult Christians, responsible both for themselves and for their church. "I attribute to Vatican II a whole new emphasis on personal responsibility for religion in your life and what it means to you," said Margaret Patrice Slattery, a Sister of the Incarnate Word who is chancellor of San Antonio's Incarnate Word College.

The question of what it means to live one's faith as an adult is alive in Catholic circles around the world, but I was struck in interviewing the women by the particularly American flavor of their responses. Free speech, freedom of assembly, freedom of religion, and participatory democracy have left their mark. So too have individualism, free enterprise, and the habit of participating in voluntary associations. Accustomed to these realities in their society, American Catholics at the end of the twentieth century look for them in their church. When they do not find them, they begin to feel restless.

In her speech to Pope John Paul II during his 1987 visit to San Francisco, Donna Hanson, bishop's secretary for social services in the Diocese of Spokane, Washington, gave voice to the sentiments of many of her peers: "When I come to my church," she said, "I cannot discard my cultural experiences. Though I know my church is not a democracy ruled by popular vote, I expect to be treated as a mature, educated, and responsible adult." American Catholics, increasingly, are neither obedient children nor adolescents in revolt in their relationship to their church and its leaders. "In my cultural experience," Donna Hanson continued, "questioning is generally not rebellion nor dissent. It is rather a desire to participate and is a sign of both love and maturity."

Firmly grounded in her American identity, Marlene Jones also has strong cultural ties. The influence of culture and ethnicity on Marlene is obvious because she consciously brings to Catholicism what she names "the gift of blackness." But all of us are shaped by—and shapers of—culture, though we may be more or less conscious of it. "We belong to our culture before it belongs to us; we are not culturally neutral beings," says the theologian Lucien Richard, O.M.I.[14] The hold of culture is stubborn because culture is a function of the senses and how they were educated. Culture is what we speak and eat and sing and what we think is beautiful. It is the shape of our house and the way we break our bread. Culture is what we remember, from the collective stories passed on by family, teachers, and community leaders. It is the way in which we imagine what it means to be a people.

The Second Vatican Council recognized the crucial role of culture in the shaping, healing, and fulfillment of the human person. At Vatican II, the Catholic community "appeared for the first time as a world Church in a fully official way," said the Jesuit theologian Karl Rahner.[15] No longer was Catholicism synonymous with Latin or even Western culture. "We are finally becoming truly a 'catholic' church," Archbishop Rembert Weakland, O.S.B., of Milwaukee wrote a decade later. "Our unity will no longer be sustained by the cultural expressions of Western civilization. The bond of the Western empire now makes no sense to Catholicism."[16] Since the Council, this "new world order" of Catholicism has emerged as a major issue within the American Catholic church and in the Church at large, as Catholics seek to live their Christianity in ways that are faithful to their cultures.

Always ethnically diverse, the U.S. Catholic church has grown even more so in recent years following the immigration of Catholics from Vietnam, the Philippines, Haiti, and Central America. Hispanics now make up the largest and fastest-growing cultural group in the American church. They are in fact people of many cultures—Caribbean, Central American, Mexican, and South American—and not all are immigrants, contrary to popular misconception. "The Anglo world is the latest invader of these parts, not the Indian, Mexican, and Spanish," writes Joel Garreau of the area of south Texas where I conducted many of my interviews with Mexican-American Catholic women. "It's the borders that have moved, not the founding cultures. There are great numbers of Hispanics in the Southwest who can't be told by ignorant Anglos to go back where they came from. They *are* where they came from."[17] This accounts for some of the resistance to cultural and linguistic assimilation among Hispanic Americans.

"We Hispanics have never melted down," Mary Esther Bernal said to me, "because of our culture and our language. You can't take it away from us. I cannot buy the melting pot concept," said Mary Esther, who is director of bilingual education for the San Antonio Independent School District. "I believe in the tapestry, or the tossed salad, that which gives us diversity." Preserving cultural traditions, Mary Esther asserted, "doesn't lessen Hispanic allegiance to the U.S.A.; during the war, you could walk down the streets and the people who had their sons at war, like my mother-in-law, would hang out the flag on the front porch [and you'd see all these flags]. And to this day you pass the houses of people who have sons in the service, the poorest of the poor, and you'll see the U.S. flag. We are patriotic, we believe in the U.S. because we have a country for the people, of the people, and by the people. I think it's the greatest system. But I still can't buy that you've got to become like mainstream America, whatever that is."

Among the women I interviewed, the women we now call minorities, but who will soon form the majority of the American population, asked me repeatedly to write about the importance of culture to them as American Catholic women. While most of them felt strongly about the roles and rights of women, the issue they tended to stress above all others was that of cultural identity.

The Mexican-American women I interviewed in Texas attended segregated schools through the 1950s, drank at "colored" water fountains, and were made to ride at the back of the bus. Often, as in Marlene Jones's early life, racial discrimination was part and parcel of African-American women's experience of church. In the same church, laity, sisters, and clergy became active in the civil rights movement. All of these experiences are part of the American Catholic story.

But women's point, when they stressed the importance of culture, was not that they had suffered prejudice. Rather, they emphasized time and again that they could maintain their distinctive cultural identity and be concerned about the common good. In fact, they said, one enhances the other. "God put us in different cultures, right?" Nicaraguan-born Rafaela Canelo said to me in Spanish as we sat in her apartment in San Francisco's Mission District. "All cultures have important values," Rafaela said, "and those cultural values are like a mosaic within the Kingdom of God. So there is a dialogue between one and the other. The Filipino, the Hispanic, the Anglo-Saxon, the Chinese—

all have values and a tradition and all those things are an individual richness, and I believe you have to preserve them."

Rooted in her culture and shaped by her relationships with her loved ones, Marlene Jones also maintains a vital relationship to her religious tradition. Critical yet positive, she remains affiliated with the institutional church and finds wisdom for her life there. She knows what has been destructive to her and what has been redemptive. She tests her tradition against her experience, as most women do, and has made a decision to contribute to this tradition, as some women have.

Marlene does not see herself as a dissenter. Nor does she use the word *dissent,* favored by both the Vatican and the American mass media. It is not part of her vocabulary. The overwhelming majority of the Catholic women I interviewed share this trait.

An observer of American Catholic women for decades, Sally Cunneen writes in her most recent book, *Mother Church: What the Experience of Women Is Teaching Her:* "The voices of women . . . are often interpreted—as it appears Pope John Paul apparently interpreted the polite but firm voice of Sister Theresa Kane*—as voices of opposition, threats to authority, rebels who want to overthrow the divinely mandated role of men. Such a picture fits easily into the framework of popular journalism, because it offers a public image of dramatic conflict. As I hear them, however, these women are actually offering constructive insights on common problems."[18]

It is no longer unusual for a layperson like Marlene to found and coordinate a church group such as the Black Separated and Divorced Catholics Group of the Diocese of Oakland. The rise in leadership of the laity is not simply or even primarily a consequence of the growing shortage of priests but a fruit of the post–Vatican II spirit. (American initiative and women's concern for the care and feeding of human relationships surely play their part as well.)

When the Second Vatican Council began to speak of the Church as the people of God, its words fell on welcoming ears in the United States. During my years as a Catholic campus minister and church staff member, the major developmental transitions I witnessed involved a sense of ownership, a move from understanding the Church as "they" to experiencing it as "we." For Marlene, the Church is home. It is "her

---

*During Pope John Paul II's first visit to the United States, in 1979, Sister Mary Theresa Kane, president of the Sisters of Mercy of the Union and of the Leadership Conference of Women Religious, appealed publicly to the pope in these words: "The church in its struggle to be faithful to its call for reverence and dignity for all persons must respond by providing the possibility of women as persons being included in all ministries of our church."

people." It is *her* Church, flawed as it is. She belongs to it, but it also belongs to her.

"I like being a Catholic," Marlene said to me. The same sentiment appeared a few years later in the opening pages of Andrew Greeley's *The Catholic Myth*. Greeley recounted a guest appearance on the Phil Donahue show: "Now, Father Greeley," Donahue said, "don't you think it would be better if all these dissenting Catholics left the Church? Wouldn't it be better for everyone if only those who agreed with the pope remained Catholic?" He added, "Why don't they just leave?" "Because," Greeley answered, "they like being Catholic."[19] Marlene's inconclusive attempt to find a home in the Baptist church, her attachment to the sacraments, especially the Eucharist, her humorous relish of pomp and ceremony, her stubborn membership in the body of the Church ("It was something that was innate") support Greeley's contention that the tie that binds, for Catholics, is not just institutional but poetic.

What makes these women Catholic? What keeps them in and draws them back? I agree with Greeley. The memory of the liturgy sits deep inside the body and soul. Treatises and declarations about Jesus, God, and the human community may be written in the language of rationality, but it is movement and smell and music that imprint upon the being. The Creed is true, not as "one plus one equals two" is true— the truth of mathematics—but as "I love you" is true—the truth of poetry. The poetry of Catholicism, Andrew Greeley argues in *The Catholic Myth,* is what makes American Catholics Catholic—and what keeps them Catholic, whatever their relationship to the institutional structures may be.[20]

More deeply than theological arguments, then, what holds the fractious body of the Church together is "the message in the media," in the words of author and theologian David Toolan, S.J.: "The lighting, smells, rhythms, incantatory sounds, the polyvalent density of Catholic symbols salted our souls, the earth itself, with a grandeur we could hardly name. In contrast to the Protestant stress of the Bible's literal word, we Catholics were a pre-Gutenberg phenomenon with a bias for the charity of God made palpable to the five senses and the sympathetic nervous system. It is this earthy 'taste' of God that has been our glue, the source of our adhesion."[21]

Women's relationship to the sacramental life of the Church is passionate and double-edged. "I think," Ellen Reuter said after speaking of the centrality of the Eucharist in her life, "that what connects women with the Church is women's sensitivity toward ritual. Women are more sensitive to all that taste and touch and smell stuff and that's why Eucharist has such holding power." The sacramental nature of the Church is what gives "the women's issue" in the Catholic church its particular intensity. The message of faith, the erotic power of ritual, the language, authority, and structure of the Church, the respective positions of the ordained ministers and of the laity—all coalesce in the celebration of the sacraments. Sacraments are sources of healing, symbols of belonging, times of feeding, places of peace. For some Catholic women—not all, but a growing number—the sacraments also wound, exclude, starve, and distress. For these women, the sacraments become freighted with contradiction, evoking all these realities at once—belonging and exclusion, satiety and deprivation, peace and distress—a painful twist that Greeley does not address.

The Church's worship reflects and engenders a vision of the world: The earth, not just the soul, is salted with heaven's taste. Catholics, Greeley writes, "are more likely [than Protestant Christians] to imagine God as present in the world and the world as revelatory instead of bleak." To a colleague who asserted that Catholics were "becoming just like everyone else" by questioning traditional teaching on sexuality and authority, Greeley retorted: "We *imagine* differently." Greeley calls this Catholic imagination "sacramental" or, borrowing theologian David Tracy's word, "analogical." It is this imagination, Greeley says, that accounts for the Catholic emphasis on image and art, community and institution, and devotion to Mary and the saints.[22] American Catholic women, shaped by the songs, stories, and sacraments of their church, embody this form of imagination: For them, God is present—*present,* not suggested, not reflected, not evoked—in nature, in the bread and wine of the Eucharist and of family meals, in friendship, celebration, suffering, and the human community. Creation does not veil God but reveals God. Everything—at least potentially—has religious signifi-cance.

The belief that God is present in the ordinary life is characteris-tically Catholic. It is also typically female (as Elizabeth Dodson Gray has vividly shown in *Sacred Dimensions of Women's Experience*).[23] Mar-lene's trust that God lives and moves in her life and in the lives of her family and friends is characteristic of the women I met. Like all of them, she has a rich inner life, and like a majority of them, she has a comfortable relationship with God, Jesus, and the saints that sustains her through difficult times.

Marlene's spirituality, her church affiliation, her cultural identity, her relationships with her family and friends, and her concern for the common good of society are overlapping commitments. There is not, in her life or in the life of most Catholic women, one compartment for God, another for love, and a third for work and public life. Faith and spirituality are the means of her connecting her many commitments and concerns.

Catholic women are reexamining what it means to live a godly life. Can one be a good woman, a holy woman, and fully sexual? Other religious traditions have their own version of this question. American Catholic women wrestle with it in the context of their own upbringing, in which marriage and celibacy (either as a single woman or as a nun) were presented by church teaching as the only options for living a holy life. For those women who are single and sexually active or those whose partners are women, this framework often creates conflicts both internal and external; some women, like Marlene, simply bypass official teaching in certain areas. Many, including women whose lives followed more traditional paths, spoke to me of the relationship between sexuality and spirituality and of their efforts to integrate in a healthier way these two vital dimensions of their being. What I found everywhere, among women of all ages and life-styles, was a reluctance to live a life in pieces, a yearning for a life in which one can be, all at once, spiritual and sexual, smart and good, and not have one exclude the other.[24]

I found few crises of faith among Catholic women and much hunger for the life of the spirit. Where there was a crisis, it was a crisis of institutions. Whether they embrace or deplore the shape of the institutional church, Catholics are rarely neutral on the subjects of structure and authority. When I asked the women how they would change the Catholic church if they could, they invariably mentioned the need for structural change. They spoke of the inflexible nature of church government and, even more frequently, of their desire for smaller, more personal communities of faith.

Like Marlene, the women were strongly aware of belonging to a universal church, grounded in two millennia of history and reaching to the ends of the earth. Nevertheless, the pope was less of a concern than the local pastor, the curia less than the parish council, the theological disputes on the world scene less than the experience of prayer in the local community. For most Catholic women, the local church is where the questions of Catholic identity, mission, participation, and responsibility are played out.

The documents of Vatican II speak of the Church as a pilgrim people, always on the way, open to new insights from a God who is alive in history and present as Holy Spirit in ever new revelations. The same documents also continue to affirm the hierarchical nature of the Church. To this day the tension between these two perspectives plays itself out in the Catholic church throughout the world. Beneath the rise of grass-roots "base communities," beneath the conflicts between liberation theologians and the Congregation for the Doctrine of the Faith, beneath church women's growing insistence on sharing leadership and decision-making responsibilities, are questions about the nature of the mysterious and messy reality called "Church." What is the Church? Is it a "we" or a "they"? Who is a Catholic? Who defines and decides this? What is the relationship of the Church to social, political, and economic realities, to poverty and violence? What is the heart of the Gospel message? What is the Church's mission in the world? Does the current shape of the Church help or hinder this mission?

Concern for the common good pervades the Council documents, which speak of the need for Catholics to "read the signs of the times,"[25] looking at historical events and social realities of the contemporary world in the light of faith and looking to them for challenge, warning, and hope. Less than a decade later, the world's Catholic bishops would declare that the work of transforming society is a "constitutive"—that is, central and irreducible—dimension of the preaching of the Gospel.[26] For Marlene Jones, morality involves social structure and politics as much as sexuality. It is about intimate relationships, but also about public life. When asked about sin, Marlene speaks of war and homelessness. Though not every woman shared this perspective, I found it to be widespread; it is certainly typical of the direction in which Catholic moral thinking has moved in the past few decades. And inevitably, many of the women brought to bear the same standards of justice and fairness in their judgment of society and of the Church.

In interviews with women around the country, I heard not only longing for personal integration, but urgent yearning for the mending of the world. Why bring muffled voices to speech and marginal people to the center of the human circle, why examine painful and complicated inequities of power, if not for the purpose of healing?

"Does the center hold?" This is not women's question. The questions preoccupying American Catholic women sound more like this: What is the right way for us to be in the world? Can our church help us to answer this question? Are we as women full, adult members of this church and of our society? What legacy will we give our children?

Catholic women do yearn for unity, but spoke of rifts in society due to violence and prejudice more than they brooded over the unity of the Church. For them this unity is a given. They are more concerned with imbalances and abuses of power both religious and secular.

When "different voices" like Marlene's begin to speak—"This is how it is, for us"—and to ask, "What is the right way for us to be in this world?" other voices worry aloud: "Does the center hold?" Explicitly or not, the "different voices" ask: "Whose center was it, really?" When new partners enter the public conversation, the center may shift. The story we tell ourselves about who we are is going to change.

THREE

NANCY VITTI

"Okay, God, you're the pilot."

Nancy Vitti attended public schools through the tenth grade. Except for the first few years of her children's life, she has worked outside the home since the age of sixteen. Nancy has been a file clerk and a child-care worker, made tags for women's blouses, and worked as a beautician; she now drives a school bus for handicapped children. Her husband sells foreign cars, owns a body shop, and manages a catering hall. Nancy was in her mid-forties when we spoke at the kitchen table of her home in Brooklyn, New York.

I'm born in Brooklyn. My father was born in Italy but was brought here when he was twenty-two months old. My mother was born here; her mother came from Sicily. My mom was a homemaker and my father worked in a shoe factory. My father finished grade school, that was it. Any book that we brought home from school he used to take. We'd say, "Daddy, we have to do our homework." "All right, I'll get it to you in a few minutes," [he'd say]. And he would read *everything*. He was a self-taught man.

[In my family] there's three girls and a boy—and you know who's spoiled. My grandmother spoke Italian in the house. I used to frustrate her because I understood everything that she said but I wouldn't speak it. Now I'm sorry, especially I'm married to a man that comes from Italy and when we get together with his family it's like I'm from another planet because half the time I don't know what they're saying unless it's sign language.

My grandmother was very religious. She sat and she read her prayer book every night, every day, whenever she could sit down. She went to church every night. I guess we picked up the importance of it through her. It's so normal in our life that it doesn't seem different. You prayed to God for whatever was going on. My parents didn't go to church but my mother made sure that we did our catechism.

I didn't make my communion or confirmation until I was about eleven because I was a big chicken: I had a nun that was a heavy and a big mouth and she scared me. She had a bell. When you answered a question wrong, she used to ring this bell. So I never wanted to go. I feared going to church. I didn't want to listen to Sister Thomasina. Then, when I was about ten or eleven, my mother says, "You *have* to make it." So I went and I made both of them [communion and confirmation] two weeks apart. And I looked like a big dummy: all these little kids in their white dresses and me and my big, lanky self.

The day that I made my confirmation, my mother was wondering where I was. I was washing windows in the church. Sister Thomasina said, "Oh, the bishop can't pass through here and see these dirty windows." It was like a hall that you had to walk through and maybe eight or ten windows. So Nancy washed them. I was making confirmation at two o'clock and it was one o'clock and I still wasn't home. And I was *filthy*. My mother was going to kill me, I think: "You have to take a shower and get ready for your confirmation and you're washing windows, which *I* wouldn't ask you to do, but you're doing it there!?"

My mother always prays to Saint Anthony; he's her patron saint. At the time my father's father died, my brother, who was named after him, Anthony, was very sick. My mother swears that she saw Saint Anthony in front of her rising with the child. She got scared; she thought it was a sign that my brother wasn't going to live. Then the next day, she heard my grandfather [Anthony] died. She's religious in her own way. She believes in God. But as far as going to church, no, outside of weddings and funerals.

My parents were very open if we had a question [about sex]. It wasn't, "Shhh, you don't talk about that." We could sit at the dinner table and discuss it. [My parents said to us,] "Be a good girl." Which meant, "When I say come home, be home." If you were with the wrong one that they didn't like, [either friends or dating,] you had to break that relationship. I was kind of stubborn. I was the black sheep, more or less. Many times my mother came after me. And she didn't care if we were in front of friends or not: If we did something wrong, she'd smack us. At eleven years old she caught me smoking. She made me eat two cigarettes. It cured me for a while.

I met Raymond [,my first husband,] on a blind date. Raymond worked on the racetrack. [He was an] exercise boy. When we knew each other two weeks, we were engaged, and married eight months later. He was Baptist and a Heinz 57 as far as [I know]: I had asked him once, "What are you? I mean, we're going to get married and have children. The kids are going to want to know what they are." He said,

"I don't know. You could ask my mother." Maybe there's Irish because her great-grandmother's name was Kelly; we figure there's Irish, French, German; they've been here since the *Mayflower*.

I had two children. I was married three months, pregnant with the first. They had told me I'd never have a baby. Twenty months later, had another one. I was married ten years. Then Raymond had a heart attack, the first one; six months later he died. He was thirty-three. I was twenty-seven. My kids were seven and nine.

[I got remarried in] '75. My husband's nine years younger than me. Keeps you young. He was engaged to my father's friend's daughter and the marriage didn't go and he happened to come around. I said, "I go out on Friday nights. While you're here in New York, if you want, tag along." [So I went out with him and we got engaged.] I tried [to have kids with him] but no luck; went through an operation, everything. I have a grandson, so I make up that way. [My kids are] twenty-eight and twenty-six. One has a five-year-old and she's expecting another one; she stays home and takes care of the kids. [The other daughter] is a career girl. [My daughters aren't churchgoers.] They never really were.

You marry for better, for worse. Too many marriages today, kids get into and they say, "Well, if we have an argument, if it doesn't work out, we'll get divorced." When my girls were getting married I told them, "Before you go into marriage you sit and you understand the vows you're going to take: good, bad, and whatever, you're going to be there." [But if you're divorced and you want to get remarried and the Church makes it hard on you—] that I think is foolish. This is a man-made law. I think you should be able to go in front of God. I'm probably contradicting myself [here].

[Homosexuality] is okay. Whatever people decide. How they want to live sexually is their business. Some of them I feel can't help it because they're born that way. [It's] hormones; then you know when you're very young that you're gay. But there [are some who are] because they chose to be lesbian or gay; they found more happiness, more contentment.

[After I got married I didn't go to church as much,] not as steady, every Sunday Mass like I did before. It wasn't because my first husband was Baptist, because he used to take me to church when we were in Kentucky. It's just that I went when I wanted to go; I used to go some Sundays and I always made December eight, Immaculate Conception Day. [Mary was important to me.] They all were. Mary; Joseph [,who] was my patron saint; and Saint Lucy. Saint Lucy gave her eyes for somebody that couldn't see and I thought it was terrific that you could be that unselfish. My church that I grew up in was called Saint Lucy. I always felt very peaceful with that church. I was married and baptized there. It was more than my parish. It was like my second home because that's where I was most of the time [as a kid], either at Confraternity* or just sitting down in front of the church.

Later on in life I went to Saint Jude because in the hospital somebody gave me Saint Jude oil. My first husband had six coronary arrests in one day, and the doctor told me, "Go in and pray that he dies. He's just going to be a vegetable and he'll never come out of this coma." There was a woman there, her father was dying. She gave me a little bottle of Saint Jude oil. She said, "Just keep putting it on his forehead, make the sign of the cross, and the little novena card, just keep reading it over and praying." And the doctor says to me, "Please stop." I said, "No, I want to do it," and he said, "Okay." And my husband came out of the coma, and the doctor said to me, "It worked. You really needed a miracle for him to come back." I feel that Saint Jude did help me because he astonished *everybody*. I brought him to classes for the interns and they asked, "How many coronary arrests can you have in one day and still talk about it?" They all said "Three, four." And [the doctor] said, "Here's a man had six." And he made him walk up and down.

Another one of my saints is Matthew. He was the tax man. I think we learned from him that money isn't everything. He gave up the money in order to be a follower of Jesus. They always want money [in church] and I don't go for that. And I hear stories. Like this girl, she wanted to marry a divorced man and she spoke to the priest. She came back and told us if she had $10,000 he would marry them. And she said, "For money you're going to marry me? Forget it." She wound up getting married in a Protestant church.

When I got married we got married in a Catholic church. Raymond was Baptist so we couldn't get married on the altar,[†] we had to get married at the rail.[‡] I told the priest, "I want to marry him. He's not Catholic. He's not going to change his religion; I'm not going to ask him." He said, "Okay, you have to sign a special dispensation," which was, he didn't object to my practicing my religion, and if anything

*Confraternity of Christian Doctrine (CCD), the traditional name of the Catholic program of religious education for children.
[†]Catholics say "on the altar" to mean "at the altar" or "around the altar," e.g. "there were three priests on the altar."
[‡]Before the Second Vatican Council, people in ecumenical marriages were permitted to be married in the church sanctuary, but at the altar rail rather than up at the altar.

happened to me my children would continue being raised Catholics.*
We signed it. [The priest] said, "If you put fifty dollars in the envelope
to the bishop, he'll approve it faster." I got mad. I said, "If I don't have
the fifty dollars to put in there, what is he going to say: 'No, you can't
marry him'?" But my husband said, "Fifty dollars. We're spending so
much now, what's fifty dollars?" [It took] a week and a half [to get
approved.] It might have gotten approved in a week and a half anyway,
but we'll never know.[†]

When I was pregnant with my daughter I wanted my sister to be
godmother. My sister was pregnant and the priest wouldn't let her
become godmother—because she was "carrying original sin." And my
sister said, "If I didn't get pregnant I would [have] committed a mortal
sin;[‡] but because I have a child in me and this child is not baptized
yet, I'm carrying original sin?!" So my aunt had to be the godmother.
[This was in] 1961.[§]

I believe priests should get married. I don't see anything wrong
with that. It might do some good because a priest that has a family
will be more into what we're going through. On the outside it's very
easy to say, "You should raise your kid this way." I was always taught
that they used to get married, but then [at one point] this pope decided
they shouldn't get married anymore; he must have had a lousy marriage.

[I started going to church even less] after my kids were in their
teenage years. The changes, the Latin to English and shake the hand,[‖]
not knowing what to do. . . . I felt I could stay home and if I wanted
to go to church, I could put on the TV and really see the fullness of

*Before 1966, ecumenical couples were required to be married in a Catholic church and to make
an explicit promise that their children would be raised as Catholics. The non-Catholic partner
was required to take explicit instruction in the Catholic faith. Currently, if a marriage between
a Catholic and a member of another Christian church is to proceed with the blessings of the
Catholic church, it can take place in either church (say, in a Methodist church if one of the
partners is Methodist). The couple must participate in a marriage preparation program (several
options are available) and the Catholic party promises to do "all in my power" to raise the children
as Catholics, which allows for the possibility of other options.

†As far as I know, this is highly unusual, but I have no reason to believe Nancy Vitti was lying,
and I have heard of a few other such instances. Normally it does not cost anything to get a
dispensation, except in some cases for a small fee of no more than five dollars to cover handling
costs.

‡By using birth control, which was considered a mortal sin at the time.

§Even at this time—immediately before the Second Vatican Council—this priest's statement was
a rather outrageous one, based on a distorted theology of creation and a faulty understanding of
the sacraments.

‖A reference to the Greeting of Peace before the reception of communion, during Mass, when
members of the assembly turn to each other and shake hands or embrace with the words, "The
Peace of Christ be with you" or "Peace be with you."

the Mass. And I didn't like a lot of hypocrites out there; they go to church to look like goody two-shoes. Meanwhile they're [saying], "Oh, look at her dress, look at her shoes." I go because I want to go. When I feel I want to, I have [the] church around the corner.

When the [changes in the Church] came in, I remember first no more Latin Mass. And then it became guitar playing, which I didn't care for. I still like the old Latin way. It's like listening to any other language; after a while, you kind of grasp. I think it was more religious or something. Now, it seems like they change whenever they want. I don't know what to do when I go to church now. I have to watch everyone.

At the time they stopped where you can't eat meat on Friday I couldn't understand. It's God's rule you don't eat meat on Friday; now all of a sudden you can. But as you get older you realize these are man-made laws; and they change them to the way they want, when the Vatican comes down.

I don't really [pay much attention to the pope.] He's a lovely man. I think he should stay home a bit, though. I think John XXIII was the best pope, [because he was] loving, accepting.

I think the bishops are stepping into things that are out of their religion. They go over to all these other countries. They seem to be making the Church look like the tough guy. I don't think they belong in politics. [It's okay to talk about] poverty, yeah, if they could help other people. And unemployment, if they can also back up their words by trying to get them work.

The bishops can make a statement [about abortion] but I think they get carried away. I don't think religion belongs in politics. I think someone has to make a decision on their own. I feel at times it might be right and at times it may not be. You have to look really deep into yourself. I don't think you ever forget it. I don't think it would be an easy decision. Like you see on television, babies are fully formed; that's murder. It comes down from the Ten Commandments: Thou shalt not kill. But if the baby is going to be deformed, I don't think it's right to bring that baby into this world. Or if a girl is raped, I don't think she has to go through that trauma too, of having the child unwanted. But to go and have fun with a guy and then you get pregnant—"Oh, I'll get an abortion if that happens"—that's killing. [Better] to use birth control. Birth control is something each person has to deal with, [make up their own mind.] I always felt that way. The Church teaches you it's a sin, but to bring a child in the world that's not wanted is more of a sin.

[If I could change the Church] I'd go back to Latin. I'd let the priests get married. I wouldn't give this impression of being money-money-money-money. I'd make people feel we're a family. That's how I felt when we were growing up, that church was my family. Maybe because I used to stay in church and get close with the priest. [I don't feel that way anymore]. It got a little cold. They were more compassionate then. Now they seem to be concerned with your little envelope:* "Oh, you belong to our parish. Did you get envelopes?" They used to come bless your house once a year. They aren't doing things like that anymore. Now you have to request it, and if they get around to it, maybe they'll come. And you have to give them a reason why you want your house blessed.

I had it out with a priest, about twenty years ago. I said, "I have something to ask you. Why is it a sin to eat meat unless you tell me I can eat it? Or it's a sin to not go to confession: Why do I have to go through you to go to God? Where in the Bible it'll teach you where Jesus says, 'Come to me.' " He's saying, "I think you better come in." When I went he said to me, "You're the girl who wanted to cut the middleman out—me." I said, "I just cannot see why I have to come to you to go to God." His explanation was, "Because if you do something wrong and you have to tell someone else, it's going to stay on your mind—'The next time I'm not going to do this because I have to say it again and it's embarrassing.' It's really degrading to have to tell somebody."†

[The last time I went to confession] to a priest was the day my [first] husband was being buried in '68. [The last time I went] to God himself was two years ago. [The last time I received communion‡ was] about a year ago, when my neighbor got killed. [I don't usually receive when I go to Mass] because I feel I ought to prepare myself to speak with my God. [I set aside time to go to confession to God, by myself,] and then I receive. I have to sit down and cleanse myself. [I feel that way] because of my upbringing. The only thing is, I eliminated the priest.

I got a job on the school bus in 1975 as a matron; I'm driving since '80. I like working with children. When I first took this job I used to come home crying because these are all handicapped children. I used to come home and thank God that mine were normal. My closest

*Dated envelopes in which parishioners turn in their weekly contribution to the parish.
†This is not the official theological rationale for the sacrament!
‡Catholics tend to speak of "receiving" communion, Protestants of "taking" communion.

friend is my matron. We're together all day five days a week. We're so close that sometimes I'm thinking something and she'll come out with it. Or she'll go, "Ah, you know . . . " and I'll know what she means, and people look at us and say, "You two work together a long time!"

I could write a book on my work; nobody would believe it, though. This one boy gets on the bus at seven o'clock in the morning and he's crying on my shoulder. He said, "I have to go to the hospital." I said, "For what?" He said, "I have to be sabotaged." I said, "What do you mean, sabotaged?" He said, "They have to cut my penis." I said, "That's *circumcised*." So he says "Oh," and now he's got himself across my lap and he's really deeply crying. I said, "What's the matter now?" He goes, "How the heck am I supposed to pee if they take off my penis?" I said, "I don't believe this; seven-thirty in the morning and I'm explaining circumcision." So then I explained it to him and he was fine. I don't know [why such an old kid was getting circumcised.]

The women's movement affected everybody: As far as work goes, I get the same salary as the guy who does the same job as me. Some things I don't like about it. I don't like to be fully liberated. I like to have the car door opened, I like my cigarette lit. I like to be able to ask my husband, "Could you do this, because I can't do it." I can come and go as I want because of the marriage I have; if I said, "I'm going away for a week," my husband would say, "Go ahead!" But I like that feeling of the husband comes first. Could be the upbringing I had.

When it comes down to lady firemen—she's 115 pounds: She's going to be able to carry 200 pounds out of the window? The same way for cops. You wonder where are they going to stop. What would they actually do if there was a man against, like, my husband? You give her one punch and she could be finished.

[I don't think women should be ordained.] Because Jesus picked men as apostles. I don't think they would get through to a parish the way a priest would. I never dealt with [Protestant women ministers]; I might feel different if I had. It probably all stems from how you grew up. Right now the way I feel is, besides being a cop or a fireman, now they want to be priests. I can't see them wanting to be a priest, because they're still serving God as nuns, and they're devoting their lives that way, the same way a priest does. I don't think the Church will [change on this]. Don't ask me why.

[Jesus is a] very lovable man. I picture him as a very soft, contented man, someone that you could sit and confide in. Mary had to be somebody really special in order for God to pick her to be Jesus' mother.

She had to be a very strong woman to see her son nailed to the cross, and a very loving woman. I think of her as very soft and gentle.

I pray by myself. Sometimes I'll take a walk around the corner [to the church] and I'll sit and I'll go light candles. I pray in my bus. Every morning I say, "Okay, God, you're the pilot; I'm just the copilot." I thank Him every day that I drove the kids to school safe and back home and that my matron's home and that I made it home, too. I just couldn't do that "thee" and "thy." I speak to God the way I'm speaking to you. Sometimes I'll ask why and ask for things. Say, maybe I don't deserve something that I want; I ask Him, "If you see fit, if you think that I deserve it, give it to me. Give me my way."

My first husband died on a Wednesday. The Sunday before, my daughter, the older one, came into the room and she said, "Mommy." I thought she wanted to sleep with us and I said, "No, you can't get in bed with Daddy and Mommy." She said, "No, I just wanted to tell you Daddy is going to be fine. He's going to be all better. I just saw him with God," she said, "and God had his arm around Daddy. Daddy was happy. He was smiling."

Well, my husband died [three days later]. My neighbor downstairs had the kids. The priest came and I said to him, "How do I tell my children?" He said, "I'll go with you. If you want, I'll tell them." I said, "No, I think it's my place." He said, "Well, then all I can say is God will find a way for you." The only thing that came into my mind was this dream that my daughter had and explaining to them, "You saw how Daddy was, how he was no longer sick." Naturally, not seeing their father the usual way, knowing he was a very sick man and [seeing how] he aged in six months—he wasn't the father they knew. So this dream was reassuring for her. I believe God goes through the innocent. [That was God's way of] preparing her.

I'm not afraid of death. I used to be. When I was younger, naturally, I feared the unknown. Now, I don't know exactly where you're going, if you stay in the ground or whether your soul goes to heaven. I just feel that if I really feel in need, any one of them, my husband, my grandmother, anybody, I can get some kind of reassuring feeling that they're with me; and no matter how tough things are, somehow they will help me find a way.

My friend has this sister that changed her religion from Catholic to I don't know what; they get rebaptized. Her religion has made her a different girl: She's very peaceful and very happy. The difference between Catholics and [other kinds of Christians is], maybe I'm wrong, but they're into their religion more than we are: They have Bible classes; they're together. We probably have it in the Catholic religion and I just never got into it.

My first husband took me to Mass once, and he came out and said, "You damn Catholics don't know whether you want to sit, stand, or kneel." And I gave my daughter tuna fish one day and we took her in the car and she got sick and he said, "You damn Catholics and your fish."

[I'm a Catholic because] I was born a Catholic; and then as I got older, it was my choosing. I was happy with it. [It gives you] a sense of security. I don't really think there's any difference [among religions]. If you believe in God, that's the main man, right? Whatever religion you have and you find peace [in] . . . it all comes down to one God.

[People who say they don't believe in God] are full of baloney. I've met atheists, and if anything happens they say, "Oh, thank God, thank God." Well, if you don't believe in God, why thank Him? [And if something bad happened] they'd be the first ones to say, "Why did God do this to me?"

A lot of people blame God if something goes wrong. I can't. I think it's just part of life if the good comes with the bad. And He's there to help if you go to Him. Whether you go to church or not, if you were raised to believe that there is a God, then wherever you'll go, He'll never fail you. Just ask now, and He will help you.

I put an alarm in the house. I don't want to come in and find out it's violated. [If I could change the world, I'd have] no guns, no fighting, peace. [Nuclear arms make me] scared. I was never really deep into politics. [I've never voted. I'm not registered. Why?] Because my decision will be the wrong decision. I have an insecure feeling that maybe my vote would bring in the wrong guy, you know, that one vote. —That it could bring in the right guy? Never thought of it that way.

FOUR

BECOMING A CATHOLIC WOMAN

It was very tight, a lot of controlling by shame, but there was definitely security, and colors, smells, awe, magic, the votive candles. I remember as a child being in church with my hands covering my eyes, thinking if I looked up I would see God, and did I want to do that? What would I do?

—Maureen Dallison Kemeza

Great is this power of memory, exceedingly great, O my God, a spreading limitless room within me. Who can reach its uttermost depth? Yet it is a faculty of my soul and belongs to my nature.

—St. Augustine

All the women, of course, spoke about their childhood. What began to arrest and puzzle me as I sifted through their accounts, trying to find the common threads and make sense of what I heard, was how often the stories contradicted one another. There were stories about nuns, for instance, in almost every Catholic girlhood. But in some the sisters were sadistic authority figures, in others extraordinary role models. Some women complained of a lack of intellectual stimulation in their Catholic schools; others blossomed intellectually in Catholic educational institutions. For some women, the God of their childhood (in all cases the ever-present maker of heaven and earth) was benevolent, for others fearsome and punishing. For some, the structured, secure world of Catholicism was enveloping and nurturing; for others it was repressive, even traumatic; for many women, it was a mixture of both. Nancy Vitti lived in terror of Sister Thomasina, but she experienced her parish as a comforting home.

What all the memories had in common was a set of themes or images, present in virtually all the stories but arranged in different ways, as in a kaleidoscope, or a series of watercolors that had begun with the same set of paints but ended with the colors running into one another and combining in different ways. The nuns, the life of the mind, the love of God, fear and security: What I found was a mixed picture, neither a ferocious *Sister Mary Ignatius Explains It All for You* nor a sentimental *Bells of Saint Mary's*. The way the themes combined hinged on many factors: the health of the family environment, ethnicity, social class, geography, the historical times, and each woman's personality and ego strength.

Catholicism was, in fact, both constraining and emancipatory. The Church set up boundaries that helped people to grow as well as boundaries that stunted. Growing up Catholic, for some women, was a dispiriting experience. For "Jeanne Dupont," an artist raised in a small New Hampshire town, Catholicism early became synonymous with the repression of emotions and sensuality, with lack of attention to the individual, and with abuse of authority. "[It was so] top-down," she said. "Growing up Catholic cured me of organized religion." For a few women, the memories of Catholic childhood were overwhelmingly positive. "Louise O'Connell," a generation older than "Jeanne," loved her Catholic upbringing in Connecticut and remembered it fondly; in her life, Catholicism provided comfort, color, meaning, and reassurance. But for a majority of the women, regardless of age, growing up Catholic in America was a mixed picture: a blend of shame and guilt, rules and control on the one hand, and mystery, warmth, and security on the other, a structured and meaningful world that could be both stifling and reassuring.

Hardly a Catholic will speak of his or her childhood without mentioning guilt. In fact, while many of the tales about "Catholic guilt" really are about guilt, that abiding feeling of perpetual responsibility, some of them are actually about shame, the feeling of being unworthy, sullied, less than whole. While both were burdensome, guilt was easier to deal with, and to laugh about later on. It was even, in some ways, a useful emotion, fostering a sense of responsibility for others. Shame fostered only low self-esteem; it wounded more deeply and was slower to heal. When young girls received from the pulpit or the schoolroom the message that they, their bodies, their thoughts, their whole selves were bad, they took years to gain self-confidence. Self-love and self-esteem were recurring themes in the interviews of these women; often they had gone outside the Church—to other religions, to therapy, or to the self-help and human potential movements—for healing.

For those women in whom the Church had nurtured a more robust sense of self, the burdens of guilt could still seem formidable. At the age of seven, ten, or fourteen, one was accountable not only to self and others, but to God for the state of the world at large. "I was taught," said Ellen Reuter, "that if you had prayed harder some war wouldn't have started. Talk about feeling responsible!"

For those women—a clear majority—who escaped the experience of deep sadness and shame, Catholicism was often a rich source of comic material. The massive institutional realities of Catholicism seem to develop in people a finely tuned sense of the absurd. Women's childhood stories often contained a mischievous irreverence. "Catholic schools are really very blasphemous," said Caryl Rivers. "When we had a beer party in our senior year and the nuns found out about it, one nun, with a straight face, said that the Holy Ghost had told her about it. In our homeroom class there was a picture of the Holy Ghost as a dove, so we drew a little convict's cap and a stool on Him, [and turned Him into] the Holy Ghost as stool pigeon." "I remember deciding in the second grade that I would go to hell," said "Serena Townsend." "The nun had said that everybody who threw spitballs and talked in class would go to hell and that all the good persons would go to heaven and play little musical instruments. A number of us in the room looked around at each other and I think we all made the same mental assessment: Hell was obviously where we were headed and it would be a lot more fun than sitting around on some cloud whanging away at a harp."

But the critical factor in women's upbringing was the family matrix. Of all the variables—generation, class, culture, geography—this was the most influential. The family, after all, is the first place we learn to trust (or not to trust), to belong, to believe, to love, to care for the common good. Despite the well-defined role played by the parish school, parents were their children's first teachers, a fact that today's Catholic religious education curricula have finally come to recognize. Family, church, and Catholic school usually reinforced one another, but in cases where the parish imparted one message and the family another (say, about sex or relationships to non-Catholics), the family message prevailed in women's minds and hearts.

Catholic women learned to pray, quite literally, at their mother's knee. "The foundation was laid in my mother's faith," said thirty-eight-year-old physician Mariette Murphy, speaking of the Christian values she embraced as an adult. Women's teachers and models were most often mothers and grandmothers, but fathers were present as positive religious figures as well. Diane Williams, a twenty-nine-year-old theology student and parish worker, the daughter of a machinist and a homemaker, remembers both her parents as "strong models of Christianity. The teachings of the Gospel were very much upheld in my family. My father," she said, "is a very compassionate and understanding man. I rarely have heard him talk badly about anyone. I can remember getting up one night and passing by my parents' room and seeing my Dad on his knees saying his prayers. God is a very important source of strength for him." "Genevieve O'Rourke," a contemplative nun in her sixties, attended public schools and went to Sunday School at the local parish. "I remember every Saturday sitting on my father's lap and how he would question me on the catechism for the next day." Her memory of religious learning is associated with her father's love. "For all I knew," she said to me, "all fathers did that." It was not till later that she realized there were other kinds of Catholic families.

"[My father] was a real bad alcoholic," thirty-two-year-old "Regina White" remembered. "He kept leaving, my mother would take him back, they'd fight, he'd beat us up. Then he'd leave again." She joined a street gang because "they didn't send me away; I felt like I was accepted; I felt like I was wanted." Raised in a violent family, she found no comfort in the local church, which reinforced the messages she was receiving at home: "They made you feel bad [about yourself]," she said. "I felt bad enough; I didn't need nothing else to make me feel worse. If you weren't perfect you were no good. I felt bad every time I went to church." Women raised in cruel homes struggled much longer with a punitive image of God and a negative self-image than women raised in loving homes, regardless of what any of them had been taught in church.

The liturgy of the Church continued to affirm, Sunday in and Sunday out, that God was alive in the things of earth. Simultaneously, alongside the sensuous worship celebrating the sacredness of creation, came the negative messages about the body and sex. I asked "Joanne Grace," the mother of grown children, about her view of her body and her sexuality as a young girl. "Really mixed," she answered without any bitterness, "because the nuns, bless their souls, were really hung up on sex, and save yourself for marriage and all this nonsense. I had a real hard time trying to sort the whole thing out." "I don't think it's possible to have been a pre-Vatican II Catholic and have a positive view of your body," Sandra Mondykowski Temple remarked. "Gradually over the years that grew and changed," she added with a happy smile.

"So much of fifties Catholicism at the parish level was bound up with obsessive trivia," Caryl Rivers remembered. "I mean, we spent all our time agonizing about necklines. Most of us didn't *have* anything [to show]: Even if we had worn low necklines, it wouldn't have mattered! Morality came down to sexuality. The world was going to blow itself up, there was an atomic bomb, and we were arguing about necklines!" During the 1960s, "Kathleen Daly" said, "The priest used to preach all the time about 'the passion pits,' which meant the drive-in. It was so funny because he was having an affair with a woman in town who owned a liquor store; they used to go to Florida [together]. I remember confessing to him my first orgasm; I didn't know what it was! I must have been about fourteen. I was trying to describe it to him, and he was very quiet. We used to go all the time and confess sexual sins.

"When sexuality became really established in my life I left the Church," "Kathleen" continued. "The most important thing was the Vietnam War, and Father M. kept on preaching about the passion pits." She attended Quaker Meeting until early in her marriage, when she and her husband, also a questioning Catholic, traveled to France, where "the liturgy was freer for us, in French culture and away from the Irish emphasis on sex, and very intellectual. That's when we became Catholic [again]."

"I don't think I was raised with a positive view of my body," said Pamela Montagno, a journalist in her thirties. "It was not very joyful. The messages we got in Catholic grade school were just terrible. The girls could not play with the boys on the playground; they were told to keep their legs together in the classroom; there were lots of little messages that said sex is dangerous, your body is something you should keep chaste at all costs. Some of that," she said, "is that Catholicism came down very harsh and heavy on the body, but some of it is just part of the culture too, [an American thing]." Other women too felt that American culture discourages pleasure and healthy attitudes toward sexuality, especially female sexuality. "I was brought up like all good American girls to hate my body," "Jeanne Dupont" said when I asked about her early views of her sexuality.

Family attitudes toward sex counteracted some of the messages

Catholic girls received in school. "A lot of Catholic women talk about [receiving negative messages about sex]," Ann Richards Anderson said to me. "I never felt *any* of that. My mother was certainly not open in the sense that sex was a common topic of discussion, but I remember when she explained to me about menstruation and how babies get born, she also said, 'Sex is a wonderful thing. It's God's way of having husbands and wives express their love for each other and it's very beautiful.' [She also said] that's why you shouldn't go—she definitely didn't use the words 'sleeping around,' [but that's what she meant]." Susan Dyer Johnson of Corpus Christi, Texas, a woman in her forties whose father was a physician, spoke of the contrast between her home and her Catholic school: "I got a positive message at home and a negative message at school. My mother and father were very sexual. Sex was discussed and you could ask any question you wanted at any time. But at school it was very repressive. My father was one of the first [physicians] prescribing birth control," she added.

Athletics in girls' schools and in the Catholic Youth Organization (CYO) also mitigated the negative messages about the body. Without exception, the women who had been active in youth sports grew up with positive body images and remained athletic as adults, and all spoke of having satisfying sexual relationships with their partners. Caryl Rivers, asked about her image of her body as she was growing up, answered, "It was really positive because of sports, no question about that; because I was a little girl jock and a tomboy. Certainly parochial schools tried to reverse that in that whole silly business of don't wear [this or that] kind of neckline. That promoted a real hostile view of people's bodies. But I think the fact that I was into sports at a very young age made the rest of that stuff slip off."

"It was a funny mixture," Sandra Mondykowski Temple recalled. "Your body is the temple of the Holy Spirit, therefore you should respect yourself, you shouldn't be exploited. That was the positive aspect. The negative aspect was that these acts were dirty: Kissing and French kissing and touching and petting and intercourse were dirty. And then all of a sudden you were married and they were clean. That caused a tremendous conflict for most of us." She added: "There was no such thing as questioning or free choice or loopholes. You were either pure or you weren't. My nickname in high school was 'Ivory Soap,'" she laughed.

Sexual restraint did have its positive aspect, Sandra said. "In the late fifties, early sixties, that was the norm. I really feel for the kids today. We were able to take our time. You had peer support to stay 'off the bases,' which really did give you more time for your own growth and reflection and identity. We had the same hormones, but got a chance to sublimate a little more. So it's a trade-off: I grew up with terrible guilt about doing anything other than holding hands, but also with a long opportunity to be a kid and a teenager and see what else that meant for me besides sex."

Next to parents, the most important adult influences in Catholic girls' lives were the nuns, less distant than priests and present every day in the classrooms and hallways of Catholic schools. They evoked vivid memories. "I could tell you the names of all my teachers," said forty-two-year-old Evelyn Reichman. Women's memories of "their" nuns varied widely because the sisters came, Maureen Dallison Kemeza told me, "in a variety of flavors: some really soulful, some totally sadistic who must have been enormously unhappy. I had Sisters of Mercy as grade school teachers. They wore black and were totally covered and we didn't know if they had hair. We always used to wonder." Maureen's fifth grade teacher was especially influential. "She was very sensitive and had a talent for language, and could recognize that in me and others. She used to lead us in meditation: She would have us put our heads on the desk and meditate about God's love. I remember feeling God's love. Sometimes the nuns went crazy, so there was a fear of their repressed anger; they were furious ladies. I have very mixed emotions about my nuns. Except for family, they were the most formative influence in my life—those furious tender women with all this mystery about them and all this repression."

Some women remember more fury than tenderness: "I was brought up to revere my authorities," said Evelyn Reichman, who grew up in Philadelphia. "The nuns were very brutal. I was filled with terror. I got my hands slammed in a piano once because I didn't practice. We didn't have a piano! How could I practice? I was in such a heightened emotional state in grammar school," she added, "I could tell you what the convent smelled like. I felt so scrutinized by my family and by the structure of the school that I grew up terrified of making a mistake. I witnessed some brutal beatings with dustbrushes, children beaten around the head and shoulders. I was sickened." "I don't think we saw women as powerless," Sandra Mondykowski Temple observed. "The nuns were very powerful figures to us, though often for negative reasons."

For Caryl Rivers, the nuns were a kinder presence, and conveyed to her "an optimism that may be particularly Catholic. One of the things you got, particularly in elementary school—it may have been a very female thing—was that nurturing and loving were equated with God and religion; the nuns were very much a vehicle of that."

While a few of the women I met chose to enter a religious order, inspired by teachers or members of their family, the majority, of course, did not. Many had considered the possibility as young girls. Some had never wanted to emulate the nuns. "Nuns were kind of the servants of priests," said "Elena Martinez Wise," an officer in a San Francisco corporation who grew up in Mexico. When I asked Boston business-woman "Anne Marie Quinn" whether she had ever thought of becoming a nun when she was growing up in an all-Catholic neighborhood, she answered emphatically: "I wanted to be a priest. Nuns were sissies." But for many, the nuns served as models and inspirations through their independent spirit, their altruism, and their professional accomplish-ments. "I grew up with great-aunts who were very well educated," said Ann Richards Anderson, a human services administrator in her early forties. "One of them, probably the most influential person in my life, was a Mercy nun, and she had two Ph.D.s, one in English and one in French." Mariette Murphy, who grew up in the housing projects of Brooklyn, New York, was sent to a private Catholic girls' academy after her intellectual gifts were recognized by her parochial grammar school teachers. She still remembers "the really brilliant principal who could see beyond everything I was doing" when she misbehaved, and would send her "to the desk to read Ovid—and not in translation!" She is still grateful for those days. Through the nuns, she said, "the Catholic educational system responded to me, saw me as a whole person, [and imparted to me] the concept that human dignity and respect are the ultimate priority. I was completely identified with [the nuns]," she added. "That was going to be my life." She attended Harvard Medical School and developed a specialty in adolescent medicine; her profes-sional priority is the care of low-income adolescents and young women who do not have access to adequate health and prenatal care.

Many of the women's stories reflected the radical shift in the aca-demic training of American nuns that took place thanks to the work of the Sister Formation Conference.[1] As Catholic school teachers in the 1940s and 1950s, American sisters seldom had a college degree and their theology was often primitive or outdated. After the 1950s they were equally as likely to have studied at the master's level. The renewal of sisters' communities in this country preceded Vatican II by a full decade, giving them a head start on the rest of the American church. Even before this, in the early part of the century, nuns with doctorates from the best universities in the country and abroad educated several generations of Catholic women at institutions like Minnesota's College of St. Catherine—the first Catholic institution to be awarded a Phi Beta Kappa chapter.

The younger women I interviewed grew up with the new generation of religious sisters, more highly educated and theologically sophisticated than their elders, no longer dressed in habits, now working side by side in Catholic schools with lay faculty. For women under thirty, Catholic education is no longer synonymous with nuns as it was for their elders. Since nuns entered a broad array of ministries after Vatican II, younger Catholic women have encountered them early on in many other roles besides that of teacher: They know them also as retreat leaders, campus ministers, prison chaplains, and parish administrators. The stories they told me held more familiarity than fear. "We were friends with the nuns," said twenty-nine-year-old Brigette Rouson, who grew up in St. Petersburg, Florida. "The nuns in my high school, Sisters of Notre Dame, were just great, very upbeat women, almost every one of them." Twenty-three-year-old "Jenna Santini" became active in church youth groups in her mid-teens. "I got to meet and get close to a couple of Sisters of Saint Francis," she remembered. "When I turned sixteen I went up to their mother house; it was one of my better experiences. A lot of people in their teens put priests and sisters in these categories by themselves, like they are really square or hard to get along with, not normal people, above other people. I got to see they really are neat people, and they just have a beautiful life. They seem at peace with themselves, so open and easy to talk to, they pray so easily. I got to walk around with them, and I got to visit the house where the retired nuns were, who all wore their habits."

Many women said that girls' and women's schools run by religious orders of women helped them develop leadership skills, independence, and athletic talent. Sarah Hofheinz's high school fostered "a lot of freedom and individuality" and "encouraged leadership in women," she said, "and for that I'm grateful." "Joanne Grace," now in her late fifties, found that "going to school in a girls' academy and a women's college is really a reinforcing element for a young woman because there, the women do everything and you're not in competition with men who are dominating the classroom. So I emerged quite confident that I could do what I wanted to do." For Caryl Rivers, one of the advantages of attending a small Catholic girls' high school was that "girls' sports really counted. In public schools, girls' sports were *nothing*. But here you were a *star*. I can remember being in a packed gym with three hundred people screaming their lungs out for me as I went to the foul line. That's the kind of stardom few girls get."

Some Catholic women are still choosing girls' schools for their daughters. Angela Rodriguez said of her daughters' high school: "The girls are trained to be leaders more, and they have more freedom to be who they are. The other thing I really appreciate is the friendships they develop among themselves; their girlfriends are really important to them. They just seem to have a better self-esteem."

At least half the women I interviewed had attended Catholic schools from kindergarten through twelfth grade. Women often contrasted the education they received from independent Catholic schools run by religious orders of women and men with the education they received in the local parish school, which they found far less satisfying both intellectually and theologically. Many women had attended public schools, but had gone on to Catholic colleges and universities. For many of the women who disliked parochial schools for their narrow-mindedness, Catholic colleges were the redeeming factor in Catholic education.

Parochial school students' creativity—and their teachers'—was often more constrained by the sheer numbers in crowded classrooms than by teachers' ideology. "I recall there was an awful lot of having to be quiet," Maureen Dallison Kemeza said, "and not saying what you thought. There were fifty-two kids in my class, grades one through eight. You can imagine, one nun and fifty-two kids. So discipline was the thing."

But many women had memories of being forbidden to question the truths they were taught and the people who taught them because questioning itself was wrong. "Because I went to public school," said fifty-six-year old "Rose Mazurkiewicz" of Milwaukee, "we had to take religious instructions [at church] and I was tossed out of class because I accepted nothing, I questioned everything. The same thing occurred at two other churches and [after that] my parents gave up on me."

The youngest women told a different story. Camila Alvarez was a seventeen-year-old student in a Catholic high school in Milwaukee when I interviewed her. "Our religion teacher is a rather liberal teacher," she said, adding with some alarm, "I hope she doesn't get mad at me to label her liberal. She agrees with the church on abortion but she believes there should be a different way of handling sex education in the school. She talks freely about sexual things. She's very easygoing. She's also a counselor. She strongly believes in the Church; there was a time, she told us, when she had broken away from the Church, when she was at a difficult period in her life; she didn't know if the Church was right for her. She thinks that we all go through that and we take that time to evaluate our lives and see where does God fit in."

While nuns were ever-present, daily companions in schoolgirls' daily lives, priests were more remote figures, presiding at the holy mysteries of the liturgy and representing ecclesiastical and divine authority. Sometimes their intervention brought about decisive changes in Catholic girls' lives. "Joanne Grace," born and raised on an Iowa farm in a family of German immigrants, now lives near a university campus in Minnesota with her husband, an academic administrator. A college graduate, she also attended graduate school and has combined motherhood and part-time professional work. "The parish priest told my father when I was in seventh or eighth grade that it was my father's duty to see to it that I went to school," "Joanne" remembered. "Most of my peers stopped after ninth grade, which was what our little parish school had. But the priest said it was my father's duty to send me to school because I had more brains than any girl he had encountered; and my father and mother at that time, as everyone else, believed that God spoke directly through the parish priest and they would no more have said, 'No, Father,' than anything," she laughed. "So I was guaranteed an education, whereas everybody kind of drifted off to farm life and no more school."

Most childhood stories of priests were confession stories, and few of them were happy. "It wasn't the sacrament of Reconciliation," said "Serena Townsend," using the post–Vatican II term to emphasize her point. "It was *confession* and it had everything to do with rules and regulations." Though many Catholic women still go to confession today and experience it as a time of healing and new beginnings, many decried their childhood confessors' preoccupation with sex and sexual sin. While most of the women who related this kind of experience were over the age of thirty, even the youngest of the women I interviewed complained about it. "Two guys in my junior class last year," said Camila Alvarez, "were asked by the priest if they masturbated and if they had gone to bed with their girlfriends. It was none of the priest's business." Camila stopped going to confession after hearing of this incident.

Negative experiences of confession also marked the transition into young adulthood, and, at least temporarily, away from the Church. I heard several stories like Sarah Hofheinz's from women looking back on their college years. In the late 1960s, as an eighteen-year-old student at Indiana's DePauw University, Sarah went to confession one day at the college town's local parish. "I decided this particular confession was not going to be like the childhood confession, that I really wanted to discuss my positioning in the Church with the priest, have a mature chat about contemporary Catholicism and being a young woman facing four years of college and some of the challenges it might bring me. So I started into this little spiel, and the priest stopped me and wanted to know whether I had had sex with anybody, was I swearing, was I drinking. The tears started rolling down my face and I said no, I hadn't done any of that, and got out of that confessional as quickly as I could and called home and said, 'I can't go to that church anymore.' That was the last time I went to confession in my life."

Priests functioned as hosts and gatekeepers, in some cases driving young women out, in others welcoming them and helping them to feel at ease in the Church. Sometimes they even helped young women to shift their focus of authority off of Church leadership. A few years before the confession incident, during her sophomore year in high school, Sarah found the priest who taught religion classes to be "the first religious person who made sense to me. He gave us a fabulous course in Old Testament. He was the first one who said you don't have to buy into all of this to be a good Catholic, your relationship with God is not based on the fact that you go to church every Sunday or do regular confession. You don't have to take everything literally and you have a conscience you can rely on. It had an enormous influence on me," said Sarah. "It made me relax about my religion. I have been relaxed about it ever since." Today Sarah and her husband are members of their local church; their children attend the parish school.

Religion in Catholic women's childhood was both central and taken for granted. "Religion was always there in the family," Caryl Rivers remembered. "You believed in God, there were right and wrong rules, and you went to church. It was a baseline: Under everything there was religion, but it was by far not the major part of life." When she was growing up in Ireland, Angela Rodriguez remembered, "It was like eating and sleeping, your religion was so integrated into your life. The big event of the week was going to church on Sunday. We had lots of religious objects around the house; my mother had all these different saints, [she had] novenas going, and of course [we said] the Rosary every night as a family. And you would never turn away somebody who would come to the door looking for alms."

"It was just part of them," Abigail McCarthy said of her parents' faith, "not something they reflected about a great deal. It was half real belief and half that's the club you belonged to." Either way, the practice of faith required discipline and effort during her youth. She remembered "strenuous daily Mass and communion during Lent and Advent. You used to rush to Mass, then rush home to get breakfast and rush back to school. It was very athletic in the Minnesota winter. Depending on whether you took the shortcuts or not, it was seven or twelve blocks to church and back and often below zero. So it was kind of like 'dying for the faith.' It's hard to tell now how genuine one's piety was at that age," she added.

For some families, the parish played a minor role; for others it was the center of life. There were also ethnic variations in the relative influences of parish and family life, or at least in styles of relating to the parish. Nancy Vitti remembers spending many hours at the church as a child; her mother, on the other hand, rarely went to Mass; this was true of other adults in the family. Devotions were centered in the home, as they were in many Italian-American families; public celebration was focused on festivals, saints' days, weddings, and funerals rather than Sunday Mass. As an adult woman, Nancy has developed a pattern of church attendance similar to her mother's.

"I can never talk about the spiritual or the religious life," the novelist Mary Gordon writes, "without talking about early memory, which is anything but disembodied. Whatever religious instincts I have bring their messages to me through the senses—the images of my religious life, its sounds, its odors, the kind of kinesthetic sense I have of prayerfulness. These are much more real to me than anything that takes place in the life of the mind."[2] The Church was a kind of sensory womb, a place of mystery, planting in Catholic youngsters the desire for a religious experience that was direct, prerational, and sensual. To impressionable girls this was a magical world, almost a taste of heaven, both wonderful and fearsome.

"I just loved my religion," said "Louise O'Connell" of her Catholic childhood in the 1920s. "We were always in processions; we'd have to go to practice weeks ahead of time. They'd have banners for all the mysteries of the Rosary. In May there was the crowning of our Blessed Lady. It was gorgeous, absolutely beautiful. Everything was in Latin. We had little May altars in our home, we had lovely pictures. It was wonderful." "I liked the ritual," said Angela Rodriguez of San Francisco, born in Ireland at the beginning of World War II and now a U.S. citizen. "I would spend a lot of time in church. I liked Benediction. Incense—it did something to me. It still does something to me. It's mystical, otherworldly." Twenty-nine-year-old Bridget Palmer was partly raised in the Byzantine Rite of the Catholic Church, whose churches are similar to the Orthodox churches in their liturgical practices: "I always liked when they hung the icons, and the incense, and the old ladies with their babushkas who were praying and saying their Rosaries; there was an aura of mysticism and spirituality connected with it." When she goes to church today—sporadically, to both Episcopal and Roman Catholic churches—it is this atmosphere of mystery for which Bridget hungers.

For Maureen Dallison Kemeza, faith, sensuality, fear, and wonder blended together: "I remember being in choir, the incense, the Latin, singing, being very small, everything else was very large. I remember thinking it was entirely possible that Jesus would step down from the crucifix and talk to me, so it was very magical, but it was very serious. We always had rosary beads in church. There were so many kinds; my grandmother had crystal ones, or glass, transparent [beads]; the nuns wore long black ones down to the floor. With the incense there was a lot of fainting," she added. "We used to fast [before Mass, of course]. I remember the thud of bodies. The ushers would come running up. No one paid much attention."

Boundaries on behavior and belief were not the only limits Catholic women experienced as children. One of the major external boundaries in their lives was the one between the Catholic enclave and the outside world. "Anne Marie Quinn" grew up in Boston's Dorchester section, where people announced their affiliation not by neighborhood but by parish, as Catholics also did in Chicago and Philadelphia. "It was a very structured life," she remembered. "Most social activities revolved around the church and the school. I loved grammar school, the feeling of kinship," she added. "It was real warm." Catholics in major urban centers socialized with other Catholics, identified as Catholics against the world, rarely knew people of other faiths. A friend in her fifties who grew up in Boston told me that when a Protestant family moved down the block, "we went peeking through the fence to see what a Protestant looked like. We'd never seen a Protestant that we knew of."

Ann Richards Anderson, raised in Chicago, spoke of her Jewish neighbors as "our second family" and was the daughter of a Protestant man who converted to Catholicism while she was at college. She attended parochial elementary school, where Catholicism was defined to young students as a privileged identity. "I remember teachers talking about [the fact] that Protestants could not go to heaven. They weren't necessarily going to hell; they would just end up in limbo. After all, they *had* been exposed to the True Church and it was only their willfulness that made them refuse to see that that was the truth. I remember thinking that that was not right. Nevertheless, I used to say a prayer every morning, on my own, that my father and my grandmother would become Catholics."

Some rural and small-town settings mirrored the insularity of the big city. "Jeanne Dupont" remembers "the French Canadian *curé* [pastor] as the main authority in the community and the image of the *paroisse* [parish] against the world isolated in cold, rural Québec" which was preserved in the Franco-American New England town in which she grew up. Not so in the Midwest. Ellen Reuter, in her thirties like "Jeanne," grew up in Avoca, a Wisconsin farming community of three hundred people. The town had several churches, one Catholic and three or four Protestant, but "nobody was that much identified by what church they went to. Everybody went to their church on Sunday and that didn't keep people from doing what they did with their neighbor on Monday." In Ellen's opinion, "rural Catholics are healthier than urban Catholics. They see more of the world. Their church affiliation doesn't become their label because so much else goes on: There are a lot of other things as intense as church affiliation in rural farm life."

Besides sexuality, relationships to non-Catholics were the area where the family ethos prevailed most often over that of the Church. Sarah Hofheinz is the daughter of a Catholic father and a Methodist mother. Like Marlene Jones, Sarah remembers "doing double duty" when she visited her grandparents, attending two church services each Sunday. At home, her mother attended the Catholic church in which Sarah and her siblings were being raised. Sarah remembered telling her mother one day after school: "Mother, you're going to be thrown straight to hell because you're not a Catholic." The nuns, Sarah said, had told her that her mother was a heathen. "A lot of women would have responded in a very different way than she did and gotten upset and angry," said Sarah. "She was just very calm and explained that of course, that wasn't the case. I don't remember specifically her words to me but I felt assured that the nuns were wrong and that God's love went beyond what I was being taught in school." Some of the women I interviewed had themselves imparted this message to their children: Dolores Reuter, married to a Lutheran man, remembers her children coming home from school during the

1950s and 1960s with the question, "Mom, is Dad going to hell?" "No way," was Dolores's simple answer, and with that she laid the issue to rest.

Usually these discussions stayed at home. In a few cases, parents went public with their disagreement. "Serena Townsend," married to a man whose father was Protestant, recounted a scene from her husband's childhood. "They said during some sermon that people who did not belong to the Catholic church would go to hell, and 'Ed' came home in tears. He was a tiny boy. His mother marched right down to church and she had the priest retract [his statement] at every Mass the following Sunday."

When there were adversarial relationships with non-Catholics, they often went in both directions: Many women—more than half—had experienced anti-Catholicism when they were growing up, in subtle or overt forms. "I remember being called 'Catholic' as an insult in grammar school," said Victoria Bowden of Raleigh, North Carolina. "I used to get teased," Mary Olivanti said, remembering her school years in Sheboygan, Wisconsin. "They called me a 'cat-licker' [and yelled], 'You worship statues!' " Adults in the community shared those sentiments, though they may not have screamed them on the streets as their children did. "Children don't come up with things like that on their own," Mary said. Later Mary's family moved to Grand Rapids, Michigan, where, she said, "We had neighbors who wouldn't talk to us because we were Catholics. I had friends whom I met at the public school whose parents would not let them come over and play with me because I was Catholic." Catholicism, "Serena Townsend" remembered, was "the underdog, the negative religion, the one looked down upon." In her upper-middle-class, mostly Protestant neighborhood in the suburbs of Chicago, anti-Catholicism "was very subtle but you were aware of it." "Serena" was scolded by her parents for running instead of walking around the pool of her family's country club. "We're one of only two Catholic families in the club," her parents reminded her. "Somehow," "Serena" laughed, "I felt the survival of the whole Church including the pope of Rome was on my shoulders."

"The outside world" was not only the world of non-Catholics but that of the broader society. What were these women taught to do with an unjust world? Creation may have been filled with the presence of God, but affliction and evil were real. For some women, social and personal suffering were part of the same reality; while they might have meaning—and therefore a redemptive quality—they could not be transformed. But not all women were raised to be passive in response to injustice, particularly social injustice.

"We have to know our place," Mary Esther Bernal's mother would say to her daughter, who argued vehemently with her about segregation in mid-century San Antonio. Beatrice Cortez, like Mary Esther, grew up poor in south Texas, the daughter of a construction worker. "My parents knew discrimination and inequality. They were not ignorant: They used to listen to radio a lot and my mother used to read the Spanish paper, but it was like not knowing what to do. They never knew of an effort or an organization or a group of persons who could correct those wrongs." "Elsa Colón," a young woman of mixed Irish, French, Puerto Rican, and Cuban background, came from a family of artists and social activists: "I grew up with a sense that my life and calling were to do service in the world, to help change the world," she remembered.

Family was not the only formative influence in this respect: All three women became social activists as adults. For two of them, the Church eventually played a decisive role in this development. The church of Mary Esther and Beatrice's childhood did not involve itself in the economic and social problems of San Antonio's poor neighborhoods; but later, with the coming of parish-based community organizing in the 1970s, both women found an institutional connection between the life of faith and the work of justice. For "Elsa," who was politically and socially active early in her life but whose connection to the Church had been tenuous, the same kind of church-based organization was a path back to the life of faith in her young adult years.

For other women, the connection between Catholic faith and social change came much earlier. Mary Hunt's Catholic high school in Syracuse, New York, sponsored work programs in poor neighborhoods of the city, on a Native American reservation, and in Appalachia in conjunction with the Christian Appalachian Program. Mary took part in all of them. "Those were very important formative experiences," she remembered. "My view of the world became much larger. [And I saw this work was] being done by people who were coming out of the churches, not just politicos: This was all connected to what it meant to be a Christian, what it meant to be a Catholic; this was the way one expressed one's faith."

"[There was an] optimistic world view," in Catholic education, said Caryl Rivers of her upbringing in middle-class Silver Spring, Maryland. "Human beings *could* be better; even though you were born with original sin, you *could* be good, you could be better, and the imperative to help your fellow man or woman combines [with that], I think, to make you very much oriented toward changing rather than conserving the old status quo." She added: "Catholicism really imbued you with a sense of duty toward other people—and that you don't accept an unjust world, that you try to remedy things when they're unjust, and that things should be fair, and God is fair."

The question that remains with many women is not about the true nature of their Catholic childhood, but about what they will do with their inheritance. What use have they made of their early experience during their adult life? "Elizabeth Heilig," a yoga teacher and psychotherapist whose connection to Catholicism loosened during her early adult years, began reclaiming her Catholic identity when her child was born. For years she had found spiritual sustenance in yoga and meditation, which she continued to practice after her decision to move back toward the Church. "Catholicism does have that mystical component that I gravitate to," she said. "For me it was fun and necessary to experiment with different religions, but look where it led me: right back to base one! . . . I was raised Catholic," she added, "it's my tradition, and I'm proud now of my tradition." I asked what she was proud of. "The tremendous emphasis on doing what's right and examining one's conscience," "Elizabeth" answered. "At a very early age I was taught to think critically. Catholicism taught me how to look deeper. It was very important for me. It made me who I am."

FIVE

KAREN DOHERTY

"I will hear that music in the mountains."

Karen is in her mid-thirties, an articulate, calm woman with dignity in her bearing and a steady gaze. She is assistant director of membership for the American Management Association (AMA) in Manhattan, which she describes as "the largest nonprofit management education organization in the world," serving the major Fortune 1,000 companies, small businesses, entrepreneurial ventures, and large nonprofit organizations.

I said to the *National Catholic Reporter* [when they interviewed me for] a series on "Catholics at the Top," "Why don't you write something that business people can understand and that they can relate to? They're *hungry* for this! Speak to them in a language they can understand because they really want to do good." Religious people don't understand that most people in business are not dirtbags. There are some dirtbags that just care about the bottom line and they're greedy and they're rotten. But most people in business *would* care about justice if they could, *would* do the right thing. But you've got to not hold them in contempt.

[Catholic clergy are no help to] people in the corporate world. They don't know about us at all. [In their homilies] you get nothing but the "bad business leader" diet. It doesn't make one receptive. I think clerical people have missions to people they can control; they don't have missions to people they can't control, where they would have to talk to you on a peer level. There were Jesuits who had a mission on Wall Street and I heard they were *packed;* people wanted to come in and talk to them. I wish they would do more of that. Nobody cares about working people. Everybody cares about wretched people and poor people or hates rich people, but nobody talks about the average middle-class working person. I think Catholic clergy, whether they're liberal or conservative, are held in very little respect by the average layperson, because they're not a part of the community.

They don't face the same kind of life decisions.

You're really put to the test working in a corporation. I long to go back into the relative simplicity of a not-for-profit or "movement" kind of job where you don't have to make the little choices every day: Do I say something or not say something? Do I speak up for poor people? Do I speak up for alcoholics? Or do I let it go? Being faced with those little choices regularly is hard; but it also reaffirms my decision to be a Christian and follow the Christian way. It's not a very easy way, but it also can be a very joyful way. I think this kind of speaking up has made me more of a Christian and more of a Catholic than when I was [working for the] Sierra Club. There I didn't have to go outside myself to see who I was. I could just define myself by being in Sierra Club and therefore a good person, fighting the good fight. Here you have to take stands.

It's absolutely [appropriate for the bishops to have written a pastoral letter on the economy]. I think they should speak up on issues. But when the bishops said, "Let government do it," everybody went "Unghhhh." It was sort of a "Good Ship Lollypop" approach. As a business person, I would say government doesn't have any background of accomplishment in terms of people: Bureaucracies get in there and perpetuate themselves. I think what the bishops should have said, rather than coming out with a lot of platitudes, is, "Here's something you can do, business people; you can get a pilot program and start hiring some poor people, and if you don't want your taxes raised, then start training some people in-house." Which some companies do, as a matter of fact, Texaco being one of them. [I know the final draft of the pastoral paid more attention to the concerns of the business community, but] there was not really a strong follow-up to that version. The one which made the impression was the "let government do it" one.

The other thing that people hee-haw at the Church about is that, as I understand, the salaries that people in the Church make are absolutely a bomb. They're just slave wages. So business people were cackling away saying, "These high and mighty people are coming out and talking about economic justice and we wouldn't hire a dog to work for what their employees make." So the Church doesn't have any credibility and people partially ignored what the bishops had to say.

I was born in Elizabeth, New Jersey. Both my parents grew up very very poor, during the Depression. They had come from money, old family money, and both families had lost it all. I grew up listening to my father tell me about my grandfather, who in the Crash of '29 lay on the floor for three days, mourning the fact that he was [suddenly] destitute. [I grew up] knowing that it was a family of working people, but surrounded by old furniture which obviously had come from another day; people had hung on to it. There was always pride in the family and [the notion of] holding on to one's heritage no matter what the cost might be. That certainly influenced me in terms of my Catholicism—to hold on to my heritage no matter what.

One thing that was to tremendously influence my spirituality was a family curse. There was a family myth [on my mother's side] that when my great-grandmother renounced her titles and left [Prussia] to come to America, a witch had put a curse on her that would follow her descendants, the women in the family, to the fourth generation; and so far, everybody had died absolutely in accordance with that curse. The curse was to die before you were forty. So usually all the women, once they hit the fortieth birthday, breathed a sigh of relief, because it was at thirty-nine that they went. There was one from each generation who died, and supposedly mine was the fourth generation. I grew up worried that I would not make it to forty, because I would fall victim to the family curse.

My father is an English teacher. My mother always wanted to go to college, but her Prussian grandfather, with whom she lived, believed that a woman's place was in the home, so she never did get the opportunity. My mother's expectation was that both of her daughters would go to college. She said to me, "When you graduate, you're going up for all of us." That was sad. I'll always remember that about my mother.

I can't say that we were really Sunday-going kinds of Catholics. We were Catholic two-timers, going to church Easter and Christmas. We had to say our prayers when we were little and had grace [before meals]. We went to catechism, which I hated because I had to sit still. And because I really wanted to get to the bottom of things and I got answers like, "It's a mystery," or, "Because we say so." There were lots of things that didn't make sense. The first breach of faith I had was when I asked the nun, "Could I bring my dog to heaven?"—it was really important—and she said, "No, because dogs don't go to heaven: Dogs don't have a soul." I was really upset about that, so I went home and cried to my mother and she said, "If you want to bring your dog, bring your dog." The other thing was trying to understand how someone could go to hell for eating a bologna sandwich on Friday, but a bad person like Hitler, if he made a confession, could go to heaven.

All the changes in the Church in the 1960s didn't have an effect on me, because at that point I had stopped going to church. The only thing I remember is the priests used to walk up and down the aisles to make sure people sang, because they were changing the liturgy, and I absolutely and adamantly refused to sing. I think that was because I was so tired of being told what to do and it was just one more thing.

I got married in 1972, my sophomore year [at Trinity College], to a law student at Georgetown University. I don't know if I fell in love with him, but Jon was about as good as anybody to marry, because he was a really smart man, and as an attorney, he would certainly provide me with a lot of the social things I needed. When I was eighteen, I fell desperately in love with a woman who was my best friend, and I think the marriage was part of trying to deal with all these lesbian feelings I didn't want. I became aware of them when I was twelve years old; I wanted to get rid of them or bury them or pretend that I wasn't going to be that way. I was really homophobic. And I thought marriage was the ticket to convince myself that I was okay. So we got married. And we ended up in Juneau, Alaska, with our St. Bernard and our wedding bands.

Well, I was a dutiful wife: Get up and get auxiliary employment with the Alaskan Department of Fish and Game. I was an administrative assistant; I had majored in English. One day I came across a document called the Native Claims Act of 1971. I read it and brought it in to my boss, who was chief of habitat protection, and said, "This had something to do with the Indians." And he said "Yes," and I said, "It seems to me that they really got cheated," and he agreed with me. I said, "Is it too late to do anything about it?" And he said, "Yes, it is." And I said, "Well, I don't believe that." That got me involved in the environment and Native Americans' rights. "Habitat protection" was just that: Protecting from mining and lumber companies and everybody else. I saw how much destruction there had been. The destruction of the land is the destruction of the native culture, because their land is their culture and their religion.

My work brought me in contact with the Tlingit people of southeast Alaska. I got to know some of the women and men in the village of Angoon, which is the most traditional of all the villages, meaning they live the Indian ways: They didn't have television and many didn't have cars and telephones. Many of the people spoke Tlingit as their first language and English as their second, ate Indian foods and hunted and fished for a living. In 1976, I had one of the greatest honors I probably will ever have, which was to be formally adopted into the Tlingit tribe. They give names to people who are adopted. I still for the life of me cannot pronounce mine. I received a friend's grand-mother's name. Their belief is that you have the name and you bring it honor during your lifetime and then it goes on. It isn't something that's yours; it's something that you hold for a while.

I was adopted during what's called by laypeople a potlatch. A potlatch is a ceremony and a time of feasting to thank the members of what they call the opposite tribe for burying the dead: There are two tribes in Tlingit, the Eagles and the Ravens. The ceremonies and rites of the dead are not handled by your own tribe [but by the other one]. The potlatch is a thanking; they themselves call it a payoff. The family of the dead person puts it on. But that's only one reason for it. The other reason is a redistribution of wealth, because at the potlatch, the family literally gives away everything. Great honor is brought to the family by doing this.

There were many other people involved in the lands claim movement. That wasn't the reason I was adopted. The reason that was given was they felt that I was a real human being. Whatever that means, I'm yet to find out, but that was it. The only thing I could think of is that they felt that I really loved the land like they did. They just said, "We adopted you because you're a real person." I was, as far as I know, the only white person ever adopted into that family, but once I was adopted, I was considered to be a full-blooded Tlingit and not a white person from that day forward.

When I spoke to members of my Tlingit family, I spoke in English, but I had gotten to a point where I could follow Tlingit and at least get the gist of it. Tlingit is a much more developed language than English. If I had children I would make them learn Tlingit first and English second, because they would have a view of the world beyond anything I could ever give them: It seemed to me the Tlingit could see things in total, where we see things in pieces. There's a Tlingit word, "a rock with seaweed on it above high tide" and how many words in English just to get that one image?

That would make my children, in a way, more American and less European-influenced. And I don't know that I would bring them up Catholic. I might, if the Native American spirituality and having a spiritual affinity for the land could be compatible with their Catholicism. But the most important thing would be for them to have a spirituality that was home-based, and not foreign. Catholicism is foreign in some sense, so long as it's directed to the Mideast being the Holy Land and the spiritual father being a person in Rome, Italy. The desert in Israel is less holy to me than the deserts of the American Southwest. That might be a holy land because of where Christ walked, but that's not the Holy Land as far as I'm concerned.

Both Jonathan and I testified in front of a congressional subcommittee on Alaskan lands in July of 1977. The word had been given underground that state employees were to stay away from testifying in favor of the Alaska Lands Bill because the state would tend to lose if a lot of mineral rights were gone. I was harassed and lost my promotion and left Fish and Game by September. Our marriage at that point was in trouble, because it was a marriage in some ways based on convenience: Jonathan wanted a nice wife, and I wanted a husband to convince me that I was heterosexual, and we didn't like one another, really. So we did less and less and drank more and more, both of us. I couldn't go on anymore and finally I was divorced in October of '78.

I had a very bad experience with a priest in Juneau. My husband was drinking heavily and it was horrendous. I wanted to get a divorce, but I didn't want to be a divorced Catholic. I said to the priest, "When I walk through the door tonight, I don't know if my husband isn't going to be there with a gun and blow my head off. Can't I just leave and not worry about my standing in the Church?" And he said, "I'm sorry, but there's nothing I can do for you." I went home and said to myself, "Looks like I'm on my own." Within a day or two I just said to Jonathan, "I'm getting a divorce." I remember being in shock that this priest would go ahead and let me get my head blown off but not get divorced, and that was part of what made me very angry with the Church, the keeping up with the form as opposed to problems that individual people were encountering. Now, I saw the look of agony in his eyes, and years later I thought that he was as much a prisoner in that system as I was. He did have a lot of feelings and he didn't want to say it, but he had to go by the book. And by the book, it was, "You can't get divorced no matter what." It was, "Keep up the form no matter what is rotten underneath." I was very, very, very angry about that.

[After I left Alaska] I was dating men to the point of being engaged to be married again; I almost ended up a housewife in Stamford, Connecticut! But he dumped me, because I spent New Year's Eve with my best friend. She loved me dearly but wasn't in love with me; she's never had relationships with women. It's the classic business of falling in love with a straight woman and never saying anything because you're so afraid of rejection. I got home from St. Louis where she lived and said, "I think I'd better really think about this whole business and come to terms with it." So I went through a period of being celibate, which

I remember fondly as being one of my most creative periods, and came out in May.

It was really very scary. I fortified myself with a lot of liquor. I ended up going to Dignity*: I knew somehow that I had to confront the Catholic part, and really take the bull by the horns. That marked a departure for me, to just go into whatever was going to give me the most trouble. Dignity was the main group I connected with. That was also where I met Christine, who became my lover and with whom I live and am in love to this day.

To say that my parents took it badly would be the understatement of the year. My mother threatened to have Christine deported, because Christine at that point was not an American citizen. I said to my mother, "If you do call Immigration, I will never set foot in this house again," and my mother knew that I meant it. My parents got to know Chris but they had to change themselves. They came a long way and I give them a lot of credit for that.

I went to work as a lobbyist for the Sierra Club here in New York. I realized and accepted the fact that I was an alcoholic, and I could not put up with the stress of being a lobbyist while dealing with the stress of going cold turkey. So I quit the Sierra Club and came to work in a basically clerical position at AMA, because that would give me time to work with my hands and build my confidence up. You definitely need that when your identity is at ground zero, to take the stress away, in order to deal with the stress of kicking that addiction. I came to work at AMA in November of 1981. I had kicked alcohol a month before that. I moved into a managerial position two years after I came here.

Thirteen different councils, groups of business leaders, meet twice a year and advise AMA on where American business is going, whether marketing, manufacturing, or human resources, and we turn around and translate those latest trends into books, periodicals, and courses. I'm going into what's known as the controversial management issues. [I had] us do a program on drugs in the workplace. That meant me coming out as an alcoholic. I [had originally] made a vow that I wouldn't tell people why I didn't drink, and I didn't care who asked. But the first person to ask me was our CEO. I said, "The reason I don't drink is because I'm an alcoholic." He said "Good," and I think he was pleased. Getting over those little fears and saying, "Well, the heck with it," really does break down the stigma of who an alcoholic is. You can be an

---

*An independent national organization of gay and lesbian Catholics.

alcoholic and not in the gutter; it's a disease that can be handled.

Now I would say, to take it one step further, that I wouldn't give up being an alcoholic, because it showed me what strength I have and how sensitive I can be. I would go through it all again. In some ways alcoholics and other addicts are people who take life full blast; there isn't a filtering system. You feel life very deeply. You can learn compassion for people. When I see people on the street, I go, "Well, that's me too." I don't feel superior to them, I feel very much with them.

I was one of the original organizers of the Conference of Catholic Lesbians. [A few of us realized] that lesbians weren't ever going to be full partners in Dignity. I was trying to find a sense of women's bonding in Dignity and remembering the bonding I had in Alaska in the tribe which was so strong. It was a tiny little village on an island way out in the middle of nowhere and because they were so connected with one another and with their spirituality—which was their land—they literally fought to a standstill I don't know how many major corporations, the United States government, and the state government. A tiny little village of four hundred people, with no educational resources to speak of, but their faith was so strong that they prevailed. That was a lesson that really struck home. If you have faith and a real good strong spirituality there isn't anything you can't do. I knew that women weren't getting that connectedness in Dignity, with each other, or anything. They were just haggling over inclusive language and fighting for every little image of God they could get from men and it was just zero. It just wasn't any spiritual food at all.

So I banged at a typewriter and punched out a memo about what possibly could be done about bringing the women in Dignity together, bringing Catholic lesbians together, to find out who they were and [how] to get that [nourishment] from one another. Then a group of us sat down and planned a conference. We wrote to a number of speakers including Theresa Kane who, in our minds, was really the Catholic woman of America, because she stood up to the pope and that was really something as far as we were concerned. That's how it got started. And it took on a life of its own. Everything would point to the fact that it wouldn't succeed. We had no money. The first brochures [were printed with] a Xerox machine. But over one hundred women came [to that first conference and today the national organization is going strong.]

I have a spiritual director in Tucson, Arizona, and I work individually with her. We speak over the phone. I also go on retreat [out there]. I started off being very angry at God, angry at God for the loss of Alaska, for alcoholism. So the first retreat I went on was trying to get me to pray, and it was being angry at God. My second retreat was [focused on] dealing with the witch and the family curse. The third retreat, which was this year, was dealing with and coming to honor the feminine within myself, the patience and the waiting and the gentle and the compassionate. My male side, in terms of being very action-oriented and decisive and independent, is really very well developed and I think it's part of the reason why I've been so successful in the business world. But I realized with this retreat that I was out of balance: I was often searching for the feminine in other women and needed to search for it in myself. You would think as a lesbian you would automatically honor your own womanhood. I found out that in ways I was contemptuous of my own womanhood, much having to do with our own society being contemptuous [of women]. So some of my spiritual journey now is finding and honoring what my woman hood is.

I found out that the witch represented some psychic power I was ignoring. I mean, I really buried my spirituality; I kept so busy with my religious activism that I didn't look at my spirituality. The witch was my spirituality that became destructive when I didn't take a look at it. It was the negating of the spiritual power which really destroyed the women if they did not take it and make it their own. I think that was one of the lessons of the witch, that [this power] will kill you if you don't recognize it and honor it. I don't fear it anymore because I recognize it. It is now a part of me.

I have set up my own altar at home where I am starting to go and pray by myself, every day, and learning to let go of things, as a way of relaxation, and getting to what I miss so much and which I had in Alaska, which is the stillness. Especially living in Manhattan, you don't have the stillness.

When I pray it's kind of a mix. It's speaking interiorly, because I still haven't gotten to the point where I can even whisper a spoken prayer. On my altar there are symbols that are sacred to me. I meditate upon these symbols and in some way relate them back to my day or my life. I don't have a crucifix within my altar, but then I never liked the suffering part. Humor gets me through the day. One thing I always remember is not to take myself too seriously, but just to enjoy living fully. The best picture I ever saw of Jesus was a laughing Jesus. It's so much healthier, I think, than to have the symbol of the crucifixion.

The crucifixion means a lot of suffering, and growth comes from suffering, I understand that. [But] I would much rather have the laughing Jesus.

I consider myself a Catholic. I define myself as a Catholic. I was born and baptized a Catholic; it's a religious tradition that I have made a very conscious choice to continue. When I pray in a community with the symbols and traditions I've been raised with, they speak to me. I continue to identify myself as a Catholic because I care enough to want to shape the church that shaped me. And I see myself as being perfectly able and within my right to do just that. So I have no qualms about identifying myself as a Catholic.

Often on a business trip I'll go to church in a strange town, a five o'clock Mass, with a bunch of other business people, or little old ladies, or people who have just wandered in from the street, and we all pray together. In some ways I get my greatest sense of community from praying together with those strangers in a church, more than in any other [setting, even] a women's conference. There's a rush I get from praying with women, a sense of being a part of something. But in terms of going back to the stillness again, I find that when I go to that five o'clock Mass.

I probably alternate between praying to the Great Spirit and praying to Jesus, who I think is a very human, warm type of person, very loving. If I want that feeling of being loved, I would bring in my mind the image of Jesus. Besides Jesus, the Great Spirit would be my primary way of experiencing God. God for me is a tremendous, dazzling illumination, a dazzling white light. I am sort of ambivalent to the fray over the sex of God, because God to me is neither male nor female.

For the good and bad, Catholicism brings me a sense of continuity. There was life before and there's life after. So the sense of life is what I get from Catholicism, and being part of something. And the jokes: the humor, the sense of irony. And the sense of continuity, the communion with strangers. The sacredness and the communion, which makes you related to other people, not just that we've all got our butt plopped in the pew to listen to a sermon for a while; Catholicism is less intellectual than Protestantism. That sense of the sacred to me is something distinctly Catholic. I don't find Catholicism intellectually satisfying. If everything's a mystery, I don't know how it can be intellectual: You can't understand the un-understandable. [But that's] not a problem for me, because a lot of my spirituality comes from feeling and sensing and doing nonintellectual things.

The women's movement had an influence on me, in terms of making me aware that I was discriminated against and thinking about the use of the term *girl*. But I wasn't a movement person; I was in Alaska for a lot of that and it kind of passed me by. But the Tlingit society was a matrilineal society and certainly that influenced my spirituality. They didn't just go out and adopt you; you had to pass muster in terms of character in front of these old women that really ran the tribe. Men had a lot of powerful positions, but the final word on any life-or-death issue was reserved to women because they considered men too frivolous to deal with life-or-death issues. You knew the men were saying what the old women told [them] or let them say. The guardians of the clans were these old women. Because they held the insignia, the symbols, they held the spiritual life for the clan and the tribe. The woman who became my [adoptive] mother had to go before them and tell them about me and they decided whether I was going to be in the tribe or not. And one thing that prompted me, when I came back, to found CCL, is that no self-respecting Tlingit woman would permit someone to tell her who she was as a spiritual woman. She interacted fully, and Catholic women did not interact fully, they had their spirituality told to them by men. How corrupt and evil that was and how degrading, how "not being whole," in comparison with all the Tlingit women I had seen.

I'm absolutely for the ordination of women. And I would say, let's not wait for a "renewed" priesthood. Let's ordain them now and see how the priesthood evolves. If I could change the Catholic church, I would change that first for a major impact on the common woman and common man. Not for the elite or intelligentsia, but people like Mom and my sister and my friends. I think to see women as priests would give the common woman hope that we are fully spiritual people and I think it would take that symbol to do it.

Then I would hope that the Catholic church would address the whole issue of sexuality, looking at it for what it is and for its spiritual connections. Because now it's kind of warped: It's either nothing or babies. I think that looking at sensuality and looking at pleasure in a different way would be a help. When I was twelve and realized I had feelings toward girls, I wanted to hide my sexuality and run away from it. My father especially was very strict with me in terms of harping on the whole virginity thing; that wasn't healthy. But I grew up masturbating and by the time anybody thought to tell me it was bad, I had been doing it for years and years. So I always found that part of myself— my sexuality—extremely pleasurable, and it was something I always enjoyed. I knew I didn't want to be a nun precisely because I would have to give up sex and there was never a thought in my mind that I would give it up.

Birth control should be a shared responsibility between men and women. I used birth control when I was married, and my husband did from time to time, because I had a problem with birth control pills. I'm opposed to abortion. One of my closest friends has had two of them and I had very mixed feelings about that. But what the base came down to is I said, "I love you and I want to make sure you get the best, and if you need money or you want me there, I'll be there, without the moralizing. Or if you want me to take the baby, I will take the baby." But she would have been fired from her job for being pregnant. I think [abortion] shows a basic disregard for human life— a little scrape to get you out of a little scrape. [I probably feel this way] because I saw so many "inconvenient" Indians. When [people] wanted their land, they just got rid of them.

I would vote pro-choice because I think women will get an abortion one way or another and I would much rather see them be healthy. My grandmother and my aunts who had abortions, what they did was jump off dressers, or they did something to induce a miscarriage. Women are going to have them, so being a realist, I say, okay, let's have it done in the hospital. Especially poor women should have first-class medical care.

I'm for abortion in some circumstances and I'm also in favor of capital punishment under some circumstances. If it was a socially heinous crime, raping and killing for example, I don't know why we should keep a person alive, or a person who has killed once, served their time, and goes back out and kills again. I would say society has given them their chance and we don't owe them anything beyond that. We have a finite amount of resources and I don't think that poor people are given enough at this point. I think that they should be given good medical care and that they should be given enough to eat. You can't ask a child to go to school and eat hot dogs at night. Keeping a mass murderer alive, we pay $25,000 or $30,000 a year. The person did have a choice to kill or not to kill. But that baby or those aborigines had no choice, and I think that's where the evil comes in. We owe everybody in our society health and medical care, food, shelter, and in some way, love.

Christine always tells me that my bark is worse than my bite. She and I visit two women in the maximum security prison in Medford Hills; one is in for murder and one is in for homicide in the course of armed robbery. You always put your theories to the test when you meet someone face to face. They are both good women in their own way; but certainly under my own definition of justice, at least one of them would have been put to death.

My definition of success has changed. I always thought success was a series of accomplishments, especially great change-the-world accomplishments. In Alaska, we had these beautiful, beautiful mountains that surrounded us, and the mountains seemed to have a language that was always just beyond my ability to hear it, just beyond the wind in some way. About two weeks ago my spiritual director said, "What is your goal in life?" And I said, "My goal in life, and my definition of success, would be to be able to hear the music in the mountains." I think once I reach a state of harmony with my surroundings there will be that click, and I really will hear that music from the mountains.

Two years after our initial interview, Karen was diagnosed with chronic immune dysfunction syndrome (also known as chronic fatigue syndrome). After a period of disability leave, she returned to work at AMA. She said of her illness, "It has shaken me up to the core of my identity. I lived for my work and was very interested in all the status symbols: having a corner office, being in Who's Who, having an expense account. Having to learn patience, having to learn humility, that was a terrible lesson, to learn not to be in control, to live in the moment and day by day. [But] if your legs hurt and you can't walk, you learn to enjoy sitting, and watching the birds and insects and people, which I never had time for. I was too busy marching along from project to project and purpose to purpose. There was a whole life I would have passed by. So the illness gave me my life back."

SIX

KNOWING GOD, NAMING GOD

When I think of Jesus I think of someone wrapping their arms around me and being safe.
—Susan Dyer Johnson

God, the beginning and end of all things,
can be known with certainty
from created reality
by the light of human reason....
Those religious truths which are by their nature
accessible to human reason
can be known ... with ease ...
even in the present state of the human race.
—Dogmatic Constitution on Divine Revelation
(Dei Verbum), Second Vatican Council

Prayer is at least as intimate a reality as sex; for many people, it may be an even more delicate topic of conversation. Yet all of the women I met spoke freely about God and prayer. Catholic women are people who pray. They are Christians. Their reference is Jesus much more than the pope. Whatever their relationship to the institutional Church, all but a few prayed, or, in some cases, engaged in another spiritual practice such as meditation. All had rich inner lives. The few who did not pray, with one exception, were socially or politically active women who regularly engaged in considered reflection on their actions and decisions, reminiscent of the "examination of conscience" they had learned as Catholic children.

I discovered that Catholic women share a set of assumptions about

God and prayer, assumptions so basic that most take them for granted and do not articulate them. At first I took them for granted as well. They remained unspoken, lying under the text of our conversations, until it occurred to me that they needed to be spelled out. Five especially stood out. The spiritual life, Catholic women believe, is real. God is accessible. God is generous. Spiritual development is possible in this lifetime. And the imagination is a good thing, useful to that development, part of a mature spiritual life.

The spiritual life is real. Underlying Karen Doherty's rich and winding spiritual journey, underlying everything Catholic women said to me about God and prayer, is the premise that the spiritual life is not a projection, not an illness, not something one outgrows after coming of age. It cannot be reduced to something else, a social or psychological phenomenon. *"Lo principale Dios"*—"the most important thing is God," Colombian-born Marlene Mydy answered when I asked what was most precious to her. Spirituality is not only the act of prayer but the practice of living one's life under the gaze of God. "My life," said feminist liturgist Diann Neu, "rests in the arms of the Holy One." The spiritual life, for these women, is not just how they pray but how they live with God. To talk only about the act of prayer when talking about spirituality would be like talking only about the act of making love in a conversation about sexuality. Both sexuality and spirituality are ever-present realities, which suffuse all of life.

The women spoke repeatedly of God as alive in the world, as a reality, person, or presence they perceived as accessible rather than "out there." For Catholic women, God is Other, but there is no unbridgeable chasm. God can be known. For Karen Doherty, the mystery and presence of God are a given. The question for Karen about God and the spiritual life is not whether, but how.

Catholic tradition tends to view reason and faith as compatible rather than opposed. For most Catholics, mystery and intellectual inquiry coexist; they are not contradictory. Gallup and Castelli found Catholics to be more willing than their Protestant counterparts to accept "the compatibility of the evolution of physical life with the existence and creative power of God."[1] Many of the women I interviewed were highly educated and intellectually curious; they were not people who neglected the life of the mind. But their way of knowing integrated personal experience, book learning, and community life. I also found few Catholic women to be preoccupied with doctrine. This is not to say that Catholic women are not concerned about truth, but truth for most of them (there were a few strong exceptions) is not so much a proposition as a path or way of life that rational statements cannot embrace. Faith is not a formula.

Carmen Benavente de Orrego-Salas of Bloomington, Indiana, raised in a privileged Chilean family prominent in politics and the arts, moved to the U.S. several decades ago with her husband, the composer Juan Orrego-Salas. She returns to Chile regularly to work with women from a small village who practice the art and craft of embroidery, a project she initiated which has enhanced the women's cultural pride and economic self-sufficiency. "Why is this spiritual work?" she asked. "To me, Christianity is a very physical, bodily, practical practice. Christ had to do with people, people that live here, that have needs, that have to live with each other." "Holiness is full human wholeness," said "Genevieve O'Rourke," a cloistered contemplative nun. "It's to go through people to God, to realize the dignity of each human person."

To Catholic women, the spiritual life is anything but static. It is an ongoing process that has its ups and downs. Although a striking number of women spoke of dreams, visions, revelations, and other "peak experiences," theirs is not a spirituality of "being saved". Crises of faith—times of doubt about God's presence and power—are not absent from the lives of Catholic women, but they speak of these episodes as part of their journey of faith rather than interruptions in it. Their views are in keeping with the traditional Catholic view of the spiritual life, which is a developmental one. This perspective is shared by converts and "cradle Catholics" alike.

As the women spoke of changes and fluctuations in prayer and the spiritual life, they assumed there was no single way of being a person of prayer. Mary Olivanti, a practicing Roman Catholic until her mid-twenties, is a Lutheran pastor; she is married to a former Catholic priest who is her colleague in the Lutheran ministry. Although she prays privately on a daily basis, she said, "what I need to have a healthy spiritual life is not only a regular Sunday sacramental life but some kind of small prayer and Bible study group. My spiritual life is almost always people-connected." She added, "Jim's spirituality is real different from mine. He's kind of a monk at heart. I often go over to the church and find him on his knees at the communion rail." Mary did not perceive this as better or worse than her own practice or as an obstacle to spiritual companionship with her husband, but simply as a difference in temperament and style for which there was plenty of room.

For Catholic women, growth in the spiritual life occurs in community as well as in solitude. "Without the people," "Jenna Santini" said to me, "you can't really have God, because you don't have anyone to show you peace and show you faith. You have to have that community, you have to have that sharing with people to feel God sometimes. You can't always do it by yourself." A majority of the women spoke of the nourishment they found in the sacramental life of the Church. "The liturgy, the Eucharist, the Mass will always be central to my life," "Joanne Grace" said, "and in good times and bad is a source of joy and comfort to me. The Eucharist is what it's all about. From it we draw strength, and the teaching possibilities of homily, of prayer, of song are really mind-boggling. They're not always that well used but the possibilities are there and I've seen them succeed." Many women echoed "Joanne's" feelings. "The body and blood of Christ in the Eucharist, that's where I feel connected," said Mary Olivanti, who now presides at Eucharistic celebrations as a Lutheran pastor. "Madeleine Mitchell," a bank clerk, is an active member of one of Southeast Washington, D.C.'s black Catholic parishes. "At certain parts of the Mass, at the offertory and at the consecration, I just get this lightheartedness," she said, touching her chest, "and I know I'm all right."

"The sacraments," "Serena Townsend" explained, "are really important for those times when you have neither the energy nor the courage. Whatever is going on in your life publicly or privately, it's there; it holds you. I regard it as a sort of safety net. There are times when prayer simply consists of abandon. You say, 'There is no way I can pray, *You* take over, *Your* job.' The Mass is like that. I don't mean that you don't have an obligation to be attentive but when at times in your life you're not at your highest peak of efficiency, it's there."

"I like the ceremony," said Barbara Kern of Indianapolis. "I like the ritual. I like the aspect of being together with the community of people." But, she added, "It's so rare that you hear a good sermon." Barbara's complaint about the poor quality of Catholic preaching was echoed around the country.

Of the women I interviewed, virtually all those who went to Mass received communion at every liturgy. There were two exceptions. I went to church with Camila Alvarez and her mother in Milwaukee on the Sunday I interviewed Camila, noticed she had not received communion, and asked her why. "Because I felt that I'm not worthy to receive his host," Camila said, voicing a sentiment more characteristic of a mid-century Catholic than a seventeen-year-old in the late 1980s. "When I feel that I have totally done good [in the] past week or feel good about myself, I feel worthy of receiving his body, his bread. It's something that grew through my mother. She does not go to communion either, only when she feels that she has done something good under the eyes of God." Camila and her mother were atypical. For the other churchgoers I met, the Eucharist was a sacrament of healing, to which one may come broken as well as whole.

The other exception, Aurora Martinez, told one of the most poignant stories I heard in the long months of travel and research. A night custodian at the University of Texas at Austin, Aurora is illiterate; she cannot read or write except to sign her name. She attends church faithfully but does not receive communion, I discovered, for the same reason she does not read: Her parents were migrant workers, and economic necessity forced them away from education, both secular and religious. "We would go to school a couple of weeks," Aurora remembered, "then when they found work they would take us out." Without continuity there was no chance to learn to read and write. For the same reason, because of the lack of a stable residence, Aurora never received religious instruction to prepare for her First Communion. She and her husband went to a justice of the peace to be married, although they are both baptized Catholics, assuming mistakenly that they could not be married in the Church. To this day she does not receive communion. "Why?" I asked. "Because I am ashamed that I am so old," she answered. "I think I am very big to be making my First Communion."

A small but growing number of Catholic women choose to worship in informal, lay-led groups, as Karen Doherty now does once a month. "They're very participatory, held in a circle, which implies a certain equality," she said to me a year after our original interview. "Our liturgy leaders come from our community, our friends, not someone who is thrust upon us. Whatever you have is drawn from your own experience and not somebody lecturing at you. There's time for shared reflections, time for silence, we sing together, we pass bread and grape juice in Eucharistic commemoration of our faith. I don't think they have the richness and tapestry of a High Mass," Karen added, "but High Masses were developed over 1,500 years; when you have that kind of history behind you, five years is a short time. But [our liturgies] are very touching in their own way. We don't always sing on key. It isn't so polished that you feel excluded. Everyone's a part of it."

Since it is well known that confession is on the decline among American Catholics, I expected to find that American Catholic women celebrate the sacrament of Reconciliation (as it is now called) only "very occasionally," in Abigail McCarthy's words. In fact, many women do celebrate it—at least half the women I interviewed—but only once or twice a year. The one exception I encountered, Ruth Pakaluk, a member of the highly disciplined and traditional Opus Dei movement, went to confession weekly as Opus Dei requires of its members. After hearing so many unhappy tales of childhood confession, I did not expect to encounter many positive feelings about Reconciliation, but I did. Women found the gift of God's forgiveness enabled them to live with renewed energy and faith. "It makes me feel more at ease with myself," said college student Leticia Zamarripa, who goes to confession once a year. "I feel better and I feel I can start all over again and get out there and conquer the world again."

Well over half of the women who celebrate Reconciliation favor the communal form that has come into practice since Vatican II. "Joanne Grace" attends such communal celebrations "maybe a couple of times a year." "I find communal penance is one of the latter-day joys of the Catholic church," she said, "because I find real meaning where a group of us gather, examine our conscience together, sing and pray, and publicly, instead of sneaking into the confessional on Saturday afternoon, acknowledge our faults and ask for God's mercy, and do it in a way that's not condemning. Somehow I always feel very joyful after."

Some women are discovering or creating alternatives to the traditional celebration of Reconciliation. Like the small Eucharistic circles, these celebrations of reconciliation are characterized by mutuality and shared responsibility. "Sometimes," said "Jenna Santini," a regular churchgoer, "I'll go to women who are involved in the Church and we'll kind of confess to each other, which I think is a very beautiful experience, because we're more open to each other. I don't really feel like someone has to be ordained to say, 'I don't think God will be angry with you.' Now, I know that we cannot reconcile them in the eyes of the Church the way a priest can, because we're not ordained; but I think it is a kind of confession. And I feel like in a way I am being reconciled."

Other women find spiritual sustenance outside the sacraments. Twelve-Step programs, for Catholic women as for so many others today, serve as a source of renewal for the spirit. For a few of the women I interviewed, groups like Alcoholics Anonymous and Narcotics Anonymous had been literally life-saving. For many Americans, including Catholic women, A.A. and N.A. have come to replace church as a primary spiritual community. Of the women I interviewed, however, most combined recovery programs with attendance at Catholic liturgy. Rather than substitute one for the other, they included in their routine what they found life-giving, adding and integrating as they went along.

For some women, church-based work on behalf of social justice has been the main wellspring of spiritual growth. Beatrice Cortez became intensely involved in COPS (Communities Organized for Public Service), the major parish-based community organizing movement in her city of San Antonio; it changed her life. Before she joined COPS, where she soon took on a leadership role, "I was like a child in my faith," she remembered. "I was obedient. I saw the Rosary side of faith. I felt protected. Since COPS I am an adult in my Christianity; I feel responsible for what happens in my church." Spiritual renewal, for Beatrice, has meant a less passive, more participatory relationship to the community of faith. Because the Church's involvement in the problems of her community has made it a more credible institution, Beatrice hears the message of the Gospel in a new way.

Women also spoke of meeting God in nature—hiking, river rafting, growing flowers in their gardens, or jogging on a quiet street. "Jeanne Dupont" remembered: "I was on the porch and there was a very soft rain, so soft that it whispered into the leaves, and I was listening to them saying 'blessed, blessed, blessed, blessed' and thinking that the air was so damp and soft I could inhale blessings. [I have] that sense of divinity being always present, we just need to be awake to recognize it, to enjoy it, to inhale it." In some cases, as women described it, their environment itself seemed to pray, whether it was nature or the work of human hands. Sarah Hofheinz said, "I don't pray much in a formal way, [but I] view Jesus through art; I love religious art. Though consciously I don't think about religion [a lot], I see it in my life all the time: I selectively seek it out through one of the things that is most dear to me, and that is art. I have holy water fountains around the house. I find a lot of humor in religious art; I like the everydayness of it. I like it around me."

The percentage of Americans who list their primary religious affiliation as "New Age" is low (less than one percent),[2] but if these interviews are any indication, significant numbers of Catholics (especially women in their thirties and forties) have incorporated Eastern forms of meditation and what is popularly known as New Age spirituality into their lives. "Elizabeth Heilig" has renewed her connection to the Catholic church, but continues to practice meditation and yoga. "I always found it easier," she said, "to go through the body." Women like "Elizabeth Heilig" and Karen Doherty are drawn to Eastern, New Age, and Native American paths because of their focus on steady practice, attention to the body, interiority, quieting and expanding the mind as well as listening to the heart, direct experience of God, healing, and a more integrated relationship with nature and earth. Some integrate these spiritual disciplines with the active practice of Catholicism; for others, this path has become the primary means of spiritual development, providing nourishment and healing they did not find in the traditions they received as children.

While women who practice yoga or visit psychic healers are a minority among Catholic women, they share with their sisters a desire not to disconnect body from soul, heart from mind, politics from the life of the spirit, the child in the past from today's adult woman, the self in relationship from the self before God. Contemplative nun "Genevieve O'Rourke" practices yoga. "I am drawn to the whole body, the whole person," she said to me. "I express it in dance and gesture sometimes, and I feel really good about this." At the twenty-fifth jubilee celebration of her vows as a nun, she incorporated liturgical dance into the ceremony, which was attended by relatives and friends from her days as an office worker. She laughed: "My girlfriend said, 'If I ever thought I would be in church doing this!' but they loved it, this body movement to express the joy of faith."

Catholic women assume that the imagination is good and necessary in the spiritual life. The capacity to make images is healthy and part of a mature spiritual life, and everything is usable for spiritual growth: dreams and daydreams, emotions and mental visions. "Madeleine Mitchell" of Washington, D.C., uses her imagination when praying the Rosary: "If I'm trying to meditate on the Rosary, I try to picture different things in the life of Christ or Mary. You can picture Elizabeth going to Mary, or the agony in the garden," she said. The imagination is also fundamental to the women's approach to the Bible. "I look to Jesus as a role model of what it means to live in the world as a Christian," said "Joanne Grace." "I try, when I have a question as to what's right and what's wrong, what's good and what's not, to look at the Gospels and try to figure out what Christ would have done, said, felt."

Catholic women read the Bible with varying frequency. Though some grew up reading Scripture or listening to Bible stories, many shared the memory of fifty-six-year-old Lucy Seal of San Antonio: "In my era, it was drilled into us not to read the Bible because you could read it incorrectly." Before Vatican II, the Bible was proclaimed from the pulpit during Mass but otherwise remained off limits; women of all ages regretted not knowing it better. But many Catholic women today read the Bible, alone or with the help of a study group. Almost without exception, the women favor a multifaceted approach—what Susan Johnson described as "a mixture of academic and emotional"—

combining a historical-critical approach with an imaginative and prayerful reading of the text.

Catholic women's prayer practices vary from contemplative to Charismatic, from the Rosary to the one-sentence Eastern Christian mantra known as the Jesus Prayer. Nearly half use the Bible as a springboard for personal prayer. At least half say formal prayers some of the time, but more than anything they pray informally, in a conversational manner, with a God who is familiar and intimate. "[When I pray by myself it's] just talking," said Ann Richards Anderson. "God as shrink: You say, 'Oh, look what I did now! I am such an idiot! Please help me learn how to handle this better.' At home we always say grace: We all go around the table and say thank you for whatever we're thankful for that day. I still say prayers with [my youngest son] at night, which, again, are just like talking to God, saying, 'Thank you for that' or 'I'm sorry about this,' or 'I can't get along with my brother, will you help me learn to love him more?' " I asked sixty-four-year-old May Kast of Madison, Wisconsin, if she spoke to Jesus: "Yes, we have straight-out talks sometimes!" she laughed. "I think that sometimes he'll say, 'Well, that woman, she's a little too sassy.' "

"Regina White" had finished serving a prison sentence a year or two before we met and was successfully navigating the difficult journey of recovery from alcohol and drug abuse. Two crucifixes hung on the wall of her studio apartment, along with a dart board and a large poster of Marilyn Monroe. She said to me: "My thinking got straightened out because I believe in God. It's like He's my best friend. I keep Him beside me. If I have a problem with somebody at work I try to hold my tongue and talk it over with my God and ask Him to help me, and so I just say, 'Help me with this person, guide me through this, because I want to crack their head open.' " In the morning, "Regina" said, "First I get quiet. And then I tell myself, 'Okay "Regina," you're talking to your maker.' I try to get real calm. And then I talk. I try and think about how I feel, what I'm worrying about, any real big problems I have, and then I go through the steps of the day [in my head]. I don't ask for material things, I ask for things for my character. And then I try to be quiet and just listen."

How do these women, who are busy all day and part of the night earning a living, caring for children, and attending to their relationships with husbands, lovers, and friends, find time for prayer? They pray late at night, early in the morning, in between and during periods of activity. Commuting time seems to have become the privileged place of prayer in North America. Betty Anne Nogan, a deputy director of the Financial Control Board of New York, rides the subway from Brooklyn to Manhattan every morning. "On the subway on the way to work I pass a church when we're above ground, and the church has a cross on it," she said. "Every morning I make sure that I look at the cross and I say a prayer or think about God. It's been years and I still do it. It's just a time to thank God for being alive, recognize that I will die, life isn't forever and it's meant to be meaningful." "My private prayer life is mostly conducted in the car," said Mary Olivanti, who pastors two churches thirty miles apart. "My best time to myself is when I am driving; I pray and I talk and I meditate." Two thousand miles due south, in San Antonio, community activist Beatrice Gallego prays in the car on her way to meetings or to her granddaughter's day care center. "Does this ring a bell?" I asked Maureen Dallison Kemeza of Boston, a Ph.D. student, part-time church worker, wife, and mother of two. "Of course," she laughed. "Jesus rides in the passenger seat!"

Does God answer? More than this, the women are concerned about whether God is listening. They do not necessarily expect answers, but they hope and believe that they are heard. Prayer calms, soothes, strengthens, gets them through, helps them to let go. When Joy Duffy's father was ill with cancer, she found herself praying a lot, but, she said, "My prayers were not so much, 'Let him not have cancer,' but, 'Give us the strength to get through this ordeal.' " Prayer, "Regina White" said, has made her life "more for other people." She works as a dietary aide at a state psychiatric institution. "I work in the kitchen but I always sneak upstairs to the patients. I feed 'Barbara,' she's been there for fifty years and she sits in a chair all day long. I tell her I love her. She tried to break my arm. I like them all in there," she said fondly.

From conversing with God or praying throughout the day, the women slip easily into contemplation, simply being in the presence of God, a gratitude without words. "It's like this awe," said Diann Neu, the codirector of WATER, the Women's Alliance for Theology, Ethics, and Ritual. "I feel my eyes are totally open. I have the overwhelming conviction of being totally loved." Some times of prayer become moments of heightened awareness, peak experiences, coincidences too intense to be accidents. The women spoke of them with wonder, but also without any doubt that the miraculous could happen in daily life. On the first retreat she ever made, an ecumenical Cursillo, Angela Rodriguez "felt a oneness with things. Everything was very vivid," she remembered. "Flowers were very bright. Pain was more painful." Maude Lancaster showed me the short stories and plays she had written over the years; she had worked as a housekeeper during most of her adult life and, at the age of seventy-five, was caring for her grandchildren, whose fathers and mothers all work outside the home. "One night," said Maude, "I had a dream. It bothered me so the next morning. I saw Our Lord. I woke up at four in the morning and I went to get up and it seemed like all of a sudden something came over me, like I was there and I wasn't there, and I looked over to the door, and I don't know whether it was a dream, but He was standing in the doorway. I reached up to my eyes and I felt water coming down and [my husband] said, 'What's wrong with you?' and I said, 'I've just seen Our Lord.' "

As a young woman, Carmen Benavente de Orrego-Salas experienced "a sort of vision, a Damascus Road thing. Suddenly the oneness of life was there. Everything that had been simmering [in me] came together—a feeling there is no death, there is only transformation." Many years later, Carmen sat in her room one morning saying the Lord's Prayer. She began to ask, " 'Who are you, Jesus? Who are you, Christ?' And the answer was right there," she said. "The answer was a very physical presence sitting next to me. I didn't see Christ; I felt Christ, but as a physical presence of somebody who would always be with me. I would never know loneliness; aloneness yes; loneliness no."

Victoria Bowden was living in a housing development in Raleigh, North Carolina, when we met, working in an office and raising her children alone after disengaging herself from an abusive marriage and living on welfare for several years. The first day she was able to have day care for all three of her children, toward the end of her time on welfare, Victoria went down to the city's Capitol Square. "I remember sitting under a tree. I wanted to write, I wanted to read. I took the Gospel of John with me. I'd heard somebody saying something about 'God is in every living thing' and I remember stopping to dwell on that, and suddenly God was. I was aware of it. Everything took a different form. Everything was alive with God's presence. It was almost suffocating." Victoria wrote a poem about this experience. "I sent it to the North Carolina Catholic and they put it in there," she said happily.

To speak of God, Catholic women use language of acceptance, welcome, and protection. Even the stern Father-God with whom a sizable minority of the women grew up was approachable, though the friendly mediation of Mary and the saints may have been required. Only for a few has God remained a faraway, punitive judge. For most, God is the One who takes you in. Ann Richards Anderson remembered: "A bunch of us were having drinks one night [after work]. We were talking about how difficult it was getting away from the guilt and the restrictions that our various religious upbringings had given us, and how we were all going to raise our children differently. And one of the men, who was raised a Fundamentalist Protestant, said, 'Yes, there was always the thought that you wouldn't be saved, or that you were damned, or that you couldn't quite make it. Always the great fear.' I spoke up immediately and the other Catholics in the group said the same thing: That is not how it feels to be a Catholic at all. Particularly [if you're] an Irish Catholic, you are definitely raised with the notion that you are a sinful failure in life, but that you are *loved* nevertheless: You never need to worry if you'll be 'saved.' That's not even Catholic terminology. You know you're a terrible sinner but you know you're loved. I don't think that's the way most Protestants are raised. I mean, they really worry about whether they're going to be loved. I don't think that question enters a Catholic's mind."

Presence was the word that occurred most often when I asked women about their understanding of God. "I don't necessarily think of God as a person," said Ann Valdez, a public health administrator in Texas. "I think of God more as a presence. I really believe that God is reflected in each of us," she added, "and so I think about God as being many people. I believe that each of us is a part of God and each of us is called upon to be God to the people we come in contact with."

Daughters of a tradition that treasures the imagination, Catholic women do not spontaneously visualize an image when they hear the word *God*. A few even make a conscious effort not to envision God: "I try not to have [an image]," said seventy-six-year-old Ruth Bolan, "because I think some of them are so bad—the solemn-faced man, always very kindly, with the beard and the long flowing robe." (But, she said, "God is a person.") "God doesn't have any face," said Angela Rodriguez. Most of the women I interviewed stressed that the God who can be known by mortal beings is also beyond human imagining. "I feel very deeply," said "Joanne Grace," "that God is going to be a tremendous surprise to me, and it's really impossible for me or anyone else to comprehend God."

To speak of God, the women drew on the language of the senses, but it was more kinesthetic than visual. "I never really pictured God with the beard and the blue eyes," said "Jenna Santini," "just peace and a warm warmth." "I don't really hear a voice or anything," said college student Patsy Weser, "but I feel more relaxed and calm after [I have prayed]. It's like a fresh breath." "It's like a cloud," said Nathalie Nepton, a student at the College of Saint Elizabeth in New Jersey. "If anything," said theologian Mary Hunt, "my God experience is more like smoke, sounds, and light than a creature or being. It's more amorphous, a process, much more of a dynamic, or force, or presence. There's movement, there's change, but there's also protection. I have a real sense of divine protection over the world—I think we would have all blown ourselves to smithereens [otherwise]." Many women, like Karen Doherty, experience God as light. "God is like a prism of light," said fifty-seven-year-old Dolores Reuter, "and everyone is a part of the light." "God," said "Jeanne Dupont," no longer a practicing Catholic, "is what pumps our blood, what makes us take our next breath."

"I don't feel particularly close to God at this point in my life," said thirty-six-year-old Sarah Hofheinz, "but I just always have the feeling that He's there and I'm very comfortable with Him. I can't imagine not having that belief in my life."

The image of God as father came up with some frequency in the interviews, but far less than God as presence. For some women, the term *father* was filled with positive connotations: God was like the father who had loved them or the loving father they had never had, writ large. Dorothy Wodraska, a physical education teacher in Indianapolis, said, "I often picture myself sitting at His knees talking to Him. I do that with my own dad." For Janet Kanitz, a mother and farmer's wife in Michigan's Upper Peninsula, God evokes "kind of warm fatherly images, someone that would cuddle. My family aren't cuddlers; I have always missed that," she added.

To "Anne Marie Quinn," the young businesswoman from Boston, "God or Jesus is just some fatherly all-knowing creator." When she prays to this God, the feeling she has is "a good safe feeling, almost womblike." "Anne Marie" spontaneously came up with both male and female images of God, though she is not especially preoccupied with current debates about inclusive language in prayer.*

Some women have begun to use female language to speak of God, though few favor its exclusive use. "Lately, mostly in my dreams," said journalist Pamela Montagno, "I have experienced an earth mother im-

---

*For nearly two decades, the language of prayer—both the words used to talk about human beings and the words to name God—has been under discussion in many parts of the Christian and Jewish communities. The conversation about "inclusive" God-language, that is, language that is not exclusively or predominantly male, is highly charged because it is, in part, about the nature of God and the nature of the human person. Within it lie the ticklish questions of what constitutes maleness and femaleness and how these qualities are related—or not—to the divine. At the root of the move to change the language of prayer is a desire to pray more deeply, a search for words that might better convey the depth and fullness of the love of God and the relationship between God and humanity.

age, nurturing and assertive, very loving and very much in tune with the earth and taking care of the earth." Community organizer "Elsa Colón" said, "I have a real mother vision of God, not a father vision of God. I pray when I'm afraid and I pray to God to guide or help me find the strength to do what I need to do. I also pray before eating; and that's very much identified with mother as the source, mother earth, God as the creator of all that's around us [who] has brought us the food that's on the table for us to share. And I pray in that moment too that other people will be able to eat as well as myself, and there [I have] a real strong vision of God as a mother, a giver, a life-affirmer. Maybe that's just my life experience, that I don't perceive men in that same way." Marie de Porres Taylor, the Sister of the Holy Names who directs the Pastoral Center for Black Catholics in the Diocese of Oakland, told me her image of God had changed from that of an old black man with white hair to that of a black woman nursing her child.

For "Jeanne Dupont," the conscious use of the mother-image is a corrective, part of her recovery from the trauma of incest by an older male relative which she remembered only a few years ago. She envisions a female God, she said, "to recover my own dignity as female in the sense of 'to make sacred what was violated' but also to recover an image of Mother, capital M, that was capable of nurturing, as I came to realize that I'd never had any such thing from my mother, zero, none. It is important to stress the relationship with the divine that is nurturing, that is not just correct. I was brought up with God as a rule-giver; I have gone over to the nurturer. That is really a good thumbnail sketch of the journey." Diann Neu remembered moving from the image of God as father to that of God as woman and God as friend, "but now," she said, "it really is more of a sense of being-in-the-presence-of."

Concern about the language of prayer is not universal among Catholic women, but it is on the rise. Most of the women who struggled with or rejected exclusively male images of God were in their thirties and forties and defined themselves as feminists. Women in their late teens and early twenties took for granted the need to make the language of prayer more inclusive. But a few older women spontaneously mentioned the language issue. Sixty-four-year-old "Kitty Riordan" was one of the first lectors and Eucharistic ministers in her parish in the Midwest. "I'm one of the few that changes the language and gets a lot of flack for it," she said. "I started doing that early on, [back in the seventies]. I say the Creed in a language that I can live with. I remember saying, 'I feel invisible in this church,' and they started saying, 'Would you like to wear a robe when you're a lector?' They don't know what you mean when you say 'invisible,' when it's all 'him, him, him,' forever, and 'he, he, he,' and God is a 'He.' I don't let myself get on this topic too often," she said. "It's too painful." She added, "Isaiah has given me wonderful womanly images of God."

For Catholics, of course, Mary the mother of Jesus has been the feminine face of God. To be sure, Mary is not God according to orthodox Christian theology. "We honor Mary, we don't worship her," Christine Beckley said, wanting to make the distinction clear. Nevertheless, people pray to Mary. She may not be God in their spoken creed, but in the language of the heart she functions as God. "I think it's important that there's a woman in heaven," said Gaye Lott, a forty-nine-year-old sales manager from Texas who is no longer a practicing Catholic. "As a girl, that made me separate from my Protestant friends. I remember slumber parties where we talked about, was she really a virgin, was she really as important as we said she was? I remember defending her and thinking how important she was." For Camila Alvarez, a Mexican-American high school student from Milwaukee, God sometimes has the face of Our Lady of Guadalupe, the brown-skinned madonna of Mexico who is said to have appeared to the Indian Juan Diego. "Guadalupe is God," she said, adding that she also envisioned God in a number of other ways, all aspects of one reality. Three years later, as a college student at the University of Wisconsin, she wrote me a letter about her junior year abroad in Spain and the various options she was considering after graduation. "We'll see what *la Virgencita* has in store for me," she concluded, using the affectionate diminutive of the Virgin's name.

For every woman who had a strong devotion to Mary I found one for whom Mary had no meaning. The widely diverging relationships to Mary seem to reflect the variations in Catholic women's views of women and of God, both of which are currently in flux. Many of those who had no special relationship with Mary were active, practicing Catholics. "At this point in my life," said "Joanne Grace," raised in a rural environment and now living in an academic community, "Mary does not play a major role and I see that to be true of almost all my Catholic friends: farm women in Iowa, cousins, university people [here]. It may have something to do with the fact that, with a few exceptions, we don't hear anything about Mary in homilies anymore."

For some women, Mary has simply faded into the background. Others reject her more actively. The miraculous events associated with her birth, the birth of Jesus, and her death are no great stumbling blocks for them. The problem lies in Mary's image as a woman. To many she seems either an inadequate or an impossible model of womanhood: too mild, too good, too pure, too silent, nonsexual, and a mother all at once. "Virgin Mother!" Ellen Reuter exclaimed. "What kind of an example is that for us?" "[Mary was] the perfect model, the angel mother," "Serena Townsend" laughed. "Never did she misslice a tomato or drop a bean on the floor instead of in the soup. That kind of perfectionism is so unrealistic and so unreal. I suppose if I worked on it I could get Mary to be a real person, [but] Mary is not somebody I have any interest in at all."

Catholic women who do relate and pray to Mary see her as one who knows the human situation, who is infinitely compassionate and highly accessible, more so than God. "You can tell her things you wouldn't bother God with," social science researcher "Sylvia Presti" said. "During my childhood," Caryl Rivers remembered, "I prayed to Mary a lot more because she was just more accessible. [She has] no [place in my life now but she] was certainly a part of shaping my idea of God. She was a mother figure. She wasn't austere and forbidding—[which God was] to some degree. You approached Him slightly on tiptoe." Maude Lancaster recites the Rosary every day. "I have a book on Mary that I read," she said. "Her whole life is just wrapped around me. To me she was just like one of us."

Mary also seems accessible because of her appearance (far more often than Jesus) in a variety of cultural forms. Many of the Latina women, but also women of Chinese, European, and African ancestry, spoke with warmth of Mary as Our Lady of Guadalupe. "She's *morena* [dark] like I am," said Mary Esther Bernal. "The thing that strikes me about her," said Beatrice Cortez, "is how she, in her appearance to Juan Diego, was challenging the system, the Church. She appears to an Indian who is ignorant and poor and says, 'I want a temple in this place,' and she already knew what the bishop was going to say [to Juan Diego], [so] she says, 'but I want you to insist.' She knew where the power was and she was role-playing with him about how it was going to go."

The Rosary is still a popular devotion, functioning in a way like a mantra; women spoke of reciting it during thunderstorms and personal crises, as a comfort or an aid to meditation. Kathy Kasza of Milwaukee, a medical office manager raising her children alone after a bitter divorce, began to cry when speaking of her concern for her children and her prayers to Mary. "She is the person I discuss things with," Kathy said. "She is the person I reach out to and ask for help. When my husband left, nightly my prayer was the Memorare" (one of the traditional prayers of supplication to Mary). "She got me through those initial years of desertion, when I was going to school and being a mother. When I don't know what to tell my children, she is the one who taps me on the shoulder and says, 'Tell them you need time to think about it.' I always have a Rosary with me. It's a crutch, and when times get tough I pull it out. And I use it in desperation, too, when the [Green Bay] Packers are losing," she laughed.

The figure of Mary heartens some women about the dignity of their life-style. "Being mostly at home with my children running a household," said Ruth Pakaluk, "Mary becomes very important because sometimes you simply have to remind yourself, you have to say this like a little formula, that the greatest of all created beings was a housewife. She swept floors, made dinners, did laundries, the same things that we do were done by the Queen of Heaven and Earth. In modern America," Ruth continued, "being a housewife and a mother is not respected. In many circles you are just completely scorned and you're pitied. It's emotionally draining work and physically tiring and a lot of repetitive work, it's just hard to remember that it's service, physical, very direct service to human beings. Thinking of Mary and how she would have been doing these exact same things helps very much."

When Catholic women mention Mary's life as a mother, they speak not only of raising children but of letting them go. Commenting on the New Testament passage in which Jesus is brought to the Temple as a baby, Ellen Reuter noted how Mary looked into Jesus' eyes and felt sad. "She felt a pang in her heart. I related that to looking in your child's eyes and realizing that as much as you love him, you can't keep him, and that she had that experience very intensely, that here was this child who was probably the embodiment of love, and she couldn't keep him. He wasn't hers to keep."

Some women have reexamined Mary and come to a new understanding of her. "She had to be a very, very strong woman," Ellen said, "none of this plaster sweetness, because a plaster sweet mom wouldn't have lasted, couldn't have done what she did. I think about her as the ultimate woman, who did it all with style and grace, and it was real painful for her. It makes me real angry when people talk about Mary as a sort of sweet wimp who can get around Jesus and get him to do things for you. I pray to her especially when I'm dealing with mothering things, 'Help me to be a better mom,' or, 'Mother me,' when I'm feeling the need to be mothered; she's sort of the God that can mother. I think she is God's feminine image." In an update interview, she said, "Mary and Jesus have kind of melded into one. That's how I can do a male/

female God. I find myself praying to them as a team: 'C'mon guys.' "
The women for whom Mary is a model rarely see her as mild-mannered.
"She stood at the foot of the cross," said "Genevieve O'Rourke." "She
was there all the way; she's a strong woman of faith."

To these women for whom God is most of all a presence, Jesus
manifests this presence in the flesh; he is the humanity of God. "Jesus
is the invisible God revealed to us," Ruth Pakaluk said. "Contemplating
the humanity of Jesus and his life and his teachings, that's how we're
going to understand who God is." "Jesus," said Sarah Hofheinz, "is
God's way of demonstrating Himself to me in a concrete way."

The women spoke of Jesus less as the crucified one and more as
one who was alive, who walked and talked with them. When they
mentioned Jesus' crucifixion, it was almost inevitably when I asked
them about Mary: The topic of Jesus' suffering and death came up in
the context of relationship. Although the body on the crucifix has
influenced their view of Jesus (and of God) as one who "suffers with,"
they experience Jesus as alive, not dead. For them, he is the trustworthy
one, the confidant who is no stranger to pain or joy. The words *brother,
companion,* and *friend* came up repeatedly in answer to my question:
"Who is Jesus for you?"

"Whenever I read the New Testament it touches me," said "Caroline Wong." "Jesus had to go through a path like human beings, joy,
suffering, and had to die. When I go through my daily life then I can
identify with Jesus. I see Jesus like a human being, but he has his God
nature. Jesus is part of God, Jesus is God. Sometimes I cry—say, I fear
death—[then I say to myself], 'He was scared too, he cried.' " "[I talk
to Jesus]," said Vietnamese immigrant Hang Vu. "When I was young
I talked to him like a God, very powerful. When I grew up, I [began
to] talk to him like a friend." "I know that God and Jesus are the same
thing," said "Jenna Santini," "but I feel like Jesus is kind of the little
guy I can pull down to my level." Many women identified Jesus with
the poor and with all suffering people. "Jesus?" said seventy-six-year-
old "Louise O'Connell," sitting by a credenza adorned with a doll-faced
statue of the Infant of Prague. "He's everything. He's in each one of
the people that comes to [our town's soup kitchen], and any poor
soul."

"Jesus is the person who does all the things I'm afraid to do," said
college student Madeleine Msall. "Like when you see a wino on the
street who's falling over because he's sick, Jesus is the person who goes
up and makes sure that he's okay. A friend once told me that she was
riding a train with only two other people on it, two men, one of whom

was a wino who had fallen asleep, and they were getting toward the end of the train ride and the other guy bent over the wino and put his hand inside his coat, and she thought that he was checking his heart. [She] said [to me], 'I never thought this guy could be dead, I thought he was just falling asleep.' So she walked over and said, 'Do you think he needs help? Should we summon help?' And the guy said, 'Just go sit down,' and she realized he was robbing him, and she was very shocked. Jesus for me would be the person who was actually checking [the man's] heart to make sure he was okay."

Many mentioned Jesus' relationships with women in positive terms. "Jesus always recognized the value of women," said Rafaela Canelo. "He did not reveal himself to anyone more than to women. He never left the woman behind. He always valued her. Not for one moment did Jesus marginalize the woman. Maybe it is for that reason that we women [were there], until the last moment when he carried the cross. And at the resurrection? We were present there. No, we were not afraid."

After friend and brother, the women referred to Jesus most often as teacher and guide. "He reminds us of what we can be," said "Elsa Colón." "He's an example of how we could live," said forty-four-year-old Sara Whalen of Madison, Wisconsin. "We're just too much into our own selves. Jesus challenges [us] to do more." "Jesus," said Rafaela Canelo, "shows a style of life that is very simple. We can live so as to be able to share with one another. But we make it problematic."

For some women, Jesus blends with God to such an extent that they answered my question about one by talking about the other. "Who's Jesus for you?" I asked Mary Wunnicke, the dairy farmer from Wisconsin. "God our Father," she answered. "They are the same but different," said Thao Truong of Hayward, California, in a simplified version of the classic creedal statement. A small group of women questioned Jesus' divinity—but not the example or inspiration of his humanity. Anne Burke of Raleigh, North Carolina, considers Jesus "a prophet, the man who loved deeply. I think we've twisted him, made him into something he never meant to be. I work among a lot of Pentecostal, Evangelical, [and] Fundamentalist people who throw Jesus' name around in terms of 'personal savior,' 'being saved.' They feel they've bought a ticket into heaven as far as I can tell, and they can sit back now and not worry about a whole lot. It takes the human struggle out of the concrete and puts it up in the air somewhere so that you don't have to touch it; it removes people from reality. I reject that. The loving, touching, believing, challenging real person is the person I believe in. But he's not the be-all and end-all." When I asked Betty Anne Nogan, the government administrator from Manhattan, "Who is Jesus for you?" she answered: "I really don't know. I don't know whether I believe Jesus was God. I do believe in what he did," she said. "Even if he wasn't the son of God," said Christine Torrey, awaiting release from a long prison sentence, "I would follow him."

The Holy Spirit was not always a significant dimension of God for the women. When they did have something to say about the Spirit, the words that came tumbling out described a constellation of qualities: warmth, courage, consolation, inspiration, communication, serendipity, strength, enlightenment, movement, change, and power.

The most intriguing images of the Holy Spirit were occupational: "Jenna Santini" sees the Holy Spirit in a role similar to hers as a police officer, one who watches and protects, ensuring community safety: "I always think that the Holy Spirit is kind of like the policeman would be for a community. The Holy Spirit is the guardian and that's how I relate to the Holy Spirit. So we're kind of in the same occupation sometimes," she laughed. Mary Esther Bernal, the director of bilingual education from San Antonio, was originally trained as a musician and volunteers her time as a choir director at the city's cathedral. She said of the Holy Spirit, "I liken that to the feeling you get when you hear a beautiful piece of music, when you get that feeling in the soul." As a leader in the Massachusetts pro-life movement, Ruth Pakaluk is a frequent public speaker. She believes the Spirit resides in the Church and its leaders, but also spoke of the Spirit as "the one that actually acts within me. When I'm about to speak, I pray to the Spirit."

For many women, the Holy Spirit is the moving, active dimension of God, the energy of God, "the change agent" as one woman put it. Dorothy Wodraska spoke of it as "the power, an aura, almost like an energy source around me." The Spirit seems especially to be the dimension of God that does not sit still, the dynamic, historical part— "the fire at the core," said "Jeanne Dupont."

"Unlike God," says the historian Jay Dolan in his history of the American Catholic people, "saints were human; they walked the earth, and lived and died like other mortals. Consequently they were more approachable than the unseen God of the heavens. People treated the saints like distant relatives, heavenly aunts and uncles whose pictures hung on the walls.... No more complex than the family tree, the network of heavenly relatives was there to call on in time of need."[3] Dolan's observation about the saints' role in past generations still holds true today. In the Catholic world, there is a lot of company. At best, the saints can be a wondrous crowd of companions, exemplars, friends of God who serve as models in the spiritual life—"one of the smarter things to come out of Catholicism," said feminist theologian Mary Hunt. "They are very much a part of my life," said contemplative nun "Genevieve O'Rourke," "dear friends cheering and leading me on."

On a walk with her granddaughter, whose parents left the Catholic church to join an Evangelical Christian congregation, Dolores Reuter heard the child suddenly say, "Grandma, we don't like Catholics; they worship idols." "How so?" said Dolores, remaining very calm. "They worship statues," came the answer. "No, we don't worship the statues," Dolores answered. "We don't *worship* the saints. We keep the statues around to *remind* us of these people who were good and holy and show us what it means to follow Jesus." Andrea Sherlund, the twenty-six-year-old daughter of a Catholic mother and a Lutheran father, explained: "We don't pray to those figurines; they're just there. It's like a lamp. It's a reminder of who they are."

Women had their favorites of course, as people have favorite relatives. Aurora Martinez's bedroom was entirely occupied by two pieces of furniture, a king-sized waterbed and a dresser serving as an altar with a colorful assortment of *santitos*. "My favorite saint is Guadalupe," Aurora said, speaking of the brown madonna of Mexico who is now the official "Patroness of the Americas." "She is the one I pray to the most and also to St. Joseph, that handsome one there," she said, pointing to one of the statues on her altar. "She performs many miracles; you ask her and she grants them. I believe in that."

Thérèse of Lisieux, "the Little Flower," was the clear favorite among the canonized saints, beloved for her common touch, depth of prayer, and demonstration of holiness in everyday life. Anthony was another popular saint, a practical chap with a specialty—several women swore by his efficacy—of locating lost objects from keys to wedding bands. Some women prayed to Jude, the patron of desperate causes, and a great many, including a disproportionately high percentage of the Italian-American women, were fond of Francis of Assisi. One knew he was her favorite but momentarily forgot his name. "Who's the guy with the animals?" she said. A few women were especially attached to saints with conspicuous flaws. San Francisco city treasurer Mary Callanan favors Peter: "St. Peter was always blowing his top or going off the deep end," she said with some relish.

Sandra Mondykowski Temple, now a member of the Episcopal Church, finds the saints "a bit of a neurotic lot. I never could stomach the Little Flower," she said. She admires educators and founders of religious orders and medical institutions. "I wouldn't pray to them," Sandra added. "I think they'd laugh. Their inspiration for me is imitation."

At worst, the canonized saints seemed like poor role models to some women. Unlike most of the Catholic population, most of the canonized saints were celibate, often members of religious orders. Of the nearly four hundred saints recognized by the papacy between the years 1000 and 1987, fewer than 20 percent, according to historian Catherine Mooney, R.S.C.J., were laypeople; only twenty of the four hundred were laywomen. Sixty-five percent of all papally canonized saints during this period came from the territory of modern-day Italy, France, and Spain.[4] "I asked a priest last week, 'How come there's no Chinese saints?' " "Caroline Wong" complained. "He said there are lots. [We never hear about them] I would like to [learn about] Chinese saints." Some women remedied the gap by adding to the pantheon holy women and men who were not canonized. Their list expanded to include Dorothy Day and Mother Teresa, Sojourner Truth, countless grandmothers, and theologian Pierre Teilhard de Chardin, S.J. As Marlene Jones does, many women pray to loved ones who have died, or think of them as members of the company of saints—which they are, according to the fundamental theology of the saints.

There is a new fascination today with the strong and spirited women of the Christian tradition, like Julian of Norwich, the medieval English mystic, and other holy women whose history is becoming known to a wider circle. "I have been fascinated by the mother foundresses," said Abigail McCarthy. "They were women of great capability. An amazing number of them started what they started in mid-life. What they accomplished within such narrow confines [was remarkable]. More than fifty religious orders were founded in the seventeenth century to educate women or girls and poor children, and they were all forced back into the cloister. It took two hundred years before nuns were even allowed to teach. These women kept trying, and they finally did achieve marvels. I think they're a tremendous part of the history of women."

"After childhood and being steeped in the saints," said Diann Neu, who plans, designs, and leads creative liturgical celebrations, "I quickly broadened the communion of saints, and that happened when I was young, about six years old. My very best friend from childhood died of leukemia. I realized that she was a saint, and my mother used to say, 'You know Jeannie's a saint.' Often I will sit and have a chat with my grandmother, who died in 1980, particularly when I have difficulty with the ways my parents react, and have this wonderful little con-versation which I find very healing and helpful. Now, in the litanies that I create, Mary Magdalene is always very important—she received the call as Peter did, and many people forget. I name Ruth and Naomi because of the powerful relationship between them. I name Catherine of Siena and Teresa of Avila because they were Doctors of the Church. I name the house church leaders [of the earliest Christian church], Phoebe, Prisca, because of the importance of women in house churches. I name the justice makers: Ita, Maura, Dorothy, and Jean, the women who were killed in El Salvador. I'll name Theresa Kane, Dolores Huerta of the [United] Farmworkers, our own theologians, women ministers and pastors, and also children who will be born this year, because I have this sense of the passing on of generations. And also the unnamed women saints," she added, "the women who have been raped and battered and killed. I have a cousin [to whom] that happened."

Saints, for Catholic women, are the link between past and future generations, companions through space and time. Bridget Palmer, a twenty-nine-year-old human resources manager at Morgan Stanley, lights candles for her parents and grandparents. "It's sort of like wishing on a star," she said. "It's bringing in the saints' and God's care. Maybe it's linking me to the people who have lit candles and have these hopes and desires. Maybe it's just saying that there is a little star or saint or God looking out for this person."

"The notion of having saints and the abundance of saints is a real plus," said Mary Hunt. "Catholicism is on the right track here. Saints are real people, role models people can look to. The four women who were killed in El Salvador function that way. This is a very important thing to tell children: 'You belong to the tradition of these women. They came from where you come from.'"

SEVEN

CARMEN BADILLO

"This is wrong; these people are suffering."

Carmen Badillo, a divorced mother of five, works as a consultant on parish development for the Archdiocese of San Antonio, but the formative experience of her adult life—which led her to working for the Church—has been her involvement in Communities Organized for Public Service (COPS), a church-based community-action coalition. Carmen Badillo was forty-five years old when we met in her office at the archdiocesan center in San Antonio.

I was born and raised in the inner city, in the *barrios* downtown.* My parents' parish was the Cathedral of San Fernando. My dad was a boarder in the rectory, my godfather was a cook, so in my early life I got to see the other side of priests: They could be kind.

I'm the firstborn of parents that had been rural and came into the city. My maternal grandparents used to work for my paternal grandparents. On my dad's side, my grandmother was Navajo Indian, my grandfather was Scottish; going back another generation there was somebody that was Spanish, I think. On my mother's side, they were all Mexican-Americans.

The first of the freeways knocked out the *barrio* where we were living, so we were forced to move into another. Things were very hard for us. We lived in a shack with dirt floors and cold-water showers and a community rest room. Then we moved to another neighborhood. We had floors and we were all excited; we still had the joint rest room but we had electricity. I lived there till I was nine years old and my dad came back from the war.

---

*Joel Garreau writes in *The Nine Nations of North America* about the destruction of the *barrio* by highway construction in another Southwestern city: "what the Anglos saw as a blighted area given over to junkyards, sandblasting, and arc-welding shops, Mexican-Americans who lived there saw as their homes and their jobs. More than that, it was their 'barrio,' and a barrio is not the same thing as a ghetto. It means neighborhood, but often is translated as community, and a community is not something you flee, much less casually tear down."

My dad had a decision to make; either to move outside the city limits, to the *colonias,* or [to take] public housing. My dad always used to say, "I don't care for handouts." So rather than go into a public housing unit where you were guaranteed all the niceties, he said, "We'll go out to the outskirts." When we moved out there we had an outdoor rest room, [but] it was all ours! We had no electricity; we had to go half a mile for water on a daily basis. We had a wood-burning stove. It was a very small house, maybe two rooms, and it cost 2,500 dollars. [My dad said,] "I have my piece of property, I have my house and we're better off this way than being dependent on anybody."

I remember growing up in a household where church was mandatory. My mother was a *Guadalupana,* which was the women's society in our churches. When we moved to the outskirts there was no development, so there was no parish; we would come into San Alfonso, the mother church for the whole West Side, or my dad would bring us in to the Cathedral. I was baptized and confirmed there; I made my First Communion there when I was in the third grade.

My parents never said very much; they just wanted me to be good. I found that very frustrating. "Be good"—what does that mean? We didn't grow up in an environment where parents would encourage you to be something. My dad used to say, "If you ever want to learn something, there's always going to be a book." But I think way down deep he just wanted me to be a good wife.

I'm the first on either side of the family that finished high school and that was a big hurrah; everybody was all excited. My mom was saying, "Why don't you become a nurse?" so I took one year training— only because that's what my mom suggested. I got married when I was nineteen, almost twenty. He was in the army. I decided that I wanted to be a good housewife, a good mother, and a good child. We didn't have any children for three years so we decided to go to Germany— and came back with two children. [Once we got back] we lived where I live now, on the West Side. I remember [that was] a very dark time in my life; there were too many restrictions. I began to be involved in the school and my husband said, "No, you belong at home. The women don't belong outside the home." Very very *Mexicano* and macho in attitude. [And I had no resources.] There was nothing that supported a person wanting to look at what happened to the children, what happened to the family, what pressures you were under.

I was drawn into the school situation with my firstborn. I had prepared him, so when he was tested he was ready to take on the first grade instead of kindergarten. But when I took [him there], he was disturbed about the environment, he did not want to go: The school was a very dark, very dreary, very very overcrowded place. Our district is the poorest. I started getting involved in PTA. We went to the school board to get some remodeling done but they wouldn't [do it].

By the time I was pregnant with my fifth child, the people at church started looking at the needs of the community through COPS. COPS is an organization of leadership within a community; it's institutionally based, [mostly in parishes]. People come together to be able to have credentials and power to work on the needs that the families have. The majority of the people at the elementary school were Spanish-speaking and they couldn't articulate what they needed. Because I was a PTA president and also on the bilingual parents' council, I was interviewed as a community leader and asked what the problems were; then the [COPS] people from church said to me, "Would you be interested [in getting involved]?" and I said, "No thanks, I don't want to pray; church can only light a candle and say a Rosary." I didn't see the church as being involved in community needs; I thought church was a very personal type of experience—until there was a little crisis in the neighborhood.

There had been a drainage project in the neighborhood and the excavation was eight feet by ten and it was running along a whole block: the people that were living on the northern side of the street had to go into the ditch and out just to cross the street. Trash was piling up, the sewer was overflowing, the mail service wasn't there, and an elderly person fell down and broke his leg. When it rained, people couldn't go to work and the children couldn't go to school. So the parents that were being harassed by the teachers because their children were absent from school came to me as PTA president and I was swept in, I mean sucked in, to the COPS organization. The people that helped me in the school were saying, "We can't do it ourselves." I remember saying, "Okay, we'll try to get help, but you've got to stay with me. I'm not in this for myself. I don't live on this street." And I took ten ladies to a COPS meeting. I just wanted somebody to listen to us.

The COPS organizer said, "You want to do something about this? Here, pick up this phone and dial this number." I picked up the phone and dialed. He said, "You ask for Mr. X., he's the one that can get it for you." After I picked up the phone, I thought, "what am I going to say to this person?" And I said to myself, "Never mind, he said that this is the person that is going to get it done." So I ask for the man and the secretary gives me the runaround. I remember saying, "Look, I am Carmen Badillo and there is a problem in our neighborhood and

I've been told Mr. X. is a person that can correct this situation and I want to talk to him right now."

We eventually got the man down there and it was my first experience with power and the power structure. He was a city official. So he comes down with his team of people and we're there with the PTA people, the neighborhood people, and the three pastors from the neighboring parishes, and I'm saying to myself, "What did you get yourself into?"

The man comes down from a big, very luxurious car and his shoes, they look patent to me, they're so shiny. He starts looking at the project and everything's overturned, there's mess, mud and everything, and the guy is worried about his *shoes* getting soiled, and that gets me angry. Internally I say, "What's the matter with this man, can't he see the mess here?" So I say, "Mr. X., I'm the one that asked you here and I want very much for you to understand what our problem is." So we walk the whole block. We get him committed to resolving the problem, and he says, "Anything else you want?" I say, "Yes, we want three bridges," because there were three intersections, "one here, one there, and one over here." "You've got it," he says. I said [to myself], "My gosh. I was able to do this much; this COPS organization is really something. I'd better listen to it."

I think the most difficult thing about accepting COPS has to do with where you come from: When you begin to want to understand power and to deal with it, you have to use confrontation, and by tradition we're not taught confrontation as a people. We're not taught to be vocal, to be assertive, we people who are all those things: I am Hispanic, I am poor, I am woman; I'm a minority many times over. We're taught to sit tight and not get angry. It is difficult for me to remember my parents wanting me to be anything, because we were conditioned to be passive, to be humble, to be respectful. When you come out of that environment, it's very difficult to be assertive. "Assertive" is very much like "aggressive" and "aggressive" is very much like "confrontation." So you just aren't those things, because you're supposed to be *nice*.

COPS has secured monies for the poorer school districts in the whole state; it has done a lot to improve the drainage system within the community; it has worked at keeping to a minimum the utility increases. But I think the most important thing COPS has done for us is that it has shown us that we *do* have power. We do have a role to play in what's going on in our lives. And that was something the Church never taught us, and we Hispanics always looked to the Church.

I was still very skeptical. I was saying, "We were just lucky." But [at the first city-wide COPS convention] I saw the archbishop of this diocese take out a check and say, "I'm more than just supporting you, I'm making this contribution to you." So I thought, "My gosh. The Catholic church is making this kind of statement—it has definitely got to be the best thing that happened to my being a Catholic." I really had not seen my church involved in things of my community. I had seen it very much as something that just took care of personal needs. It was like an awakening. I call it a conversion. I actually came back to the Catholic church because of this experience.

What the Church was saying [was], "We're going to *act* out what we believe and what we're saying we should be about." It wasn't till much later that I realized there was such a thing as Vatican II. In effect that's all we really were doing.

[Before COPS] I would take my children to church because of the discipline—you know, you want to do the right things for your family. My husband was never churchgoing, but that didn't mean he didn't have a commitment. I went on my own. It was a lot of going into a Sunday service, hearing a sermon, having it come down on you. "You're sinners, you're this, you're that," all the negative side of what church used to be. I didn't need to be told, "You're bad." I knew I was doing the best I could with what I had. So I would go purely for a personal thing. I would say, "Okay, I am Catholic. This is my church." I listened to the Gospels. I listened to the homilies; I always wondered why they were so negative; I always wondered why they talked about things in the abstract. I always wished they could say, "Hey, this is how this Gospel applies to how we're living today in this world." And that wasn't happening. It wasn't happening during Sunday services and it wasn't happening outside.

We never saw the priests involved in the community until COPS. Then we had some very good priests that supported us. They were up front with us. If it hadn't been for a priest who stood by me the first time I went to City Hall, I wouldn't be who I am. I go up there and I've got a priest right in back of me. That gives a lot of confidence to a person.

I've been working for six years now [in this job] at the Office of Parish Development. The COPS experience was picked up by the diocese and was put into this office: the archbishop learned [from COPS] that if laypeople look at their needs and at the role they can play, they begin to find solutions to their problems. So [the staff of] this office goes out to the rural areas which are the poor areas in this diocese. We do training sessions, reflection on what is church:

What does it mean to be church? Who is church? What's the business of church? What does baptism mean? What does it mean to be priest, prophet, and king?* What is a disciple? What does the Last Supper mean? We do role-playing with the Last Supper. We provide leadership training skills so people begin to look at their parish and do an analysis and profile of the parish. Eventually we wind up with a parish assembly where they adopt a statement of purpose and an action plan.

We don't start Bible classes in a structured way. We use Scripture more in a reflective way. [Say we're talking about] discipleship. We take the word itself, what it means in the dictionary; we look at what is said by Scripture; we look at what Vatican documents are saying; and we try to come up with a situation at the level of the people, where they can understand and begin to see themselves as called [to discipleship].

We begin to help the parish look at the roles. Okay, here is a pastor, what is his role? Here is a layperson, what is their role? We have societies, what are their roles in the parish? The Holy Name Society, at least for this diocese, was a group of men whose sole purpose was to go out and convert other men. They no longer do that. They just do fund-raising [and they] go to communion once a week. We need to help the men rethink those things and they need to make a decision: Do we continue to just be this way or do we move into what our real purpose is? And if it's difficult for them to move that way, they deal with it as a parish: How do *all* of us as parish reach out? The focus of the parish will no longer be internal, it will be external. It will be how to reach out and include other people.

In this process we've done with parishes, we try to focus on diversity. To be a parish and a community means we have to accept diversity. We have to begin to accept all those things that we were never familiar with. Diversity is very important because it helps us rethink our values. Diversity. Relationships. Accountability. It's a whole new terminology, very much a part of what we're trying to do in the parishes.

We're losing people to other denominations. We're losing people to the Pentecostal churches. The economy in the rural areas is real bad and there's a frustration, no hope sometimes. The leadership is burned

---

*Titles taken from the Hebrew Bible and applied to Jesus by the early Christian communities. These titles are often applied to the entire people of the Church in contemporary spiritual and theological reflection and are part of the rite of baptism in the Catholic church.

out. For the pastor that invites us in and works with us, those are the things he really has to deal with. All too many times the pastor, in his preparation for priesthood, was never trained in relationships, how to deal with people and bring out their gifts. So our priests can't deal with the people, and the people look for the preacher who's going to give them a high, or for a church that gives emergency help in a time of need.

[When I was growing up,] every time we went to the grocery my mother would buy some Pet Milk for whoever had a baby in the parish and she'd sew a couple of extra dresses for whoever needed, but that was the extent of how we helped poor people. [There was] nothing ever organized. People depended solely on the *Guadalupanas* and what they wanted to contribute. [The other Christian churches are] definitely [more organized]. One of the things we do in our work as consultants is encourage families and friends to come together and talk about the church, the community, and the family: "What do you think the needs are and how can the church help?" In one parish one of the ladies said, "We need to wise up. I work for a Baptist church. Every Wednesday night I cook a meal and they provide nursery service for the couples. They're given an assignment to go visit one person: They go out, visit for an hour, come back, eat dinner, and evaluate how the meeting was; and if the person needs something they give [the request] to a committee." That's something we've never done. It's always been the festival, always money, always a new roof, always the physical plant.

So we need to begin, as a church, questioning the priorities we have. Look at a parish budget: You don't have a budgeted item saying "For education and laypeople, for scholarships." If any layperson wants to go outside of what's offered by the diocese [for training of some kind], you have to have a fund-raising activity. And we lose the people, the young people especially. I mean, you can't deceive the young people nowadays; they're so wise. The kids are exposed to so much that you have to be able to be up front with them, to reason the thing out, or you lose them. In one parish I had a young lad that was recognized by the archdiocese as the outstanding youth. But his pastor was the most negative type of person. The young man eventually started his own church and he drew people in. He carries a Bible and he preaches and people get high. It's one of these Pentecostal Charismatic type of situations. Nobody [in his original parish] paid attention to that resource, that talent that was there. The Church has never given us [laypeople] any decisions to make. It has kept us at a third-grade level of education: "We will tell you what to do, and this is what we think."

It's never said, "What do you think and how can you contribute?"

I'm more concerned right now about TV ministers than I am about anything else. I cannot believe that you can build a church through TV. That's not what we should be about. It's anti building community. Anti relationships. Anti getting people involved with people. And I think if our faith means anything it's being involved with people. How could I know what the least of my brothers is suffering unless I'm right there with him and involved? How could I help him? Mail him some money through the TV tube?

Jesus to me is those people who are out there wanting to be involved in the suffering of people. Anybody that's involved is Jesus—whether it's the clergy, the lay, the woman. Because it's very difficult to just stand up and say, "This is wrong. These people are suffering." As a people and as a church we're all right with the ceremony and the rituals and the singing and all this kind of stuff. We know the power of being church. We're very good with the liturgies, with the *Posadas*,* with the *Via Crucis*†; I mean, we can really play that up. But as a church we still don't understand that little piece of standing up and actually being involved with and suffering with people. Until we begin to look at that prophetic piece, we'll be stuck back in the other place.

[I was brought up with] a fear of God. My mother would always say, "If you're not good God will punish you," and it would cause tensions in me. I'd say, "If God is the person who made me, then He should love me. He shouldn't punish me. He shouldn't hate me." But we weren't allowed to dialogue with parents. If I learned a public demonstration of what it meant to believe in God, it came from a widowed lady who lived in the neighborhood. We didn't have CCD classes because we didn't have sisters, we didn't have a parish. This lady would draw the kids together and tell stories about Jesus and the saints. She would tell us that Jesus was born and he was a child like us; he had parents. She would [talk about] St. Joseph, the father, who wasn't really the father. She would tell us about Our Lady of Guadalupe. She never did anything with rosaries or anything like that. It was just telling the stories.

Mary has had an influence in my life. A lot of influence. She's a role model. She's a super lady. All that she had to deal with—the rejection she exposed herself to, [having this child,] I mean, that was gutsy. That

---

*Posada means "inn" in Spanish. The Posadas processions commemorate Mary and Joseph's search for lodging before the birth of Jesus.
†The Way of the Cross, a traditional devotion commemorating the passion of Christ.

required a lot of faith, a lot of courage. If I look at Mary's reappearance as Our Lady of Guadalupe I can better appreciate what she was about at the beginning. [As Our Lady of Guadalupe] she appeared to a people that had been oppressed, abused; she was giving a message to the Church that the Church did not understand. "Build my temple"* did not mean, "Build a basilica," but, "Be concerned about these people that you're doing these things to." I think more and more our people are beginning to understand that. As a church we're moving in that direction—understanding what is being said to us instead of moving in the ritual of things. We're still struggling, but we're in the right direction.

I have one [favorite saint]: the name of my parish, Saint Martin de Porres, the black saint. Even though he was a minority, an outcast, he fed, he healed, he was hope, he was a teacher. You always hear about saints that they pray and pray. I'm not saying that it's not good, but I'm much more drawn to someone who is out with people doing things.

I worry about water, the resources we have. Right now the city is involved in building over an aquifer which is our sole source of water and it can be polluted. Who's going to pay for that pollution? I am concerned about nuclear type of issues. I look at what that means for future generations. Sometimes, I laugh at myself because there was a time when I wouldn't think about *any* kind of issue. I'm concerned about nuclear energy. It's a monster. I think it's something we never learned how to control and to me there is great danger in that, whether you use it for weapons or you use it for electricity. We tried in COPS to get involved in the utility aspect of nuclear energy, but money controls, power people control; I don't think it's an issue that can be resolved by any one group. I think more of the people have got to be educated and aware.

I feel very strongly that too many times we don't appreciate the gift of life. So as an adult and as a mother I think it's very important to not only give birth but also be responsible, to be able to meet the needs of that child. Spacing children or looking at a limited number [of children] is something that's acceptable to me. I don't know what the Church says specifically about it in detail. I know I have a lot of tension in me when we start talking about abortion as a method of limiting family. If I understand correctly, the Church is saying we are against abortions. I am. There's a real bad tension in me about who

---

*Part of Our Lady of Guadalupe's message to Juan Diego.

deals with this particular issue. I think the government is the system for this world and of this world. I don't think the government gives life so I don't think it's something that can be legislated or not legislated. I think the whole decision really needs to be dealt with with the person and God. So to me, a law in a docket someplace is not going to make that much difference. It's not going to have as much impact on me as what my church is saying about it. If I was being asked to vote on [abortion] I would not vote for it. I probably would not even vote.

At Christmas we have a birthday cake for Jesus and we sing "Happy Birthday." My older children say, "I wish that you would continue doing that, even when we have our children." It's not anything religious; it's just "Happy Birthday, Jesus." I know I have [raised my children differently from the way I was raised.] I've tried to help them be prepared for this life. I've tried to include them in what I've learned about how we operate. My children have been to City Council meetings. They have been able to get a different perspective from church because of my work. My parents never allowed interaction, dialogue. We never questioned. I allow that within my family.

It's important in the United States that we all have the freedoms. So in that sense [the women's movement] has been very, very helpful. In the Church we still struggle with it. I think things are getting better as the Church moves in the direction of reflecting on what it means to be church. There is a dialogue which hopefully will lead us to that point where women will have more of a role. I would like to see women more intimately involved in the decisions and the ministries on the parish level. [I would like to see] more formation, more education [for us]. We're still very limited. If we really reflect on Jesus and what he was about and what he did when he was here, there's no way you can avoid dealing with women. They were there.

I think we're fighting the man on his grounds [when we say] the woman should be the priest. We're making a mistake when we want to take the place of men in the same way. I think the structure needs to change. I don't particularly see myself as being involved in a church that stays structured, [in which] there are priests, there are deacons. If we need to have it for administration, that's fine. I don't have a problem with that.

It's the whole thing of being prophetic again. The prophet is that person who is able to read the signs of the times and then call up what we are supposed to be about. So if as a church we begin to look at where we're at and begin to raise questions, the answers are going to make us change.

EIGHT

THE COMMON GOOD

Action on behalf of justice
and participation in the transformation
of the world
fully appear to us
as a constitutive dimension
of the preaching of the Gospel,
or, in other words,
of the Church's mission
for the redemption of the human race
and its liberation
from every oppressive situation.
  —"Justice in the World,"
  Statement of the World Synod of
  Bishops, 1971

The Catholic church, known in other eras for preaching "pie-in-the-sky" and disengagement from the world, now holds as an official teaching that the transformation of unjust social realities is an integral part of the preaching of the Gospel.[1] In other words, for Catholic Christians today, changing the world—what the Jewish tradition calls *tikkun olam,* the mending of the earth—is as important to the Christian vocation as the proclamation of Jesus' life, death, and resurrection. A strong message, and one that Catholic women have absorbed in varying degrees.

Catholic women do not mention Catholic social teaching a great deal ("our best-kept secret," a recent book calls it[2]), but the values underlying the social documents of the Church are clearly a part of their world view. Human dignity was the social and moral priority

Catholic women articulated most often, whether they were speaking about racism, abortion, violence against women, or access to decent housing. The dignity of the human person, for them, was an article of faith. In restating· the Catholic teaching on the intrinsic worth of every human person, they expressed a kind of radical egalitarianism, which their American belief in democracy enhanced and reinforced.

"To a Catholic," said Caryl Rivers, "every question is a moral question." *Sin* is no longer a frequent word in many Catholic women's vocabularies, but they continue to be preoccupied with morality. Gail Benjamin, at the age of thirty-two, was director of the Office of Environmental Impact in the New York City Department of Environmental Protection. Gail is no longer a practicing Catholic, though she still attends Midnight Mass at Christmas. "I think a lot," she said, "about what's right or wrong, what's fair. It's part of everything I do."

Catholic women take for granted the reality and possibility of the moral life. For Catholic women, a moral order is possible; the world has structure, purpose, and meaning. This outlook remained true of women who had left the Church. "Jeanne Dupont" no longer considers herself a Catholic and is actively involved in contemporary pagan spirituality. Nevertheless, her language was unmistakably Catholic. "There is a drive within all creation," she said, "to come to moral growth."

When asked about sin, Catholic women defined it in a variety of ways, from fifty-six-year-old Dorothy McFadden's "having sex before marriage, stealing things, especially from the poor, not going to church" to thirty-five-year-old Mary Hunt's "structural and/or personal choice to act in ways that destroy rather than enhance human community." Many mentioned the Ten Commandments as fundamental guidelines or rules, a different understanding from Judaism, which sees these commandments in the context of the whole of Jewish law, and the law as a path of life rather than a set of regulations. Even younger women like Brigette Rouson often spoke of an evolution in their understanding of sin: "I used to think sin was breaking the Ten Commandments or doing the things the Church says are wrong," Brigette said. "But basically sin is not using the gifts God gave you to accomplish His will. I no longer think of it as if there is some big scoreboard in the sky, and God's gonna rack up all your sins and if they outweigh your good deeds you're in trouble. I think we shouldn't put so much emphasis on avoiding sin as in achieving our good. Sin is not being in tune with God's will, not being willing to listen, not willing to be an instrument." "I don't think it's a mortal sin anymore to miss Mass," fifty-seven-year-old Dolores Reuter said. "A mortal sin is one that really takes you away from God. I personally commit very few of those."

For most, conscience and individual will figured strongly in the definition of sin. "Sin," said Dolores Reuter, "is deliberately hurting someone else or yourself." Her simple statement summed up the main themes in other women's definitions. The words "deliberately," "consciously," and "intentionally" came up again and again, a persistence, no doubt, of the *Baltimore Catechism*'s explanation of sin as requiring "grievous matter, sufficient reflection, and full consent of the will," which presumes the presence of a conscience and not simply the obedience or disobedience of an external rule. "Grievous matter" alone, in this view, merely constitutes wrongdoing, not sin: "Before it could be a sin, you had to realize what you were doing, and do it anyway. I still believe that," said seventy-six-year-old Pauline Johnson Jones, a lifelong member of St. Augustine's church in Washington, D.C.

Almost as often as they spoke of the importance of morality, Catholic women talked about their consciences. Some women, like Caryl Rivers, were taught about and encouraged to search their consciences at an early age. Caryl found this feature of her Catholic education "pretty revolutionary. In fact," she said, "the bottom line in Catholicism is still that—the primacy of one's own conscience." Other women were adults before they learned or realized that this internal authority was an essential component of their spiritual and moral life as Catholics.

Women frequently equated "hurting someone else" with "offending God." Sin, for them, involved relationships: In broken connections was the breach of trust with God. From the notion of sin as harming others, some women had moved to an understanding of sin as social or structural, beyond what *Cross Currents* cofounder and editor Joseph Cunneen has called "the 'Jesus and me' scheme of the world."[3] Sin affects structures as well as individuals, says contemporary Catholic social teaching; not only individual hearts but also institutions cry out for healing. One of the major components in the U.S. bishops' 1986 pastoral letter on economic justice[4]—often overlooked in the flurry of responses to specific policies—is their fundamental definition of morality as public and communal and of human life as essentially communitarian. It is impossible, the bishops contend, to talk about the dignity of the individual without talking about the shape of the human community. This view also underlies the educational and lobbying work of NETWORK, the Washington-based Catholic social justice lobby founded nearly two decades ago by Sister Carol Coston and sustained in great part by the efforts of Catholic women. Many women shared this perspective, though it seemed to grow out of their experience rather than a familiarity with church documents.

"In the old days," Pauline Jones said, "we used to be taught how bad sex was, yet we weren't taught how bad racism was." Pauline's parish, where she is clearly what the Afro-American religious tradition calls a "mother of the church," was built by emancipated slaves. "Now I feel one is just as bad as the other," Pauline said, "because to hate your neighbor because of their ethnic background, there's no worse sin than that. Hating people because they're different from you, hating Jews for no reason, hating blacks because they're black, it's just as great a sin as any other and maybe worse. I suppose it's covered in the commandments: 'Love the Lord, and your neighbor as yourself.' You can't hate a person and love them as yourself. But we were never taught that way, and that's always been a failing of the Church, the social teachings and teachings of justice and fairness."

Several women included sexism among the social dimensions of sin. "Feminine values have always been trampled upon," said Rafaela Canelo of San Francisco. "Since the beginning with Adam and Eve, the woman has always been marginalized completely. It has always been the man who is in charge, always the man who is the head of the house, it has always been he [who] governs all, the nation and the Church. But it is not thus in the Kingdom of God, because we are all equal in the Kingdom of God. And we women have abilities to govern a nation. We have abilities for everything. Jesus always recognized the value of women," Rafaela added.

Dolores Reuter's "hurting others or yourself" included the harming of self in the definition of sin; she was not alone. Sin, said Andrea Sherlund, is "when you defeat yourself, [when] you let yourself down." Mar Londo, a counselor in Green Bay, Wisconsin, said, "We sin against ourselves. I want my daughters not to accept second best and not to sell themselves short." She added, "To me, it's sinful not to grow. I think a lot of people sit on their energy and don't make good use of it." In the past two decades, women of various religious backgrounds, not only Catholics, who were taught that sin was pride and lack of attention to others, have begun to challenge this definition, realizing that they often attended to others at the expense of caring for self, and that lack of self-esteem rather than pride was their abiding wound.[5]

A few women also spoke of sins of omission, which they often defined as standing by while others are being harmed or oppressed. Beatrice Cortez, a colleague of Carmen Badillo at the Office of Parish Development of the San Antonio Archdiocese, was also introduced to public life through COPS. Through this community organizing work, Beatrice said, "I learned that sin was not doing. And that connected with when we go into Mass and say in the prayer, 'Forgive me for the things, not only that I do, but that I do not do.' To me the greatest sin is the things that we do not do. Many of us, educated and uneducated, just hope things are going to go well because we have good hearts, we have good intentions. That doesn't happen. Good doesn't come out of people just thinking; you need to get in there and take leadership."

"I have come," said theologian Mary Hunt, "to a more nuanced understanding of the incredible capacity for evil that lurks in society. I had spent a lot of time at least passively denying it. The Holocaust is just another example. People *did* that to one another. People *justified* the killing of six million Jews on the basis of their background. It's unthinkable, yet it goes on on a regular basis. I think there's an enormous capacity for evil as well as an enormous capacity for good in the whole society," she said, "and choices about that really can be manipulated. It's part of what religion is, it's part of what good government is, it's part of what education is: It's to try to manipulate in the human community those forces of good and evil."

Beatrice Cortez directly related her work for social change to the prayer she said with other Catholics at the beginning of Mass ("I confess . . . that I have sinned through my own fault, through what I have done and what I have failed to do"). A few other women made this conscious connection between social responsibility and the words of their tradition's communal prayer. Much more frequent, however, was the identification of the person of Jesus, and of God, with other people, especially those in need. "I firmly believe," said Pauline Jones, "that if you don't see God in your fellow man you can't see Him. I think Vatican II has brought that out more than anything," she added. The life and teachings of Jesus also exerted a strong influence. Dora Yelk of Madison, Wisconsin, said: "Jesus was concerned about people, and that's what social concern is, it's being concerned about people, it's being concerned with what's happening to people because of the economy."

I asked the women whether they knew about the U.S. Catholic bishops' pastoral letters on various social issues—racism, peace, the economy—particularly the latter two, which involved a broad consultative process and received a great deal of publicity during the past decade. Over half the women had heard about the pastorals, but few had read them. The bishops' stated purpose in writing the pastorals was twofold: to speak to members of the Catholic church in the U.S. and to contribute an additional voice to the public debate about vital social issues. They appear to have been somewhat more successful in their second goal. "I don't see the people in our church being influenced," said "Joanne Grace." "I think it makes the national news and then for all intents and purposes it's a bit lost. But at least it makes a statement." In general, Catholic women approve of the bishops' speaking out on social issues ("It helps the rest of us stand up and be counted," said Marlene Jones), though there is an undercurrent of concern among some of them about "the Church meddling in politics" and a few felt the bishops were "leaning too far to the left." Interestingly, women who had left the Church were some of the most enthusiastic supporters of the pastorals.

In the pastorals on peace and economic justice, the bishops distinguish between authoritative moral principles and policy proposals that are open to debate. In their comments, women tended to make the same distinction, somewhat more vehemently. "As religious people, we're called to be prophets, to say 'This isn't right, this ought to change,'" said Ann Richards Anderson, who, with her husband, was one of the neighborhood peacemakers in Boston's Charlestown section during the busing crisis of the early 1970s. "I'm more reluctant to endorse particular prescriptions. I always get worried about people having the eternal truths mixed up with putting the tax rate at twenty-five percent. That dilutes the force of the message. [And] it [makes it] too easy for *The Wall Street Journal* to say, 'This solution is idiotic,' or 'This solution is socialistic,' and then they don't ever have to deal with the problems."

Women implicitly raised the question, "Who is the Church?" when discussing Church leaders' participation in public life. "I think the bishops should certainly give moral leadership," said Abigail McCarthy, "but I think they're usurping the lay prerogative when they are specific about legislation or foreign policy initiatives. That is an area in which they don't have the expertise. I also feel that they are resorting to political intimidation when they all go to the White House in their black suits. The image they give of the Church is not the image I like to see. I would like to see the application of Christian teaching done by those whose vocation it is, and I don't think it's the bishops' vocation."

Words are always tested against deeds. Catholic women did so when evaluating the pastorals, often wondering aloud whether Church leaders' actions within the institution were consistent with their official statements. "In the economic pastoral," said Abigail McCarthy, "I would have really liked to have seen a spelling out of how this could be done in the Church: how the Church invests its money and pays its employees. As one who was a lay teacher for many years I feel very strongly about this. I've been on the board of [Catholic] colleges and they say they have these wonderful benefits, but they were forced into it by the unions—it was not something they did out of moral concern. I think the Church is a long long way from justice in its own organizations."

Many Catholic women experience the pastoral letters, this generous strand of the Catholic tradition, as a blessing and a curse. They notice a massive contradiction when they place the bishops' talk of "interdependence" and "human solidarity" and their call for efforts "to overcome the effects of sexism in our society"[6] side by side with women's exclusion from decision-making roles within the institutional Church. "The Church seems to be a very male-oriented organization," said "Elena Martinez Wise," an officer in a San Francisco corporation, who has raised her daughter as a Catholic but does not attend church because, she says, "I feel left out." She observed: "You can't talk about social issues [and justice] if you're not practicing that in your own organization." For women like "Elena," the Church teaches in two ways: through its pronouncements and through its institutional behavior, and its behavior speaks loudly.

Church institutions and leaders seemed most effective in women's eyes when they responded concretely to social problems and supported the laity's efforts to respond to them—or when they put people to work in some way, as Mary Hunt's high school did by sponsoring projects that brought its students in contact with rural and urban poverty. "Social activism *is* the role of the Church," Gail Benjamin said firmly. "The Catholic church has done tremendous things for immigrants and poor people all through [its history]. They gave people an entrée, via Catholic schools, to a larger piece of the world. If you look at the number of blacks in this country who have achieved, you will find an abnormal amount of Catholic blacks," said Gail, who is black. "The Catholic church is one of the few institutions that don't leave the neighborhood when the neighborhood gets bad. They take their investment in souls very seriously. When every other major institution left the South Bronx," she said of one of New York City's most devastated sections, "the Catholic church stayed. They have stayed as forces in people's daily lives."

What social problems concern you? I asked. And how would you change the world, if you could? Women from their late teens to their early nineties gave remarkably similar answers. When I asked what social problems preoccupied them, women across the generations, races, and socioeconomic classes began by decrying the unequal distribution of resources in this country and around the world. "I worry about the trend in our country for the rich to get richer and the poor to get poorer," said "Joanne Grace." "[I wish] there would not be this gap between the very rich and the very poor." "All that stuff about some people have and [some] have not," said "Inez Garcia," a student at Incarnate Word College in San Antonio, "—make it as equal." Poverty and economic justice are first among American Catholic women's social concerns, followed closely by violence and war.

Why is poverty more troubling to American Catholic women than any other social issue?

American Catholics look at poverty and economic justice in a new social context: Catholics have a higher socioeconomic status than ever before in U.S. history, while the gap between rich and poor in this country has grown, especially in the past decade. At the same time, the immigrant experience is not far removed for much of the Catholic population, even those people who are now economically comfortable. The memory of poverty was vivid for many of the women I interviewed, whether they had grown up poor like Carmen Badillo or come from university-educated professional families whose forebears had left Ireland during the Potato Famine.

Catholic women also felt the pinch of regional economic woes. At the time of the interviews, the nationwide recession of the 1990s was barely on the horizon, but the economy was suffering in several parts of the country. Department stores were closing in Texas. Wisconsin and other parts of the Midwest were in the midst of a bitter farm crisis. Unemployment was at a record high in Upper Michigan's Mackinac County. And in the large urban centers, Catholic women saw growing numbers of hungry and homeless people on the streets and at church-based meal programs.

Even before church documents on the rights of workers and the "preferential option for the poor,"[7] American Catholics had a sense of connection with the other side of the world—and the other side of the tracks. The fact that the Catholic church spans the globe has influenced Catholic women's attitudes toward economics, human rights, and peace as much as the social teachings of the Church, or it has, at least, paved the way for these teachings. When I asked Wisconsin farmer Mary Wunnicke whether any social problems bothered her, she answered, "I really worry about some of the people that live in the missions." "What do you mean by that?" I asked. "The poverty is really a problem in those areas," she answered, mentioning the persistence of hunger in Bolivia.

"The missions," of course, were what we have come to call Third World countries, "mission countries," where one of Mary's relatives was a Maryknoll Sister working among the poor. Earlier in this century, Catholics acquired global awareness in an unsophisticated but empathic way: They were presented with visiting missionaries, pictures of hungry children, even collections for "pagan babies," a thoroughly offensive concept today, but a way in which Catholic children felt linked to children on the other side of the world. They made the connection not only through prayer but through financial donations: There was always economic responsibility alongside the spiritual communion. Cultural awareness and support for the self-determination of peoples may have been low, but the relationship—if only through the collection for the missions and *Maryknoll* magazine on the coffee table—was clear: We are one body, and part of the body is hungry.

Another factor in women's attitudes toward poverty involved their beliefs about Jesus. Mother Teresa of Calcutta is not the first in the Catholic tradition to base her work and prayer on the presence of Christ in the poor. "Meeting Christ in the poor" is not the same thing as "being good to the poor," but rather a statement that Jesus Christ himself is present in society's disenfranchised people, and that their human dignity as God's creatures is equal to that of the rich.

Women's experience of economic vulnerability may well be another factor in Catholic women's concern about poverty. Many of the women knew poverty firsthand or were aware that women, in the U.S. and around the world, are economically in a far more precarious position than men.[8] Several of the women mentioned divorce as a factor in women's economic fragility. Writer and lecturer Abigail McCarthy, who is separated from former U.S. Senator Eugene McCarthy, said of divorce, "I see it from a feminist point of view. Wherever I go to speak women think I have some kind of secret that I've been able to survive so well. But I couldn't survive so well if my husband didn't contribute to my living. I think the laws allow men to dispose of wives in middle life and not be responsible for their financial well-being. I think that's wrong and I don't think the Church has really zeroed in on that side of [things]. The statistics are that the man two or three years after a divorce is living better, [whereas] the woman's [standard of] living [is] worse, much worse—not just a little worse." Anne Burke, director of the Urban Ministry Center in Raleigh, North Carolina, a drop-in center for the city's poor, spoke of what she had observed at work: "What poor women have to face is different from what the poor population in general has to face. Most of them aren't educated; they don't have the earning capacity the way men have. And they always get stuck with the kids, always. They get left holding the bag. The men face obstacles as well, black men particularly, yet I still see the women assuming full responsibility."

I interviewed women at all income levels, from highly paid managers to women on welfare. Two of the women I interviewed had previously been on welfare—both after leaving abusive marriages—and were now employed, one as an administrative assistant to a state representative and one in an office job where, she told me, "I'm making a lot of money now—$7.50 an hour." Getting off welfare was difficult even for those with the energy and will. Iris Palmer, a single mother of several children living in a public housing development in Raleigh, North Carolina, and active in her community and her church, said to me: "The system is not made for you to get out. Like if I went to get a job, it's going to take me two weeks to a month to get paid. I'm going to get all kinds of eviction notices because it's so far between the last check that I got from [welfare and the first check I get from my job.] That's what happened to my neighbor. She lost her job and she had to go on welfare. Then she found a job, but before she got paid they had cut her lights off, they had cut her phone off, her water off, and her rent was past due."

One thing I did not find among Catholic women was the notion that financial success is in some way a reward for holiness or devotion. Catholic women who are financially successful tie their good fortune to hard work, but not to virtue. They do not view riches as a reward from God for being good. Several women did speak of developing greater self-sufficiency and of freeing themselves from guilt about earning, having, and investing money. I have seen this shift in attitude among women of other religious backgrounds, but there may be a particular Catholic twist to it: "Our Catholic upbringing says you should only want the absolute minimum that you need to survive," said Ann Richards Anderson, "and to want more is sinful or greedy." "I thought to behave in an ethical manner meant to deny myself money," said performance artist "Jeanne Dupont." "I'm now making changes in my life. I'm actively choosing to succeed, for the first time in my life."

"I used to be really antimoney when I was in college," said Brigette Rouson, the young Washington attorney. "Like, oh man, I never want to be rich, because money just brings trouble and people who are rich are unhappy, and I don't want the temptation of having all that money at my disposal. I've since come to believe that money, like any other resource, be it wood, fabric, people, ideas, is something to be used to carry out God's will, and that we are given gifts and the ability to bring resources to ourselves so that we can distribute them in a way that fits into God's plan and makes the Kingdom closer. The power's in us, not the money, and it should just be a means."

While they were no less concerned than other women about the common good, some women from poor and working-class backgrounds wished for a material security that had eluded them in their younger years. Success, to "Elizabeth Heilig," is "being the best, better than anyone else, whether it's being a plumber or a yoga teacher. I want to feel like I really did a good job. And better [yet], to do the job real well and get paid a lot, because my husband and I never had any money in our family, we're really working class. I deserve money. It's time. I don't feel guilty. I don't feel poverty is sexy anymore. I feel it's okay to have money and I'm going to go for it."

Although all deplore the inequities between rich and poor, American Catholic women analyze the reasons for this discrepancy in varying ways. Kathi Bowers Wallis of Washington, D.C., summed up the conflicts many of them expressed. "I do believe in capitalism," she said. "I think it's the only system that works. It unfortunately leaves a lot of have-nots in a very precarious situation." Catholic women also vary in their approach to solutions. A majority of the women I interviewed favored entitlement programs and felt government should play a strong role in helping the economically vulnerable. A vocal minority, mostly registered Republicans, disapproved of government social programs.

Divided in their opinions on the role of government and the causes of poverty, Catholic women are united in their position on government spending priorities. Their comments frequently linked economic issues with the question of war and peace, comparing military and domestic spending. Even women in favor of maintaining a strong defense disapproved of the size of the military budget. For Catholic women, funding basic human needs—health, education, housing—is not negotiable. "I get real offended," said Ellen Reuter, "when people say, 'We can't do this because it costs too much money.' I just get incensed with this administration: 'We can't feed women and children, it's too expensive!'" "The U.S. bombed the hell out of West Germany," said Beatrice Cortez, "and then they put something like $3 billion into rebuilding it. And I say hey, they're not willing to do it for their own country. I want a Marshall Plan for south Texas!"

"Serena Townsend" mused: "I think if people could just step outside themselves and see this beautiful little planet and that there is nowhere else to go. . . . Everybody thinks that there is another block, there is another place, there is another country. There isn't. I also feel," she said, "that every officer in the military ought to take two years of broad humanities training and be forced to work with people before they're permitted to become an officer. By which I mean, do things like work in day-care centers, centers for the handicapped, centers for the elderly, on a one-to-one, person-to-person basis. Then let them go and be military officers. I'm not saying you don't need a defense. But they would certainly have a sense of wanting to balance the military judgments."

"The last years of the Vietnam War," George Gallup and Jim Castelli write in *The American Catholic People,* "marked a major turning point in the way American Catholics viewed defense spending: They shifted from being more likely than other Americans to believe the United States was spending too little on defense to being more likely to say the country was spending too much."[9] The Vietnam War "caused a sea change among American Catholics," Gallup and Castelli continue. "When it began, they were more hawkish than other Americans. When it ended, they were more dovish. And they have remained that way for a generation."[10]

Peace and war came a close second to poverty among the social issues of concern to American Catholic women. Most expressed a strong opposition to violence as a way of resolving conflict. Worry about the nuclear arms race was widespread; among the women under thirty, it was universal.

Dolores Reuter, Ellen Reuter's mother, who spent much of her life in a small Wisconsin town, exclaimed: "They have enough nuclear weapons for centuries. It's stupid. It's really stupid to have the power to kill somebody ten times over. We don't need it." "We are in this big technological fix," said Caryl Rivers, speaking of the Strategic Defense Initiative (SDI) or "Star Wars," which she called "the fantasy that somehow we're going to build this magic shield with magic buttons that's going to protect us." She added: "If we don't realize that solutions come out of political arrangements and agreements between people, not out of technology, we're going to blow our butts off and the entire planet [too]." "We don't need all these weapons," North Carolina office worker Victoria Bowden said simply. "It's like solving sin with sin."

Some of the women felt, as did Sandra Mondykowski Temple, that it was "really naive to carry on about disarmament." But on the whole, Catholic women were more likely than not to favor negotiation as a means of settling conflict and to support arms reductions. Those who were familiar with the U.S. bishops' 1983 pastoral on war and peace[11] felt the document was too moderate and would have preferred stronger language about disarmament and less of an endorsement of deterrence. "It didn't go far enough" was a typical response.

Though women who were mothers and women with no children were equally likely to name violence, war, and world peace as primary concerns, mothers spoke with particular poignancy. "The arms race is a big concern," said Ellen Reuter. "It became an exquisitely painful concern when my child was born, because now it wasn't just my life that I was worrying about but his and his children's lives, and I'm not going to be around to protect him. And if the Bomb goes off there's nothing I can do to save him, and that's a horrible, horrible feeling."

"Elizabeth Heilig," thirty-five years old, married, and the mother of a little boy, told me she had registered her son as a conscientious objector soon after he was born. "As soon as I saw that he was a boy, I saw that penis, and I said, 'This child is not going to be cannon fodder,' so I went to register him." She added: "My heart's desire would be that more men would be involved in taking care of tiny little babies, little helpless babies, so that they would learn how it is to nurture and give life and take care, and think of others, and think of the well-being of the whole; then we'd have more of a peaceful world."

"The clearest impact of post-Vietnam Catholic dovishness can be found in attitudes toward Reagan administration policy in Central America," Gallup and Castelli write of their findings. Both the "fear of turning Central America into another Southeast Asia and the pivotal role the Catholic church is playing in the region" have been factors in Catholics' opposition to U.S. policy in Central America.[12] Although I did not ask any specific question about Central America, Catholic women spontaneously and frequently mentioned U.S. policy in the region during our discussions of war and peace. An overwhelming majority opposed the policies of the U.S. government.

Catholic women may not see themselves as a voting bloc, but on issues pertaining to human services and arms control, the women I interviewed show a clear consensus. "I tend not to vote for someone long on war and short on social services," said sixty-year-old Ann Bright of Corpus Christi, Texas, summing up the opinions of Catholic women around the country.

Abortion was third among the social issues mentioned most often by Catholic women, though it came up significantly less than poverty and peace. (The environment was fourth on the list of Catholic women's major social concerns.) Very few women were single-issue voters, although abortion was, for several, the decisive factor in their involvement in public life.

On policies concerning poverty and peace, the direction of Catholic women's position is very clear. I found no such political consensus on the issue of abortion. As a public policy issue, it was far more murky. Antiabortion sentiment runs very strong among Catholic women—a clear majority—but does not always translate into the desire to see the abortion laws changed. Slightly more than half the women I interviewed felt abortion was morally wrong, but perhaps acceptable under certain circumstances, and when asked whether the law ought to reflect their convictions, were hesitant. The most prevalent position was one combining antiabortion sentiment with support for legal access to abortion—a combination of the "pro-life" and "pro-choice" positions. "I am against abortion," Mary Esther Bernal said firmly. What about the law, I asked; did she feel it ought to change? "No," she said, "I think the law is fine, because you have a large group of people who do not believe like I do on abortion; and I am a firm believer in the rights of other people."

When discussing abortion, women often spoke of the need for consistency. Their definitions of consistency varied. Women opposed to legalized abortion favored the U.S. bishops' "seamless garment" or "consistent ethic of life," which views abortion, capital punishment, euthanasia, and war as intrinsically related and condemns them all. Women in favor of legalized abortion complained that pro-life activists seemed more concerned about unborn babies than about growing children and tended to reject the umbrella ethic of life as too abstract. A few women wondered whether the bishops were consistent in their stated distinctions between policy positions that are open to discussion and fundamental values that are not. "At the end of the peace pastoral," said Ellen Reuter, "they say 'everybody should make up their own mind, this is just for discussion,' but when they write about abortion there's no room for discussion. So when you're talking about blowing up the earth and killing five billion people, that's for individual consciences to decide. But if you're talking about having an abortion, that's not for an individual conscience to decide. Now, either they're both wrong, or they're both for individual consciences to decide." Many of the women, "pro-choice," "pro-life," and at every point on the spectrum, voiced concern about society's neglect of children and about the social context of abortion—the circumstances and attitudes that lead women to choose abortion. Pro-life activists were frequently involved in groups offering emergency assistance to pregnant women such as Birthright or Pregnancy Help. Pro-choice activists were often on the forefront of movements and groups helping poor mothers and young children to gain better access to health care, nutrition, and housing.

Nearly all the women who expressed strong antiabortion sentiments also opposed capital punishment, but women who expressed pro-choice sentiments were equally as likely to oppose it. On the whole, there was more consensus around capital punishment than around abortion, though it was not as strong as the consensus on disarmament. Betty Anne Nogan, who thinks abortion ought to remain legal, said of people who commit murder, "They are wrong to kill, but society has no right to kill them for that." "Capital punishment is murder," said Sister Margaret Patrice Slattery, the chancellor of Incarnate Word College, who also believes abortion is murder and "hard to justify on any ground." "I do think the Catholic view of life is that people are good," said Abigail McCarthy. Remembering the teachings of her youth, she said, "Of course we believed in original sin but it certainly wasn't the Calvinist idea [of sin]. That's why I think we should be against capital punishment, and I'm so glad we are: You have to believe there is always the possibility of a person being redeemed."

Only a few of the women I met lived an existence devoid of communal connections. They were significantly more concerned about the common good than the sample of white, middle-class Californians studied by Robert Bellah and his colleagues in the landmark *Habits of the Heart*.[13] They viewed themselves as interdependent more than independent, though not all were involved in reshaping the life of institutions.[14] The vast majority were involved in some kind of service to others. Even women holding down full-time jobs made time for volunteer work. A greater number gave time to social service projects— for instance, serving food at a shelter for homeless people—than worked for institutional or social change—for instance, working to support or create social policies that address the causes of homelessness such as lack of affordable housing. A few women spoke about the difference between these two forms of community work. "I was [always] a person of values," said Beatrice Cortez, "a person wanting good will for family and friends, but COPS taught me about power."

In addition to their faith, women cited many reasons for involvement in the social concerns of their community, ranging from motherly love (which led Beatrice Cortez to her first COPS meeting and Carmen Badillo to the PTA) to sheer frustration. Claudine Schneider of Rhode

Island, a Republican member of Congress at the time of the interview, ran for office, she said, because "I became very frustrated by the way politicians were failing to pay attention to the citizens of the state, and I had learned that our country was a democracy of, by, and for the people, and that we really all had a role to play in making this place a little better than we found it."

For Gail Benjamin, who is making a career in city government, the moving force was gratitude. Before directing New York City's Office of Environmental Impact, she served as director of the city's Board of Estimate staff. "The only thing I've ever wanted to do was work for government, for this particular government," Gail said. "New York City gave me incredible things when I was growing up. We could have opportunities that, given our income, we couldn't have gotten on our own—really simple things like the libraries. From the time I was five I went to the library every day. My parents both did the same thing. Every year we would go to the opening of the Botanical Gardens in Brooklyn and the opening of the Botanical Gardens in the Bronx to see the cherry blossoms, and that was always a big special day. Now, we have a fiscal crisis; it's really important that people go into government who remember what it was like and who would insist, who would care enough, [who would] know how important it is that those things happen."

Gail also named another reason for her work in public life, one that seems to underlie most Catholic women's active concern for the common good. "Once you're here," she said to me, "you can't close your eyes; you are responsible."

NINE

CHRISTINE BECKLEY

"If he's Lord of all, that includes me."

Christine Beckley, a forty-three-year-old woman of Scottish, English, and Welsh ancestry, was living with her husband and three children in Allenville, a tiny community in Michigan's Upper Peninsula. The Beckleys' house was spacious and cluttered. Pictures of their children, relatives, and the classic soulful, brown-eyed, bearded Jesus looked down from the walls. Kittens crawled in and out of the kitchen. Christine's youngest child, Ian, then fourteen, was with us during most of the interview. Born with renal tubular acidosis, a kidney disease affecting brain and body growth and causing retardation, Ian is also visually disabled. He hovered around affectionately as I interviewed his mother at the kitchen table.

The Bible doesn't show Jesus as a warrior or a soldier, but I believe that God has established man over all things on the earth. And that gave him territorial-type instincts. We have to defend our land and our country. I think that's a God-given *right* and a duty. So I [feel] very strongly that we need the military. Right or wrong, the Vietnam War happened, and to blame the fellows who fought in it is wrong. And to blame the military overall is wrong. The military only answers to its authority. I think the Vietnam War was inevitable. But they should have just gone in and won the war and got out. I think a lot of it was [people] playing a political ball game. All that fighting was so futile in the end—to have us just backing out and letting them have the country.

I remember something that came around [from the bishops that said] if people were working in a place that had anything to do with nuclear arms, they were encouraging them to leave their jobs. I'm not totally convinced that it is fair to the people, simply because they work with nuclear arms. Anybody who works with the military, if they work in a company that makes tanks, I mean, why don't you just tell them they have to leave their jobs too? I think of nuclear arms in the same terms as I think of arms in general. I think arms are a necessary thing for defense. Nuclear arms are just another type of weapon, not better or worse. If you're going to kill eighteen thousand people it doesn't matter how you kill them. It's the killing and the death and war itself that's bad. I don't think about nuclear attacks; I don't think it really bothers me.

[If I could change this country] I'd probably change the spiritual and moral attitude of people. I'd have them getting back to more biblical principles and more Christian-oriented life-styles: for instance being less abusive of the body, like alcohol, drugs, things like that that you do to yourself; plus sexual and physical abuse and all kinds of abuse that we do to other people.

I feel strongly that the Church has a responsibility toward providing for its people that are in need and it cannot all be placed on the government. I believe the government has to shoulder some burden, but I don't think it should have it all. What did we do before all these government programs? Who took care of the people? The people did. They took care of each other. I think what has happened is that everybody's gotten so comfortable they just sit back and let the government do it.

I think of myself as a Christian first and a Catholic second. Being Christian to me means that I have a very deep and personal relationship with Jesus as my Lord, but also as my Savior: I think about how much he's forgiven me. Some of my family members say, "I don't know if I'm going to heaven or not." That bothers me. I think they don't have enough faith and assurance in Jesus. Having Jesus as Lord means that I want him to be first in my life in everything and that I trust him in and through all situations. If he's Lord of all, that includes me. I can trust him for guidance by giving everything over to him. Before I had come to that point in my life, I worried more and I had to be much more in control. I think there are personality types who are that way. I always will want to maintain a certain amount of control, but I also feel like I have given that control over to the Lord and I continue to be able to let go and give it over to him each and every day.

My mother was very open-minded: we used to attend Vacation Bible School at the Methodist Episcopal Church every year in her hometown, Maynard, Massachusetts; I'd always go and stay with my aunt [there] for a couple of weeks. I remember even going across to the Assembly of God—I think it was Assembly of God; it was some type of Pentecostal [church].

When I was in school we had a Jewish teacher. He wanted us to read from the Bible each morning, and how ignorant I was: "I'm not reading from no Jewish Bible." I mean, it was the Old Testament! I think about that now, how silly I was. I think a lot of people are very ignorant of other religions and denominations.

When we moved to Holliston, Massachusetts, Catholics were the minority. There was quite a bit of prejudice against us. We were very visible. When you had to go to church on a holy day, kids would make fun of you; you were late for school. The same thing with ashes.* [It was] probably done in joking but you had to put up with the ridicule.

People are raised with certain religious and cultural beliefs, and if they've never had the opportunity to hear the Gospel or to learn about Jesus, I don't like to say they're going to hell. I think our God is a much more loving and forgiving God, and I just wouldn't presume that. I just feel that they're going to be given an opportunity to make a decision. I really believe that God intends for us to be Christian.

I was married after high school. He joined the air force shortly after. We were married for five years and during that time we lived in Mississippi, South Carolina, Georgia, [and Alaska]. The marriage was real shaky right from the beginning. He filed for divorce and I left, and started dating Vince. Vince, who had been in the air force, decided to go back to it and went over to Germany. I flew over in '67 and we were married over there. [We stayed] three years and we adopted our two girls there as babies.

Because I had been married before, Vince and I were only married with a civil ceremony. But in the air force everything goes through the chaplain whether you're going to be married by him or not; you still have to go and be counseled; that's part of their regulation. At that time there was a priest who was quite contemporary, way ahead of his time. He challenged us to make our marriage work. He said, "Five out of ten marriages like yours end up never stepping foot inside the church again." It was almost like he *dared* us to be faithful to our church inasmuch as the rules would allow us. He was very thorough in explaining to us where we stood: We were allowed to attend church on a regular basis and to be active and involved in whatever ministry a pastor would allow us to be active in. The restrictions were on the sacraments. No sacraments except in the event of death. For the kids it was no problem receiving the sacraments. He said to us, "You can always live like brother and sister and stay practicing Catholics."† He

---

*A reference to the ashes which Catholics and members of some other Christian churches receive on their forehead on Ash Wednesday.

†Christine and her husband clearly were practicing Catholics, but could not receive commu-

was being facetious. But he did challenge us, so we remained faithful.

That was right in the big changes. Our parish wasn't very big, but we were probably very progressive compared to many of the other bases. We immediately instituted all the changes: the turning of the altar, the going to English; Father V. was also running a Bible study, which was very new to Catholics. I became a reader [at Mass]; I was one of the first lay readers. Women at that time were not particularly called upon. [Father V.] put in a request for lay readers, didn't get a whole lot, and there were some women who were interested so he allowed us to [become lectors]. The Military Ordinariate* do pretty much their own thing. If there's a change that needs to take place, they just do it.

The chaplains are always rotating. When [this priest] left we had a real elderly Polish priest come in. We backed off a little. I continued to read, but I also had the children's choir and I used to do the children's Sunday School—we called it "children's church"—which went on at the same time as Mass was going on upstairs. He mentioned something to me about [going to] communion and I explained to him, and Vince went and talked to him about our marital situation. He was just as good as could be with us. He was also very helpful to us in our adoptions. We had to have a recommendation from our pastor and he gave us a very high recommendation. And he baptized both the girls.

When we left Germany we went to San Antonio. We wanted to continue to be active in church but we were a little bit afraid, because we were the ones coming in new rather than a new pastor coming in. So I held back. But the pastor approached us. He encouraged us to make sure I had filed for annulment, which I had, when I had first gotten divorced four years before. Within three months he did what is probably not acceptable in the Church; he invited us back to confession and back to the sacraments, in conscience. We just had to, in conscience, before him, say that we felt that this was the true and valid marriage, before God. This was very special to us. Because one of the prayers we both had as the girls were growing up was how nice it would be some day, especially when they made their First Communion, if we could go to communion with them. But it happened even before

---

nion. The military chaplain may or may not have used the expression "practicing Catholics" to signify "participation in the sacraments." Whether he actually did or not, Christine's use of this expression reveals how central the sacraments are to Catholics' sense of belonging and participation.
*The Military Ordinariate is a nonterritorial diocese—under the jurisdiction of a single bishop—made up of all the Catholic chaplaincies at American military bases around the world.

that, which was really a blessing. Because that happened it seemed to draw us closer together in the Lord.

Then Vince got his orders for Vietnam, [in] 1971. His job in the air force was in a top-secret security-type thing; he was in what was called "security service," not like the military police or security police but more like what you would think of as FBI or CIA, intelligence-type security. He was there for a year. I had my last miscarriage just shortly after he left—I lost seven altogether. Then I had a partial [hysterectomy], so I can't get pregnant any longer. Vince was able to come home for the surgery, which was really a blessing.

The Vietnam War didn't affect my politics at all because I'd always felt very strongly about the defense of our country. I wasn't one of these antiwar type people at all. It increased my faith. But the thing is, no matter how much faith you have, when you're apart for a year and then you come back, you're two different people. And we both now say, "Hey, somebody needs to warn these kids [in the military] that you need to be prepared for that." We had a rough time there for a while. But we were able to work through it.

[After Vince got back from Vietnam] we went back to Alaska, [where we had met]. We were up there for three years. We were very active with youth ministry and with the CYO* and the folk music group. It was also at that time that I first became involved with the Charismatic Renewal.†

---

*The Catholic Youth Organization (CYO) is a parish-based national organization founded in 1930 and focused on religious, cultural, and athletic programs. In the memories and minds of many Catholics, it has become especially associated with its athletic component.

†Many Catholics, like Christine, have found in this spiritual renewal movement a freeing of the heart, a more intimate relationship with Jesus, and the opportunity to pray with greater enthusiasm. The Charismatic Renewal movement began in the U.S. in the late 1960s, after a group of Catholics had a religious experience characterized by prayer in tongues and the utterance of words of wisdom which they described as "Baptism in the Spirit." The Charismatic experience bears some similarity to Protestant Pentecostalism but, in contrast to Pentecostals, who tend to break into small independent congregations, Catholic Charismatics have remained part of their church's mainstream (though they were viewed with suspicion at first) and resolutely Catholic. In the early days of the movement, Charismatic prayer groups were often based outside the parish (for instance, at retreat centers) but now exist both in and outside parish settings. In the early days of the movement especially, it was not uncommon for groups to burgeon from three to three hundred people. The Renewal is essentially a lay movement whose centers of gravity are in the Midwest, though clergy around the country have become involved. At least one major strand of the Renewal, influenced by Evangelical and Pentecostal Christianity, advocates "male headship" and limits some of the ministries open to women; other strands of the Charismatic Renewal support a broader leadership role for women. Catholic Charismatics tend to be ecumenical, since their central focus is the experience of prayer and "being set free in the power of

There was no Charismatic prayer group on base at first; my first exposure was through a young [airman] in my folk music group. The bishop was coming from New York for Christmas Eve for Midnight Mass, and the folk group was asked to do the Mass. This fellow came in and he was almost three sheets to the wind, drunk. Mass went fairly well considering his condition but I was just a wreck because of it. [After that episode] we didn't see him for the longest time, and then all of a sudden he'd start showing up at practices, every once in a while. Pretty soon he started coming back and doing Mass with us, and we were using the songs he was teaching us as part of our meditation music. I knew something was different about George and he had truly changed. He explained that he had really had a rough time and had gone into a coffeehouse downtown in Anchorage one day, a Christian coffeehouse, and that they had helped him. And then he had visited this Christian commune out in Palmer, Alaska, called the Bread of Life, and he had given his life to Jesus and was now a different person. George invited me to go with him to this Bread of Life commune, so we packed up the whole folk group and CYO and we took them out there. Later we had a seminar on what Charismatic Renewal was and our prayer group began.

I felt an immediate attraction [to the Renewal]. My husband would tell you that they developed the Charismatic Renewal just for me because he says that's the way I was all the time. Even before hearing about the Charismatic Renewal, when I would do the children's Mass I would have the children clapping their hands and waving their arms and doing little motions to songs, and singing in rounds; I didn't know until later that this was something that was very typical of the Renewal. *Everything* about it turned me on: the love, the *freedom* in expressing themselves—that was probably the biggest thing. I believe it comes from my association as a kid with the Assembly of God; when I found myself in that situation again, and people were raising their hands and singing and clapping, and even when they started to sing in the Spirit,* I [thought it was wonderful]. No fear whatsoever.

---

the Spirit," an experience shared by Christians from other churches. In addition to a freeing of heart and voice, Catholic Charismatics often speak of a discovery of God as primarily loving as the central revelation of their Charismatic experience; they also speak frequently of physical healings and direct answers to prayers. Christine's son, Ian, was completely healed of his kidney disease a year after we met, after attending a healing Mass during which a priest anointed and prayed over him. As a result, Ian's physician took him off the medication he had been taking all his life.

*In addition to the words that come to people who are "speaking in tongues," a melody comes spontaneously to those who are "singing in the Spirit" or "singing in tongues."

My experience [of Baptism in the Spirit] took place by myself. I had been in my rocking chair and I was reading my Bible and praying and saying how I wanted to just give myself totally over to the Lord and love Him so much more than I felt I could. I didn't seem to be able to do it, and I was trying to express my love for the Lord. And I remember a peace coming over me; it was almost as if somebody breathed on my right shoulder. I even remember turning my head to see if it was the dog. That's how much I felt it. After turning my head I saw my picture of Jesus way up on the wall. The picture caught my eyes and it was like whatever had happened, had happened. The next day I was standing out in the kitchen doing the dishes and kind of praying or singing, and all of a sudden these funny words came out of my mouth. That was the beginning. [I began to speak in tongues] before I really had an understanding of it being a gift that you could ask for. I went right to the prayer group leaders and they just got so excited. They prayed with me and said you didn't have to go to some specific place and have somebody pray over you [to have this experience]. So I wasn't in church—it just happened to me right there in my chair.

From Anchorage we went to Michigan, right up here to Kincheloe [Air Force Base], which is closed now. I started playing the guitar and we became involved in the |Charismatic| prayer group at Kincheloe, a very large, very active group. [It was] ecumenical and we had sixty-five members. In 1979 Vince retired from the air force. We ended up staying here. He works for the school system in community education.

I'm the liturgy coordinator for our little parish out here, Immaculate Conception. I do all the music. But it just closed three weeks ago. No priest. We would love to [have a sister in charge* but] getting somebody is so difficult. There's a possibility that we will go back to mission status: That means a priest would come out maybe twice a month and say Mass out there and then [the rest of the time] they'd have lay-led communion services.† I think it would be better [to stay open under mission status than to close], to keep the community together.

---

*A growing number of sisters—and occasionally laywomen or men—have become administrators or pastors of parishes in the past decade, particularly in Christine's part of the country, which is experiencing a shortage of priests.

†A "communion service," in Catholic parlance, is a service of worship at which the Scriptures are read and hosts or bread consecrated at a previously celebrated Mass are distributed. These services may be led by a layperson and have increased in frequency as the number of priests has begun to diminish in the U.S., France, and other countries.

We've always had a Bible study going which Mary now [leads].*
Even before Pastor Mary, we always had a group of us women that
met. It really is special. There really isn't any emphasis on the denomination; Mary can teach us from such a broad perspective. There are
mostly Lutherans and Catholics, because those are the only two
churches we have in town.

I'm involved in Women Aglow. It's based on that Scripture, "Now
be aglow with the Spirit," and it's basically to provide women with a
chance for fellowship and spiritual growth through guest speakers and
worship. It would be like a counterpart of the Full Gospel Businessmen's
Fellowship. Also prison ministry, that's my favorite. They changed the
air force base to a men's prison. My husband and I go with another
couple and have prayer meeting. If somebody had told me I would go
to a prison and minister I would have found it very difficult [to believe].
My mother worked in a prison as a nurse and I used to go there with
her, so I never had fear. But as a child I had been sexually molested
[by a neighbor and a male relative] and I had never told anybody; I
was never even able to tell my parents. So to go to a men's prison
where I knew that's what some of them were in for, I didn't know if
I could handle that. But I also knew the Lord had really healed me
[from that experience I had]; [it wasn't through counseling], just
through prayer. Now I feel I can go into that prison and it's the Lord
that gives me just love for those fellows. Some of those guys were able
to share how it was such a big help to them to know that the things
they had done, somewhere out there someone could really forgive them,
that person they had robbed or whatever. That somebody out there
was helping that person to forgive them too.

We adopted Ian when we were at Kincheloe. He was four and a
half. When you already have two they don't give you much hope; some
places wouldn't even take our name to put on the waiting list. The
girls happened to see this movie *Mixed Company*, about this family
taking in all these kids of different colors and backgrounds, whether
they were handicapped physically or mentally. I had always told the
girls, "There just aren't any kids." Well, they saw that movie and they
really challenged me. They said, "Mom, you keep telling us there's no
kids, but look here, this lady's bringing kids home because there's kids
that people don't want." So I explained to them about "hard to place"

*Mary is the Rev. Mary Olivanti, another of the women interviewed for this book, an ordained
Lutheran pastor who was raised a Roman Catholic and was serving two rural parishes at the time
of the interviews; one of these churches was in Christine's community of Allenville.

and they both said, "Well, that's what we need to do, Mom, we just need to get one that no one wants." And that's what we did.

Right now the girls are both seventeen; there's only ten and a half months between them. People say, "You adopted them and you still got 'em that close?" [I say], "I don't believe in birth control." I do and I don't. I think it's abused but I think there's a time and a place for it. I think the Lord's promise about never giving us more to handle [than we can bear] is sometimes abused when it comes to having a ton of kids. You can quote Scripture out of context for a lot of different things. But birth control has to come from an unselfish decision. I think people saying, "I don't want more than two" because they want to maintain a certain social status or live a certain high life-style [isn't right]. I don't believe in abortion at all. I tend to be very pro-life.

Very Puritanistic attitudes of New England prevailed when I was a kid growing up. So my mother didn't talk to me about that three-letter word, whereas I was much more open and talked about sex with the girls. I've always tried to give them a healthy attitude, knowing that in today's society promiscuity is very prevalent. Premarital sex is something that's almost accepted. My older daughter, Andrea, has had cousins that have been very open about the fact that *their* mother put them on *birth control pills.* I've told Andrea, that sex is a special gift from God and that it's for her and her future spouse. It's not something to be done casually or loosely.

I think the Lord wants me to have a healthy body, that's the primary thing, and I'm trying to get that through to the girls. Society tells them how to look and dress. They're always worrying about their weight and how their hair looks and I try to reassure them that the important thing is that you're healthy and that you look natural. I try to encourage them not to be obsessed with how their body looks.

I feel that if God can forgive *all* other kinds of sins He can certainly forgive you for making a mistake in your choice of mate. And I am *against* divorce, don't get me wrong; but there are times when there just isn't an alternative. Now, this is a question that was presented to me and I have to answer it honestly: Someone said, "Okay, you were divorced. What if you had become a Christian as you are now* when you were married the first time? Would you still have gotten divorced?" I have to be very honest and say no, I wouldn't have. It wasn't a question of sticking it out, since he divorced me; I didn't have a whole

---

*Meaning the conscious commitment to Christ which Christine experienced as part of her involvement with the Charismatic Renewal.

lot of control over that. But I think that had I come to that spiritual point in my life [sooner], it would have had an effect on my marriage and we probably would have been able to make our marriage work. I think divorce is wrong. But when it comes down to where there is no choice and divorce does take place, there needs to be a change in policy and attitudes. [I did get the annulment, by the way.] On our tenth anniversary we had a regular [Catholic marriage].

There are certain things about the Church that make me sad. We expect our priests to be human, but many of them do not set good examples for our young people. Their life-styles don't always reflect what should be, [for example] the freedom and ease with which they can just go out partying at bars. I would rather see them setting an example that says you don't have to do that to have a good time. It bothers me because many of our young people are being led away; those who have come to some knowledge of Jesus on their own will be led to another denomination because of ministries provided for young people and because of the example set by the pastors.

[Another thing bothers me.] The idea of priests not marrying was a man-instituted type of law; I think they should be allowed to marry; I really feel strongly. I could think of people that would have made excellent priests, excellent pastors, excellent counselors. But they also were drawn to married life; they wanted family. I think we wouldn't see the shortage of priests today if they were given an option, as in the Orthodox Church.

I would prefer to see men continue in that role within the Church. I feel that God really did establish an order of headship. There is a place for women in ministry but I'm not sure it's through that particular role. I really believe that women make excellent teachers, excellent preachers, I have no objection in that sense. I just believe that order of headship is there. You know the way the Scriptures refer to Christ and the Church, you know, the Church is the Bride of Christ. And where Paul says men are to love their wives as Christ loves the Church. That sets Christ over the husband over the wife, and I don't mean that in an authoritarian type thing. I feel that male spiritual head is important, almost like it's instituted by God from the beginning of creation. Yet I have no objection to women ministers [in other denominations] at all, that's obvious; so it almost sounds contradictory. Even in Christ's followers there was a place for women. In biblical times women were deacons; that's why I believe there's a place for women in ministry. You still are *ordained* a deacon. But I think that specific priesthood as we see it in our Catholic church should remain for men.

Knowing the type of personality I am, I think women can become very domineering. I think that would have a devastating effect on the Church if all of a sudden the Church were to be run by the women. I'm not saying the men are all good men either. I'm just saying that overall that's what was intended: women leading to a degree, but always under that covering, that protective authority.

I definitely feel that way about marriage too. I think the husband should be the head of the household and the spiritual head as well. It all comes down to him having the final say. I believe we have to talk things out, but there needs to be *one* with that final authority. Because if you want to know the honest to goodness truth, if you want to talk women's lib, I have never been freer than when I finally came to the point where I was able to say, "Vince has the final word."

Did you ever get called up to do this, and then asked to do that, and then somebody wants you to do something else, and you want to do it all? And you think, "How do I say no? How do I say no?" and you just say, "I'm sorry, but my husband says I am doing too much." It's so much easier to say, "I'm sorry, Vince says no and that's it." I don't mean that in a copout sense either, I mean it in a real sense. He has the final say. Whether it's right or wrong. Sometimes he makes a final decision that I don't agree with. But I don't have to let it bug me because he made it. It has taken a lot of burden off me. I think it's a lot easier to be a wife and mother when you don't take all that on you.

I think the women's movement hasn't swayed me at all. All it did was confirm and cement my own feelings. My first thought when I think of women's liberation is an attitude. I don't think of it as being a movement. Being liberated is an attitude of being free. I don't think it has anything to do with any laws or principles or movement. Real women's liberation has got to be an individual thing. The *movement*, as we call it, is a bunch of hogwash. Because they're doing it from a self-centered and—I don't know how to explain it; I don't *care* about the women's liberation movement and I don't *care* about feminism and I don't *care* about this attitude they stick on men because they want to be polite and open the door for a woman. I don't think about those things. I don't think it's worth my time. It probably almost sounds like a copout, but I got very tired of hearing that business of equal pay for equal job. I don't think of that as women's lib. To me, if you do as well as a man, the laws have always said you'd get paid. Whether you did or not, I realize that's another story. If they were just concentrating on those aspects—but the idea of all this freedom of choice and wanting to get this amendment, the ERA, I just don't think it's coming from the right attitude of the heart and I don't think it's headed in the right direction.

If a woman has a valid case [about job discrimination], okay, then they're justified. The company should be definitely made aware of the fact that they're discriminating, if in fact that's the case. I don't think that has anything to do with women's lib.

[The bishops are thinking of writing a pastoral letter on women?] I'd tell them to go out and get married and then talk about women. I'm serious. Really and truly, what right do they have to say anything about women?

TEN

A WOMAN'S WORK

A strong woman is a woman in whose head
a voice is repeating, I told you so,
ugly, bad girl, bitch, nag, shrill, witch,
ballbuster, nobody will ever love you back,
why aren't you feminine, why aren't
you soft, why aren't you quiet,
why aren't you dead?
　　　　　　　　　　　—Marge Piercy
Housekeeping ain't no joke.
　　　　　　　　　　　—Louisa May Alcott

"There is no subject about which the women disagree more than woman herself," Sally Cunneen wrote in *Sex: Female; Religion: Catholic* in 1968.[1] More than two decades later, Cunneen's observation about American Catholic women still holds true. Nowhere did I find more variety, ambivalence, and contradictions than in Catholic women's opinions on the nature and role of women, feminism, femininity, and the relationship between women and men.

There is often a kind of cosmology implicit in women's understanding of the distinct roles of the sexes: Women's relationship with men is, for them, intrinsically related to the order of the universe. Some women, like Christine Beckley, made the connection explicit. "I just believe that order of headship is there," she said. "I feel that male spiritual head is important, almost like it's instituted by God from the beginning of creation."

Like Christine Beckley, Ruth Pakaluk is strongly opposed to both the feminist movement and the ordination of women. For both women, hierarchy in marriage, hierarchy in the Church, and hierarchy in the universe are logically connected. If women were ordained, Ruth said, "I guess I would completely have to alter my picture of what it means to be a priest because I think the Roman Catholic priest is another Christ, and Christ is the head of the Church as the man is the head of a marriage. There's a very profound reality that we don't understand too well right now in our culture because we are so confused about what men and women are and how they should relate to each other. To have a woman priest completely upsets reality, it just gets everything out of kilter. Understanding how maleness and femaleness relate to each other is in a way a picture for us of the relationship of God to the created universe. Initiator/receiver, that's how I think about it. . . . It's as if in the Church the whole created universe is summed up. To have a woman get up and be the priest and speak the words of Christ— 'This is my body, this is my blood'—and be the Christ for the Church completely wrecks the picture. You have to believe that the pictures we use and the way you express reality really matter. You can't just change it and think you're going to get the same reality. If you were to have the woman be the priest it would be like you'd be ruining the symphony, you'd be wrecking the song."

Though few of the women I interviewed would agree with Ruth (and those who agreed did not use such vivid language), her words point to a reality most Catholics understand: Changing the shape of the liturgy and of its leadership does in fact alter the way the world appears and the way God is understood. This holds less true in religious communities less wedded to symbol, structure, and ritual. In all religions but in sacramental traditions especially, changes in the roles of women and men may feel literally earth-shaking. If they do, it is because they shake up the imagination: Underneath established roles and symbols are the beliefs about God and the world that support them, beliefs embedded in the gut and the unconscious as much as the conscious mind. Small wonder the cosmos feels out of place and the ground no longer firm underfoot.

Supporters of the women's movement were less inclined to favor institutional or cosmic hierarchies. They did not view as a challenge to the order of the universe the shift in symbols set in motion by new forms of leadership, language, and community. Rather, they believed this shift set on its head a (literally) man-made structure harmful to the human beings it purports to help. Theirs was a straightforward, less highly structured theology of creation: God created all persons with equal dignity; all else follows from this fact.

While the women's movement has influenced the religious life of

Catholic women, their Catholic faith has also, in many cases, influenced their feminism. The belief in the creation of all human beings in God's image and in God's love for all (rich and poor, female and male) has shaped views of women as much as attitudes toward the poor and disenfranchised. For most of the Catholic women I met, this radical equality of all human creatures before God is the theological bottom line.

Several women gave theologically based answers when I asked for their definition of feminism. "Definitely, I am a feminist," said Abigail McCarthy. "It means that you are committed to having women reach their full potential and to the idea that women are intended by the Creator to be equal to men." For Margaret Slattery, who describes herself as a "moderate feminist," "it just goes back to basic religious principles: If you believe in God, and you believe that God created all of us, men and women, then you believe that every person has an equal right to respect. Then it's your responsibility to give it. It's all very simple. Of course it's simple to accept intellectually," she added. "What dies hard are the customs and the practices and prejudices that are so much more deeply rooted than the intellectual [understanding]—emotions rather than reason."

Some women's feminism was "negatively fostered" by the Church—a reaction, they said, against a male hierarchy insensitive to their concerns. But Catholicism also contributed positively to women's awareness of their own gifts and to their solidarity with other women. The presence of women as institutional leaders and role models has left its mark: Virtually all the women who had attended Catholic women's colleges described themselves as feminists. For some women, too, the existence of a strong women's movement in the Catholic community during the past two decades has been decisive. This movement has not simply taught women to be critical of their tradition. It has also been a healing and creative force in their lives, offering women alternative theologies, forms of worship, and styles of leadership.[2]

The women's movement did not affect all American Catholic women in the same way. The differences seem to have little to do with generation: Among women in their forties, for instance, I found responses ranging from Christine Beckley's disapproval to Sandra Temple's statement that Betty Friedan's *The Feminine Mystique* was "the most formative book in my life next to the Bible." The women I met often lived in subcultures that rarely communicated with one another. Military wives, single urban professionals, suburban mothers, university women often seemed worlds apart, and nowhere more than in their views of women and feminism. Their opinions were often shared and reinforced by their neighbors, colleagues, and friends. Television sometimes seemed to have shaped their views of feminism almost as much as personal experience.

Fewer than half the women I interviewed defined themselves as feminists.

I had asked women two separate questions about the women's movement and feminism, thinking I might receive different answers to them. I did. Our conversations typically proceeded like this: "Do you feel the women's movement has had any influence on you?" I would ask. "Yes," was the usual answer, and women would speak warmly of increased self-esteem, greater economic opportunity, a broadening of options for themselves and their daughters. Yes, the women's movement had influenced them, and positively so. "Do you consider yourself a feminist?" was the next question. The answers were mixed. "Yes," some women said happily. "Oh, *no*," many more answered. No, I'm not one of those women.

Ambivalent about or disapproving of women who overtly speak their grievances, challenge discrimination, and appear to act selfish, Catholic women are grateful to the women's movement for fostering in themselves those very same qualities: being more vocal, rejecting injustice, and taking better care of themselves.

"Jenna Santini" said she valued the opportunities the women's movement had begun to provide. She spoke of the challenge of being one of a handful of female officers on a largely male urban police force. She strongly favored the ordination of women in the Catholic church. Asked whether she was a feminist, she said that she was not. Being a feminist, she said, meant "someone—female or male—who is all out for women and women should do everything. Some feminists go too far overboard to dominate the male," said "Jenna," who lives with her female lover. "Most of the feminists I know are so gung ho, women everything, it's overbearing sometimes. They are very aggressive— which is good. But sometimes it harms the women's movement."

"The women's movement," said sixty-four-year-old, Australian-born May Kast, "made you realize that you may be, as they say, 'just a woman,' but you have your right to speak and let your views be known, and men aren't always right." She laughed, then grew serious. "And if you see an injustice and a wrong, regardless of whether you're treading on territory that a man usually does, if you don't speak up for justice, you are nothing. You may as well not pray, if you don't stand up and speak up if anyone does something to another. The women's movement has made me more assertive. They just don't put up with things the way they used to be. 'Woman's place is in the home.' I don't agree with that." "Do you consider yourself a feminist?" I asked. "No," she answered, "just a little rebellious. I'm not one, because there are so many good men in this world who love God, who do so much good for people. A feminist can never see a lot of good in most men for some reason. They're more likely to condemn or to think a woman does it better."

"What is a feminist?" I often asked, wondering what the women were thinking of when they said they were or were not. Their definitions diverged widely, particularly in the way they defined feminist women's relationship to men.

To the women who said they were not feminists, "feminism" held connotations of either disliking men or (in complete contradiction) of wanting to be just like them.

Dolores Reuter defined a feminist as "someone that is loudly proclaiming women's rights and won't let anyone open a door for her because she's a woman, who goes overboard, antagonizes people." Yet, when I asked how she would change the Catholic church if she could, Dolores responded, "I would put in some women cardinals. And," she added, "recognize women as people. I think women are second-class citizens in the Catholic church," she added with irritation. The words *feminism* and *feminist* elicited from many women adjectives like "extreme," "aggressive," "angry," "strident," "pushy," and even "fanatical."

Women who said they were feminists defined feminism in an entirely different way.

"Oh yes," forty-three-year-old Marty Woodward answered when asked if she was a feminist. A feminist, she said, is "a woman who is on a journey toward wholeness, who has come to accept her feminine self as an authentic, important part of who she is; one who sees women as truly made in the image of God. There's not a part of my being [that] does not make me feel equal to a man. The concrete part of being a feminist is to be a person who not only declares that about herself but has determined a way that she can work that out and call others to it. It cannot just be a statement. The statement must move you to some kind of personal action. I am really committed to working with women," said Marty, who is the Catholic chaplain at Hollins College, a women's college in Virginia. "And I've always found it very comfortable to work with men." Marty is married and the mother of two children.

None of the women who said they were feminists appeared to

hate men or to think of feminism as antimale. They did talk about valuing women, which, for them, was not the same as devaluing men. "My definition of *feminist* is that women are very important people— and that their lives, their issues, their perspectives should be paid attention to," said Caryl Rivers. Angela Rodriguez, born in Ireland fifty years ago, is a full-time homemaker and a volunteer at San Francisco's Coming Home Hospice for people with AIDS. She is in favor of the Equal Rights Amendment. Her daughters attend a Catholic girls' acad- emy run by the Religious of the Sacred Heart. Asked whether she was a feminist, Angela said, "I think so. Being a feminist would be allowing me to feel myself taking an equal place, with me being respected, being honored."

Women who said they were not feminists often felt that feminists were trying to emulate men; yet women who identified themselves as feminists spoke repeatedly of the need to acknowledge the distinctive experience of women and to encourage women to chart their own paths. "My colleagues and I talk about this," said journalist and jour- nalism professor Caryl Rivers. "We say to [young] women, you don't have to follow the male model, you don't have to become just like men, you shouldn't."

At the same time, self-identified feminists shared a belief in equal partnership with men, whether at home, in society, or in the Church. "[My husband and I have an equal relationship] because I demand it," said "Elena Martinez Wise," the Mexican-born corporate officer from San Francisco. "I find I have to continuously assert myself, but I also find that when I do there's a certain respect [I receive], not just at home but in my work. I believe in complete equality in the political arena and the social arena. [And in the Church] too," she added in a gentle, determined voice.

Catholic women defined the women's movement's main focus in several ways. For some, it broadened women's options in personal relationships and public life, opening the door to opportunities formerly reserved for men. For others, it helped to infuse feminine qualities and perspectives into a world dominated by men. For a third group of women, it had more to do with working for a change in the power equation—not only between women and men, but among groups that have limited each other's well-being on the basis of race or other factors. Some women I met combined two or three of these definitions.

One of the prevailing views in our culture is that feminism aims simply to move women into male roles and male institutions. Many of the women who opposed feminism defined it in this way. But here again, women who were feminists did *not* view the women's movement—in church or in society—as an effort to "add women and stir," in Mary Hunt's words.[3]

Women strove for achievement in their chosen fields and many were highly accomplished. But I heard few grandiose expectations of "having it all" as a result of the women's movement. Catholic women's definitions of success—which were remarkably alike—always included one or more of these four goals: using their gifts and talents; using them for the common good; attaining inner peace and a sense of comfort with themselves; and sustaining loving relationships. A great majority of the women said they felt successful.

"First and foremost in my life right now," Sarah Hofheinz said, "are to be a good mother and a good wife—which is more than a full-time job; to derive personal satisfaction from doing those things; to have a network of friends [with] a sophisticated relationship, not just a superficial relationship; and to be helping my community." For Ruth Pakaluk, success is "using the gifts and talents that God had given you to do as much good as you can where you're placed." "To do a bit of justice here and there," was Mary Hunt's answer. Ann Valdez defined success as "knowing yourself to the best of your ability and achieving the goals that you set for yourself; but achieving them without sacrificing people who are important to you along the way." "Following my conscience and being at peace with myself," Mar Londo said in answer to my question.

Women who had struggled with addictions were especially likely to speak of success as inner serenity. "I try to accept this time in my life as three years of soul-searching," Christine Torrey said of her stay in prison. "Success for me would be to be in a career where I was looked up to and respected and had a tremendous sense of purpose—as far as success in the world goes. But true success is to find inner peace." For Sandra Mondykowski Temple, a recovering alcoholic, success "means feeling secure with your inner self. If everything around you dropped off, your job or your position in life, if you lost everything tomorrow, that you would still feel whole."

For some, feminism meant the entry of women into traditionally male occupations or institutions. A second group of women defined feminism as a conscious feminization of society, usually focused on replacing "male aggression" with "female nurturing." These women, and many more who did not view themselves as feminists, felt that women had special qualities, often related to listening, nurturing, and a cooperative approach to working, leadership, and solving problems.

While many women felt the differences between the sexes were socially conditioned, others, like Kathy Kasza, attributed them to divine plan. "I fully believe that God created us differently," she said, "that He gave us qualities to nurture and care, to help grow and guide. That doesn't mean we can't lead. But I do not believe that men are capable of nurturing people the way a woman can. There are distinct differences and they are there for a reason." "There are many variants in person-alities but if you [could] take the perfect man, he would be stronger, more aggressive," said Carolyn Booth of Cary, North Carolina. "If you could take the perfect woman, she would be gentler, the nurturer, the rudder that steered the man and his aggression. That's the kind of life I aspire to. God created man and woman so God intended that. [But I don't think] man is superior to woman, they have the same level of intelligence."

Women who stressed the distinctly "womanly" qualities of women often seemed to consider them superior. "Women are much more intuitive," said fifty-seven-year-old "Sylvia Presti." "Women are in many instances much more clear-sighted, they hear, they listen, they are able to make good judgments, able to communicate much more effectively. They have much greater patience for detail." Dorothy Wodraska is a physical education teacher in a Catholic school, where she also teaches a course on sexuality to junior high school students; she chairs her parish's Right to Life committee. I asked if she considered herself a feminist. Yes, she said, "because I think women are wonderful; I think women are the mainstay of the world. We have strength beyond that of men in so many ways. Our insight is superior. I'm so proud to be a woman; I think we've been given the greatest of the gifts in pro-creation. I think the nurturing part of our nature is so important and so much more godlike than the conditioned experience of a man that he has to be macho. I often think that if women were leading the world there wouldn't be wars. It's easier for a woman with a nurturing nature to sit down and say, 'Hey look, let's not hurt each other, let's work this out,' than it is for a man who has been brought up to think that hard means strong." Sales manager Gaye Lott, a strong pro-choice advocate, spoke of her feminism and her view of women in much the same way. "I don't want to be like a man," she said. "I think we wouldn't have wars if the world was run by women. We would handle problems differently. We *think*. It's very important to my brother to make a decision and *do it*. It's more important for me to talk about it, think about it. He thinks that's weak. I think it's great."

But others felt that "women's nature" made women more suited to certain roles and less suited to others. Inevitably, the examples they gave pertained to four areas: political office, the ordained ministry, physical strength, and the relationship between women and men in marriage. "I don't think I'll ever accept a woman president of the United States," said Janet Kanitz. "That's just a position that a man should fill. Maybe women would become too emotional." Almost all the women, in fact, returned again and again to these subjects, whether they felt women's roles ought to be restricted or expanded.

In their emphasis on infusing "feminine values" into institutions, the second group of women differed from those feminists who stressed the need to change a complex array of power imbalances within those institutions, though there was some overlap in their views.[4] Feminism, for this third group, was about social change and social justice. They examined social realities through the lens of women's experience, saw discrimination and abuse, and concluded that something must be done—and that they would take a share of the responsibility for that "something." Feminism is "putting things in terms of women," said Anne Burke, the director of the Raleigh Urban Ministry Center. "It includes recognition of oppression [of women] as a group and recognition that we have to do something about that; we have to change that." Feminism, "Jeanne Dupont" said succinctly, is "setting things back in balance."

"Growing up," said Ellen Reuter, "I knew that things weren't fair but I didn't have a way to articulate it; I didn't have the words. And then when the women's movement started rolling I could feel I had kindred spirits and I could say, 'Oh yeah, that's right!' When I was in college my brother and I wanted to go to summer school. Because he was male, he could get a larger summer loan than I because they figured if he had worked that summer, he'd have earned this much money and if I had worked I'd have made that much. I was really furious. So I didn't go to summer school, I worked." Iris Palmer, who was unemployed when we met, said to me, "I look at the way that men get paid and women do the same job, and most of the time women have to work twice as hard to get the money that a man is making—if they ever get it. I was not aware of it [before]; it was just something you accepted."

These women criticized the impact on women of specific institutions, policies, and relationships in much the same way the San Antonio social activists spoke of institutions failing the needs of the poor in their community. They sometimes spoke of the fact that most of the poor today are women and children, linking their concerns about poverty and women's rights. Feminism, for these women, is a move-ment concerned about the common good. "One thing that worries me," Caryl Rivers said, "[is that] I see all these young women who think that feminists were all these crazy people and man-hating ladies [from the sixties and seventies] that went stomping around in combat boots. I talk about women who went up front and filed the [law]suits [against employers that discriminated against women]. And I say to the young women, 'The reason you people are walking in [to these institutions] is that a lot of women took tremendously courageous stands for which they suffered their whole professional lives.' Feminism is a human rights movement!"

Paradoxically, some of the women who spoke most easily about power and its abuses—the COPS leaders from San Antonio—said they were neither particularly influenced by nor particularly interested in the women's movement. "Putting things in terms of women" was not their primary concern. The rights of the poor and the cultural identity and survival of the Mexican-American community were foremost in their minds. Speaking of the U.S. bishops' proposed pastoral letter on wom-en's concerns, Beatrice Cortez said, "It's not that it's not something good, but I don't know what a woman's concern is. To me a woman's concern is a man's concern and a man's concern is a child's concern. I always look at the whole family."

"These women that are so vocal feel everything in society is a discrimination," said Mary Kay Leicht, a mother and community vol-unteer in Indianapolis. "I have a bad picture of them. All they want to do is complain about how they are being discriminated against in every part of their life and throughout history, and I just don't see that that's the case. I do believe that women are capable and I'm just as intelligent as my husband," she added. "He just happens to get paid for his job and I don't and that's okay. I think women are capable of doing everything and I would be delighted to have a woman president or to have my daughter be a doctor." She made no mention of the barriers that might keep women from medical institutions or from the White House. "My sister is a strident feminist," said Bridget Palmer. "She alienates a lot of people; they shut her off."

"I think you need to express your views," said Betty Darko, "but I don't think you should do it in a way that's offensive or rude. That holds true for a man too. I do think sometimes women, in being too pushy, do more harm in the long run. Being offensive is not the way because it tends to make opponents. Maybe a little more tact is what I'm saying [is needed]." Sometimes, as in Bridget Palmer's case, women's observations were based on experience. In other cases they were not. I asked Betty Darko for a concrete example from her own life of "pushy" behavior by a woman with feminist concerns. "I'm not sure I can give you something specifically," she said, adding, "Of course, television tends to dwell on the worst part of anything to try to sensationalize it."

Much of the negative response to the word *feminism* (among Catholic women and elsewhere) seems to come from apprehension or ambivalence about women's anger. Women have traditionally been the soothers, the bridge-builders, the reconcilers, those who calm the anger of others. Women's anger is not only frightening for those who stand on the receiving end, but for the women who experience it. "I was afraid," said Caryl Rivers, "that people wouldn't like me if I got angry. Nice girls don't get angry. I've learned to get angry in a rather nice way," she added with a twinkle in her eye. "My voice drops and my tone gets a little bit more steely. Because women's anger provokes such terror in men, women have to know when to use it." Two decades ago, Ann Richards Anderson said, "I very consciously did not read feminist books [at first]. I remember when *Ms.* magazine began I really wanted to buy it. Then I thought, no, I'm not going to buy it. Because if I buy it or read any of these books, I'm just going to get mad, and I'm in a place right now where I can't change my situation."

Many women said it was difficult for them, because of their upbringing, to experience and express anger. This seemed more related to being female than to being Catholic. "Women in general have trouble getting angry," said psychotherapist Ellen Reuter, who works as a counselor at Sacred Hearts of Jesus and Mary Parish in Sun Prairie, Wisconsin. "Anger is what lets people feel their power. It can be what says, 'Hey, you can't do that to me anymore.' " The women she knows, Ellen said, "often try feeling anything but anger, and end up depressed."

In expressing their disapproval of "angry women," some women seemed to confuse anger with hatred. Yet of all the women I met who were angry about women's place in society or the Church, none spoke from a hate-filled heart. Their anger was obviously a sign of love, born of intense caring, commitment, and pain. People who do not care do not get angry.

Women exercising an assertive rather than a long-suffering strength seem to strike terror in human hearts. Part of the terror may be a fear of losing a softness and gentleness traditionally associated with being female. "What concerns me about the feminist movement is they want to share in the power that men have," said Eunice Staples, a secretary at Cincinnati's Xavier University. "I don't like the idea of power. I don't like to feel I control other people; I like to feel in control of myself. The women I know who want to be part of the structure tend to lose some of their nurturing qualities, some of their femininity. I think women have a great deal to contribute because of their sensitivity and their ability to nurture, and we need to bring that into male structures. Unfortunately too often—maybe because we're in the early stages—women who get into the power structure become very male. I think men need to learn nurturing too," she added. "We haven't educated our sons not to be afraid to cry, to be sensitive to other people, to be caring, not to feel they have the macho image."

Power, for Eunice and many others, has become attached to traditionally "masculine" qualities. If women gain more power, will the world lose its caregivers? Will there be enough gentleness to go around? Some women felt the women's movement fostered a different kind of power. "Power doesn't mean control," said Anne Burke. "Power means being able to enable people. It means taking charge of your own life and helping people to take charge of their own lives. It doesn't mean oppressing, it means raising up. And it means doing it in an inclusive way, a nonhierarchical model. Women have had to live like that: We never had power. Women are good mediators, they're good organizers, they're good workers from the ground up. They are inclusive because they've been forced to be."

Nice girls, Caryl Rivers said, do not get angry. Raised to attend to the needs of others, many women have trouble attending to their own needs. Feminism, with its emphasis on the well-being of women, may threaten women's sense of their own femininity. "Liking yourself first," as one woman put it, can make a woman feel like a bad girl. Nevertheless, women were grateful to the women's movement for instilling in them a new sense of confidence and inner power. When they spoke of its benefits, they mentioned increased self-esteem at least as often as the broadening of economic, religious, and professional options.

The women's movement, said Kathy Kasza, "gave me the okay to have my own feelings, my own needs, my own wants, and the permission to get them [met] in whatever way I could." Susan Johnson, at the age of forty-six, contrasted her life with her mother's, saying, "I've fought to be myself, to go to school and to have my own little section of life that's me, that's not mother, that's not wife, that's not daughter—and not to feel guilty that I've carved out time for myself. It is necessary for my mental health," she said. "I'm convinced it is for all women, and it really doesn't matter what it is you do, but you've got to get your strokes somewhere other than the family—'good job, well done'—whether you're serving food at a soup kitchen or you actually have a job. You cannot be dependent upon your family to go, 'Gosh, Mom, that was a fabulous meal.' "

For twenty-eight-year-old accountant "Caroline Wong," who emigrated to San Francisco from Hong Kong at the age of nineteen, "the women's movement especially helped the Chinese woman, because traditionally Chinese women have been really passive. Some parents still say, 'If I have sons I will spend my money in educating *them,* not daughters, because after they marry they're not carrying my name.' With the women's lib my parents are open-minded: They give more room for their girls to achieve their own personal goals, and I can freely speak my mind and do more things."

"Oh gosh, yes," Gaye Lott answered when asked whether the women's movement had made an impact in her life. "It's been the most wonderful thing that happened to me. It made me feel important as a woman and I had not had any of that anywhere in my upbringing." "I learned to love myself," forty-year-old "Alice Schwab" said simply.

Women are invested in human connection; it is the stuff of their lives. Their sense of self is rarely determined in isolation. Jean Baker Miller, M.D., and her colleagues of Wellesley's Stone Center for Research on Women have charted for over a decade the central place of relationships in women's adult development.[5] It is partly because of this, they write, that "when women contemplate the use of power on their own behalf and for their own interests, many of them equate the prospect with destructiveness and selfishness—characteristics that they cannot reconcile with a sense of 'feminine identity.' "[6] Kerry M. Thompson, a Catholic psychotherapist in Boston, observed: "Whether they are Catholic or not, for *all* the women I see, the biggest issues are the lack of self and the fear of finding and using personal power. And fear that finding and claiming and developing it will mean you'll be alone, will disconnect you from others, particularly from men."

Women who said they wanted the door held for them (a fact many mentioned in the same breath as their distaste for feminism) may have wished to retain the small courtesies that make daily life bearable. But the holding of the door may be symbolic of deeper connections, economic and emotional. Invested above all in relationships, women (lesbian and heterosexual) fear what challenging their existing connections with men could mean: loss of love, loss of approval, loss of sexual partners, loss of economic security or support, loss of employment.

Women have been schooled in indirection. Their mothers' voices ring in their ears: "If you are too aggressive, no man will ever love you." To stand up and say "This is wrong" is a shock to the system, especially when women say it to men they love or to men who have power over them—who may well be one and the same.

Some women found it difficult to reconcile the notion of "putting things in terms of women" with the loving relationships they experienced with men. Asked about the women's movement, Beatrice Cortez responded by speaking about men: "I'm a woman and I'm very proud of who I am and what I am, but some of my best friends and people who have influenced my life are men. My husband is very supportive. He's very proud of being Hispanic, he's very proud of being a man, he's very proud of being my husband, and he loves me. He just says, 'You're a more exciting woman when I know that you're doing what you want to do.' He's very secure. The negative piece is when women begin to separate themselves. Hey, men have power, you've got to work with it." Women of color often stressed their positive connections with men, aware of the fragility of their survival as a people and of the grave injustices the men in their communities had suffered because of their culture or their race.

Feminism raises a tangle of questions about power and love, affection and eros. I wondered if the dislike of "being exclusively for women," as more than one woman defined feminism, did not also reflect a fear of lesbianism or of being called lesbian.[7] Women's identity often derives from their life in relationship. Could it also be that women who view feminism negatively think it limits their ability to love, and women who view it in a positive light believe it broadens and deepens this same capacity for love?

Many women did, in fact, attribute to the influence of the women's movement positive changes in relationships with both women and men. For many Catholic women, the women's movement begins at home: The transformations it has wrought are domestic as much as public. Mary Wunnicke, the Wisconsin farmer, nearly sixty years old, smiled when I asked whether the women's movement had influenced her. Oh yes, she said, it helped her to stand up for herself and ask for what she needed. And she liked all this sharing in marriage that seemed to happen nowadays—she thought the young men would be much better fathers than their elders.

Carolyn Booth, who spent most of her adult life as a full-time homemaker and mother, now works as a freelance photographer and food writer for her local newspaper in Cary, North Carolina. The mother of grown children, she received her college degree a few years ago. "I've had this hunger always," she remembered. "When I would mention going back to school and getting my degree, my husband was very negative because his picture of a wife did not include working outside the home. Those were very difficult years, trying to convince Dick that what I wanted was for myself, not so that I could be as good as he was. I just wanted the education for my own identification. He's a doll," she added, "he's a wonderful, wonderful husband. But he was definitely of the opinion that man is superior to woman in every way." "Do you believe that?" I asked. Carolyn laughed. "I don't think so at all. I very much believe that in the traditional marriage a man is superior to a woman in his ability to take care of the family. I like to be the wife of a man who takes charge of me and protects me and takes care of me. The hard part has been to convince him that I have a mind and I can do things and be productive."

Some women were sympathetic to the changes required of men in the new dispensation. "[The women's movement has] done two things," said Ann Richards Anderson. "It's made me appreciate that I have some value and something to contribute and that there's nothing wrong in wanting to do that. And it's made me see what a trap men are in. It's very tempting to say, 'Oh, what's the matter with them? Why don't they just shape themselves up? What do they think women did?' But I think it was much easier for women to change because life is bound to be better [for us if we change], whereas for men I don't think it's so clear that life would be better if they changed. To be a whole, caring, aware person is probably worth trading all the privileges they've got," she added. "But it's hard for a person who has the privileges."

Catholic women are not only renegotiating their relationships with men; their relationships with women too have changed since the advent of the women's movement. Many have joined or founded women's organizations to find support in their professional life. Bridget Palmer of Morgan Stanley joined the Association of Women in Banking "because of the old boys' network," she said. "The old boys' club is very strong. When you try to knock down the doors it causes the men to barricade." Many spoke of a new commitment to friendship with other women. "My relationships with women have changed," said forty-two-year-old Evelyn Reichman. "I used to look to men for the kind of support that I now look to women for. Women are far easier to be around. I find that I choose their company more frequently." "I wish," sixty-four-year-old "Kitty Riordan" sighed, "that women could trust each other enough to know that we really are sisters and that we need to be loved by each other. The women friends we have, if we could really go on nurturing these friendships, really make them a priority . . . I'm doing that now and it feels so good."

Few women thought the changes brought about by the women's movement were sufficient. Not one woman expressed the opinion that we were in the "postfeminist" era. Economic change was a recurring topic. Around the time she was reading *The Feminine Mystique,* Sandra Mondykowski Temple's parents separated. Sandra's mother lost her credit rating and her car insurance premium doubled when the insurance agent decided her boyfriend would probably be driving the car; Sandra's mother had no boyfriend. "It was the bread and butter issues," Sandra said, "that got me into the women's movement: equal credit access, insurance rates, education opportunities." "I'm a traditional woman in many senses," said Susan Johnson, "but [the women's movement] has opened up so much for me. I was a very dependent wife when I married. I went from a loving father to a loving husband with the same sort of relationship. But I'm not that same person any more. I have my own VISA card in my own name because I felt it was important to establish my own credit. I wouldn't have even dreamed of doing that [before]—that would have been disrespectful to my husband."

Abigail McCarthy, now in her seventies and "very much part of the women's movement," served on the first board of the Women's Equity Action League (WEAL). "It was really an eye-opener," she said, "when we began to examine how we were disadvantaged economically: in mortgages, in credit. . . . And it took a real struggle to open up the professional schools. I joined the struggle enthusiastically when I discovered it. I have always thought it was much more important that the financial and educational aspects of the women's movement be our concern rather than the biological issues," she added.

One of the obvious changes in this generation of Catholic women is a more highly charged relationship to the workplace. Many women define themselves primarily through their work, sometimes more than through their Catholicism. On the other hand, the women I met had little connection to organized labor. A few were union members and one was professionally involved in a labor organization. They seldom mentioned unions unless I asked about them, despite traditional Catholic support for organized labor. They reflect a trend among American Catholics, many of whom have moved to the suburbs and become more affluent, entered the professions, and lost their ties to the labor movement.[8]

Catholic women have worked outside the home for several generations. Unmarried women, of course, rarely had a choice; the real differences I observed were found in the work patterns of married women. Class, race, and culture made a great difference in women's relationship to paid employment. Ann Richards Anderson was raised in a white middle-class family in Chicago; she has held both full- and part-time jobs during her adult life and has also spent a period of time as a full-time mother. "I remember my mother saying that it was morally wrong for a woman to get a job and work," she said, "that no matter how little money you had a woman should never work because that was a real insult to men, that [men] needed to feel responsible for their families and that women should never, *ever* suggest that whatever they earned was not enough." "It had never been intended that I would work," said Gaye Lott, the sales manager from Corpus Christi, who went to work after her first divorce at the age of thirty-four. "I would get married, or Daddy would take care of me."

Sandra Mondykowski Temple, who grew up in a working-class Polish-American family in Union, New Jersey, laughed in amazement at these notions. Her culture assumed that married women were partners with their husbands in economic responsibility for the family. For working-class women, the women's movement has never signified "opportunity to work outside the home," though it has meant a widening of educational and professional opportunities.

Virtually all the African-American women I interviewed, spanning three generations, worked outside the home while raising their children. Hispanic women in their forties and fifties had often stayed home to care for their children, but their mothers had worked in fields, factories, and retail businesses. Their daughters planned to stay home during their children's infancy but otherwise to hold down full-time jobs. Irish-American women of the older generation stayed home after marriage, but often married late and worked for at least a decade as nurses, like "Louise O'Connell," or teachers, like "Mary Sullivan."

The women's movement has broadened women's occupational options. It has meant, said Barbara Kern, a full-time mother and former actress, "thinking of new roles for myself to play." "My kids get to do a lot of things that I couldn't do as a girl," Iris Palmer said. "When I was in high school I would have liked to have taken woodworking and auto mechanics, but if you were a girl you couldn't take those subjects. Now it's not taboo any more, you can take them." "Women can do all kinds of work," Aurora Martinez said to me. "I think feminism is this: that the men do not say that women cannot. Because women can."

But some criticized the movement for what they saw as neglect and disparagement of traditional women's roles. Sarah Hofheinz considers herself a feminist and defines feminism as "equal opportunities for all people." She is an active member of the Junior League, the mother of two daughters, and the wife of a supportive and loving husband who respects her intelligence and abilities. "I always assumed I was going to get married, I would not work, I would have children," Sarah said to me. "Since the women's movement there are many times where I don't feel real comfortable. I'm embarrassed to say sometimes that I'm a housewife and that I don't have an occupation. I am not disappointed in the women's movement. I am happy for my daughters, because I think there are opportunities for women that were never there before. But in my own personal life it has caused turmoil. I sometimes don't feel like I justify my life because I'm not bringing home a paycheck."

Ruth Pakaluk considers herself a full-time mother and housewife, though she is also active in public life through her leadership in the pro-life movement. She finds "the glorification of traditionally male careers" a major irritant. "Whenever I get the Radcliffe newsletters," Ruth said of her alma mater, "or correspondence about alumnae get-togethers and class reunions, all the women are professional women. All the seminars are geared toward them. There is nothing that would be of any interest to a graduate who maintains an active intellectual life but is not in the public world. There is nothing that would appeal to anyone who is raising children, as if raising children means you shut off your mind. It's as if we are invisible. Nobody knows we exist, nobody is interested in us, and we're like the failures; they can't write up little blurbs about how we're the illustrious graduates who are achieving all these fantastic things in the traditionally male world. I graduated *magna cum laude*. We're not the leftover schlepps. We've made a different choice for our lives."

Mothers, nurses, physicists, or police officers, what women wanted was respect for women's work—all of women's work, paid as well as volunteer, in the home and in the marketplace. Much of this work was undervalued long before the advent of women's movement. Driving school buses, milking cows, writing legal briefs, changing diapers, sweeping floors, arranging flowers, preparing food, solving mathematical equations, addressing envelopes, teaching art—all of this is work, and Catholic women do it, as other women do, with and without compensation or public recognition.

Women's work is the work of forty-eight-year-old Angela Rodriguez, who, "struggled," she said, "with 'just being a homemaker' and finding my own self-esteem. I went through a period of being very defensive. Now it's okay to be Angela the homemaker and mother and involved in the girls' school. Nowadays they really need parents in the school, helping in the library and volunteering at the store the school runs to [raise money] for scholarship funds for the children who can't afford the tuition. And I just love to be at home, I enjoy making bread and making soup and doing things at a slow place, that whole home feeling. It's really important for me to be home.

"I've been very blessed," Angela added, "in having had the freedom and the opportunity to go slow. There's something in me that says, 'Angela, you need to get out and share this,' so I've been listening for how I can do that." The year before our interview, Angela became involved in Coming Home Hospice, a home for people in the final stages of AIDS. "I felt that I wanted to respond to a need in the community, and I just had a lot of compassion toward AIDS patients," she said. "I help to feed people. I've started to use my massage skills again. [I can] be there for family members. If there is somebody who is in the final stages and actively dying, I'm very comfortable to sit in the room with that person and just be there. Just my presence, that's enough reason for me to be there; something happens when two people are together like that, even though a person may appear not to be completely with you."

Women's work is the work of thirty-three-year-old Betty Anne Nogan, a deputy director of the Financial Control Board of New York State, set up when the City of New York went into fiscal crisis "to make sure the city doesn't go into bankruptcy and complies with all the rules," Betty said. She and her staff are responsible for analyzing $22 billion of expenditures and about $5 billion of federal and state monies. Betty described her work as "managing and motivating people and doing a good deal of analytical work." Women's work is what Dolores Reuter did as a young married woman on a small Wisconsin farm: "There was a big garden, a lot of canning and freezing, washing clothes three times a week with a wringer-washer. For ten years we had no water in the house so it was carry the water in, carry the water out. I don't know how I did it," she grinned. Women's work is the work "Maria Ricci" did before she went to jail in a midwestern state, in the parallel world of the drug ring to which she belonged, with its suppliers, bosses, babysitters, and runners, a highly structured organization that gave its workers $1,000 per week, paid vacations, and company cars.

Housekeeping, child-rearing, volunteer work, and paid employment: All of these are labor and most of this labor is skilled, even if no economic recognition is attached to it. The Gross National Product, of course, measures things differently. Sometimes the women themselves did not name their labor as work. "I never worked a day in my life" said ninety-two-year-old Sylvia Park, who raised four children, taught them to pray, cared for a sick husband, cooked, cleaned, and fed hungry strangers who came to the door.

Though some women tended to undervalue their work, many more credited the skill involved in homemaking and child-rearing. "I certainly think running a household is as complicated as most things that most men do," said Ann Richards Anderson. "I think that's why women are such [good] managers. And raising children is a growth experience. You never know your depths till you're dealing with a bunch of preschoolers. I think in our great fury at the injustice of the way we were treated and were never allowed to do anything else, we accepted men's devaluing of what a lot of women were doing. People are now coming around to see that is important." Vicki Bowden, a bookkeeper, spoke of her work as a mother using explicitly religious language: "I'm a basic shaper and molder of my child's personality and who they're going to be in the world and that's a tremendous [responsibility]—it's like taking on a church. I'm the minister for this little church. I'm the one that's bringing God into it."

While many praised women's traditional labor, several women also spoke of how dispiriting it could be. White middle-class and upper-middle-class women whose husbands' corporate jobs required them to move every few years were most likely to share tales of stress, depression, and sadness. After five years in Columbia, South Carolina, Susan Johnson and her husband moved to Corpus Christi, Texas, when he was offered a "tremendous opportunity" to be general manager of the city's newspaper. "I was thirty-one," she remembered. "My mother died in January, my third child was born in April, and we moved in June. So I had three major traumas in the year of '72. It was very, very difficult. The older children were eight and ten, I had not been a new mother in a long time, and I arrived in Corpus Christi like a ship without an anchor. He had an exciting new job and I had two little boys and a new baby. There was a book out at that time with a catchy title, something like *Corporate Wife, Corporate Failure* and it was about people like me. At the time we moved I was working on my master's, I had my nursery, I had my home, and then whammo, gone." "Serena Townsend" slipped deeper into depression as a young corporate wife, although, she said, "my surface was marvelous. Nobody would have known it. I was doing this magnificent cope bit: I was supermom, running the car pools, seeing to it that the kids were in their swimming classes, putting on the perfect little wife-and-mother parties." Finally, "Serena" said, "I was literally at my wits' end. I was *giving* everywhere: I was giving at the church, I was giving at social things. . . ." Things got worse when "Serena"'s husband accepted a new position in another city. "I lost all my feeder things," she said. "I lost the groups [I belonged to], lost all my contacts, I lost everything that I had built up. This is what happens to women when you move. The men have the continuity of the job and the office, the women lose."

Women's work is often taken for granted. So too is the complex skill it requires. Christine Beckley, during the two or three hours of our interview, answered my questions attentively and thoughtfully; she also watched her son, Ian, out of the corner of her eye as he played in the next room, and conversed with him on and off when he came to join us at the kitchen table. The work Christine does is assumed to be a labor of love and therefore not specialized labor. Child care, says the sociologist Elena Stone in her study of life in a community day-care center, "calls upon many capacities that the culture seldom names as skills" although they require exquisite perception, planning, and pedagogical competence. "The low status and abysmal pay that are typical of most women's occupations," Stone writes, "are largely a function of the characterization of women's work as an extension of personality rather than the product of effort and skills."[9]

I was struck by how varied the women's commitments were and how they were able, as Christine Beckley was during our conversation, to attend to several levels of activity at once. "The basic model of women's traditional role," Mary Catherine Bateson writes in *Composing a Life,* "has always involved the traditional tug of different tasks. . . . There is a heritage here of responsiveness and interruptability."[10]

"Women have been regarded as unreliable," Bateson writes, "because they are torn by multiple commitments; men become capable of true dedication when they are either celibate, in the old religious model, with no family to distract them, or have families organized to provide support but not distraction, the little woman behind the great man. But what if we were to recognize the capacity for distraction, the divided will, as representing a higher wisdom? . . . Instead of concentration on a transcendent ideal, sustained attention to diversity and interdependence may offer a different clarity of vision, one that is sensitive to ecological complexity, to the multiple rather than the singular. Perhaps we can discern in women honoring multiple commitments a new level of productivity and new possibilities of learning. . . . [11] It is not unreasonable to suppose that the kind of synergy we associate with the Renaissance man can develop in the lives of men and women who multiply their spheres of sensitivity and caring."[12]

Mariette Murphy, a member of the church I attend in Boston, is a woman of multiple attention. Initially a public health nurse, she attended medical school as "a woman with a mission," determined to establish systems of primary care for adolescent women, especially poor young mothers. The Catholic teaching of her childhood, she said, gave her the unyielding belief "that dignity and respect are the ultimate priority." Her work is also, she said, "based in a feminist understanding." Mariette started a teen health center at a local high school and cofounded a project delivering maternal and child care to residents of Mission Hill, the neighborhood surrounding Harvard Medical School, which has the highest infant mortality rate in Boston. She was paid a small consulting fee for five years of free work, training the project's community health workers and serving as consulting physician. "One can't simply pray and say one lives those values," she said to me. Today Mariette works at Massachusetts General Hospital and affiliated neighborhood clinics and at a small private practice "to pay for my daughter's education," she said. She volunteers on the advisory board of her church's family religious education program, keeps house, and raises her daughter alone; her former husband has moved to another city. She jokes about her "vow of involuntary poverty" and calls it "a consequence of the choice [I've made] to do this kind of medicine. It's real painful. [My daughter] doesn't understand why her mother's a doctor and is not making a lot of money." Like many of the women I interviewed, Mariette lives her "women's work" somewhere between the creative synergy Bateson describes and sheer exhaustion.

At the end of our interview, I asked Mariette for her definition of success. "The ability to live without compromising my integrity," she answered, "and to provide a foundation for that integrity in my daughter." The hour was late and Mariette's daughter had fallen asleep on her mother's shoulder during our conversation. "Do you feel successful?" I asked Mariette. A radiant smile lit up her face. "Enormously," she said. "At great price, though. I never would have anticipated how much it cost."

ELEVEN

MARY WUNNICKE

"We are a close family."

Mary Wunnicke and her daughter-in-law Andrea have fixed a generous lunch in the kitchen of the family's farm house in Bear Valley, Wisconsin. Mary is a slender, lively woman close to sixty years old. Her husband, Gene Wunnicke, a gentle man with a sunburned face, has suffered a tracheotomy and walks with crutches from a recent accident; his voice wheezes softly as he welcomes me. Mary, Gene, their children and grandchildren, and several members of their extended family welcome me to the table. After the meal Mary and I sit together and talk. It is the summer of 1986; the drought has not yet parched the Midwest. Outside, the corn is high in the fields. The landscape is lush, a rich rolling earth.

If anything goes wrong in our community, it seems that everybody's there. There's somebody you can go to: You can share your problems with other people and sometimes that doesn't make them seem as big. On two occasions our neighbors have come. Once Gene was sick and had been hospitalized for a long time, and one day about eighty people came here and did our crops, pretty much all the people from our parish. And this time, he got hurt on a Wednesday and [our son] Mike went to Mass on Sunday morning and the neighbors approached him about what can they do to help. So they came the following Thursday with their tractors and mowers. Four of them came and baled or mowed down our hay. Saturday morning came, the women started arriving with food; the men started arriving with tractors; and by two thirty that afternoon they had all our hay up. It was really something. We have a new pastor, so I called him and I said, "Father, how would you like to come and witness some real community spirit?" [The people were] from two parishes. Mike doesn't belong to the same parish as we do.

I've always been a Catholic. I couldn't imagine being anything else. Growing up I had a lot of friends that weren't Catholic. Some of them didn't go to church at all, and there always seemed to be something lacking in their lives. We had a Lutheran church and a Congregational church in Spring Green and I had friends that belonged to both parishes. But the ones that didn't go to church, even their family life seemed so much different than ours. Our life centered around our family. Our parents seemed concerned about what we were doing. They were pretty strict, in fact.

[My faith gives me] strength. Without my faith, maybe I wouldn't even be here. We have problems with alcoholism in my family. I think if it hadn't been that I could go to Mass or talk to God and pour out my troubles [things would be different now]. And I think by both of us sharing the same faith it made us try a little harder to keep our marriage going. We had something to strive for. That always meant a lot to us. Another thing: when you live in a rural community, I think the whole community enters into your faith life.

I don't have structured prayers so much. But my evening prayers are still the prayers I said as a little girl. Before I go to sleep I say one Our Father and three Hail Marys and the *Memorare* and an Act of Contrition. And then I always have this little jingle that I pray, "God bless my mother and father and everybody else in my family." That just sticks with me. That's automatic before I go to sleep. My parents are dead now. "And Grandpa, and Grandma, and John, and Scott." All the people that were important to me as I was growing up; they're all dead. I still pray for them.

Sometimes I think my work is my prayer. I'm so busy. It seems like I'm always asking God's help when things are going wrong. Sometimes I don't stop to give thanks. I don't have a picture of God in my mind. Jesus for me is God Our Father. It's the same thing. I think the Holy Spirit gives us strength, enlightens us. When we were having problems with Mike not going to church I used to pray a lot that the Holy Spirit would help him.

I was raised about seven miles from here. I was the second of six living children; my mother lost four children, three babies and one six and a half. My mother was an only child and she was only seventeen when she and Daddy married; he was thirty-four. My grandmother never liked my father because he was a city boy and Mom was a farm girl—a very protected little girl. He was a man of the world; he had been around. [But] his folks were farm people. We're all Irish, full-blooded. My Daddy was from a large family and I had lots of aunts and uncles living very close by. My [maternal] grandparents had an adjoining farm so we were just like Mike and Andrea are here, we could run to Grandma's. My older sister and I would draw straws to see who was going to sleep at Grandma's house. We grew up always with older people with us.

My grandmother used to tell all kinds of Bible stories. We didn't have a parochial school. My parents were very strict Catholics, very faithful about going to Mass on Sundays and getting us to religious instruction. We'd go in the summertime: We'd have the nuns come for a two-week summer session and I don't think we ever missed.

My mother was a very caring person. If anybody had any problems they came to Mom even though she had a big family of her own. She had a couple of foster children. She took one girl who couldn't get along with her stepfather. Then we had a young neighbor girl whose mother had a mental illness; the girl never really had a mother she could go to and she came to Mom and she was pregnant. So Mom took her baby when she was just out of the hospital and we kept him until he was nine months old, allowing the mother to go back to work; she was only nineteen. And Mom took care of my bachelor uncles. One was bedfast for nine months, one was bedfast for six months, and the third one died the day of our wedding. And then she took care of her father and my grandmother and she ended up taking care of my father. So she was almost a saint in my book.

My sister [Betty] is eleven months older than I, eleven days short of a year. We weren't allowed to date but we would sneak out. We had a grandmother that was unpredictable; we never knew what she was going to do. We would go to a basketball game and leave a little early to go down to a bar [where] they had a back room where the kids could dance. Grandma was always one jump ahead of us. We thought we were pulling the wool over *her* eyes, but we'd get there and five minutes later she would come through the front door: "Ready to go, girls?" She'd take one on each side and out we'd go.

During high school I took typing and shorthand and all the business courses I could. I took a civil service test and placed well on it; I graduated on the twenty-fifth of May and started work on the twenty-ninth for the U.S. Armed Forces Institute in Madison; [that was] 1944. The next June I went to Washington, D.C., on a temporary duty assignment. I worked in the Pentagon for three months. Then I came back to Madison.

I met Gene the night before I graduated from eighth grade. Our teacher and his wife took us to a dance. He was a freshman at Loras College in Dubuque and he was six years older than I was. When I was a sophomore in high school in 1942 he went into service as a pilot. So I dated other kids but we corresponded. He got out of service in 1945 and we were married in 1946. He had enrolled at the university in Madison as soon as he got out. I worked and he went to school. He graduated in 1948 in chemical engineering. By that time I was three months pregnant, so that ended my career for a while.

After he graduated we came out to his folks' across the valley and he helped his dad farm. Then in the fall we went to Worland, Wyoming, [where] he worked in the derricks; Mike was born there in 1949. He was the first baby of the year so we got all the prizes. . . . We lived out there for two and a half years. We came back and Gene worked seven years [in engineering] and then we bought this farm. Gene always liked farming. He liked being his own boss more than anything. And we liked being close to family. We made lots of good friends in Wyoming, people we still correspond with, but we were glad we made the decision because Gene's parents only lived about six years after that.

We had seven altogether that we helped raise. We were married two and a half years and we didn't think we were going to have any children. Then I started doctoring and I got pregnant. Then I didn't have any more children for about five years. I started doctoring again and found out that my uterus had torn in two when I had Mike. I had two miscarriages; I lost one baby when Mike was five, a baby four and a half months along. Then I had surgery and I lost two. When Mike was five years old we took two foster children. We went to apply for adoption and at that time they didn't have many babies for adoption but they needed foster homes. So we took a little girl, Dottie, she was nine months old when we got her, and a year later we took her little brother. We had those children for seven years. The parents always had visitation rights. Finally the parents remarried [each other] for the third time and petitioned the court and got the kids back; it lasted five weeks. The kids ended up at the diagnostic center in Madison.

Mike must have been in eighth grade when we adopted Peggy. Then Mike went into the seminary. He only stayed a year and then he came back. He went to Loras College first and then into the service; he was in service for two years and when he got out he finished school. When Peggy was seven, Gene's first cousin's children came to visit Fourth of July. Their mother had passed away when those kids were two and four; they were the same age as Peggy. Their father needed help and they came here just to spend a little vacation and they never went home for three years. Then in September [of the year they came] I found out I was pregnant with Kathleen. So our family grew from Peggy at home to three more within a short time. Kathleen is now sixteen. Peggy will be twenty-four at Christmastime. Mike's thirty-seven. It's spread out.

We had four foster children and they added a dimension to our lives and we still consider them to be a very important link to our family.

When Mike went to college it was such a disappointment: We knew he wasn't going to church. We had lots of battles. But he still had something there that he wanted to remain a Catholic. He wanted a Catholic wedding even though he didn't attend Mass and didn't believe a lot of the things the Catholic church was doing. I think it all started in the army. He had a lot of trouble with the poverty in the world, the Catholic church being so wealthy. I'm sure Mike didn't see the slums where some priests do live, but he thought a lot of the priests had pretty plush living. They do around here. They all have nice rectories, and he thought that some of the money could have been handled someplace where it was needed a little more. I think they should have a good standard of living. They have a hard life; I know our priest does. He's taking care of three parishes; he should have a few comforts. He doesn't, though; he lives in a new building but it was a convent at one time so his rooms are down long corridors, it's not really a home atmosphere.

We belong to St. Killian's right down in Bear Valley; we're like a mission parish, but we do have a weekly Mass, on Saturday night. Lone Rock has an early Sunday morning Mass and Keysville one at ten thirty; our priest takes care of three congregations. We're not daily Mass attenders because of the distance and because of farming chores. Mike goes to St. Pat's at Loreto. Andrea goes with Mike but she's not Catholic. I'm not sure if she's a confirmed or a baptized Lutheran; her mother used to take her to the Baptist church and then I think as she was growing up they used to take her to the Unitarian church; her grandfather was a Lutheran minister.

I don't think Mike ever would have stayed away. His roots were there. He wasn't even mad, really. I think it was a phase that he went through. And he just didn't think Mass attendance was that important. Mike's been back at church for about three years, back to the sacraments. He went to church a long time before he went to the sacraments; now he receives communion. The parish they belong to is just wonderful for young people because everybody supports the whole family. [The children] hadn't been baptized until about two months ago. They talked about having the children baptized for a year and they just weren't doing it, but Aaron and Claire [,the two oldest,] both go to

Sunday School after Mass. In second grade they're old enough to be receiving First Communion, and Aaron was beginning to ask questions about why he wasn't a Catholic. You know how little kids are. They had a priest who was really great, and he was leaving, and the morning I went down to the barn to tell Michael, "Did you know Father R. was leaving?" Mike said, "I've got to get those kids baptized." So they made arrangements and it was a beautiful baptismal service. They had all three baptized at once, and Andrea's parents came and it was a big family celebration.

When Aaron was little, Andrea asked me what I would think if he wouldn't be baptized. I started to cry, and I said that was something I had always prayed for, that my grandchildren would be Catholic; but I said, "I would certainly respect however you want to raise the kids. They're your children." I have a lot of respect for Andrea. I have respect for anybody; they don't have to believe what I believe. She said, "Maybe some day I'll be a Catholic." So then I started hoping for that. Our priest was offering instruction and I approached her about it and asked if she would be willing just to learn a little more about our faith and I offered to babysit if she wanted to take the course and so she did. We never really discussed it when it was over. She just said there were some things she got a lot out of, she learned a lot more about what our beliefs are, and there were some things she couldn't agree on. I think she did tell me that confession [was one issue], and I think the Blessed Mother was another thing she couldn't quite relate to.

I don't go to confession often, twice or three times a year, not every month like we used to go. We usually have a communal penance service, but then we have individual confession too. When I was growing up I had such a *fear* of confession. And I used to go in the confessional and make up sins. You were supposed to have something that was a grave matter. But we were taught to even confess our venial sins. I didn't get real comfortable with confession for quite a few years. Now I'm not afraid to talk to a priest at all.

I didn't like the changes when they first happened. I still thought the Latin Mass was beautiful although we didn't understand it. Then it changed and went to English, and after a short period our priest was getting everybody involved, where you could be a lector; I was one of the first lectors in the church. [And there was] more participation with the singing. When we were growing up, if you couldn't sing, you couldn't sing in the choir. Then when they changed, everybody could, whether you could sing or not. As a young girl I wanted to sing in the choir and they told me I couldn't, because I couldn't sing. It wasn't like singing praise to the Lord, it was if you weren't a good singer you just weren't supposed to be up there. [After the changes] more people started singing and participating in the Mass. I liked it when I could get involved. I don't think Gene liked it as much as I did because he's quiet; he never participated. Now he's a gift bearer. That's about the extent of his involvement; he's just more reserved.

When I was growing up a nun told me one time that if you say three Hail Marys every day to the Blessed Mother you'll have a happy death. I think because we've had a lot of deaths in our family I've always had a fear of death; so when I say my three Hail Marys it gives me a little bit of comfort. I still believe that the Lord will give me a happy death because I pray to the Blessed Mother. When the kids were littler, we [said the Rosary] as a family; like the month of October, that was the month of the Rosary, or the month of May. As Gene was working and we were getting more involved in school things it was something we just dropped and we really never knew when it was dropped. I say it by myself quite often. I think Gene probably does more than I, when he's not sleeping at night. Gene has an aunt in a nursing home, she's ninety and they have a Rosary group, so when I go to town sometimes I drop in on them. There's five Catholic ladies that live in the Lutheran home so they get together and say the Rosary.

I'm not fighting for any cause. I'm not in any movements to get women priests in or anything like that, although if that happened I would accept it, and I think it's going to happen sometime, but maybe not in my lifetime. I do belong to Wisconsin Citizens for Life. That's mostly women. When certain bills are coming up before the legislature I write letters. They have fund-raisers to raise money for Right to Life [and] I help with that; and they have an annual banquet where they bring in a speaker, and we've promoted having someone come to show movies at our church on the abortion issue, showing the fetus at different stages. One of the times that I was pregnant, I guess that was my first time, I was very upset, because I was pregnant and I wasn't losing the baby and the baby was dead; and the doctor took the baby. I had to go into surgery. I wanted the baby baptized, and I was really sick, I had a high temperature. I had to struggle for a while, wondering was the baby really dead, should I have gone on [with the pregnancy] for a while, but the doctor assured me that the baby *was* dead. That was before there were a whole lot of abortions too. I'd like to see abortion banned completely. I really think that life does begin at conception and I don't think anybody has the right to terminate another life. It's murder. There are so many people wanting to adopt children.

And our society is accepting things like that better; a lot of young girls have the choice of keeping their babies.

I don't believe in birth control. I just talked to Peggy about that last night. I think that your marriage is so sacred. I think if people studied the natural-planning birth control, it would be just as effective and a whole lot less danger than taking pills. I guess [there are exceptions according to] each one's circumstances; I'm not going to place judgment on that.

I think we live in a pretty good country. I haven't traveled out of the country but just from what I've read, I think we're pretty privileged. If I could change things in the world I'd divide the wealth up a little, so that we wouldn't have people starving to death. Sometimes I think we could do more. We could maybe do with a little bit less. I worry about some of the people that live in the missions. The really poor people. We live in such an affluent society. Gene had a first cousin, Sister Rita, who was a Maryknoll,* and she spent about fifteen years in Bolivia. [The poverty] is really a problem in those countries, really bad. We get missionaries here three or four times a year, someone from away. We get *Maryknoll* magazine and the *Catholic Digest* (that one doesn't talk much about what's going on) and we used to correspond with Rita. Every time she came back, she was like a missionary [to us].

[Our] families [are Democrats]. It's passed down. I can remember asking Gene's mother, "Who am I supposed to vote for?" and she said, "Vote Democrat." No questions asked, just vote Democrat. Mike said yesterday when we were talking about our assemblyman, "I wouldn't vote for a Republican." It must stick. I haven't yet voted Republican but I think I could. The first time I voted was Truman, just before we went to Wyoming. We voted absentee because we were going to be gone, and we got to Wyoming about the third of November and picked up the paper to see if our vote counted.

We had Lutheran friends and we were told when we were kids that we were not to go into their churches, but we used to go anyway. I think if people live a good life, if they're good to themselves and good to other people, I can't see that one religion is any better than any other. It's just that I happen to be Catholic. Gene's part Irish but he has a German name. It was pounded into us that we *had* to date an *Irish Catholic*. But I don't feel that way. Andrea isn't Catholic, Peggy's boyfriend isn't Catholic.

---

*The Maryknoll Sisters are an American religious order working overseas, mostly among the poor.

I think there's too much permissiveness in our society. Nothing is a sin anymore. I think premarital sex is wrong. We've had it in our family. Nowadays I don't know if the kids think about what the consequences will be; they don't think about the hurt they're causing their parents. When our kids were growing up times were changing and there was so much free sex and everything that it was scary. Our kids are all different ages so they never had the companionship of a sister real close like I did.

I think they got very relaxed about [divorce and remarriage] and I think it's good. We've had divorce in our family. I don't know if it's different dioceses or different priests but I can't understand why sometimes one person can get an annulment and another can't, and why one person can receive the sacraments and another one can't. Just because they're divorced I don't think it's right that some can and some can't. If they want to remain Catholic [they should be able to receive the sacraments].

Mike and Andrea belonged to a peace and justice group in Richland Center. I thought [the bishops' letter on the economy] was a long time in coming. I think a lot of it is good. They were a little slow coming on for peace and justice. They've got some small groups going now where they are training farmers, people that have filed bankruptcy and have to leave the farm. They've got grants that people can get; some of it's from the Church. I think they're trying to solve some of the problems for some of the people. Going through bankruptcy or losing your farm, it's almost like a divorce and the whole family suffers. I thought the [bishops' letter on war and peace] was good. I think it's a good thing to oppose nuclear arms. At our parish we saw those movies—it was devastating, the burns and all. I do think we have to keep our defense up but not with nuclear arms.

I think that they don't want to get the women too involved in the Church. My daughter was a Mass server. We had three girl Mass servers and [the priest] said, "The bishop says that we are not to have girl Mass servers." The priest then said he would make an exception because we don't have any boy Mass servers.

I'm more assertive now. I stand up for my rights better. I think that you can be happily married but if you want a career, you can have a career. I like the *sharing* a lot better and I think that has come from the women's movement, because I think women just demanded that men share the responsibility of the kids. It used to be that it was a man's place to work and provide the living; it was a woman's place to raise the kids. I don't think it's that way anymore. I think it's good.

The young men are going to be better fathers because of their involvement with the kids. I like what I see with Mike and Andrea. If she wants something she does it. She doesn't question whether it's going to be all right with Mike. She just assumes it's going to be. [In my day] it was [different].

I'm not a feminist. I still hold to some of my beliefs that I had before and I think being a feminist is being a liberated woman and I don't consider myself really that liberated. A feminist is going to stand up for every right of being a woman, equal all the way. Equal opportunities, equal pay, job sharing. I guess I still think that some things a wife does and some things a husband does. I used to think it was up to the man to be the sole support; I don't feel that way anymore because I work now too. When I was raising my kids I probably wouldn't have gone out and gotten a job; I felt my place was at home. I think it's not so much the quantity of time that young mothers spend with the kids, but it's how valuable the time is that they are with them. That's what I would do myself probably. These girls are doing their own thing. That to me is a feminist. [I think] it's good.

Success is having a comfortable life, not a lot of material things necessarily but to be comfortable with your husband, how you feel about yourself, and your family. And in the monetary sense, not having to worry about paying your bills. A lot of success is just how you feel you can deal with other people and deal with yourself. I [feel successful]. I feel loved by my family. I have the respect of my neighbors. All that is success.

We are a close family. We're having a wedding the twentieth of September and just in our immediate families, Gene's and mine, we have 125 people, all invited. On my side of the family we have an annual Christmas party and that is about as important as getting to Mass on Sunday. It's pot luck. And unless somebody is out of state and can't possibly get home, ninety-nine percent everybody is there. My kids are really close to their first cousins. They have an annual first cousins' party—this summer will be the fourth one. They really have a good time together. They all seem to have the heritage that my folks passed on to them. My dad lived till he was eighty-seven, and from the time he was seventy-five on, he had an annual birthday party which was really the social event of the year. Everybody came. Then when he died, he was buried on his eighty-seventh birthday and it was a celebration, because Daddy always celebrated.

TWELVE

LOVING WELL

*A woman builds relationships around herself
with the commitment and devotion with which
a monk prays.*

—*Elizabeth Dodson Gray*

For many people, the topic "Catholic women" conjures up the issue
of sex. "The pelvic issues," one woman said to me, "are biggies for us."
Catholic women are also subject to more stereotypes in this area than
in any other: the "good little Catholic girl," the sexually repressed
woman, the obedient follower of church teaching. Catholic women do
live with a mixed and sometimes painful inheritance where sex is
concerned—"the pebble in the shoe," one woman called it. But neither
this legacy nor the stereotypes constitute the whole story. Though they
may have lived with conflict and guilt about sex (who has not?), most
of the women I met viewed sex as good and experienced pleasure in
it. They also rarely considered sex outside the setting of love: Relationships, not sexual activity in itself, form the context of Catholic
women's attitudes toward sexuality. It is with relationships that the
story begins.

Catholics who disagree with official church teaching about sexual
matters are often described as "defying" church teaching. This is not
how they define themselves. While I met many women who expressed
such disagreement, not one considered herself in defiance of church
teaching. Catholic women make their sexual decisions not out of defiance or revolt, but in the context of their relationships. They search
their consciences and test the truth of church teaching against the truth
of their experience. The strongest motivating factor in their decisions
is their desire to love well.

Some Catholic women, like Mary Wunnicke, live inside a rich
network of human connections: in Mary's case, a large but closely knit
extended family, a life partner who is also a coworker, adopted, bio-

logical, and foster children, friends and neighbors, a robust community and church, all interacting with one another. For other women, the circle of loved ones is more narrow: husband, lover, children, housemate, colleagues, best friend. A majority of Catholic women are or have been married, but, like the rest of the American population, only a minority fit into the traditional pattern of husband at the workplace, wife at home, and children. Catholic women today live in committed partnerships with men in marriage and in some cases outside of marriage. Catholic women are divorced and remarried. They include single women with an abundance of friends and associates ("I talk to twenty people once a week," said "Anne Marie Quinn") and single women who are more isolated; some of these single women have never married, others are widowed or divorced. A fraction of Catholic women share their lives with another woman, a roommate or lover. Some women live with aging parents and others with young children. The smallest group are religious sisters living in community ("I live with two other sisters, two dogs, two cats, and six kittens," Margaret Slattery said when I asked about her living arrangements).

Many women—most of them married—expressed appreciation for the Catholic church's support of family life. Others—most of them unmarried—complained that the Church defined family too narrowly. Sermons delivered on the feast of the Holy Family, immediately after Christmas, seem to have caused more alienation than any others. (I remember hearing one in 1980 that linked divorce, working women, and child abuse.) Pamela Montagno has almost entirely stopped going to church because, she told me, she feels excluded as a woman; on a visit home in Chicago, she decided to go to Mass "as a conciliatory gesture" to her family. It was the feast of the Holy Family. The liturgy deepened her sense of estrangement. "The people in the congregation are largely single or elderly," she said, "and the whole sermon was on the traditional family. I thought, 'This is so out of touch! Where are they coming from?'" Ellen Reuter and her husband lived together before they were married. The children from his previous marriage stayed with them on a regular basis and Ellen had already begun assuming her responsibilities as a stepmother. On the feast of the Holy Family, Ellen remembered, "We [happened to decide] the kids might behave better if we sat in the front pew, so we sat right in the front, and the pastor gave the homily; he said, 'The Holy Family was just like yours.' And I looked at Phil, and Phil looked at me, and here we were, not married, two kids, in the front pew, and I thought, 'Right.'"

"Society is changing," said Anne Burke, a single woman who is divorced and the mother of four sons. "The structure of the family is changing and the Church has to change in order to meet the needs of its people: It needs to be open to different family structures. Why is it when we talk about family we think about Mommy, Daddy, and two children? I don't have that family structure, yet I'm part of a family and I feel excluded when family is talked about in that way. Divorce is a reality and is not necessarily bad. People blame everything on family falling apart. I don't know that the family *is* falling apart, I think it's just changing shape. The nuclear family is a relatively new social phenomenon. You can't blame drug abuse on breakdown of the family. I'd almost blame television: Relating to people has become secondary to being entertained." "Family is important to me," said Gail Benjamin, who is single, has many friends, and calls her mother "the best woman I know." She added, "That word, though, doesn't connote to me 'nuclear family.' We have Thanksgiving dinner and Easter dinner always at my house, and my whole family comes, not just my nuclear family, but my friends who have become family. I think I'm a good family person."

Single women frequently voiced feelings of discomfort and alienation. While divorced women often felt wounded and exiled, single women felt invisible. Many of them, especially women who were single and sexually active (the majority of the single women I met) wondered aloud whether they existed in the eyes of their church. Single by choice or single by default, many felt they were second-class citizens, viewed as misbegotten celibates or not-yet-married wives, rather than whole and holy women on a par with their sisters. Outside of campus ministries, which received high praise from many of the young women I met, single women found little recognition of their life-styles in homilies, parish programs, or Catholic literature.[1] None of them had ever heard a sermon on the single life as a place of encounter with God, a life-style in which people engage in relationships that have meaning, depth, and commitment.

For most of the women, friendship, that most egalitarian of relationships which any human being can have with any other, was the unsung heart of life, and it was holy ground. Several women said they found God revealed in their human friendships; they also spoke of God as a friend. "If there is a God," said "Cara Marini," a woman in her thirties who has grown discouraged with her local parish, "God speaks to you through your friends." "I treat God and Jesus like my buddies," said twenty-eight-year-old "Caroline Wong," who is active in her local church, a largely Chinese-American urban congregation. "Most of the time I sense God through my friends."

Intergenerational friendships were not uncommon; younger women especially reveled in relationships they had built with women old enough to be their grandmothers. "I *love* older women," said twenty-nine-year-old attorney Brigette Rouson, "because they just have so much to offer and so much to tell you. Right now I'm sort of best friends with Ma Jones," she said, speaking of Pauline Jones, a woman in her seventies whom I had also interviewed. "I don't know when she adopted me, but I suppose it's when we were on the parish council together. She'll fuss if she doesn't see me at church for a few Sundays in a row. I am constantly amazed at how much she does, and how she just lets criticism roll off her back. And she became real close to my family especially after my father died. It's not like we have any kind of regular contact [these days] other than seeing each other in church and hugging and kissing. But every friend I've ever brought, she's just so welcoming, she's always interested, wants to know how things are going, wants to pray for us." For some women, friendship is a stroke of luck in an atomized, individualistic, and somewhat hostile world. But for others, friendship is born in and creates community. This is true of Brigette and Pauline, both active members of Washington, D.C.'s St. Augustine's Church, which is the matrix for their relationship, as it is true of Mary Wunnicke, whose friendships are rooted in the neighborliness of farming and small-town life.

"Friendship," said Mary Hunt, "provides a model of mutuality and equality. Marriage does not."[2] But many women spoke of friendship with their husbands. Marriages in which husband and wife saw each other as friends were invariably happy. Though a sizable minority (perhaps one quarter to one third) of the married women stated that their husbands were the heads of their households, a larger number spoke of marriage as a partnership of peers. "Peter is my very best friend," said Ann Richards Anderson of her husband of twenty years. "We enjoy doing outdoor things with each other. We both love music, though our tastes are totally different. We're a good team; we sit down and figure out what the problem is, what we've got to do to take care of it, and divide the tasks between us." "I have been blessed with a *beautiful* man in marriage," Mary Esther Bernal said of her husband of three decades, a former teacher, state representative, and state senator, "[who] from the beginning not only preached what he believed but lived by it: equal rights for women. I tell you, this respect from day one to the present day is the key to a successful life together. When you lose that respect then I think you start having problems. That has been the key thing [for us]."

In an update interview after the birth of her second child, Ellen Reuter said of her marriage: "It's hard work, there's not much time for us, there's a lot more to disagree about—but we have more of a sense of partnership, and it feels good to be the parents of this family. I feel my husband is one of five men in the U.S. who does more than his share of the housework and child care and I feel lucky and appreciative of that. And between you and me," she joked, "it's real hard to live in a constant state of gratitude." She added, "I need friends more than ever. It's hard to keep them because there's so much less time and it all has to be scheduled. We have to get out our calendars and make appointments. Phil and I have a real understanding that we need to see our friends, so I can have brunch on Sunday with my friend and he'll take the kids, or he has a beer after work with a friend and I take the kids. I think all that is really good for my marriage," she concluded.

What makes for a good couple? The themes of friendship, respect, fidelity, communication, and common values recurred whether women were heterosexual or homosexual: The language of relationship was not much different for the women who were married and for the much smaller number whose life partners were other women.

Giving together to the world, bringing forth something or someone beyond the couple itself—what both psychologists and the Catholic theological tradition call generativity—was another frequent theme. Friends, lovers, and colleagues, Diann Neu and Mary Hunt are founders and directors of the Women's Alliance for Theology, Ethics, and Ritual (WATER), a religious feminist think tank and resource center. "Love really is a generative experience," Mary said of their relationship, which was thriving, she said, "in a community of friends. Generativity is a hallmark of love. What you generate is community and ways for more people to feel more included and more cared for and more encompassed and nurtured. Many people whose relationships break up break up because they don't have the time or the energy to generate out of their love." A generative relationship, Mary said, "is always open to more and more and more rather than closed. It's a tough thing to do. Love has to generate something; it can't just generate good sex. Although it shouldn't be without that, either," she added.

Shared Catholic affiliation is no guarantee against divorce, nor is marriage to a non-Catholic a recipe for an unhappy union. Well over one third of the women I interviewed had non-Catholic partners, in keeping with the high rate of ecumenical and interreligious marriages among Catholics today. A few mentioned difficulties due to religious differences, but most spoke of happy and fulfilling partnerships. At the same time, some of the most solid couples were those whose members were partners in faith. They shared assumptions about God and the world and a language to articulate these assumptions, a kind of bedrock below them, underlying their companionship and commitment to the shared journey, however stormy the journey might be.

Women's perspectives on authority in marriage reflected not only diverging views of male and female roles but a variety of attitudes toward disagreement, conflict, and autonomy. "I utterly reject and abhor the 'wife as an ornament' mentality," said Ruth Pakaluk, "and the notion that men completely take the lead and women just docilely nod their heads. But I do think there is a natural built-in relationship between men and women and something that is masculine and something that is feminine. In the relationship of a husband and a wife there just is a certain appropriate leadership the husband exerts and a support the woman provides. I hate to use those words because people will think, 'She thinks women should be doormats,' which is not what I mean. But in all the marriages I know that work very well, there is this very subtle dynamic that goes on without the husband being domineering or the woman being servile. Like the husband tries to give the kid the wrong kind of food and the wife says, 'No, he really doesn't like it,' and the husband says, 'We'll just try it,' and the wife will stop and not keep insisting on it, and somehow it just sort of resolves. The kid doesn't eat [the food] and the husband stops. Whereas if the wife said, 'I know he will not eat it,' then the husband will try and shove it down his throat. If the woman insists, it seems that the husband insists and it just becomes a conflict that will not go away. I see it so often in my own marriage and people around me: When the woman gives way, it's as if the husband is freed up to acknowledge that she actually knew better."

Ann Richards Anderson had another perspective on married life: "Probably the strongest reason we've had such a good marriage through times of enormous change is that we're both autonomous people and respect the autonomy of the other one," she said. "It wouldn't occur to me to try and change his views nor [to him] to change mine, which is not to say that we don't have arguments all the time about politics and other things. But there's a real respect for the other person's right and obligation to make their own decisions. Maybe that's why we argue," she added.

The acid test of equality, for many women, is still the sharing of housework and child care. The vast majority of women living with a man are still responsible for maintaining a clean, harmonious, and healthy home environment; some questioned this division of labor, especially women under the age of forty-five. In the early years of her marriage, Ann Anderson remembered, "a friend of mine and I used to mutter and complain about our respective husbands. Actually," she added, "Peter is about the best there is. [We do share the housework now]. But he would say to me [back then], 'Well, tell me what to do; I'll do it,' when I would start ranting and raving about how it wasn't fair that I had [all] the responsibility. My friend and I used to say, 'I don't want to tell him what to do! I want him to walk in the house, see the place is a mess, and pick it up. At work he wouldn't wait until someone told him. Why, at home, does he wait until someone says, "Gee, those things have been on the stairs for three days. Do you think you could carry them upstairs?" ' "

The politics of housework appear to be changing among the younger generation. Madeleine Msall graduated from Oberlin College exactly two decades after Ann Richards Anderson. She had recently married a fellow student when I interviewed her in the spring of her senior year. "We're very big on sharing all the household tasks," she reported, "making dinner, doing the dishes and cleaning the house. Frank makes me really happy on that scale," she added, "because the entire time I was growing up I don't think I ever saw my brother vacuum. Now I come home and Frank has decided that the apartment is a mess and has cleaned it up."

At least half the women I interviewed felt that mothers of young children ought to stay home with them, though many admitted this was often economically impossible. "A woman," said Kathy Kasza, "should have children when she can stay home and take care of those children. Not forever, but I have a hard time with, 'I'm going to have a baby and six weeks later go back to work.' Raising a child is a process and it's not done in six weeks. Damnit, God didn't have us carry those children inside us for nine months for [nothing]. There was a reason for that. Motherhood is a role too and a job. There's a lot to it."

I asked Aurora Martinez whether she thought husbands ought to share everyday responsibilities for their children with their wives. "Yes," she said, "because the two of them made them." Though still in the minority, a greater proportion of the younger women were sharing child-care responsibilities with their husbands. The establishment of this new pattern was rarely easy. "I force myself to stand back," said "Elizabeth Heilig," "and let 'Drew' go in there and take care [of our son]. Now in the nighttime 'Drew' hears him before I do."

Women under forty, across social classes and occupations, often told me their husbands were more present in their children's lives than their fathers had been. "The major difference [in our children's life]," Sarah Hofheinz said, "is that we have two parents raising them—major, major difference. I think a father gives a girl self-esteem that a mother can never give her child." Sarah added: "Growing up, my perception of my parents and their relationship was not realistic at all. They prevented us from seeing what a marriage is like, never raising the voice, not a lot of touch. Fred and I are totally different. It's important to see the good times and the bad times in a marriage. Just like it's important for the kids to see you hugging and holding hands, it's also very important for them to know that you can get very angry at each other and still love each other very much."

Women also spoke of better communication in this generation and greater attention to their children's feelings and opinions. "We talk about everything," said Ann Richards Anderson. "[Our kids] argue all the time, and I don't recall ever arguing, with my father anyway." "I think we raised them to be more vocal than I was raised," "Joanne Grace" said of her children. "We talked and discussed and argued a lot, and there was great democracy, whereas my parents were more authoritarian. We took a lot of guff from our kids when they were teenagers and it was a very democratic family. They were a part of the decision-making."

Some Catholic mothers are consciously rethinking male and female roles in their child-rearing practices. "We did it to ourselves because we raised our sons," said Evelyn Reichman of the discrimination she had experienced and observed. Ann Richards Anderson said, "I say to our boys, 'You're *not* going to grow up to take advantage of women, and to order them around, and to expect them to take care of you.' " Susan Johnson said she raised her four sons to be "not like their father: They can all cook, they can all run the washer and dryer, they can all run the vacuum cleaner, they all know how to sew on buttons, they can all iron. I felt that it was very important that they not have to move in with a girl in order to have their shirts done." Betty Darko was driving her son and his friends home from kindergarten one day when, she said, "I heard Paul say to his friend, 'The girls become nurses and the boys become doctors.' I pulled the car off to the side of the road and I said, 'Wait a minute, that's not necessarily the case.' [This kind of thinking] is so prevalent I guess kids pick up on it."

The women's movement, said sixty-year-old Ann Bright of Corpus Christi, Texas, "has made a great difference in the way I've brought up my daughters; they're all self-sufficient, they're able to support themselves, and they don't feel that they have to get married and have children." Helen Doggett, the fifty-five-year-old administrative assistant to the highest-ranking woman in the Massachusetts House of Representatives, had to get a restraining order against her husband at the end of their marriage; their divorce left her no choice but to depend on food stamps for a year. Asked if the women's movement had influenced her, she declared, "Oh, definitely! I made sure my girls knew that they had a chance to do anything they wanted, and I'm sure that they'll never be abused. I was, both [physically and emotionally]. The verbal abuse is worse. You get to think that anything you do is not right. I tried to teach them you should like yourself first."

Women's relationships with their children are often the most passionate attachments in their lives; this is hardly peculiar to Catholic women. Raising children, said May Kast, "there were some days when you felt like running away. But then I loved them so much I stayed! And I would have fought like a tiger if anyone had tried to hurt them in any way." Some women's descriptions of their prayer revealed the intensity of their love. Often they turned to God as a protecting figure. Aurora Martinez explained: "I just say to God that He help me with my sons and daughters so that nothing happens to them. When I feel in my heart like a premonition that something is going to happen at home, as my heart tells me, I start to pray so that nothing will happen to my children. And at work I do that too because I work at night and they stay home and so I'm afraid something will happen." Aurora is illiterate; Ellen Reuter, a woman the same age, has two master's degrees. They echoed each other's emotions. "There are days," Ellen said, "when my prayer tends to be asking, beseeching: 'Keep my babies safe, don't let anything happen to them.' Sometimes I feel like an Old Testament person: 'You better not let anything happen to my babies!' "

Some women, especially the immigrants from Asia, spoke of the difficulty of passing on their values to their children. Hang Vu left South Vietnam ten days before her college graduation. She is now a U.S. citizen, forty years old, and living with her husband and children in California. "We try to keep the children more respectful to the parents," she said. "America has many good things, freedom and security of life. But," she added "sometimes [there is] too much freedom. The teenagers, you see a lot of trouble about them. I feel afraid for my children when they grow up. They will meet American girls, get too much involved with boyfriends, outside of their family, too young. In my country the center of the life is the family, so we stay a big family and everything is the family, not the individual feeling like over here." She added: "Life here is more convenient. That sometimes makes us forget about God. Whenever you have more needs, you pray more, right? But over here we can have everything we want, so sometimes we forget about the power of God."

Though virtually all the women were ardently devoted to their children, their experiences of childbearing and childrearing were not uniformly rewarding. "When I conceived [my first child] I was not ready," said Evelyn Reichman. "I was devastated. I felt trapped in my own body." "Elizabeth Heilig," in contrast, spoke of the "cosmic experience of motherhood. Part of me was blown open by giving birth and having a baby," she said. For Ann Bright, having children was "absolutely devastating" at first. "I didn't know anything about children, and I had no idea how confining it would be; you were never ever quite free again. That was a very hard thing for me to learn."

Married women also acknowledged the difficulty of remaining married. "It's very rough being married and being in a relationship," said psychotherapist and yoga teacher "Elizabeth Heilig." "The whole idea of commitment is to get through those rough times, and it's possible with people who really try, and it's great to work through that. I don't think people should quit. I know a lot of psychotherapists doing marriage counseling and most of them are divorced. The more you're into psychotherapy the more you see the problems: You focus on negativity. I think that's the wrong approach. I kind of like this Marriage Encounter stuff that the Catholic church has," she said, "because it focuses more on the positive, and building, and giving strength to a marriage, which every marriage needs. Marriages need as much strength and nourishment as they can get; they don't need to focus on the pathology. My marriage has had ups and downs, and lots of times I felt like leaving, but I didn't because I took my vows seriously. I really feel it's a sacrament. It's a true bond. If we were just living together I'm sure we'd split. And then I'd die alone, I'd die without being a member of a family, and I don't want that."

The teaching of the Catholic church upholds the permanency of marriage. But the lived reality of the American Catholic church today is that Catholics divorce and remarry—now in almost equal proportion to the rest of the U.S. population.* The divorced women I interviewed

---

*This estimate is generally accepted, though no one seems to have reliable statistics on the percentage or number of Catholics who are divorced; the available figures include only divorced people who have not remarried. Even the North American Conference of Separated and Divorced

continued to believe in commitment and fidelity; none had taken their marriage vows lightly. After interviewing this group of American Catholic women, I am not sure that the increase in the rate of divorce among them can only be attributed to a cultural shift in attitudes toward the sanctity of marriage. It also seems related to a generational shift in women's self-care and self-esteem and to a different set of responses to abusive marriages. Women in their thirties and forties like Karen Doherty and Marlene Jones were more likely to consider leaving emotionally or physically abusive marriages, and to challenge priests who advised them to stay, than women of the previous generation. "Louise O'Connell," a widow in her late seventies, closed her eyes when I asked her about divorce. "It's very sticky," she said. "I could have divorced my husband, I really could have. Because of his drinking; and I did have some abuse at one time; and there were women. But I felt my children were more important than anyone in the whole wide world and I put them above everything."

For some of the women I met, one of the most destructive aspects of Catholic teaching against divorce was its role in keeping them in unhealthy or even violent marriages long after they had exhausted all efforts to make things work. For these women, the line between faithful commitment and tolerance of abuse had been difficult to draw. Helen Doggett stayed married until the youngest of her four children was in high school despite the fact that her marriage had lost all sexual and emotional intimacy and that her husband had become both unfaithful and violent. "I guess I was in love for a lot of years," she remembered. "And I just had nowhere to turn. I never told my family. You suffered through everything yourself; nobody ever knew I was having that kind of trouble at home. You were just supposed to suffer and not tell anyone." Finally, Helen decided the situation was intolerable. "I went to court and got a restraining order [against my husband] and put him out. He was really outrageously drinking and breaking windows." Her children, she said, "were all happy when we finally got to a decision that he was going."

While not all divorces stem from the existence of substance abuse and violence, many are the result of marriages where one or the other

---

Catholics could not give me an exact figure.

I spoke with divorced women of many social and ethnic backgrounds. In a few cases I had requested an interview with them knowing that they were divorced. In many others cases I sought them out for different reasons and with no knowledge of their marital status. Because of this, I met more divorced women than I had anticipated. At least half had remained single after the end of their marriage.

is a factor. Nationally, four million women are assaulted each year by husbands or boyfriends.[3] Catholic women are no less likely than other women to be subject to this risk. In at least half the divorces of which I heard, women had been physically abused. In well over three quarters of the cases, the former husband was either an active alcoholic or physically abusive or both. But these women were not, in the long run, passive victims: Most of them had garnered the strength to leave destructive situations, raise healthy children, and rebuild their lives. Though they were left economically vulnerable by their divorces (the majority of divorced women I met received little or no child support from their former husbands and rarely received alimony), they were emotionally healthier and often physically safer.

Divorce was probably the most frequent and pervasive source of church-related pain I encountered. Remembering the times of "suffering and not telling anyone," Helen Doggett remembered: "I was angry. I don't feel the Church helped me out." Often, as Karen Doherty did during her time in Alaska, women turned to parish clergy for advice and comfort and were told to remain in their marriages, even when they were abusive. When Myra Spivey left her husband after years of problems—"he drank and stayed out," she said—and repeated efforts to have him seek counseling with her, she went and spoke to her priest. "Give him another chance," the priest said. She never returned to that parish. A smaller number of women told a different story. Isolated, neglected, nearly a prisoner in her own home, and pregnant with her third child, Victoria Bowden went to a priest against her husband's wishes to make plans to have her children baptized. "I told him about our situation," she remembered, "and he said, 'Before you get them baptized you need to get out of that situation,' and he asked me [whether I could] stay with somebody."

Women's feelings about the Catholic church's stance on marriage and divorce were almost unanimous. Most believed, with Ann Valdez, that "one should not marry without the intent that it be a permanent union." Ann added: "It's incumbent upon us to do everything that we can to know one another before we commit to a marriage—because even under the best of circumstances, it's not always a picnic." But a great majority of the women also said that if a marriage became intolerable, divorce might be the only acceptable option. "Those are man-made laws," several of the women said in reference to Church regulations on divorce.

"Jenna Santini"'s widowed grandmother, a faithful and lifelong Catholic, married a divorced man some years after the death of her husband. Because her new husband had not received a church annulment, the wedding took place outside the Catholic church and she stopped receiving communion. "She couldn't believe her church," "Jenna" said. "Because she got married to a man she was in love with, she can't receive Jesus Christ!"

"Clara Taylor" of Washington, D.C., who is separated and has two children, said, "I don't think marriage should be flim-flam, but there should be an option there. Especially if you want to keep Catholics in the Catholic faith. I don't think you were born to be miserable. I don't think God meant it to be that way. If it so happens that you can find happiness with someone else, another one of God's creatures, then that should be fine." "I don't think anyone should have to be unhappy in this life," Christine Torrey said. "I mean, the promise of heaven is nice and everything . . ." Her voice trailed off. "I used to wish my parents would get a divorce, because they didn't get along."

Only a few women were uncompromising in their opposition to divorce. "I don't believe in divorce," said Beatrice Cortez. "I think too many people are getting divorced without really giving their marriages a real try." Older women especially were unswerving in their belief in the permanency of marriage. Ninety-two-year-old Sylvia Park said vigorously, "I believe in, 'When you get married, you're married, and stay married.' "

Kathy Kasza, a few years after her divorce, told me she had "spent the last couple of years getting to know myself, what's good for me, what's bad for me; and I am perfectly content being single. I stopped dating about a year ago. I want to go back to school, I want to have time for myself, I want to learn who I am. I want to learn more than anything else in the world to love myself"—she began to cry—"and to accept myself, and I haven't mastered that, and that's very painful. When I can learn to love me, then maybe I can let somebody else love me. Right now I can't." A couple of years after our interview, Kathy wrote to tell me she was happily remarried. A majority of divorced women remained optimistic about the possibility of forming lasting partnerships. A few were less hopeful. Gaye Lott, married and divorced twice, mused: "I have never seen a relationship that allowed enough growth in it that it could last a lifetime. Someone always gives up something, and I can't decide yet if it's worth it."

In order to participate fully in the sacramental life of the Church, Catholics who wish to remarry must apply for and be granted a church annulment. Women's opinions about annulments were very mixed. While most believed that remarriage within the Church ought to be possible and that the Catholic church was unnecessarily rigid in its approach to divorce, they were divided between women who felt the annulment process was fair and healing and women who felt it to be unjust and injurious.

"[Second marriages in the church are okay,]" said Ann Richards Anderson, who has been married to one man for two decades. "More than okay. That's one of the things that the Catholic church stands for, that people make mistakes and they grow and change and are forgiven and start over. It's not like you make one mistake when you're nineteen years old and you're stuck forever. That's crazy. Even if you make one mistake when you're forty, you shouldn't be stuck with it for the rest of your life.

"I was a witness for [a friend] in her annulment," Ann added. "She said it was the most healing thing she ever did." When asked about the practice of church annulments, Ann Valdez, who has also been married to one man all her adult life, said: "I think it's a farce. Let me temper that," she added. "It seems to me that annulments are just more lengthy means of sanctioning a divorce. I see too many people who have divorced and remarried, who continue to go to church on a regular basis, and yet have been told that they can't receive the sacraments, or who believe that they can't receive Holy Communion, and who are totally alienated from the Church because of that."

Thirty-five-year-old Myra Spivey of Cincinnati, the single mother of two children and the president of her parish council, has attempted to begin an annulment procedure three times. Each time she has read through the required questionnaire and been put off by the many questions she had to answer about the emotional, spiritual, and sexual history of her marriage. "Why do they need to know all of these personal things?" she asked. "It's not any of their business. That stopped me each time. Now they just came out with an updated version, and it's like a book. It's *more* detailed. I'm going to try it again, because if I fall in love, I'm going to have to go somewhere else to get married." But, she added, "if the person I'm marrying is divorced, *he* has to go through it too. Most men are not going to want to go through this."

Kathy Kasza began an annulment procedure as soon as her divorce was final because, she said, "I knew I would want to remarry [some day], and it was best to get it over with and do it. I knew [my former husband] wanted to remarry because he had been living with someone for the last two years." Like Myra, she found the annulment process intrusive and painful. "It was like reliving the whole divorce," she said, adding, "If I had not been granted an annulment, that would not have stopped me from going to church, nor would it have stopped me from remarrying." I asked whether she would have continued to receive communion. "Yes," she answered.

After deciding to marry the man who is now her husband, Ellen Reuter went with some hesitation to speak with a priest who was equally well acquainted with her and her husband's former wife. "He was incredibly accepting and inclusive," she remembered, "while at the same time urging us to get an annulment and get married in the Church. He said, 'I know you, Ellen, and you're too Catholic to not do this; you won't be happy.' He was right, I think: Ultimately we waited for the annulment and we got married and he presided and it was a wonderful thing. But one of the things I had to struggle with was, 'How come if I marry the man I love, the Church I love won't love me anymore?' And what kind of family is this that you can be kicked out of the family? If this is the family of God how can the Church kick you out? I know that theologically they say, 'You're not kicked out, it's just that if you marry outside the Church you're still welcome to attend Mass, you simply can't partake in the sacraments.' Which felt to me like, 'You can come to the family reunion but you can't eat any of the food.' "

Of the annulment process, Ellen said: "If it's done correctly, it can be a real good thing because it gives the couple a chance to relive that marriage in one fell swoop and be done with it, religiously as well as secularly. When it's done as a contest—'You write your essay, and we'll see if it's good enough'—then it's real bad. It's kind of a travesty for the Church to insist on an annulment. It's a church divorce. It seems more of a legalistic tangle than anything else. But I think it can be real helpful in putting the past [behind you]—when the annulment is granted. I'm working with one couple," said Ellen, who is a parish-based psychotherapist, "where the woman's annulment [from her previous marriage] was not granted. Her marriage was horrible, there was no reason to remain in it. It's the luck of the draw with who you draw at the tribunal, too. She happened to draw the most conservative person there, who said, 'Sorry.' Had she drawn a different name, it's probable she would have gotten the annulment. That's when it's necessary for me to say to people, 'The Church isn't just him, the Church is the people around you, not just law and order, so don't let this keep you from your church.' "

I asked Ellen what she would have done had her husband not received his annulment. "We still would have gotten married," she said, "and we still would have continued to partake of the sacraments. But

I think it would have been difficult. I didn't come to that [conclusion] flippantly or easily."

Catholic women are more divided on the issue of homosexuality than they are on the question of divorce. Official Catholic teaching in recent years has recognized a difference between homosexual orientation and homosexual acts, but urges Catholics with a homosexual orientation to abstain from sexual acts if they are to live a moral and holy life. The Catholic lesbians I interviewed and roughly half the heterosexual women found this position objectionable. "Homosexuality, to me, is not an ethical issue," Mary Hunt said, "but a reality. It's a part of the way the world is. As a lesbian, I happen to think homosexuality is healthy, good, and natural. You can make any relationship a human, humane, loving, caring relationship. Many people would never love if they couldn't [love this way]. The issues the Church ought to be concerned about more are people who are alone or lonely than people who are well accompanied, albeit with people of the same sex." "I don't believe it's a sin," said "Cara Marini," who is single and heterosexual. "Loving relationships are loving relationships." "Homosexuality is just another way of being sexual," said Angela Rodriguez, whose husband's gay cousin lives with her and her family. "If my son told me he was gay I'd be proud of him," "Elizabeth Heilig" said cheerfully.

Mary Hunt was awaiting the return of her partner, Diann Neu, from a short trip when we spoke. "I wait with as much anticipation for her return after two weeks away as I did [when we first met], both sexually and personally, and it's so much richer. I bring so much more to that seven years later: memory, shared knowledge, shared hopes, a project, small victories."

As a police officer in a southern city, "Jenna Santini" feels she must keep her relationship with her female partner private. "I haven't been to any of the [local gay groups] because of my work," "Jenna" said. "I don't think the police department would accept that, [my] being open about it. I'm sure the people have their ideas about me being gay,* but it's never talked about, and I've never told anybody, unless there are other gay women in the department. I can't and neither can my roommate do things openly because of our occupations. And that really hurts sometimes." She added, "We're getting ready to celebrate our second anniversary and we really have talked about committing permanently to each other. I wish there could be [some sort

---

*"Up north," "Jenna" said, "they say 'lesbian,' but all my female friends here use 'gay.'"

of ceremony for people of the same sex who love one another]. Naturally," "Jenna" said, "I would wish that I could say I am gay and not have to be worried about what people might say or think; and that I could take my lover [and we] could sit in church and hold hands in praise like a male-female couple does.

"We're brought up that gay relationships aren't right," "Jenna" added, "and that is something that has always stuck in my mind when I think what God really thinks about me being gay. It is hard when you have other people in the Church saying, 'I don't really think God meant for this to be.'" "Jenna" spoke warmly of her friendship with a nun she had met in a church program for young adults. "Having people like 'Sister Cathy' who accept me for who I am and like it's okay has really helped, having other people in the Catholic religion who say, 'Are you happy? Are you comfortable with your relationship?' And I am. I have to hide my relationship and that really hurts, because [my partner] is a very beautiful person; we communicate; oh, it's incredible how we communicate. I've never had anybody that I communicated like this with. We talk everything out. We don't ever really argue, we sit and talk about it and we give and we take. It's an equal relationship. I try to support her in all that she does, so we are there for each other. It feels so right. I've never been more comfortable with anybody in my life."

Catholic women who defined themselves as heterosexual expressed a mix of opinions about homosexuality, ranging from complete condemnation to complete acceptance; they were about equally divided between the two, with strong sentiment on both sides. More than age or education, close acquaintance with gay and lesbian people was the strongest factor in their approach toward homosexuality.

"I worked with gays for years [in the theater]," said Barbara Kern. "Some were nice and some weren't. You can't lump them into a category." "Rose Mazurkiewicz," a woman in her late fifties, was in failing health when I interviewed her and rarely left her home. "I have a young man that I am very close to who comes and cooks for me, he cleans for me, he shops for me," she said. "He's a homosexual. I'm very fond of him and his lover; they're both very fine people. What the hell do I care what they do? If I like you, I like you, if I don't, I don't." Women spoke more often and more comfortably about gay male relationships than they did about lesbian relationships. Many equated "homosexuality" with "gay men." For them, homosexuality among women did not seem to exist. A few other women found lesbianism threatening: "If you have a homosexual female friend," said college student "Inez

Garcia," "she might try to make a pass at you. With a man, you know he's not going to do that, unless he's a bisexual. And I think homosexual males are better friends than your best friend; I think they're sweeter."

Many women told me they had gay relatives. "When I was seventeen years old I found out that my favorite brother was a homosexual," said "Maria Ricci," "and I was torn apart. I really had a hard time handling it." She added, "It's hard for me to imagine him with another man, but I don't have to. I just have to imagine him as my brother. I accept him and I love him." At the state prison where she was serving time, "Maria" said, "There's a lot of homosexuality, people that you would never expect decide that they might want to try it while they're here. I'm uncomfortable with it." "My youngest brother is a homosexual," said another young woman, "and I love him dearly. I'm not going to stop loving him or think he's wrong." She added, "I think that there's a difference between [promiscuity and a committed relationship]." In contrast, women hostile to homosexuality tended not to distinguish between homosexuals living in committed relationships and those involved with multiple partners.

"A number of our very close friends are homosexuals," Ann Richards Anderson said. "It's so hard to live a lie—and so hard not to live a lie. You're stuck either way. And you're controlled by people's perceptions of you. I just get mad at the whole situation. I think that the issue is the quality of a relationship between people. And to condemn any caring relationship is wrong! There's not enough of them around as it is. Where I would draw the lines is not on who's gay and who's straight, but on relationships that are exploitive or nonexploitive—[and] committed: I guess commitment is what matters to me the most.

"There are a number of gay men in Charlestown," Ann said, speaking of the primarily working-class, Irish-American section of Boston where she and her husband used to live, "and the most warm and caring discussion of gay relationships came up at the 'mothers' morning' library discussion. [The local mothers] all started talking about how, of course, they *all* knew. Of course, no one ever said so-and-so was gay. Well, of course their relationship was sexual, they weren't just sharing an apartment. One woman used the term 'covenanted relationship.' She said, 'My kids know that Bill and Joe have a covenanted relationship, and if my kids can tell then that's as good as a marriage as far as I'm concerned.' Of course these were all women," Ann added. "Men would have been flying off the chairs."

Fifty-five-year-old Mary Callanan is city treasurer of San Francisco, a city with a large openly gay and lesbian population. "As an elected official," she said to me, "you get invited to things you'd never get to see otherwise. The gay groups are a very loving bunch of people. I remember walking into one of the first cocktail parties I attended that was almost all gay men, and they were coming up and putting an arm around each other and the way they greeted each other in some way made me think of the apostles, and I thought, 'This can't be all bad.' You could just feel a love and nice relationship with these people, they loved each other, they really did. Some of the Irish men I know," she added, echoing Ann Anderson's remark on the opposite coast, "if they walked in they'd be ill, because their minds are pre-set. You wonder, what can you do to change that?"

Joy Duffy, a secretary at a large accounting firm in San Francisco, offered another perspective. "The life [in this city] has changed and my enchantment with it has gone. It might have to do with the homosexuality here. It's rammed down our throats morning, noon, and night. I have no objections to working with these people, but I resent walking down the street seeing them hugging and kissing; it's like teeny-boppers on a beach. I think they force their way of life verbally upon the heterosexual world. If that's their sexual preference, I don't know whether it's a genetic difference or not, but that's them; they are nice people, I have nothing against them. I'm not opposed to homosexuality, it's not my way of life, but it is theirs. But use some propriety, I guess, is the proper word. I think the city has changed drastically," she added. "There's more favoritism."

The women I interviewed who expressed disapproval of homosexuality sometimes expressed sorrow, other times bewilderment, and often shared their belief that homosexuality was contrary to both nature and God's will. "I just feel very sad about it," said eighty-one-year-old "Mary Sullivan," "it's really so unfortunate. They seem to have very close relationships with the same sex, but it's not normal, it's not the way the Lord intended it to be. I guess it's been around forever. They say the Greeks [had it]. So it's nothing new. But everything now is out in the open. I just think it's very sad." I asked whether she knew any people who were lesbian or gay. "I really have never known anyone that I'm aware of," she answered. She concluded: "It's a freak of nature, I guess."

"I don't think it's normal," said Victoria Bowden. "I can't see gay as being an alternative. I don't think I'll ever accept that that's God's way or that God wants that for anyone. I think there should be more compassion toward them. [And] I'm glad the Church takes a stand." "It scares me," said Beatrice Gallego. "[I don't] understand why it's happening." Dorothy McFadden was categorical: "Forget it. It's not to be. It shouldn't be."

Sex in isolation did not exist for most of the women I met. This view is hardly unusual and not particularly Catholic: It is typically female, though Catholic teaching on sexuality may have shaped or reinforced it. Heterosexual majority or lesbian minority, Catholic women always spoke of sex as embedded in emotional realities and human interactions.

Many women had happy, healthy sexual relationships as adults. Their Catholic upbringing left scars, but only in a few cases were they permanently debilitating. Sometimes sexual happiness was, in Ellen Reuter's words, "hard fought and hard won," and the Church was no help in winning it. But it is hard to tell what brought about this fulfillment: conformity with Church teaching or distance from the Church, professional therapy or simply the experience of a loving partnership. After recounting the emotions and changes associated with her coming of age, Kathi Bowers Wallis, happily married for a decade, concluded, "Being loved and loving someone back releases you of an awful lot of inhibitions and anxieties about your physical self."

Although Catholicism has influenced women's experience of their own sexuality, psychotherapist Ellen Reuter stressed the primary influence of the family. "For the lucky women who had healthy parents, Catholic or not, and then married a healthy person, their sexuality is probably quite lovely. There are a great number of Catholic women out there who are not scarred in terms of their sexuality, because it has more to do with who Mom and Dad were than who the Church was; parents really do carry more weight." Ellen also observed that the security of a committed and faithful marriage, enhanced by support from the Catholic faith, could enhance women's sexual pleasure: "The Catholic church puts such a boundary around their sexuality by the fact that they are married that they are free to play within that," she said. Official Catholic teaching today upholds both the "procreative" and the "unitive" aspects of marriage, and views married sexuality not simply as a means to have children but as an expression of mutual love.

Many of the married women, including those in their fifties and sixties, seemed particularly content: "I enjoy sex," Eunice Staples said. "It's a good part of my marriage." "I didn't know anything about sex when I was growing up. I think I was in college before I was introduced to the male body—in biology class," said Dolores Reuter. "I really didn't pay that much attention to my body [when I was young]." Now, she said, "I don't like my body because I'm out of shape. But for the most part I like my body, I like sex with my husband, I enjoy life." "Kitty Riordan" was raised, she said, with a "very distorted" view of sex. Nevertheless, her adult sexual experience was a fulfilling one. "We had a good sexual relationship in our marriage," she said. "I think it's what kept us going. We came to know each other in a very wonderful way, and I'm grateful for that. And I think I was able to give that to the children. I think they knew their parents were in love."

The general observation among women in committed partnerships seems to be, "It gets better with time." "A priest in college went through this little marriage course with us when we were seniors," forty-four-year-old Sara Whalen remembered, "and he really was reassuring and funny, and really gave me a good idea of what a sexual relationship was supposed to be like. [My husband and I] have had a very comfortable sexual relationship. Sometimes it's kind of boring and then one or the other of us will do something and challenge each other and it's gotten better. We've laughed and marveled at that over the years. When we were first married we were just chasing each other around all the time, and didn't really anticipate that it was going to be nicer as we got older." Mary Hunt observed: "You really can't sustain that sexual peak with the same partner, but what you *can* do, which I am discovering, is deepen sexual pleasure and creative sexual expression over time with the same partner—in a way that is finally more satisfying sexually and personally than the novelty of a peak sexual experience with a new person."

Several of the women who spoke of the sexual restrictions of their youth added that sex was demystified for them as they became more experienced. "Is this what all the fuss is about?" Sandra Mondykowski Temple asked herself after becoming involved with her college boyfriend in the late 1960s. Most of these women felt that the tumbling of sex from its pedestal was a positive development in their lives. Some felt that people who did not have intimate sexual involvements—especially celibate clergy and members of religious orders both female and male—tended to idealize and romanticize sex. A former nun who was single, involved with a man, and looking toward marriage said to me: "I have been involved physically. For me it was good. What it did with sexuality was take it out of that whole realm it was put in in high school: It was so sacredly preserved in marriage that it almost became a God; it was so sacred and holy that it was never mundane. To have intercourse and just laugh about some funny things about it, that's the reality of it. For me, for a long time it was like, 'The marriage night,

how wonderful and sacred and holy . . .' I do consider sexual intercourse to be holy and sacred. But it's also something you laugh about
and you do in a silly way, and [often] you're not together [in your
sexual responsiveness]. I believe that sexuality is tied right in with
healthy relationship," she added.

Women's attitudes toward sex outside of marriage varied widely,
with a vocal minority strongly opposed (a few still spoke of "living in
sin") and a majority more tolerant. Relaxed though they may be, the
views of this larger group are more thoughtful than casual. "Joanne
Grace" spoke of her daughter's decision to move in with her boyfriend:
"[My husband] has had trouble with [it]. And 'Lauren' talked about
it lots with us and agonized over it before she did it. But she felt it
was the right thing to do and I guess I just don't have as much trouble with it: I've become more liberal in my later years than 'Tom.' On
the other hand, there's never been the slightest hint of ill feeling between 'Tom' and 'Lauren.' He just tells her honestly he has a hard time
with it."

"One day at the dinner table," Brigette Rouson remembered, "I
said, 'I don't think premarital sex is wrong if you're engaged and you
love each other.' Oh, my *God*. [My parents said,] 'Let's convene in the
living room after dinner,' and my father went and got the biggest Bible
in the house: 'See right here, fornication is a sin.' I was about fifteen,
sixteen. But shortly after, my mother brought home this really good
book, it was Catholic authors on premarital sex. It went through how
difficult teenage pregnancy can be and how you expose yourself to
disease and as a teenager you're probably not going to be in a mature
relationship where sex is the right thing to do. I read that whole book
and I was convinced, so I waited until college."

A few women consciously abstained from intimate involvements
for a time in order to grow in maturity and confidence and be better
prepared for a healthy, committed partnership. "I was celibate in graduate school," "Elizabeth" Heilig told me. "I wanted to concentrate on
my studies and my personal growth. In high school and college," she
recalled, "my goal in life was to be in love as much as possible and
have as much good sex as I possibly could."

This generation is hardly the first in which Catholics have had
sex before and outside of marriage. "Virginity before marriage was the
ideal but to some extent abstention was connected to nationality and
background," Abigail McCarthy said. "Premarital sex was very much
practiced among the country people where I grew up and wasn't really
thought of as shameful. . . . Because of that it was rare to have a marriage

in our parish that wasn't a have-to. Premarital sex presupposed marriage, however. Sex for sex's sake was frowned upon." "Serena Townsend" and her husband became sexually involved before their marriage, while she was attending a then-exclusive Catholic women's college. "The guilt made it great sex," she grinned.

The mothers I interviewed were preoccupied with teenage sexuality. "The basic problem [about teen pregnancy]," said Iris Palmer, "is that people just want to be loved, they want to be needed, and parents get caught up in being rushed and pushed, they never hug their kids, they never say, 'I love you.' Those are the problems more than available birth control or low morals." Dorothy Wodraska, a physical education teacher in a Catholic school, also teaches a sexuality course to Catholic junior high students. "Oftentimes when kids get involved in sex outside of marriage it's because they don't know who they are," she said. "They want to be accepted, and they think this is a form of showing somebody that you love them. They don't really have a sense that they can have control over the direction of their life. [We teach] the kids that sexuality is everything you are as a man or a woman, the possibilities open to you, the self-esteem that you should have because of who you are, [we try to convince] them that they're important people and that they have important things to do with their lives and they have choices in their lives. We talk about roles: Can a man be thoughtful, gentle, sensitive? Can a woman step out of the traditional roles and be successful and be accepted?

"This is a Catholic program," Dorothy said, "and I teach the Catholic ethic of no sex before marriage and fidelity within marriage, and show the reasons why the Church teaches this way." Dorothy was the only woman who told me she believed masturbation was wrong. "Masturbation is wrong not because you'll turn green or break out or you'll become sterile, but because [sex] is a gift God gave you to be other-centered, and if you use it to turn in on yourself for your own pleasure, that makes you a selfish person."

Ann Valdez, a state health official in Austin, Texas, has become a leader in AIDS education and directs an HIV risk-reduction program for state employees. "It scares me a whole lot to be a mother of an unmarried young woman during this period where we're dealing with AIDS," she said. "You can feel confident about your child and what they know, but [it's another thing] getting them to practice what they know, and worrying about who they might fall in love with and want to got to bed with. My daughter and I talk about it quite a bit. She called me the other day and she said, 'Mother, do you know what it's like to be twenty-six years old and to be the daughter of the woman who probably knows more about AIDS than any other woman in the state?' I laughed and I said, 'It's a bitch, isn't it?' She certainly has front-line information and what she does with the information is her own business. I say, 'Practice safe sex.' I believe that expressing your feelings for someone else through a sexual experience is really special: I think it needs to be reserved for special people. But I am not naive enough to believe that all people are going to have only one person in their lifetime that they'll feel that way about. I'm very hopeful that my daughter will not take that experience lightly.

"A lot of my daughter's friends have been real surprised to hear that we talk about the things that we do, so we've wound up talking with a number of them about sex," Ann added. "It scares me to see some of them who are so desperately in need of affirmation and affection that they tend to jump in and out of bed with a lot of different folks. I think that's a really sad commentary on us as parents that our kids are that insecure."

The teaching of the Catholic hierarchy forbids the use of birth control other than Natural Family Planning (NFP), a method of controlling conception by avoiding intercourse immediately before and during the fertile days of women's monthly cycle; fertility is determined by a combination of observing cervical mucus and charting the woman's temperature, and requires the collaboration of both partners. At least ten percent of the women I met—though hardly any of the women under thirty—practiced NFP. Inevitably, these women—as well as the women who opposed all forms of birth control including NFP—compared NFP to contraceptive pills and expressed concern about the Pill's effects on women's health. Very few of these women mentioned barrier methods such as condoms, foam, or the diaphragm. In contrast, the vast majority of women using birth control (and their partners) were using barrier methods.

Madeleine Msall, a young married woman who was using a barrier method of contraception but whose husband, a more traditional Catholic, was urging her to agree to practice NFP, agreed to take a Natural Family Planning class with him, but raised questions about the logic behind official support of NFP. "What puzzles me about the Church's attitude toward birth control is that they come across with this idea that you should not be making God's decision, you should not put yourself in the position where you have complete control over [things], you have to see that that is something that is in God's hands, and then they turn around and try to sell you NFP by telling you how effective it is and how much control you can have . . . I'm not so sure," Madeleine added, "that I see a whole lot of difference between the artificiality of Natural Family Planning and the artificiality of using a barrier method like the diaphragm. Because once you've admitted that you can have sex for purposes other than procreation, then whether you ensure that by taking your temperature all the time or [by using] a barrier seems like splitting hairs. I could see an argument for Natural Family Planning that it's more holistic, you are more in touch with the rhythms of your body, but to say that it is morally superior, I really don't quite understand. Frank's position on all this is that because we're young and have lives flexible enough to accept a child, it's not a great sacrifice to ask us to practice NFP and that as an issue of obedience it is something we should consider. I'm not very big on obedience."

American Catholic women of all generations today take for granted the need for family planning and birth control. Though several women said the issue of birth control was a factor in their alienation from the Church, most seemed to treat it as a nonissue. For women under forty-five especially, the question of birth control is neither controversial nor problematic. The women I met were completely comfortable discussing birth control, with the exception of one woman from San Francisco who, when I asked for her thoughts on the subject, told me this was no conversation topic for a respectable woman. I did not insist.

Catholic women—whether they had agonized over the decision to practice birth control, as had many women over forty-five, or ignored official teaching, as women under forty-five often did—made decisions based on their desire to sustain loving relationships with their partners and with their children. They often felt the hierarchy's position on birth control had little relevance to their lives, and that it neither listened nor spoke to them. "[The official position] is just a joke," said fifty-five-year-old Mar Londo of Green Bay, Wisconsin, who is active in her local parish and the mother of four children. "They don't know that at least 75 percent of Catholic couples are practicing birth control. They've got to be living in a totally different world than I am." Ruth Bolan of Cincinnati, seventy-six years old and a steady churchgoer, said to me: "Today people do pretty well as they please. It was very difficult in the years past when women were not supposed to use birth control, they were supposed to have unlimited children; this is almost a horror story. I know what's taught officially but I disagree with it. I don't think anybody really agrees with it; I don't know a soul who does."

"[The teaching on birth control] is lousy," "Elizabeth Heilig" declared. "It makes people unhappy. I don't see any good in it. It causes misery. Now, 'Drew' is one of the youngest in his family," she said of her husband, "so if they had practiced birth control he wouldn't have been born, so you can look at it that way. But eleven kids is too many. He never had his own bed till he went to the army, and he didn't have a desk to do his studying and his grades suffered, his mother's body just got worn down and worn down and worn down. That stupid stance, it's the most oppressive unhappy thing. People should be proud to use birth control; it's an aid to happiness." "To me," Sarah Hofheinz said, "[Church teaching on birth control] is the human side of the Church. It's not the God part talking and I don't agree with it at all." "Do most Catholics you know agree with you?" I asked. "Absolutely," she said, adding that her parents had also practiced birth control.

The word *realistic* came up again and again in women's statements about birth control. "I'm going to do what I think is right," Susan Johnson said. "The pope didn't stop us from practicing birth control." She added, "Birth control means 'how many and when,' not 'none.' I do believe marriage is for procreation, but I don't believe some celibate person somewhere is going to tell me how to run my marriage. Until you've been married and tried to practice rhythm, you can't begin to imagine what that does to a marriage; you're told that two weeks out of the month you're not supposed to have sexual intercourse. Well, marriages don't work that way. [The official position] is not realistic." Women who favored the use of contraception spoke of taking responsibility for themselves and of their responsibilities toward others. "When you have a child it should be when there are two parents and when the parents are ready to have these children," said forty-year-old "Clara Taylor," "not ready financially but mature and being able to be a responsible parent." "Most people I know," Betty Darko said, "practice some form of birth control. Not because they don't want to ever have children or they're selfish, but because they're trying to have the children that they can financially and emotionally care for." "It's a myth that God will provide," Kathy Kasza said. "God helps those who help themselves."

"I felt a lot was their fault," Helen Doggett said of the clergy in her Boston parish, "how they can tell you that you have to keep having sex in order to have kids; it is wrong. I don't know why they can't see that. When you finally start talking to people, which I never did, you find out that most or some women practiced birth control. You wondered why people didn't have as many kids as you . . ." The priests of Helen's parish "would stand up there [at church] and talk about the dumbest things that didn't have any bearing on the hard time I was having at home. Do they know what it is to live with a guy and you can't say no? I mean, that was the thing, you're not supposed to say no, you're supposed to do it." Helen and her husband grew apart. "Things weren't great at home. A lot of years he lived in the playroom and I lived upstairs. And then I had a hysterectomy.* I thought that would be great, now I could have sex whenever I wanted—and he just didn't seem to want anything more to do with me then, it was over and he wanted to come and go as he pleased."

Helen eventually stopped going to church. Other women in their fifties continued to attend; almost without exception, these women spoke of the development of their consciences as a factor in the evolution of their views. "Joanne Grace" remembered: "Early in our marriage we didn't [use birth control]. Of course both of us, if we were being married now, would practice birth control. It's completely changed, because of Vatican II and thereafter, when we realized it was okay to start examining and thinking on our own as well as with other Catholics who cared as much as we did about our faith and were honestly asking questions. So," she said, speaking of Pope Paul VI's encyclical *Humanae Vitae,* which reaffirmed the Catholic hierarchy's condemnation of birth control, "by the time it came out we were already clear it was a matter of conscience."

"Joanne," a Midwesterner with a strong group of lay peers, formed her conscience in a circle of friends. For Irish-born Angela Rodriguez and her Argentinean-born husband, who live in San Francisco, it was a clergyman who made the difference. "The issue of birth control came up before we were married, [around] 1966. For me to do anything that would alienate me from my church was out of the question. I was a very law-abiding Catholic. [My future husband] said, 'We must use birth control,' because he was one of nine children and he didn't want to have nine children. I was more of the thinking that if we have nine children, we have nine children, and the Lord will provide, and we'll be blessed. So we explored all the different methods of birth control and what might be acceptable to the Church and we talked to different priests, and really got nowhere. This was almost [the cause of] a split. He said he wouldn't marry me unless we could use birth control, and

---

*A few women, mostly over the age of fifty, spoke as Helen Doggett did of the relief they experienced after having hysterectomies. I had heard similar feelings from other Catholic women in the years before I began my research. While this evidence is anecdotal, it is widespread. I wonder whether hysterectomies—some of them medically unnecessary—did not serve as legitimate sterilization for many Catholic women who are now in their fifties and sixties.

I said there was no way I could alienate myself from my church to marry him, so it was a very difficult time for both of us. Eventually I was invited to go on this weekend retreat where I met with this priest who talked to me about my conscience, and how it was important to me to read a little bit, and he gave me a book to read about the place that my conscience would take on this issue. Which kind of said to me, 'You need to put some of your own self into this issue, and not allow yourself to be completely dictated to by what this teaching in the Church says.' Richard had been telling me this all the time, but because a priest told me, it was okay to do. So the outcome of that was that I felt comfortable using birth control. So I got married. We had a church wedding."

"Sometimes," Ellen Reuter said, "I'm appalled that Catholic women ever ask a celibate man whether they should use birth control or whether they should sleep with their husband." In her work as a parish-based counselor, she encounters "women coming in with more children than they wanted, telling me how Father said they couldn't use birth control; or women saying they were sexually abused by Dad, told Mom, Mom went to the priest, and the priest said "pray," and it continued; and of course divorced people left and right who feel like they are outcasts. What ticks me off about the Church is this expectation women should take these issues to men." A majority of the women I met who worked professionally in the Church as youth ministers, counselors, directors of religious education, and university chaplains disagreed with official teaching on birth control. Some, like Ellen, were married and mothers; others were single; some were nuns. "Don't quote me by name," one of the nuns said, "but I disagree with the hierarchy on this." "What do you do with your teenagers?" I asked, knowing that her ministry brought her in contact with the youth of an inner-city parish. "Do you avoid the topic?" "No," she answered. "I'm straightforward with them. They have to take responsibility for what they do. I think contraception should be taught in the schools," she added. "Sure, it's the family's job. But families aren't doing it, and it's got to be done."

Besides sexual fulfillment, emotional commitment to their partners, and the desire to give their children the attention they deserve, women occasionally mentioned world population problems as a factor in their support of birth control. Marty Woodward, who studied and worked in India during her college years, told me: "My experience with poverty in other parts of the world has made me horrified that the Church is not willing to grasp what population explosion does to quality of life. Until we take that responsibility of looking at it, we are being inconsistent in our 'preferential option for the poor.' "*

As a consequence of her work with adolescent mothers in a city neighborhood health program, physician Mariette Murphy has become wary of those who advocate birth control alone as a solution to the problem of urban poverty in the U.S. Working with the young women and their babies, she said, "offered a great insight into how these young women thought and what really were the conditions that they were living under; throwing birth control pills at them is incredibly disrespectful and doesn't in any way acknowledge the profound fractures in their life." Motherhood gave many of the young women focus, structure, and purpose, Mariette found. She also heard harrowing tales of the living conditions these young mothers had to endure. "I get raped less," several teenagers from the housing project told her when discussing how pregnancy changed their lives.

A small but vocal minority were opposed to the use of contraception; many were Hispanic women over the age of forty. Most of the women who opposed the use of contraceptives did not speak of obeying church teaching so much as valuing children. They found the notion of "affording" children repugnant and did not believe readiness was or ought to be a factor in bearing children. They regarded the presence of children as enriching in and of itself. "I don't believe in birth control," said Beatrice Cortez, "because usually the reasons that people give for birth control is that they cannot afford [more kids]; that is not a good answer. There is no such thing as 'I cannot afford children.' Besides, I look at my children and my brothers and sisters and there aren't any of whom I would say, 'I would like these two or three to be born and not these other two or three.' I mean, when you don't have anything, you have family."

A few women who were using or had used birth control insisted that they were opposed to it. Most of them used contraception because becoming pregnant or giving birth would have posed a severe threat to their health. Eunice Staples and her husband first practiced Natural Family Planning to space their children's births. "We did use contraceptives later when I developed some health problems," Eunice Staples said. "I'm not opposed to the use of contraceptives," she added. "I think it's unfortunate we have to use them."

---

*This term is taken from Latin American church documents and is now widespread in U.S. Catholic cities, indicating the commitment to siding with the poor as a vital component of Christian faith.

Most women were quick to differentiate the issue of abortion clearly and emphatically from the matter of birth control. "I can't see where not starting a baby is the same as aborting a baby," Dolores Reuter said. "If the Church would stop being against birth control, it would make an awful lot more honest people," said her daughter Ellen, "since nobody that I know pays much attention to that [teaching]. And it would alleviate the problem of abortion considerably. There would be a lot less need for abortions, and also they would have a much better reason to say abortion is wrong."

Only a minority of the women were without ambivalence in their view of abortion. "It's murder," said "Sylvia Presti," a registered Democrat and social science researcher. "There are no loopholes," said another woman who opposed abortion. "It's the most important issue to me," said sales manager Gaye Lott, a pro-choice advocate, "because it's my freedom, my body, my life. Having that choice is symbolic to me." Much more frequently, women's positions on abortion fell between these two extremes and few spoke of abortion in theoretical terms. I did not meet a single woman, whatever her political position on the legality of abortion, who took the issue lightly.

In her reflection on abortion, Ann Richards Anderson was typical of many of the women I met.

"I have very, very mixed feelings about abortion," Ann began. "Before the abortion decision came down from the Supreme Court," she said, speaking of the *Roe* v. *Wade* decision of 1973, "I was part of a group that decided to recommend that a fourteen-year-old retarded girl have an abortion. I don't remember if it had to go to court or if the psychiatrist had to decide. She lived in a [housing] project. This was her second pregnancy. She had no notion of how she got pregnant. She was very friendly and all the boys in the project took advantage of her and that was not going to change. In fact, whoever made the decision decided she should be sterilized at the same time, and that was definitely the right decision. There just was no way to prevent her from becoming pregnant; she'd already had one child and she was [only] fourteen. It was a terrible situation. But by and large I think that abortion is wrong.

"I think there are situations," Ann continued, "sometimes emotional, sometimes social, sometimes physical, when it's really not possible for a woman to have a baby, nor possible for her to carry the pregnancy to term and give the baby up for adoption. In those cases I think the person should be able to have an abortion, and only the person in the situation can figure out if that's the case. No one else can say, 'Weeeelll . . . if you *really* worked at it, you could manage it.' [So] I would not want the law to change," Ann said. "But I think there are many, many abortions that should not be done. A person [I know] had an abortion. She was thirty-six. She already had two kids who were in elementary or junior high school. [She and her husband] didn't want another one. She was telling me how she became pregnant; it was an accident. She said, 'So of course I had an abortion.' As if she had a tooth out! That really disturbs me. I don't think a person in that position should have an abortion. She could have rearranged her life. There was no need to take that life—and it is a life of some sort, wherever you draw the line." Referring to the archbishop of Boston's offer of financial and moral support to women choosing to carry an unplanned pregnancy to term, Ann said: "The only thing Cardinal Law has ever done that's any good is to begin to talk and think about ways to help women not have abortions, to really support them, not just say "Don't do it." But I don't think anybody but the woman can make the decision," she concluded.

"I could never have an abortion myself," said "Joanne Grace." "But I cannot condemn people who do, either, and there are instances where I can only believe that the Lord would say it's okay—the situation is so awful that it is asking more than He would expect. So I have never gotten involved with that element in the Catholic church, the antiabortion movement, because it includes too much of this feeling that it is never right, and that we could make decisions of that nature for anybody else. I cannot condemn or find fault with those who honestly examine their conscience and then proceed." Abortion, "Joanne" said, ought to remain legal. But, she added, "[I've told] my daughters if they ever have one, I don't want to know about it."

"I don't really approve of abortion except in a rape case," "Jenna Santini" said. "I feel the conception of a child should be of my choice, and if I was raped, I don't know if I would want to have that child, because I would always be looking at that child subconsciously as pain. I don't see how a mother could not love a child, but it would always remind her of a painful thing, [that] it was conceived in pain." "I considered abortion when I was raped," said another woman, who became pregnant as a result of the rape, "but I couldn't do it. But I think that a person should have a choice," she added, "because some people can live with it and some people can't." "I think abortion on demand is ridiculous in a time when we have birth control available," said Abigail McCarthy. "But I also see some reasons for abortion: medical reasons and rape. Some moral theologians in the past justified abortion under those circumstances: It was called 'the theory of the unjust aggressor'—the fetus, in those cases, being the aggressor. And I myself would have a very hard time if I had a twelve-year-old daughter pregnant as a result of rape—that's just an emotional thing, a maternal response. I don't have any philosophical ground for it, but I think I might very well consent to her having an abortion, and if that's a terrible sin, there it is."

Women who wanted abortion to be made illegal always spoke of the inviolability of the human person. "Genevieve O'Rourke" said her perspective as a contemplative nun helped her "realize the value and dignity of human life not only from a human point of view but from the eyes of faith. We are created in the image and likeness of God. One human person is of infinitely more value than the cosmos and everything in it," she said. "You don't take a kind of utilitarian view toward human beings," said Ruth Pakaluk, who is president of Massachusetts Citizens for Life. Women who favored legal access to abortion also spoke the language of human dignity, but they saw freedom as a central and integral part of the person, an essential component of what it meant to be human. This freedom was not an abstract notion; these women tended to speak, not of life or freedom in general, but of persons in concrete relationships and situations. "I lived at a time that was quite conservative," said seventy-six-year-old Ruth Bolan, "and I could cite you seven or eight cases of people I knew, [both married and single,] who had abortions when it wasn't legal, and some of those were real horror stories, and I don't think women should have to go through that. The conditions were dreadful. [Abortion is something] serious. Any woman who goes into something like this at least should have the privilege of having it done as safely and as comfortably as possible."

When does life begin? For women involved in the pro-life movement especially, this was the decisive question. But for those who were pro-choice, either reluctantly or as activists, whether life begins at conception was not the determining issue. Many of the women who expressed pro-choice sentiments were of the opinion that life does begin at conception. Far more often, the differences lay in the way women defined personhood and how they viewed the decisions of adult women to have abortions and the place of freedom and conscience in the life of the human person. The women who were most strongly opposed to legalized abortion tended to view women who had had abortions as victims; the women who were most vocal about the legal right to choose abortion tended to view the same women as moral agents, people making a mature though painful decision.

A majority of Catholic women are morally opposed to abortion. The teaching of the Church on the sanctity of life has obviously had a profound impact on them. But so too has Catholic moral teaching on the primacy of conscience. Eighty-one-year-old "Mary Sullivan" of Queens, N.Y., a former teacher, mother, grandmother, and daily communicant at her local parish, observed: "Abortion is terrible, but if people feel they must have it, it has to be an individual decision rather than somebody making the moves for them. I wouldn't want it to be illegal. You have to give people the opportunity to make their own decisions." "I want women to have a say in their lives," said sixty-four-year-old "Kitty Riordan," the mother of seven children, "and men to trust them to choose what's important for them."

Women's views of abortion were often grounded in their experience. "You meet a lot of women in the pro-life movement," said Ruth Pakaluk, "who got there because of the experience they've had of abortion. It's a never-ending source of pain." Charlotte Giddens, a fifty-three-year-old nurse from Indianapolis and a convert to Catholicism, said of abortion, "Plain and simple it's wrong. Having been a nurse had a lot to do with it: watching a child struggle for breath lying in a bowl with his mother's placenta and knowing that child couldn't live much more than a few more minutes, but still had taken a breath. You were never really sure," she said, "[if it was an abortion or a miscarriage]: It may have been an accident of nature, or there may have been some help." Charlotte would make an exception to her position on abortion, she said, "if [the pregnancy] threatens the mother's life and she can't go on and take care of her family."

Ruth Pakaluk was alone among the pro-life activists I met in having no history of health or fertility problems. Whether this was coincidence or causal relation I am not sure, but I discovered that the women who were most strongly opposed to abortion—usually to the point of becoming activists in the pro-life movement—had, like Christine Beckley and Mary Wunnicke, experienced traumatic fertility problems and gynecological problems: multiple miscarriages (often six or seven), hysterectomies before the birth of children could take place, late miscarriages or induced abortions, or permanent infertility. Many of these women had adopted children.

Women who had had abortions usually spoke of them with sadness and—a little less often—some guilt. Most of those who were involved in the Church continued their involvement in some way. None seemed to have experienced any lingering depression or severe psychological problems as a result of their abortions. "I really am unhappy about it. I don't think I could do it again," a single professional woman in her thirties told me. "I was twenty-six. I didn't believe it was wrong and I'm still not sure today whether it was wrong. I didn't think there was life there, and I obviously didn't want to have a baby. I was in the middle of graduate school. He said he would have married me. It was not what I wanted."

"I had [an abortion]," said "Regina White," remembering her adolescence in a working-class neighborhood of Providence, Rhode Island. "Long after, I had a run-in with a nun. I got real angry. She was judging somebody that I cared a lot about [who wanted] me to go with them to New York [while they had an] abortion, and she started putting her down. So I told her, I says, 'Until you go out and have a baby, you shouldn't say nothing about it,' and kind of put her in her place, and she had to stop and think about that. I said, 'Was you ever pregnant? How do you know what you would do in that situation? You don't know if you'd have an abortion or not, you don't know if you'd have the kid. You don't know what you would do until it happens to you.' And then I told her I [had had an abortion]. So she kind of backed off and didn't say no more about it. It's an individual decision. It should be an option for people if they choose. Let people make their own damn choices!" At the time "Regina" had her abortion, abortion was illegal in her home state. "I was fourteen or fifteen; I went to New York all by myself on the bus. I almost died because it was a dirty job. When I came home I ended up in the hospital. I passed out in the middle of the street and somebody brought me in."

As a young woman with several sexual partners, "Maria Ricci" had an abortion. Years later, she said to me, "I feel that I killed my baby but I feel that it was my choice. I don't think it's good in the eyes of God. I wonder whose it was, if it was a boy or a girl. I had the abortion very early in the pregnancy. I don't like to think about it or remember it or talk about it. I'm not proud of it. I really love children. But the way my life has been I'm glad that I did what I did. I got pregnant because I wanted to see if I could and that wasn't the right reason. If I got pregnant again I wouldn't have an abortion, no matter whose kid it was. But I was really young, I had just left home, and I couldn't have dealt with it. I was a child myself, really." She added, "I think women should be able to choose, at any time, in any circumstance. The woman should be able to choose. She's the one that bears the child. She's the one that knows if she's ready. I don't see any sense in bringing a child into the world that isn't wanted or can't be taken care of properly."

A divorced mother who worked full-time outside the home to support her children said to me: "I used to say that I was totally against abortion until I got myself in a position where I had one; before that I used to say I would never have [an abortion]. It was very, very hard for me. Just sitting in the clinic and looking at these other women and young girls, a lot of things go through your mind: What's their predicament? What's going through their mind? I just changed," she said. "I said to myself, 'Everyone's situation is different, and for whatever reason they're here, they have a good reason for being here. Killing this baby is wrong but what else am I going to do? While I was in that room I talked to the Lord, I said, 'Lord, I know what I'm doing, I feel that it's wrong, but I've *got* to do it. I have no choice.' I have a girlfriend and we both have said that if our daughters ever got into a situation like that where they did not want to have this baby, we would support them and say, 'You can have this abortion.' They're the ones that are going to have to live with this and I don't think anybody else should be trying to make up their minds for them. It's judging and the Lord says, 'No one judges but me.' "

THIRTEEN

TERESITA BRAVO-PAREDES

"You have to apply that Golden Rule."

Thirty-five-year-old Teresita Bravo-Paredes lives in Concord, California, with her husband, a civil engineer, and their three children. A political scientist, she has worked as a counselor at Oakland's Asian Resource Center, as an interpreter for the Immigration and Naturalization Service, and, most recently, as a consultant on immigration issues. Her father is a member of her household and was tending the fruit trees in the backyard as we spoke.

My father didn't have much education. He was in the army, sort of an elite army for the Philippines. During World War II the Japanese went to invade the Philippines and of course America went out there to assist, so the army my dad belonged to became a component of the U.S. Army. After the war his boss, the lieutenant, suggested that he should come to the United States because by that time he had become a United States citizen. And his older brother was here already. But another reason was to really see what is America because they always talked about it, that America is a really great place to live. [He came here] in 1949. I wasn't even born at the time. He suggested that my mother stay [in the Philippines]; they were newly married. When he got [to America] he decided to continue and work for Uncle Sam on a civilian ship that carried ammunitions around the Pacific. He was a cook on the ship. Ten years later he went home and decided to bring us to the U.S. The first time I saw my father I was three years old.

On my paternal side, my great-grandfather is from Spain, so my grandfather is like a *mestizo** and he speaks the Castilian Spanish. My maternal grandfather was a peasant. He was one of the helpers of my great-grandmother and eventually he married my grandmother. My

---

*A person of mixed racial and cultural background, usually a combination of indigenous and Spanish origins. The term is often used by Latinos and Latin Americans and it is possible Teresita picked it up during her childhood in the Mission District, which is heavily Hispanic.

great-grandparents didn't like the idea because they didn't like to associate with low-class people.

My mother believed that God is always good no matter what. She had a lot of different novenas to different saints. She named me after St. Theresa, Theresa of the Child Jesus. That's her favorite. I'm the only one. She would have loved to have more children but my father was always away. Maybe that was her fate, to just have one child.

[It was my mother who raised me.] I think that's the reason why I miss her a lot, because she was really my mentor, my guardian, everything, a friend. My father would come home maybe every two months, not for very long, at the most ten days. In fact, as I remember, there was a period of time that my father never communicated with us and my mother figured he must have another woman in his life. That's when she made a novena to St. Joseph.

My mother and I always prayed the Rosary together, every night before going to sleep. My mother could not go to sleep unless she prayed. And we have this custom: They instituted a Rosary for the entire month of October, because this was the time when Mary appeared in Portugal at Fatima and she asked people to pray for peace. So every year, since my birthday is October first, they always came to our house first. It was like a big festival on my birthday; I always looked forward to it every year because Our Lady of Fatima would be coming to our house.

My mother had a lot of dreams about me. First of all, she always wanted me to become a good Christian. That was the number one: to be a good human being, go to church, and try to obey the Ten Commandments. And of course she wanted me to have a good education, because from her experience she believed that education will never change no matter what, whether you have wealth or not, you can always lose the wealth but not education. You will always have it with you.

I went to San Francisco College for Women, under the Sacred Heart sisters. During my junior year they changed it to Long Mountain College, because they started accepting males. I got a four-year scholarship. My major was political science. Nobody told me to take it, it was just my own instinct. When I was in high school I was in leadership; I was very much involved with school government and the Junior Statesmen of America. And it's a part of our family also, because my uncle's family, although they're not that highly educated, they've always been involved in politics. Our wealthy relatives on my mother's side are always up there in the national politics [in the Philippines]. My relatives in Central Luzon [province] are councilmen and mayors. It's like a dynasty. They're very concerned about people.

We always discussed politics. I think that's the reason why I became so much interested. My mother said that at election time, they always used our house as a campaign headquarters when I was a small child in the Philippines. My mother used to be like the *matrona* of the area and she would call on women and invite them to our house to have their hair done [as a way to get them there]; the fellow who was running for mayor would come to the house and speak on his platform. It was a bribery thing, which means they would say, "Oh sure, I'll vote for you." Sometimes they never did. That's the way life is.

[When I was studying for] my B.A. there was a scholarship for students majoring in political science who are interested in taking up Southeast Asian studies. I applied and I was lucky to get it; it was six months, a semester during my junior year. I went home to the Philippines. It was very rich; I learned a lot. I studied at the University of the Philippines at the height of the demonstrations of the antiimperialist movement. That's the time when Marcos first declared martial law. I stayed in the dorm of St. Theresa's College because my mother didn't want me to stay at the UP campus. I don't know why—maybe because she knew that UP was a notorious college for radicals and leftism.

While I was in the Philippines I saw the poverty, and I said, "Maybe I should come back and run for office and get into politics here." At the same time in the United States I said, "I cannot abandon the work [here]" because I saw there were a lot of things that needed to be done. At first I had this gung-ho idea of going into foreign affairs and being in the diplomatic corps. That's why I got a master's in international relations. I went to graduate school at UCLA. But my political ideology changed. I said, "I don't want to represent a country that meddles a lot with Third World countries. Maybe there'll be a time when things might change and I'll think about going, but not right now." Plus being a Catholic Christian, I think it wasn't right for me to do that. Because, for one thing, if you're going to use the Ten Commandments or try to live up to your Catholic belief, I think it's not a good idea to assist the foreign policy that would damage Third World countries. You have to apply that Golden Rule. It is immoral for someone to hurt another human being. If I'm in the foreign service, whatever my superior tells me, I have to follow, because I'm representing the United States, and I always have to look for the interest of the United States, which I cannot swallow. I cannot accept it. I'm more concerned about the interests of human beings instead of the interests of a big supernation like the United States.

I finished my master's and a lot of my relatives were teasing me: "Why aren't you getting married?" I wanted to further my studies. They said, "You better start doing something about your life. You cannot just be staying single for the rest of your life." So I decided, yes, it's better [to get married]. Besides, the beautiful part of it is that my husband grew up in the Philippines and he knew me way back when we were children. When I got back home [to the Philippines] we started getting to know each other. We were just friends. I had the ulterior motive that if I became friends with him he would give me more information about the Philippines. But it didn't work out that way; he had a different idea. Every time he wrote or called long distance he'd always say, "When? When are we going to get married?" He kept bugging me about it. So I said, "Well, if you are really interested, why don't you come to the United States and talk to my parents." I was two months from my graduation [from UCLA and] I was planning to go to Spain for more studies . . . to stay there maybe one or two years. So I went there, but I only stayed for three months, because when Jaime arrived in the United States he called me in Spain and said, "When are you coming back to the United States?" So I kind of said, "Well, maybe." I don't know what happened. I decided to come back to the United States and arrange marriage to him. Crazy. We had a very good wedding, a big, grand wedding. It was in San Francisco in our old parish, St. Paul.

I convinced myself, I guess, that I was not getting any younger. I had other things in mind at first. During my undergraduate years I sort of discussed a religious vocation. I used to dance the Philippine folk dances for our Filipino organization at the church; one of the Dominican sisters from the Philippines did all the teaching of the dances and at the same time she was trying to recruit me. At that time I thought it would be a great idea for me to enter the convent. But that's not enough, I guess. My mother said, "You can be faithful to God but you don't have to enter the vocation." I guess she was a little selfish because I'm the only child. Plus I realize now, if I had gone to the religious vocation who [would have watched] her during those two years she was ill?

My father stays with me because my mother is gone. I don't want him to be living by himself and I feel that it's unfair [for him to be alone] because he gave me the love and now it's for me to do, it's that reciprocity. It's hard for an older person to be staying by themselves; it's kind of lonely. My mother died last November. That's the way it is. You cannot stay forever. I believe that death is another life, that you're going home to your Lord, and it's a forever life. That's why I have this idea that if you do good on this earth, whether people recognize it or not, there will be a time that you'll be honored with all the good deeds that you have done. I don't feel bad about my mother's death, because it was about time for her to go to her Lord. And maybe someday we'll see each other.

Of course Jaime and I wanted to have a family, and we had it a year [after we were married]. [We had a] girl; we named her Jamie Therese, because of Jaime and Teresita. I stayed home for a while to raise the family. We had another one, Joan Margaret, two years later. I always use the saints' names, as you can see. Joan, because I almost lost her and Joan of Arc, she was a fighter for the Catholic church and a survivor, so I figure Joan is a nice name. Margaret is my grandmother's name—and of course St. Margaret too.

Then I was pregnant again but it was a stillborn. This is where I was angry to God because why me? I've been a good person, kind, we did all the things we were supposed to do. . . . This was eight years ago. It was a girl. She was healthy and she moved around a lot so the umbilical cord was twisted and she lost oxygen. When I give birth I always have a Cesarean but since it was a stillborn my OB doctor suggested I wait around until the fetus came out naturally, and it did, so I gave a natural birth. It was awful because I was carrying the dead baby for two weeks. It was just gross. My husband and I used to cry every night in bed. I was very angry. I didn't go to church for a while. But my mother always kept the faith no matter what. She kept praying one of these days I would go back again. I stayed away [from church] a few months only. I guess God had His plan, because we've always wanted a boy, and once I [gave] birth to a third child [by] Cesarean I [wouldn't be able to] have any more children. So maybe it was our chance to have another [baby, a] boy. I got pregnant with a boy and boy, I was really happy. My husband was really happy. And we named the boy Louis, because my father's name is Louis.

I'm a mother and at the same time I do consulting work, immigration consulting. My concentration is Filipino immigration services. I do counseling for people who cannot afford to hire a lawyer. If I cannot handle the problem I refer them. It's technical assistance, explaining the law. People say, "How come I've petitioned for my children and they haven't done anything about it?" Usually immigrants don't come with their children [at first], so they have to petition the Immigration here to bring their children from the Philippines, and I have to explain the reason why there are certain quotas to every country, plus they aren't citizens so they don't have priority. [I also explain] how to become a U.S. citizen.

I also deal with legislative issues. For example, the Simpson-Mazzoli Bill that became the Immigration Reform Control Act of 1986. It's a repressive piece of legislation. Historically the United States always tries to open its arms to foreigners whenever it needs workers. So now the economy is bad and they're trying to get rid of these people. It's an inhumane piece of legislation because a lot of these people from countries in Latin America and Asia, their countries are really in turmoil politically so they want to stay here. But that's where foreign policy comes in again. Because [U.S. foreign policy] changes the conditions in other countries. In the Philippines they supported Marcos for years and years and they never listened to what small people like myself had to say, that he was a dictator and you don't gain anything if you support a dictator. That's the reason I don't want to be part of the Foreign Service.

Right now I'm just concentrating on community work, because you need the time to read and do some studies at home, and at the same time I am around when my kids need me. I'm an organizer with the Filipino-American Political Association. It took me a year to get to know people. We have to look out for our interests and someday endorse politicians, but right now it's more like an educational type of organization to study issues and candidates.

I'm involved in the Church. I cannot keep away from the Church. I'm a modest type of person, but we were pretty close to the former pastor of our parish and once in a while I would invite him to come and say a Mass at home, and of course when he did, I read a reading, and he said, "Wow, I didn't know you read that great. Why don't you become a lector for the church?" This was five years ago, and I said [to myself], "No, I will not do that. For one thing, I don't want myself to be standing there as an Asian because it's a white church." Every time he saw me in church he went, "When are you going to read?" I said, "Maybe next year, Father," but I knew I was not going to do it. I wasn't truthful about my apprehensions. When my sister-in-law passed away I don't know what happened, I said, "Okay Father, I'm ready." So I went to the training for lectors and became a lector two years ago. I love it. Because I have the chance to go over the reading and read it in the Bible and try to understand it, reflect it to my life—

so I'm much closer to my God now than before.

I am also a Eucharistic minister. [I became one] last year, after my Cursillo.* My husband [made a Cursillo] because his boss asked him, "Why don't you join the Cursillo?" so of course he couldn't say no, right, because that was his boss. That's Jaime, he always has to respect the boss. Jaime went first and then after he finished his Cursillo I made it. It was beautiful. It strengthened my relationship to the community again, because I [had been feeling] like I was pouring out to the community and not getting anywhere; I felt like I hadn't really accomplished anything. The Cursillo gave me strength to come back and to continue the work. And people [talked about] their experiences: Some had divorces, [some had] lost husbands, wives; it was really a sharing, Christian sharing. It was mostly upper-class women, white middle-class women; in fact we were just two Filipinos and one Korean and that's it. But I thought that was great because learning from the other women was a really good experience for me.

I'm glad [about the Cursillo] because [after he made it] my husband was able to understand why I do community work. To him it's a waste of time: there's no monetary return so why put up with all this b.s. [Before Cursillo, he saw Christianity as] going to church but nothing else, you are not responsible, you are not obligated to go out to the community. Now he understands better. So now I have the support. At that time I did not have the support, so I did not share some of my political activities. I've always been with the anti-Marcos coalition based in San Francisco. I never shared that with my husband. Whenever I went to meetings I always said, "I want to go to San Francisco and do shopping." I never told the truth. I'd been keeping it for five years. When [Benigno] Aquino was assassinated I started revealing my activities.

[I went back to the Philippines for a visit] last year. [The problems are] not that simple to correct; Marcos had been there for twenty years and it's impossible [to change quickly], but [people] don't understand this, especially people who are in the rural area. They want to see miracles, but it takes time.

My husband's relatives are politically involved nationally. Once in a while one of the relatives who is the bodyguard of the son of Marcos used to tell us that there were Filipino CIA's coming into the

---

*Cursillo, literally "a little course" in Christianity, is a spiritual renewal movement aimed at helping participants to deepen their faith; their initial involvement is usually through an intensive weekend retreat.

United States, which meant that if you were an "anti" to the regime they could kill you. That's the reason why I've always been strong to my faith; nothing will happen to me as long as God is with me. Plus I believe I'm doing the right thing.

I think right now the bishops are speaking on economic rights, which is great. I don't know anything about that [letter about women]. But if they have [begun to work on such a document] then they should continue it. Because the percentage of poverty is coming up for women and children. Catholic women usually focus on raising their children, and once there's something wrong in the family like a divorce or a death, then what are they going to do, these women who never worked or don't have an education? They should try to help these women.

There are some men who don't have that much education and yet they earn more than women. I'm glad that [the women's movement] is around because they are really working for the benefit of women today. I like the pay equity thing and the ERA. Of course I don't go for all-the-way feminists, because we women are made differently, our physical look. I don't consider myself a feminist. Being a feminist means believing that you can do anything including carrying heavy things. I can't do what a man can do. I'm a pretty special creature because I look different. So that's where there is a boundary.

You cannot abandon doing work in the house. I think God created us to. That is our role, to be a mother, raise our children, and take care of the house. Washing dishes, that's part of your role. It doesn't mean that you're being suppressed, but basically you're responsible for those things. If I get sick my husband takes care of those things, but basically I believe that it's my role. Like choosing the kind of furniture, the interior decoration of the house, it should have that woman's touch, that maiden touch. But when it comes to equality, that's a different thing, I believe that women should be given equal rights. I want to see that women are equal, that we have a place in society, that we are worthy of something, not just being a wife and raising kids. Because we do have the talent.

I like altar girls. It's really great that girls are participating in the Church. When I was growing up I always wanted to be part of the Church—to serve, to be an altar girl—but we were limited at that time. I never had the opportunity. One of these days I hope my girls will do it. But I'm not pushing them to. It has to be from their own will.

[Women as priests?] Why not? I don't see anything wrong with it. Because, as I said, we are equal. In fact, God created us equally, right? So why can't we do the same thing? I have problems with letting priests get married. I've always had this idea that a priest would never get married because Jesus Christ was that way. I know right now we're having problems in the Church because we don't have enough priests, but I would like to maintain it for a priest to be a single man. [For women priests it should be] the same. But then, if the majority of Catholic people say, "Why not, because we don't have enough people to serve," that's all right. But I have reservations. Because Christ was able to sacrifice Himself, not to get married, so we should try to maintain that. But again, as I said, I'm open.

I was raised traditional; I got used to the old way in the Church. But then when the changes came I said well, I sort of trust the leadership so I figure if these people are experts maybe it's a good change. It was a shock because before I was taught never to hold the holy bread, and nowadays you go up to laypeople like myself holding the holy bread, so that was something I had to get over. But the rest, I thought it was really great. I don't understand Latin that well and it was just a ritual for me to go through the Mass, so when they changed it to English I said, "Wow, it's beautiful." There was a better communication with me and God. The Mass has more meaning than before. But of course my folks, they were used to the old way. They had a hard time. Going through the changes was difficult for my mother but eventually she was able to accept them.

The Fundamentalists, they know the Bible very well. They memorize it, they can quote from it. I had a bad experience with that: I sit on the Human Relations Committee in Contra Costa County and we took a stand on pro-gay civil rights. The Fundamentalists hate the idea of giving civil rights to these folks. At the hearing they brought up the Bible, and quoting the Bible to me is just a big fake. If you're really a Christian you don't have to condemn your brother no matter who they are and what they do. In the Catholic church they don't condemn. That's why I'm proud to be Catholic. Because again, going back to Jesus Christ, he never condemned anybody, even if you are a sinner like Mary Magdalene. The Catholic people I deal with, they seem to be sympathetic with people. Another thing is that they don't enforce you to be a big donor to the church. You give what you can give. You don't have to show off how much you donate weekly or monthly. But in some other churches you are required to donate a certain amount, like the Mormons; I guess that's why they're so wealthy. Everything is through your own volition [in the Catholic church] and that's what's great.

Homosexuality is bad. I'm against it. Our religion is against it. I know according to the studies they cannot help it, it's just the way they are, so you have to accept it. I supported the gay rights bill because they had been discriminated against in terms of housing and employment, they have a lot of slurs and bad words against them, they get hurt, physical violence. That's really unfair. Why do you have to hurt a person just because of the way they are? To me that's un-Christian. That's not the way to treat anybody, that's cruel. I don't think that's the way Jesus wants us to treat our brothers and sisters. That's why we have the Ten Commandments. A lot of us say we are Christian and yet we are not really practicing what we say: a lot of rhetoric but inaction.

Sex is one thing that we've always ignored. Mom and I were open to everything, but when it came to that, we hardly discussed it. You had to learn through reading books, and I was really limited in that area. By the way, I don't like the idea that you see all these things in the media, because it's a private thing between a man and a woman. I don't like to expose it; it's a sacred thing.

Before, the Church did not accept divorces. Divorced people were outcasts. But I like this idea of reinserting people. We're human, we can make mistakes, and you cannot just set people aside and say, "Forget you guys." You have to accept them. I like the idea of annulment. I know the Church is strict on this, but if we ignore these people we're not doing the right thing because we have to have this forgiveness. I know a couple who is trying to get an annulment and it is so slow that they are ready to give up, because of the bureaucracy of the Church. I've always had good experiences with our Catholic religion, but when these issues come up, I sort of blame them, because they have to be more lenient. We're just people. Don't be so hard on these people! It's a bureaucracy; we have to get rid of that.

I'm against birth control. That's why you get married, to have children: "Go and multiply." The reason we have family planning is because we have the tendency to think, "Oh, we cannot afford it," we've got to have the right time, and money, we always make these excuses. Unless it's a medical excuse like myself: It will endanger my life if I have more children. Then birth control is okay; but for economic reasons, no.

Abortion? Oh gosh, I really don't like the idea of killing a human being; you should give the human being a chance to live. Who knows, he or she might be the president or a good person. But if that's the only way you can save the mother's life then that's fine. Otherwise I'm against it.

When I pray it's conversational, very simple. I give myself fifteen minutes' reflection: What have I done today? Was it worth it? I guess I'm trying to correct myself, in terms of, "Have I really done a good deed today?" I talk to Him and ask why things, especially when I feel low. There are times too that I dream about Him. In the picture that I see He has long hair with a beard, big eyes, kind face; the color would probably be like a Jewish color. Jesus is somebody that I can lean on, a friend. I guess that's my relationship with Jesus, that I trust [him] no matter what. [Jesus and God are] interchangeable. It's confusing; I can't tell the difference. The weird part is that the image is like He's a real human being; He talks to me and He says, "Don't worry about it, everything will be okay." [In my dreams] He [talks]. Maybe I'm crazy or something. You're the first one to know this: Even Our Lady, the Madonna, I used to dream of her, floating over the ocean. Now I don't dream of her anymore, ever since we put her shrine in the backyard; it's strange. I used to dream of her, her image sitting on heaven or in the ocean, sort of dark hair with that sweet face. I am embarrassed to share this with people because they might think, "What's wrong with her?" I guess I treat her like a mother. Since my mother is not around I confide in her with my feelings and little problems. Hopefully I can raise my children and mold them into good Christians like my mother did to me.

The Holy Spirit is everywhere, I believe in that. He's always around. That's why I don't need to go to church to pray or to talk to Him. When I do something wrong I say, "Well, I know you're watching me." [I go to confession,] yes. Not so often, once a year. The reason why I do it once a year is I think that I am not a sinner. I just go there because I want to communicate with a priest. I'm not saying I'm a perfect human being. That you break the law of the Ten Command-ments—stealing, being disrespectful to your mother and father—those are the things that I consider sin; and of course killing is a mortal sin. I guess you have to expand it: like a country can be creating sin. I hate to refer to this all the time, but with [some kinds of] foreign policy, if you are a part of it you are creating a sin.

I go to church because, first of all, it's part of my obligation as a Catholic to communicate with my Lord, sharing also with other folks. It's kind of nice to see other people. The entire week seems to be not a fulfilled week unless I go to church, because that's the only time when I see everyone, and having that holy bread is very important to me. Receiving [communion], when He's inside, I feel really great.

When I vote I don't care what the party is. I study the person first and he has to carry certain values. The candidate, if she pertains to the ethnic minorities and human rights, that's the kind of thing I look for. I really study before I go to the polling place because I don't want to make a mistake. I feel that maybe one vote is not that effective, but at least I've done my share, my obligation as a voter and a U.S. citizen.

I'm against nuclear weapons. The way I see it, there should be more discussion, so that's why there is a need for a good relationship between supernations like the U.S. and Russia. Cultural exchange is one way to break the barrier. You've got to know the other country. Then you can set this friendly tone and you can start discussing the military and nuclear weapons. If you and I are not on good terms, we need to talk, we need to discuss certain things, why you hate me and why I dislike you; it's the same with big nations. I hate this idea of positioning yourself as the big guy. I'm scared with the nuclear weapons. They can kill the human race. That's why we have to put the right people [in office]. I think that's another reason why I care so much [about politics].

Some people measure you by what you have. But I disagree with that idea; I don't measure people by money. My way of success is having a lot of friends—and if you accomplish something that will benefit your community, that's what I would call successful. I hope my children will finish college. And once they start earning, I hope they will always keep in mind that money isn't everything. But it's hard; you can't tell them what to do in life. Raising them is my number-one priority. So if they are on the wrong track, probably I have to blame myself.

I wish I could change the world, but it's impossible. I wish people would love each other more, no matter what their background or their race. I want to make sure that you mention that I am for human rights. That's my big thing. I'm glad you're taking time to go to the various ethnic groups, because we are not known yet nationally. There will be a time when we will be known nationally, because our population is growing. I'm glad you did not overlook us, because we are the majority of the population.

FOURTEEN

WE ARE CHURCH (OR ARE WE?)

Gather us in and hold us forever,
Gather us in and make us your own;
Gather us in, all peoples together,
Fire of love in our flesh and our bone.
                    —Marty Haugen,
                    "Gather Us In"
                    (contemporary hymn)

Still, still with light supernal
Those battlements shall gleam,
And Peter's rock, eternal,
Confront the restless stream.
                    —L. Camatari, S.J.,
                    "Rex Regum in Splendore"
                    (English version, Ronald Knox)
                    (nineteenth-century hymn)

I was having dinner with an old friend from divinity school, an ordained minister in the United Church of Christ, when our conversation, after the usual catching up on love and work, turned somehow to The Purpose of Our Being Here. "God put us here to work," my friend said, emphasizing the word *work*. "No, no," I said to her, "God put us here to praise God, to enjoy God's creation and to take care of it." My friend and I have much in common—Christian faith, social commitments, theological training, feminist perspective, political views—but our outlooks on the purpose of our presence on the planet were radically different. I think our disparity had something to do with the difference between Catholic and Calvinist. Catholics do have a work ethic: This is America, after all. But there is something at the base of Catholicism that ultimately has nothing to do with work, with productivity, with *doing,* but with *being* in the presence of God. Alongside its focus on the works of mercy, the Catholic church has also fostered in its members the belief that the core of life is contemplation and celebration.

When I asked women what they felt were the distinguishing characteristics of Catholic Christianity, their answers were brief and sometimes vague. I realized after a while that the answers to that question were more often contained in what they took for granted, answers they had given to other questions in our conversation. It is clear, for instance, how much their relationship to a God who is present in the world is part of their religious identity, and how strongly they felt both about the dignity of the human person and about the primacy of conscience. When women did give explicit answers to my question about "the Catholic thing,"[1] they tended to give either a rather generic one about the Golden Rule or a very specific one about the Eucharist.

Women's answers were most heartfelt when speaking about the Eucharist. "God is there," Rosemary Klem said simply. Sixty-year-old Ann Bright converted to Catholicism as a young woman. "I miss communion," she said, "if I don't get it. It keeps me somehow together. It reminds me of who I am and what I'm about, what's important and what isn't." "Celebrating the Eucharist is the big thing for me," said twenty-three-year-old "Jenna Santini." "We gather together to celebrate the Lord and to celebrate the sacrifice of Jesus Christ, and that he rose for us to forgive us our sins, and we celebrate that every Sunday. I think that's real distinctive for me. I mean, I've been to other churches and I really miss the Eucharist. We have something physical that we can take within our bodies, and say, 'This is the body and blood of Jesus Christ,' and other religions don't do that. It's something for me to hold on to. It's not just something we just talk about. It's something we receive. It's like being baptized every Sunday, or being forgiven. We're kind of renewing ourselves every Sunday." "Jenna" has not read the works of Saint Augustine, but her words, centuries later, echoed his: "If you want to understand the Body of Christ," Augustine wrote in a sermon to newly baptized Christians, "hear the words of the apostle: 'You are the Body of Christ and its members.' . . . It is your own mystery which is placed on the Lord's table. And it is to what you are that you reply 'Amen.' "[2]

Faith, for Catholic women, is something bodily, appealing to the heart and senses as much as the mind.[3] "Peter's conversion was a surprise to me," Ann Richards Anderson said of her husband's decision to become a Catholic. "It's always a surprise to me when a Protestant intellectual becomes a Catholic, because that requires a transition from viewing religion as having a primarily intellectual component to recognizing that religion is primarily spiritual and has truths of a different order, truths that are just not subject to proofs or explanation. I don't think you have to give up being an intellectual to be a Catholic," said Ann, a well-read human services administrator with two academic degrees. "It's [more] a recognition that the intellectual life is only one part of life; I don't think there's any aspect of life that can be understood only intellectually. There's a place for mystery, and awe, and truths that you can't draw lines around."

Community is a central part of Catholic women's religious identity; a few spelled this out in theological terms. Ruth Pakaluk, who was raised a Presbyterian and became a Catholic as a young adult, shared her perception of the difference between Protestant and Catholic Christians: "For a Protestant it's more that you as an individual are saved because of your relationship with this one person [Jesus]. The view that the Catholic Church puts forward is much more that we are a people." Other women spoke of the central role of religious community in their reflections on the Eucharist. For them, it was, quite literally, an experience of communion. Raised a Catholic, Christine Torrey left the Church for a time as a young woman in the 1970s, repelled by its official teachings on women and sexual matters. Over a decade later, in prison, she found a compassionate friend in the sister who served as Catholic chaplain there, and a new serenity at the prison's weekly Catholic liturgy. "I like anything to do with feeling closer to my Lord," she said. "I also like it because of the community, because sometimes my enemies might be at Mass—my temporary enemies, somebody I might have had an argument with or somebody who might have made [life] difficult for me. I remember times when it was time for the Sign of Peace and I was like, 'Oh no! Who's here?' because it's such a close community: These are the people we argue with, we live with, we work with, that we're going to be offering the Sign of Peace with. I really had to forgive an enemy and that's a big growth for me and I'm sure it's a growth for them too. It doesn't mean I walk up the stairs hand in hand with them but there's that single moment during Mass where you find out all humans are alike."

For Catholic women, communion always extends in time and space beyond their immediate community. Although they often struggle with what they perceive as a rigid and authoritarian tradition, Catholic women—even those who are no longer practicing Catholics—also treasure that tradition's breadth, scope, and universality. Being Catholic, for them, is inseparable from being part of a vast body that is more than an institution, unyielding in some ways, but also diverse, inclusive, and elastic. "Catholic means you're universal," said Angela Tilghman, a Washington, D.C., schoolteacher. "What is special," said Abigail McCarthy, "is when the Church is being truly catholic, when it adapts culturally the way it seems to be doing in Africa and used to do [in many places] before [the Council of] Trent. It's organic in the way it accommodates to people's lives and gives meaning to every aspect of life. I think that capacity of the Church on the one hand to have the most high forms of mysticism and theology, and on the other to have simple popular devotion, and to include the sinner as well as the saved, is what makes it special. And I think the communion of saints is another specialness, this strong sense that you are a member of 'the Church Militant, the Church Triumphant, and the Church Suffering,' that's the old-fashioned way of putting it, but that you are part of all being, in a sense." Brigette Rouson, a generation younger than Abigail McCarthy, told me she was "very, very fiercely proud to be part of the Catholic church, because I think it's the most diverse church there is in the world. This is a church that can embrace everybody, because we have all styles of worship, we have the right wing and the left wing politically, we have every color and nationality imaginable."

Women often praised the endurance and richness of the tradition in the same breath as they criticized its faults. "I know there are flaws, God knows there are flaws in the Church," said Catholic-school teacher Dorothy Wodraska. "That's because of the human element involved. We're much too heavy on the top. Our bishop is fond of saying he's a company man—I don't think the Church should be a 'company.'" At the same time, she said, "Being Catholic to me is being part of a strong tradition that I believe was founded by Christ; the worship gives me strength, a sense of belonging to something much larger than myself." Ann Richards Anderson's husband was drawn, among other things, to the Catholic church's "history of survival," she said, adding, "However much the Church looks to us like it never changes, it has in fact changed enormously or it would never have survived. It's not as good as being Jewish," she concluded, "but it's a wonderful thing to be part of a heritage that goes back two thousand years. There's something kind of awesome about it."

While they cherished the length and breadth of the Catholic tra-dition and felt in communion with Catholics in other parts of the world, the women I met felt strongly about being *American* Catholics. They frequently spoke of the differences they observed between the modus operandi of American Catholics and the Vatican's worldview and style of operation. Inculturation—"the process of a deep, sympathetic adaptation and appropriation of a local cultural setting in which the Church finds itself in a way that does not compromise its basic faith in Christ"[4]—is the order of the day in the worldwide Catholic church. But American inculturation is often at odds with the culture of Rome. Freedom of speech, due process, open deliberations, participation in policy making—these building blocks of democracy were values shared by all the women I met, and they held to them tenaciously. Several spontaneously mentioned the firing of moral theologian Charles Curran from his Catholic University teaching post because of his perspective on birth control and other sexual issues, which many consider a moderate and measured one. An even greater number of women mentioned Seattle Archbishop Raymond Hunthausen's difficulties with the Vatican[5] and the failure of American bishops "to stand up for their own," as one woman put it. A number of women also wished for greater autonomy for the American church. "I think we ought to have a little more say about how we operate," said "Mary Sullivan," a faithful churchgoer for all of her eighty-one years.

For years, Catholics in the U.S. championed American values but self-consciously differentiated themselves from the surrounding culture. Their relationship to non-Catholics was often both defensive and hostile. Most of the women—even women in their thirties—told me they had been raised to believe that there was no place in heaven for non-Catholics.* Today Catholic women are not only tolerant but adamant in their rejection of intolerance and prejudice. Several mentioned the Inquisition with horror.

Only occasionally did women wish for the conversion of non-Catholics or display feelings of superiority. "My friends that are Protestants don't have the faith I do," said Mary Kay Leicht of Indianapolis. "They don't take it as seriously." The overwhelming majority (consistently with Gallup and Castelli's findings about American Catholics[6]) were tolerant and accepting of other religions. For the most part, their

---

*This recollection was met with disbelief by several Catholics in their fifties with whom I shared my findings. Their memories of Catholic education, they said, contained a more tolerant vision of other faiths, and the infamous Father Feeney, after all, had been excommunicated by Richard Cardinal Cushing in the early 1950s for teaching that there was no salvation outside the Church. One can conclude either that Catholic religious instruction was not consistent in this matter, or that it was filtered into the present through very different lenses.

sentiments reflected Abigail McCarthy's: "I think Catholicism is special," she said, "but I don't think it's better." "The Catholic religion is the religion I know and grew up with," said Christine Torrey, "and it was how I found God and Jesus." But, she said, "I think everyone has their own spirituality. When they used to say only Catholics would go to heaven, I never really did go for that. It just didn't seem fair to me."

Many women, like Christine, came to their tolerance of other faiths through their belief in God: A God who is generous and welcoming cannot, in their minds, be one who excludes, judges, or shows favoritism. "I have no prejudice," Dorothy McFadden said. "We are one and God made us." One of "Joanne Grace"'s children joined the Lutheran church as a young adult. "He's very happy in it," "Joanne" said. "It seems right for him." She added: "We raised our children to follow their conscience and to recognize that all faiths are good; it's how you live." "God is looking upon us and chuckling at our inability to get along with one another," said Diane Williams, a young woman studying theology at the Washington Theological Union and active in an urban parish. "I totally believe that we will be all together somewhere," Betty Darko said, "if we are together somewhere." "I don't believe," said Ann Valdez, who converted to Catholicism as a young woman, "that God is going to ask us for our ID's."

Most women also made no exclusive claims for Christianity as a whole. "Every once in a while," said college senior Madeleine Msall, "I wonder whether God might not favor Christians, and that's basically because of the Bible passage that says, 'Anyone who comes to the Father must come through me, Christ.' But I think over time I've decided that passage doesn't mean that you need to be Christian. What it really means is that you need to be in touch with the values of the teaching of Christ. You could be any faith or no faith at all and still be following the spirit of Christ and it would probably work. The whole conception of some people being saved and some people being damned doesn't fit very well with the idea of a merciful God who created all of us to be the way that we are—so then how can He blame us for what we are?"

"They have their own way of thinking," seventeen-year-old Camila Alvarez said when I asked for her view of other religions. "It's all the same." Catholic women of all ages held Camila's two-fold attitude toward other faiths, an odd and contradictory combination of accepting differences and minimizing or collapsing them. Women acknowledged the legitimacy of other religious paths yet often believed them to be virtually the same as their own, a perspective that would horrify most contemporary scholars of world religions.

What Catholic women found difficult to imagine was life without religion. They seemed puzzled and saddened by the existence of people who had no affiliation to a religious tradition, and even more so by people who did not believe in God. "I don't think you have to [believe in God] to be a good person," said Incarnate Word College student Patsy Wesel. "[But] I think it helps to be a good person to believe in God because you always have somebody there that you feel is helping you or guides you, even though you can't see Him." "As long as a human being has a religion, that's fine with me," Teresita Bravo-Paredes said. "[Having a religion] makes them better; they know what a sin is."

The only negative comments I heard about other faiths were reserved for Fundamentalist Protestants and television evangelists. "The other," for most Catholic women, is no longer the mainline Protestant, the Jew, or the Muslim, or even the Buddhist or Hindu, but the Christian Fundamentalist. Teresita Bravo-Paredes's experience on the Contra Costa County Human Relations Committee and her feelings about Fundamentalists were typical of the women I met. Women also criticized television evangelists for what they perceived as greed and an overly simplistic approach to morality and faith. "It doesn't matter what religion you are because you're praying to the same God," said twenty-one-year-old "Inez Garcia," a college student of Puerto Rican ancestry. "But there's some religions I dislike, the ones on TV like PTL. It just gets me so mad. These people are [much, much] richer than the people that go to see them."

Catholic women's attitudes toward Jews and Judaism are largely positive, sometimes almost romanticized. I found in many women both admiration for the Jewish tradition and a sense of kinship which was as much sociological and cultural as religious, based on shared memory of the immigrant experience and differentiation from the Anglo-Saxon Protestant mainstream. Women who felt an affinity with Judaism perceived Catholics and Jews to be similar in their focus on culture and peoplehood and in their membership in a rich, complex, and ancient tradition.

"I always felt if I wasn't Catholic I would probably be Jewish," said Mary Callanan, a practicing Catholic all her life and a graduate of a Catholic school which offered a class in comparative religion. "Rose Mazurkiewicz" lived in a predominantly Jewish area as a young adult.

"All of my friends, naturally, were Jewish" she remembered. "You ask a question, and they have logic coming out of their ears: There's a reason for everything. I thought to myself, 'This is the way religion should be, you should have explanations for everything.' I kept my son in Catholic schools only because I was such a poor Catholic," "Rose" said. "I wanted him to have a religious background and I had enough respect for my father and mother not to bring him up in a different religion. [If they hadn't been around] I might have gone Jewish."

"I am really very taken with Judaism," Abigail McCarthy said to me. "I feel as though there's a great mystery there and that we won't really come into the fullness of Christ's coming until we are one with the Jews: I'm not thinking in terms of converting them, but [the theologian] Monika Hellwig puts it this way: 'The Messiah is still coming and He will have come when we have reached the fullness of His message.' I think the great respect for life in this world that is part of Judaism is a value that we Catholics have to recover and I think we are in the process of recovering."

There is a great deal of talk in ecclesiastical circles about the demise of the ecumenical movement—the conscious, organized work toward unity among Christians. True, aside from commissions and consultations of scholars and church leaders, there are few formal dialogue efforts among Christians. But ecumenism is alive and well in other forms. The ecumenism of Mary Wunnicke is a neighborly connection among Lutherans and Catholics based on shared life in a rural community. "Louise O'Connell," at the age of seventy-six, participates actively in her local chapter of the national organization Church Women United, "a wonderful group," she said, of Protestant, Catholic, and Orthodox Christian women who gather for educational programs, discussions, and prayer services. Christine Beckley prays with Charismatic Christians of all denominations, many of them Evangelical Protestants, and with her friends from Women Aglow. Chroniclers of the ecumenical movement often overlook this particular form of ecumenism, but it may well be the most significant in this country and the fastest-growing.

Ecumenical and interreligious* alliances also spring from social and political commitments. I met Catholic women involved in the religious peace movement who had forged strong bonds with Quakers

---

Ecumenical refers to relations among Christians (Orthodox, Catholic, Protestant), *interreligious* to relations among members of different religions, e.g., Christian, Jewish, Muslim, Buddhist, etc.

and mainline Protestants and women who worked in the pro-life movement with Evangelical Protestants. Others had worked side by side in the civil rights movement with Jews and members of the historic black churches. African-American women spoke about their Muslim relatives and neighbors, and some of the Vietnamese-born women had Buddhist family and friends.

Over half the women I interviewed had some experience of anti-Catholicism. The misconceptions and prejudices Catholic women encounter usually involve accusations of idolatry, mocking criticism of the papacy, and the notion that because people are Catholic, they do not think for themselves. "Somehow the vibes are passed that a person's estimation of you has dropped when they find out you're a Catholic," said Ann Richards Anderson. "People are very anti-Catholic," said sixty-four-year-old May Kast, who converted to Catholicism as a young woman. "They still look at you as though you belong to another world. They don't believe you believe in God. They think Catholics don't read the Bible. Some people eye Catholics with suspicion. They think they're subject to Rome." "Do you think you're subject to Rome?" I asked. "No," May answered. "No way."

"I ran into it a lot," Abigail McCarthy said of anti-Catholic prejudice. She and Senator Eugene McCarthy "were considered intellectuals," she remembered, "so we were included a lot in intellectual gatherings with the Ivy League crowd. I've always found it totally irritating, exasperating that they assume a certain ridiculous belief on your part because you're a Catholic. They assume that they know what you believe and they have a caricature in mind. The caricature is a very limited view of what God is and a belief that you do what the pope tells you." She added, "You know that saying, 'Anti-Catholicism is the anti-Semitism of the intellectual.' "

When Dorothy Wodraska and her husband first moved to Indianapolis, she said, "I played in a tennis league, and the woman who was my partner, a really fine woman, a Protestant, said to me, 'Dotty, I really like you. You have a marvelous mind and a marvelous personality. I can't understand—how can you be Catholic?' She went on to express some of the most rude opinions: You can't possibly be a thinking person and be a Catholic; we are nothing but unthinking breeders, tyrants, we allow ourselves to be run by frustrated men and women who have supposedly committed themselves to celibacy but everybody knows about the tunnels between the nunnery and the pastor's house—she just went on and on with things like this—that the Catholic church has been the downfall of world, the pope doesn't care about the poor people, and on and on. It hurt me. That she would even say that to me was a surprise. That was my first experience with anti-Catholicism."

Some women had encountered prejudice specifically directed at Catholic women. Thirty-two-year-old "Anne Marie Quinn," who is owner and president of a small business in Boston, said, "It hurts you being a woman and being Catholic sometimes, in business and in politics. Catholic women are viewed as wimps, not strong women, women that are willing to give in to a confrontation, women that have been persecuted and feel the need to be martyred, which is totally unfair. [And the view is] if you're Catholic, you're full of guilt—well, that's true," she laughed, and added, "People can't believe I'm an Irish Catholic. [In their mind] you're home with six kids and that's all you do. Catholic women are very strong," she concluded. Psychotherapist Ellen Reuter has encountered "a lot of stereotyping, especially when a bunch of therapists get together. I don't tend to wear my Catholicism like a badge, so I hear a lot of, 'Oh, [so-and-so] is a typical Catholic woman.' [By which they mean] religious, devoted, not very strong," she said, adding, "I think that Catholic women have to be extremely strong to be as devoted and religious as they are! I don't think being wimpy is part of it. That's the image that's out there. Or that we're guilt-ridden—which is probably true. I've often had the feeling, 'Do these people know I'm Catholic? And if they do, why are they talking this way?' It's stereotyping [more than anti-Catholicism], sort of like the mother-in-law jokes and the Jewish jokes."

"Oh yes," Barbara Kern answered when I asked whether she had encountered anti-Catholic sentiments or stereotypes. "People in my working life would make presumptions: 'Oh I know you, you're one of these nice little Catholic girls'—[meaning] virginal, [following] the traditional male-female roles. . . . The kind of people that made that remark were usually men; I think they had some sort of weird sexual fantasy tied up about it. I just ignored it," she said.

"People think they know what nuns are like," said Pamela Montagno. "It's so out of date, and when I see things on TV, so stereotypical. There was a Perry Mason made-for-TV movie and the nun was wearing a habit—well, how many nuns wear that kind of habit?—and they were all living in a convent—how many sisters live in a convent anymore? And some of the cloistered women are some of the most radical women you'll ever meet, because they're so in tune with themselves and God. But people *love* the mystique and they'd much rather live with the stereotypes and the mystique despite the fact that it contradicts the reality."

Several women shared the perception expressed by "Elsa Colón": "Ex-Catholics," she said, "are some of the most anti-Catholic people I've ever met." Kerry M. Thompson, a Catholic psychotherapist in Boston, once commented to me "how frozen in time both non-Catholic ideas and old Catholic ideas are about what it means to be Catholic." Though many aspects of the Church have changed, she said, "people who left long ago with lots of wounds tend to have the attitude, 'Don't trouble me with the facts, I'm busy working out my old hurts.'"

Vatican II, of course, was the watershed that affected both the identity of Catholics and others' perceptions of Catholic identity. Most of the women welcomed the changes brought about by the Council: liturgy in the mother tongue, increased lay participation, and a shift in the image of the Church from mountain fortress to pilgrim people. Some, however, expressed concern that the promise of the Council had not yet been fulfilled. "I had such a joyful feeling after the Council that all these things were going to be just wonderful," said Abigail McCarthy, "and in a way perhaps they have been, but it hasn't really worked out quite as well [as we hoped]. I put that on the fact that the changes in the Church were imposed without explanation or education. The great numbers of the Catholic faithful had not been prepared, and I think a lot of priests didn't have their heart in it because they didn't know how to contend with it; their seminary education hadn't prepared them at all for a more participatory liturgy." Abigail McCarthy was not alone in mentioning the abrupt and often incomplete way in which changes were introduced into local parishes.

I also found a difference in reactions to Vatican II based on women's age in the early 1960s, the time of the Council. Of the women in their seventies, eighties, and nineties whom I met, all but one, a woman in her nineties, welcomed the changes brought about by the Council. Women now in their fifties and sixties—in their thirties at the time of the Council—were most enthusiastic. Women who are now in their thirties and forties were in some ways less affected and less positively influenced by Vatican II than their elders; the Council had less impact on these younger women, I think, because they were then in adolescence and early adulthood, the stage of life at which it is developmentally normal and appropriate to leave, ignore, or reject institutional religion. "I was just out of college," "Serena Townsend" remembered. "I thought [Vatican II] was long overdue and it was a good thing. I also was not a practicing Catholic. I had left the Church, so to me it was in a sense irrelevant. But it was good for all those other people who were still sticking around." "Serena" later became involved again in the Church, after the birth of her children.

The practice of Catholicism in late twentieth-century America relies less than before on external signs. Catholics no longer look or act very different from their neighbors. Vatican II shook up the identity of many of the women I met by taking away some of their identifiably Catholic behavior. "Who am I if I eat a hot dog on Friday?" Sandra Mondykowski Temple remembered asking herself after the post-conciliar changes had begun. Others paused to reflect on the change in Church rules with ironic humor. "They changed all the business about meat on Friday," Betty Darko said. "All those people with supposedly mortal sin because they had eaten meat on Friday—what happens to those people? [Is there a retroactive clause?] And what happened to all those babies in limbo?" she asked, referring to the old belief that unbaptized infants went to limbo, a place apart and between, neither purgatory nor heaven nor hell. "I think limbo is gone; they totally erased limbo. Now [that] there is no longer limbo, where do they go?"

But most loved and welcomed Vatican II, which marked a change in their relationship with God as well as their relationship to the Catholic church. In shifting the focus of Catholicism away from scru-pulous observance of rules and toward conversion and community, the Council led many women to deepen their Christian faith. For Margaret Slattery and the sisters in her religious order, "there is a whole new approach to prayer and liturgy and sacraments which has made a great deal of difference," Margaret said. "Prayer, the [Daily] Office, and meditation—before Vatican II these were [things] that you did because you were supposed to do them every day, it was, 'Get it in,' 'Get your prayers said, then we can go do something else.' The whole attitude toward that has changed. There's a totally new depth of mean-ing in prayer. I pray now because I want to pray. I never feel as if I have to 'get it in' any more."

"Clara Taylor," who is forty years old, found the changes in the Church "very traumatic" at first. "The High Masses were so inspira-tional," she remembered. But, she added, "It was so devastating the way it was taught to us that if you did something wrong it was a mortal sin—if you died, you were going to go to hell; it's very scary. Now [when] my son made his First Communion you didn't hear 'mortal sin.' It's good in that you don't have the fear." At the Jesuit university she attended in the late 1940s and early 1950s, "Sylvia Presti" "had a good course in logic and I was not interested at all in the sentimentality and being talked down to in the parish at home. I questioned the fact that God was shown always as a disciplinarian, the expectations we never lived up to, the guilt, guilt, guilt. I objected to that strenuously. So when the renewal came I was there cheering."

"Joanne Grace" was a young married woman at the time of the Council. "Vatican II really turned around my religious and faith life," she remembered. "I grew up as a very scrupulous Catholic thanks to sixteen years of Franciscans who bent over backwards to define the parameters of mortal and venial sin. There was so little joy in my faith life and in my relationship to the Church. It was so structured, so strictured. With the coming of Vatican II I got a whole different perception of Christ, of God, of the Church: Christ as brother, God as loving father, the Church as the people of God. And it wasn't what poor Sister Mary Francis said. Bless her soul, she didn't know any better. I could only feel sorry for her. I did not have bitterness."

By generalizing the practice of liturgy in the vernacular, the Council made the language of public prayer intelligible and brought about increased participation of the laity in worship. "We felt a new wave of life," Hang Vu remembered. "We had more communication between people and the priest. Not like before, when the priest just turned his back to people." "I think it made non-Catholics understand the Church much better," May Kast said, "because I have spoken to people and they said, 'When it wasn't in English we couldn't understand a thing about it. It was like a foreign God.' So Vatican II made non-Catholics believe we're all praying to the same God."

In many places the liturgical renewal seems to be nourishing both spirits and aesthetic sensibilities. Latina and African-American women especially rejoiced in the incorporation of music from their cultural traditions into the liturgy. Mary Esther Bernal, who volunteers as director of music at San Antonio's San Fernando Cathedral, spoke with animation of the cathedral's liturgies, whose music is an eclectic but harmonious mix of Latin Mass parts, Spanish hymns, and English hymns. "Every Mass is *packed*," she said cheerfully.

Other women lamented a loss in the beauty and quality of the liturgical arts. "I would like to see a church that would go back to being more aesthetic," said Abigail McCarthy. "I don't think we should have sacrificed good music and good art. Liturgical reform was never supposed to be reducing everything to the common denominator of taste. Some [new] church buildings are nothing but auditoriums. Place has a lot to do with a prayerful atmosphere, and I think we need to withdraw and have our spirits replenished, and good art and good music are part of that." She defined "good music" broadly. "I find the old plainchant marvelously consoling, that rise and fall, I think it's conducive to prayer. I love the Gospel Masses. I think spirituals are some of the greatest devotional music ever written. I'm not against the folk Mass. I love 'Amazing Grace.' And I get a great joy out of singing 'A Mighty Fortress Is Our God' because I grew up in Lutheran country and to have it come home is rather nice." She quipped: "Of course, you can be devotional with the help of bad art too, and heaven knows we have been."

A few women spoke of incidents that bordered on the ludicrous. On one of the rare occasions she went to church, for the baptism of a friend's baby, Gail Benjamin decided afterward to light a candle, remembering that the anniversary of her father's death was near. "I went to the shrine," she said, "and they were electric candles! And there was a sign that said to put a quarter into the little slot, and for the big [lights] to put in four quarters. I was really horrified and shocked and amazed. I guess I was standing there long enough that the priest came up and said, 'Is something the matter?' and I said, 'I was just looking at this slot-machine idea. I don't mean to be disrespectful, but I haven't seen one of these before.' And he [started talking] about problems with insurance and candles in a church: 'It's very difficult these days, you have to worry about those kinds of issues.' I said, 'But there's something not right about the idea.' I remember as a kid and a young adult lighting a candle for somebody, you know, a candle with a taper and a light, and watching all the candles, watching them flicker. I said, 'I guess the next thing that'll happen is that when you come in there won't be water in the font anymore, there'll be little Kleen-Wipes!'"

Of the women who yearned for the beauty and mystery of the old Church, a significant number were self-described feminists who neither went to church nor participated in the small lay-led feminist worshipping communities that are springing up around the country. "I like the color, the pageantry, the ritualism of it," said Gail Benjamin of the Catholic liturgy. If she could change the Church, she said, "I would change it back to Latin—in part because I thought it was important there was a universal language." Two years ago, a Boston newspaper columnist, consistently critical of the Catholic hierarchy's positions on women and sexuality, wrote a column positively dripping with nostalgia for the Latin Mass. "We don't want Peter, Paul and Mary," she wrote. "Bring back incense, smoke, clanging chains, teary eyes, robes and Latin. . . . We're yearning for a spiritual hit in this secular world. . . . We want rituals."[7]

A majority of the women rejoiced in the post–Vatican II focus on personal responsibility and in the greater freedom to study, question, and participate in their religious tradition. A few women were uncomfortable with the new freedom and flexibility and hankered after the old way. Mary Callanan told me her closest male friend "used to say to me, 'The trouble with you is you don't want to think for yourself. With the new rules, *you've* got to make the decisions. Before, the Church made them for you: You had to do this, you couldn't do that, and you did that, and you never had to think.' And I said, 'I know, that's the way I like it: Tell me what to do and I'll do it.'" "Do you think differently on the job?" I asked Mary, who, as treasurer for the city and county of San Francisco, supervises a staff of over one hundred people. I observed that she was a leader with many decision-making responsibilities. "I'm also bound by a lot of laws," she answered. "Sometimes I'm glad when the law says, 'You can do this and you can do that.' I like parameters. I don't like things just wide open."

For a few women, the structural changes in the Church and the aesthetic changes in the liturgy went hand in hand. They missed the security, order, and certainty of preconciliar Catholicism, and the coherent and beautiful world celebrated in the old liturgy, and they associated one with the other. Carolyn Booth, who was raised in the Baptist church, became a Catholic because "I love the procedure, the ceremony, the discipline in the Church. I like the ritual, I like the special feeling you had when you walked into a Catholic church and it was cool and quiet and very, very reverent." She added, "I liked the rules, because I think people need rules to live by, so that was what attracted me, I think, more than anything." After Vatican II, Carolyn remembered, "the altar was turned around, the statues were taken down, the vigil lights were stuck in the back corner and my husband and I didn't like it at all. . . . And the priests seemed to be taking wide liberties with the Church and it became irreverent."

The Council did not define any new dogmas for the Church; instead, it concentrated its deliberations and teachings on the Church itself. American Catholic women have followed suit. The crises they experience are institutional more than theological, and when they raise theological questions, these are often related to the nature and shape of the faith community. "What is the Church?" said Anne Burke, whose work as director of Raleigh, North Carolina's Urban Ministry Center brings her in contact with people of many faiths. "Is it the institution or people? And do we have to hang out with Catholics to be Church?"

Liturgy and governance, those two Catholic obsessions, were recurring themes in conversations with Catholic women. When I asked women what they would change about the Catholic church if they could, they always returned to questions of structure, moving back and forth between the shape of the local parish and the governance of the universal Church. Religious experience, for them, was never simply solitary; they took for granted the need for a strong community of faith. The question for them was, how much structure and what kind of structure are necessary for a vibrant life of faith? What form of community is most in keeping with the teaching and spirit of Jesus? Does the shape of the Catholic community today work—and for whom?

"Tear down all the walls," Myra Spivey said when I asked how she would change the Church. One of the most active women at Mother of Christ Church, a largely African-American parish in Cincinnati, Myra sings in the choir, chairs the parish council, runs the annual fundraiser, and serves as a Eucharistic minister. "Just have a church outside for everyone. We don't need priests. I wouldn't have any priests, just laypeople. I would have more evangelization, outreach to everyone, open arms." She waved her arms and opened them wide to emphasize her point.

For most of the women, scale was as much of an issue as structure. Catholic parishes today, except in rural areas, tend to be very large. "The average parish serves about 2,300 people, and about fifteen percent serve 5,000 or more," said David C. Leege of the University of Notre Dame's Center for the Study of Contemporary Society, reporting on the Notre Dame Study of Catholic Parish Life.[8] "When contrasted with parishes in Catholic countries elsewhere, American parishes are still rather small. But the average Catholic will compare his [sic] parish with nearby Protestant congregations, and it is almost always larger."[9] Women of all cultures and life-styles, when speaking of the local church, wished for smaller communities of faith. "What happened to the priests that knew you by your first name?" "Anne Marie Quinn" complained. "That no longer exists. I would take away all the big churches. I would build some small community prayer house where people felt more at ease and less threatened by the size of it." "I would like parishes to be smaller, more intimate," said "Kitty Riordan." "There's something in our church that we have that is catching, and it doesn't catch when the mob is so great that you don't even know the person or know their eyes or their face or know a little bit about their life. What I'd like them to 'catch' is the Christ in us, the love in us, the joy. If [churches] were smaller, they would be more equal; there would be a lot more love to go around. And maybe [with] that would come the ability to lead and serve without structures that deaden."

"All politics is local," former House Speaker Thomas P. "Tip" O'Neill used to say. The same applies to religion. As Sally Cunneen wrote in her landmark study of American Catholic women in the late 1960s,[10] "The proof is in the parish." "My concern is with my local parish," Dolores Reuter said when I asked for her thoughts on the Church and its leaders. "That's what it comes down to." The pope, for most Catholic women, is a distant figure and not a subject of intense preoccupation. Several of the women I met expressed admiration for Pope John Paul II; more often women were highly critical, or expressed a blend of criticism and admiration. John XXIII, the convener of the Council, remained their favorite pope. Some women, in their statements about the Church, spoke of the hierarchy as an unspecified "they," an amorphous combination of the local clergy and Vatican officials.

Catholic women are more preoccupied with the life of the whole Church than with the hierarchy, but conversations about the local parish were laced with comments on the leadership styles and attitudes of the clergy, especially the pastor.* Women spoke repeatedly of the weight of priestly authority in the local church. "Your parish council is as strong as your pastor lets it be," said Dora Yelk of Madison, Wisconsin. "The church is the people [who] belong to it," said Sara Whalen, a member of St. Bernard's, the same parish as Dora. "The staff should really take their direction from the people. I'd like to be more involved in liturgy planning, except that there may be a committee but it doesn't work out where you really have any say. It's still all controlled by the priest."

Despite the post–Vatican II promise of collaboration between laity and clergy, women often became discouraged about the possibility of establishing collegial relationships with priests. For forty-five years, "Joanne Grace" and her husband were "pretty heavily involved in church activities and organizations and the last couple of years we've just taken a breather," she said. "Maybe it's the feeling of disillusionment with what we have not accomplished and what is possible in the structure of the Church. We've tried to loosen up the structure to make

---

*Pastor, in Catholic parlance (as opposed to Lutheran parlance where the word refers to any member of the ordained clergy), is the senior priest-administrator of the parish, what Episcopalians call the rector and many Protestant denominations the senior minister.

it more responsive to what we perceive as people's needs and wants and concerns, and less hierarchical." She added: "I think I was discouraged by the process. It seemed to me that in the end people didn't exercise meaningful control or change. If the priestly staff was in sympathy with [something] it would get done, and if not, somehow it would be stonewalled."

Another source of dismay was priestly privilege. "Priests [say] they're for justice in the Church and for equality," said "Kitty Riordan," "but they're standing up there in robes of privilege. They're speaking from a place of power as they stand there. I find that very painful." "I think it's a credit to the nuns that [they] have chosen to try and be a part of the community," Gail Benjamin said. "I think the priests have not had a similar movement, in this country at least. Priests continue to live in a parish house and they continue to have somebody who comes in to clean up for them, even when they're activist priests." "Priests should get out and see how people live," Dolores Reuter said. "This worker priest movement in France was a real good idea."

"I don't have a lot of respect for the ordained," said Sara Whalen. "So many of them that I have met have been really self-centered, they just haven't been all that caring; there have been exceptions, but they've been set up to be these real special people and it's done them harm. It hasn't been helpful to them or to us." May Kast, another member of St. Bernard's who also supports an active role for the laity, offered another perspective on the clergy. "They give their lives to God," she said, "and sometimes I wonder how they put up with some of the parishioners."

Without exception, women spoke with deep admiration of priests who chose to work with the poor, whether in rural or urban areas, in the U.S. or abroad. Compassion and understanding, identification with the people of the Church, and the ability to convey the message of the Gospel with conviction—and act in a way consistent with the message—were the qualities women prized the most in the clergy.

Women viewed the clergy with varying emotions including respect, anger, and amused condescension. Some had built solid collegial friendships with priests, marked by a sense of equality and mutual respect. Mary Esther Bernal spoke affectionately and with deep admiration of the rector of San Antonio's Cathedral, Virgil Elizondo, with whom she has worked and prayed for many years: "We met each other and within a month's time he [said], 'You will be my music director and I have great plans.' Well, every time I'd turn around, he'd have a new idea. So I would try to beat him at his game of creativity." During the liturgy, Mary Esther said, "he is at the altar and my choir sings up in the loft and we communicate, it's like mental telepathy."

One of the women I met had had an intense crush on a priest that had endured for several years. Another spoke of a close female relative who was in love with a priest; he had moved in with her but continued his ministry and did not appear to have plans to leave the priesthood.[11] "[He's been there] about three years," the woman I interviewed commented, "and I imagine he'll be around forever." Of the two women I met who had married priests, Mary Olivanti and Sarah Hofheinz, both had begun the relationship as friends. Sarah Hofheinz met her husband in the late 1960s while he was a Catholic chaplain at the college she attended but, she remembers, "I never went to him as a priest. It was just a very healthy, lovely friendship." Her husband was laicized and they were married in the Catholic church. They have remained practicing Catholics. Mary Olivanti's husband did not apply for laicization when he resigned from his religious order in the late 1970s.* Friends and partners in marriage, Mary and her husband became colleagues in the ordained ministry of the Evangelical Lutheran Church in America during the 1980s. Each couple has two children. Both women said their husbands would have remained in the Catholic priesthood had priests been allowed to marry.

Many women commented on their parish priests' lack of aptitude for mature relationships, on their dearth of social skills, and on their inability to deal with women as peers. ("An incapacity to deal with women as equals should be considered a negative indication for fitness for ordination," the U.S. bishops wrote in the second draft of their pastoral on women's concerns.)[12] Several women suggested that seminary training ought to include education in shared decision-making, group dynamics, and communication skills, as well as awareness of the concerns of women and families. "I don't think you're going to change the males in the Church very soon unless you do it through the educational process," said Abigail McCarthy, who writes a column for *Commonweal,* a magazine edited by lay Catholics. "I have long been pushing for teaching in the seminaries that would emphasize the spirituality of women and the great women saints *as women.*" This education, she felt, could begin to remedy "the total incomprehension of women's lives by the average clergyman. . . . There has been at the same time this totally patronizing attitude toward women and this kind of

*Laicization was far more common during the papacy of Paul VI, when Sarah's husband left the priesthood, than it has been during the papacy of John Paul II, when Mary's husband left.

glorification of their own mothers, of motherhood in the abstract, which has little to do with the reality of motherhood."

This concern for human relationships was often the leading factor in women's support of optional celibacy for priests. Church discipline currently mandates vows of celibacy as a condition for ordination to the priesthood. Well over half the women I interviewed favored a change in this practice. While many raised with some alarm the issue of the growing shortage of clergy, their strongest rationales for changing the celibacy rule were relational maturity, capacity for intimacy, and the ability to understand the daily lives of parishioners. Characteristically, women spoke of sex in the context of relationships and of relationships in terms of their quality of intimacy. For them, intimate relationships were the best way of developing empathy. Betty Darko said to me: "I think a man who's married and dealing with a family would be better equipped to counsel people who are dealing with the same type of problems." "For a long time," said Caryl Rivers, "the priesthood attracted two kinds of men: one was very idealistic, burning with the desire to save the world. But it also [attracted and continues to] attract people who fear and distrust intimacy and find in this kind of life a way to avoid it. I think it's very sad that a lot of priests live without intimacy—not so much sex per se, but the kind of intimacy that [you have] when you are married and you have children."

Most of the women who favored changing the celibacy rule seemed to consider marriage the only alternative to celibacy. Many voiced the opinion that priests would be not only more effective in their ministry but happier and healthier human beings if they were allowed to marry. They tended to be women who were themselves happily married. As a child, twenty-nine-year-old Bridget Palmer attended an Eastern Rite Catholic church in which priests, as in the Orthodox churches, may marry. "[If I could change the Catholic church]," she said, "I would have there be no celibacy because I think that the pope, who is a man I respect and admire in many ways, would be a lot better if he were married. I think the priests would be a lot better." Mary Esther Bernal declared: "They ought to be given that choice. It's very difficult for a person to dedicate his or her life to religion and do it well. However, seeing how Joe and I are able to balance each other—he lets me participate in the religious arena just like I let him in the educational arena—I don't see why it wouldn't work out for a priest to have a wife." "Or a husband?" I asked. "Or a husband," she said, smiling.

Women who supported the Church's current discipline of priestly celibacy (a significant minority of about one third) often favored celibacy for practical reasons: They felt it allowed for a more complete commitment of time and energy to the work of ministry. "Their priority has to be their community," said Beatrice Cortez, who also felt that celibacy was the sign of a total commitment to God. "A priest is on call to his community at all times." A smaller number of women associated celibacy with holiness, but were often vague in their explanations. "It seems to make you more in touch with the spiritual nature of things," Christine Torrey said. Women who favored optional celibacy for clergy tended to value priests' ability to identify with and be a part of the faith community—economically, emotionally, and spiritually. On the other hand, women who supported the present church discipline tended to view separation and difference from the community as a good; they were more likely to identify holiness with being set apart.

There seems to be a direct correlation between women's lived experience of other religions and their support of optional celibacy for priests. During the interviews, I was struck by the fact that many of the Mexican-American women from south Texas were opposed to ordination of married men. When they voiced their support for priestly celibacy, they usually stated that married Protestant ministers could not handle their pastoral responsibilities because of their commitment to their families. Or occasionally—still speaking of Protestant clergy— they would comment that being celibate was a holier state for a minister than being sexually active. I wondered at first whether their view of the relationship between celibacy and ministry had something to do with culture. Then I began to follow up with another question: Had they ever met any of these noncelibate clergy? None of them had. Unlike the women who were in favor of allowing clergy to marry, they had lived all their lives in exclusively Catholic environments. Their statements about the lack of effectiveness and spiritual depth of married clergy were based on pure conjecture.

Despite the central role of the clergy, "It's amazing the amount of participation there is in the average parish," Abigail McCarthy remarked. "We take so many things for granted now that we thought we would never see, like communion in the hand and women Eucharistic ministers, lay readers. Those don't even seem very adventurous things now." "I have loved the Church more since there's been more participation," said May Kast. "You feel more a part. You don't feel as though there's the priest and you're down here, and you're praying but you really don't have much to say about all this, you got to leave it to the priest. Now it's participation and lectors and lay ministers. You do feel as though you're more part of church. Not that you were apart from God before," she laughed, "because you weren't anything and the priest was [something]."

Always, everywhere, women wished for even more participation and partnership, and took for granted the need for the laity to be involved in the internal life of the Church—not just as helpers but as policy-makers, not just as listeners but as speakers. Most of the women I interviewed felt that the faith and experience of church members ought to play a stronger part in determining the universal church's direction and identity. "Church belongs to the people," seventy-six-year-old Pauline Jones said, "not to the clergy, not to the bishops, but to the people." Having spent her life "educating people about racism and advocating voices of black people in church structure," Pauline considered "a strong laity" her greatest priority for the Church, and added, "I feel very strongly that it should be more catholic in the sense that it should embrace all ethnic groups."

"One of the things I find most offensive about the treatment of Curran and Hunthausen," said Abigail McCarthy, "is the assertion by one of the archbishops involved that you can't tolerate what will 'confuse the simple faithful.' Well, there are no 'simple faithful' anymore. We don't have the peasant Catholic; we have people who are constantly exposed to the most complicated issues on television, you have a highly educated population, and to speak of them as the 'simple faithful' is to live back in the last century."

Asked for her wishful vision of change in the Church, Mar Londo responded: "that the hierarchy of the Church would really be willing to listen to the laypeople and what causes them pain, and how they've been sinned against, ostracized, and not forgiven." She shared another vision, akin to the first: In it, she saw "grass-roots people sitting in on all the important conversations with the pope and he's really listening to them because he is so much a mirror of Christ; he really hears—hears with an open mind." She added, "There would have to be a court jester, someone who at least once an hour would make them take a break, and tell jokes and play back to them all their most ridiculous moments."

The status of women was a recurring issue.[13] "Thirty or forty years ago," Dolores Reuter remembered, "the only time a woman could go up on the altar was when she was cleaning it or when she got married. That was it. It was all right for us to go up and scrub and polish [but not to do anything else]. I think women are [still] second-class citizens in the Catholic church," she added. "The fact that girls can't be altar girls is just stupid. And as far as I'm concerned my daughter would have made a much better priest than any of my sons. I'm sure that there's a lot of other parents that feel the same way."

Still, some women were more reluctant to question church authority than to address the issue of women's role in secular institutions. Saying, "All is not well between women and men" in the workplace is already difficult; saying it about intimate relationships is harder still. To say it about the institution that has been the primary giver of meaning and moral guidance can be a fearful experience. Some women objected to the openly critical stance other women have taken toward the church hierarchy, in much the same way as they criticized "pushy women" advocating feminist social change in society. "The vocal few give a distorted view," said Margaret Slattery. "I'm for women, but I get very annoyed. . . . I see them as being too negative in their approach." "I have a hard time with the way some of the nuns and some other women have taken on the pope," Mary Callanan said. "I don't always agree with him but I wouldn't be about to stand up in public and tell him he's wrong."

When we spoke about women in the Church, the three recurring concerns of the women I interviewed were acknowledgment of women's gifts and devotion, inclusion of women in decision-making, and expansion of women's roles.

Over and over, they pointed out that churches would stand still without women, who still form the great majority of worshipers, volunteers, and participants in educational programs.[14] "Women are really the backbone," Pauline Jones observed. Often, women felt they received from the clergy and from the Church at large neither respect nor recognition. "It makes me angry," one woman said, "that women aren't given the same kind of respect [as men] and are expected to do so much." Betty Anne Nogan, the public administrator from New York, serves on her parish's finance committee in Brooklyn. "It kills me," she said, "that all the people in my parish who are really active are women; the vast majority of people at any given Mass are women. The people that do the work are women. And the fact that it's all led by men seems very unfair to me."

"When you think of what women have been in the Church," said "Kitty Riordan," "what we have done in the Church. The women's society at my parish many years ago did all kinds of wonderful programs, and one of the first ones was a participatory Mass, a Mass at which the congregation answered the prayers. This was one of the very first in our parish, spearheaded by this small group of women from the Ladies' Society. After that first Mass, the men said, 'Well, that's not a good thing for women to be doing,' and they took it over. I never knew what happened. Suddenly it wasn't ours anymore. That's called 'co-opting your work.' 'Don't let men co-opt your work' was one of the first things I read when the women's movement started. And I thought, 'That's what happened there!' "

"Women are the nurturers of religion in families," said Barbara Kern. "It seems very strange that they have so little to do with the controlling." Dorothy Wodraska hoped this book "would be a positive picture of the nurturing the Church has done for its women [and the way] it has allowed our nurturing natures to be expressed." She also wished that the Catholic church would "involve more women in decision-making positions, not just window-dressing: I think women should be [on boards and commissions] and I think they should be heading them and there should be an even balance on them."

"The Church is still run by men," said "Sylvia Presti," who also spoke of the Church with deep feeling as "the one place where I will always be accepted." "Many of the men still see the women as someone to cook the parish dinner and have the bake sales," she said.

Fewer than half the women I interviewed had heard of the U.S. Catholic bishops' pastoral letter on women's concerns, a project the bishops launched in 1983. The bishops had been holding public hearings around the country for well over a year at the time I began my research in 1986. A few of the women I met had participated in these consultations in their dioceses.[15] Others told me their diocese had no plans to hold such meetings. Many of them heard about the existence of the pastoral for the first time from me. "Are you aware that the American bishops are working on a document about women's concerns?" I would ask. "What do you think of the idea?" The most common reaction, across the board, around the country, was laughter. My notes read "chuckles," "laughs loudly," "laughs softly," "laughs long and hard." "I think it's quite hilarious," "Joanne Grace" answered when I asked what she thought of the bishops' project. "God bless them. I will certainly read it with great interest." "But you sound very skeptical," I said. "I sound very skeptical indeed, yes," "Joanne" responded.

The pastoral has met with public reactions ranging from feminists' advice that the project be dropped and that the bishops instead address the issue of sexism* to more traditional women's criticism that the bishops were being unduly influenced by secular feminism, a concern

---

*The bishops did, in fact, name sexism as a sin in the first two drafts of the pastoral, but the question of "women's concerns," not "sexism," was the pastoral's stated topic.

also raised by the Vatican. In the private reaction of women I met—laughter—I heard above all a credibility gap. Feeling that many of the clergy do not understand or respect them, wounded by official teaching on divorce, independent thinkers in their decisions about birth control, many women are not prepared to listen to what the bishops have to say about women's lives. Neither are women well disposed toward hearing about equality and mutuality from men who will not let their daughters serve as altar girls.

It may be that the pastoral was of greater use to the bishops than to the women themselves. The first draft of the pastoral, "Partners in the Mystery of Redemption," issued in 1988 (the document was subsequently revised and renamed), was above all a testimony to a conversion process: The bishops began to pay attention not only to the experience of women, but to their own isolation from this experience. The introduction to the draft acknowledged "the helplessness of minority women trapped in a cycle of crushing poverty, the exhaustion of mothers trying to maintain a family, a home, and outside employment, the frustration of intelligent women being stereotyped as emotional and incapable . . . the anguish of women who have wide-ranging spiritual and intellectual gifts that could be of service to the Church, but who are not afforded the chance to use [them]." After this enumeration, one could almost hear the bishops say, in hushed voices, "We had no idea."

"There is so much power in women that is repressed and under-tapped" said "Elsa Colón." "My anger is not anger at the Church or at individuals," Mary Hunt said firmly. "What I grieve is the lack of fulfillment of potential. It makes me weep; it really does."

FIFTEEN

KATHI BOWERS WALLIS

"It infuriates me what the Church is doing."

Kathi Bowers Wallis was just under forty-four when we met. Raised in a predominantly Catholic neighborhood in Silver Spring, Maryland, she lives in Washington, D.C., with her husband and two young sons, Gavin and Quinn. Her maternal grandparents were Irish and Norwegian and "came over at a time when you forgot everything about where you came from." She is not sure about her father's ancestry. At the time of the interview, Kathi was a full-time mother after a decade as a successful businesswoman.

My father was an FBI agent for over twenty years. The FBI recruited a lot of Catholics. Hoover was famous for that. My theory is that Catholics produced a lot of kids, so it was kind of like they were indentured slaves. I worked at the FBI for a couple of summers when I was in college and almost everybody I worked with was Catholic. I think Hoover felt that Catholics made good agents: They had certain moral feelings and attitudes—duty and hard work, the great American values. My father would go to work in a car pool from our neighborhood with other agents.

My father's a convert to Catholicism. We refer to him as "the pope." There's nothing worse than a convert. As a matter of fact, he just got back from Yugoslavia [where he went] to see the apparition at Medjugorje.* [When we were growing up] he would go to church [almost] every day. Of course with six kids my mother didn't have that option. Six kids wasn't a huge family; there were families with nine and ten. They probably would have had more kids if my mother hadn't given out: at about thirty-two she had to have a hysterectomy.

In that era you were supposed to say the Family Rosary for Peace and there would always be lots of fights over who got the rosary and

---

*A town in Yugoslavia that has become a place of pilgrimage in the past decade due to reported apparitions of the Virgin Mary.

who got to say the mysteries.* We had a rosary rack and the rosaries were all hung up and we all wore scapulars. We lived two blocks from the church, and anything we were involved in, the CYO, sports, my parents' social life, it was all through the church. I didn't feel deeply religious on any level. I went to church on Sunday, I went to confession; religion was something that was part of your life. On Fridays you knew you didn't have meat; that was just the way it was. It was what was expected of you. A lot of it was rote.

An awful lot of what was drummed into us in school was done through fear—"If you don't you'll be punished"—whether it was learn-ing arithmetic or whether or not you were going to heaven. I had Franciscan nuns; in high school I had the Religious of Jesus and Mary and—God, I can't even remember who I had in college, isn't that terrible? [I went to] Immaculata right here in D.C.. It's now closed.

Everything was wrong. Things you wouldn't even think about. Sleeveless dresses were occasions of sin. Shoes that were cut too low that showed the cracks of your toes were sinful. They were always on the lookout, particularly when you started to go into puberty. From sixth grade on, they were ready to pounce and to stop anything. Con-sequently, any parties you had then, everybody played Post Office and Spin the Bottle, because you were all of a sudden alerted to the fact [that] hey, something's going on here. You talk to any kids who were brought up in that era, we'll all have the same kind of recollections.

[After college] I packed up and moved to California. It was won-derful. It was in '64 and it was the beginning of the hippie era. I went out there with a very good friend, Tish, who was brought up Catholic, and another friend who was not. I had started asking questions to myself and considering what the Church was saying. I think out of laziness I didn't go [to Mass]. And I was away from home for the first time when I didn't have somebody looking over my shoulder: [Back home] you got up and went to church; didn't matter how old you were, as long as you were in the house. Tish was going to get married and start a family and I remember us vaguely arguing about why did you have to have children right away. We were all virgins and you know, "girls didn't," and I was questioning that. Although I was a virgin—there was no way anyone was going to touch me! But I won-dered why it was so inherently wrong, as we had been taught, and

---

*The Rosary is made of three sets of five meditations on the "mysteries" (events in the lives of Jesus and Mary): the Joyful Mysteries, the Sorrowful Mysteries, and the Glorious Mysteries. In a group recitation of the Rosary, one person announces each mystery.

purposely set out at one point to lose my virginity, to get it over with. I can remember waking up the next day and walking down to the water in Sausalito and thinking to myself, "I am alive, I have not been struck down." I was almost twenty-one. Couldn't believe the fact that I was still functioning, arms and legs attached to my body. [Of course] it was a terrible experience, as it was for almost everybody! But what I remember about it more than anything was being amazed that I was not struck down. Having been so hammered at for so many years about how wrong so many things are, particularly sexuality, it was astounding to me.

I think that being married, being with somebody you love and who loves you changes your view of your body and of sex. Being brought up Catholic, you're never totally uninhibited, because so much was pounded into us over the years. But being loved and loving someone back releases you of an awful lot of anxieties and worries about your physical self.

I probably grew up with a negative view [of my body]: When I got to that age when you start being interested in boys, seventh and eighth grade, I was so much taller than everybody else. I was very well liked by the girls and kind of the class clown, but basically pretty inept and shy around boys. I don't know if that had anything to do with the Church's teaching; I think that was just dealing with my own physical self.

And of course you were told everything was wrong. We had retreats in high school where the priest would come in and say you couldn't sit on a boy's lap; you had to sit on a telephone book. You couldn't dance a certain way, and you couldn't hold hands in public. I'm sure that probably reinforced feelings of being awkward and not knowing what to do about yourself and your relationship with a boy. And of course boys were told the same thing. You only went out with Catholic boys; God forbid somebody from a public school should even call up. You didn't get to meet those kind of people. Our next-door neighbors were Jewish and they were very close to us [but] they had no kids. There were Protestant people in our neighborhood but they were in the minority. We used to call them "the publics" because they went to the public school down the block.

I came back here and found the East Coast very provincial, very conservative, after being in San Francisco. I lived in Georgetown with a group of girls. We worked at Georgetown Hospital. We were all going to snag a doctor. Ha-ha—none of us did. I worked with a cancer specialist as his assistant with the patients, helping with the bandages and the procedures in the office. I liked it a lot but I left it. My brother, who was fifteen months younger than I, was killed in Vietnam, and between his death and the fact that I was dealing with a lot of people who were dying in that job, I left.

He was killed in 1967. I've *never* reconciled myself to that, because of the waste. We had to wait two weeks for his body to come home. It was like a two-week wake. God, it was horrible. My parents spent that period of time saying their faith, their faith got them through it. And maybe it did. That was kind of the coup de grâce for me with Catholicism and God for a long time. I couldn't understand my parents saying their faith was getting them through it because I felt that he had died so senselessly, for nothing. I can understand their saying that they were proud of him, that their faith helped them to hold on, but to me it was senseless, and I blamed God.

I was protesting and marching adamantly against the war. My parents and I were very split on it. Johnny and I talked about it but when I knew he was going I backed off. And I never let him know in the letters what I was doing here.

After all that I just didn't want to deal with anything around the medical field. I had a series of jobs, not getting anywhere, and was dating a lot of people. Then I opened my own business in 1970. It was very successful. As a matter of fact it's still functioning. A Canadian company bought it; I sold it in '79 when I decided to retire and become a mother.

My mother was delirious when David and I got engaged. "She's getting married, she's getting married, praise God, she's getting married." I was in my late twenties when I got married; fifteen years ago that was considered old. My husband's five years younger than I am and my mother was horrified. Since then my old roommate has married a fellow twelve years younger and another friend has married another guy eleven years younger, but fifteen years, ago, five years younger was not something one did. But he's old for his years. He says I've aged him.

We got married by a Jesuit—you know, Jesuits will marry anybody. We wrote part of the ceremony and the priest wrote part of it. We got married on the C & O Canal barge because we could not get a dispensation from the Archdiocese of D.C. to get married within an actual church because David wasn't Catholic and he wouldn't take instructions. We asked [our friend] Ray, [who is a diocesan priest], to marry us and he couldn't. So that's why we went and got Marty, [the Jesuit]. My father said if we weren't married by a priest my sisters could not be in the wedding.

When David very old-fashionedly went to talk to my father about getting married, my father told David that birth control was illegal. Not immoral, illegal! And we were living together at that point. My mother knew but I think my father didn't want to know. My mother has become much more adept at rolling with what goes on with her kids.

The children have not been baptized. Once again we went to Ray, to ask him to baptize Gavin, just to keep peace in the family with my parents, and he wouldn't because neither of us could stand up and say that we would raise this child as a Catholic and honestly say that we believe things that need to be said during the ceremony. Probably my parents have baptized both of the kids; we've had to travel frequently over the years and we've always figured while we were away they did it; it must have made them feel good and it certainly doesn't bother me.

I'm not raising my kids in any structured faith. My husband has a very hard time even believing in a God. He was raised Episcopal. If I *wanted* to take my kids to church I don't think he would strongly object to it. *I* believe in God. I believe, and I have always taught both of the kids about God, and that Christmas, Easter, the various religious holidays, they're not just for bunnies and presents. Gavin went through a period of time when he talked about God a lot, when he was about four years old. We would have conversations about God. I went into the backyard one day and he was looking up. I said to him, "What are you doing?" He said, "I'm talking to God." I said, "About anything in particular?" He said, "Oh no, I was just asking some questions that I couldn't get a good answer for." And I said, "Is He answering you?" [He said], "Yeah, yeah, sometimes He does." He wouldn't tell me what the questions were.

Over the past few years I have been thinking about God and my relationship with Him, and also my children's relationship to Him, because of having a lot of friends in very unfortunate, unhappy circumstances, where for me God seemed to me to be the only person to turn to. When there's no other answer, when you can't seem to figure anything out, when you see people you love suffering and in pain, [that's what you do]. I found myself talking to God. My very close friend in Boston, Bonnie, is dying with cancer; she's a year younger than I. And we have another very dear friend, a man, who has cancer.

We have several acquaintances who have terminal cancer. I have friends whose child came down with cancer. We just discovered David's mother has lung cancer. In the past two years it seems like we have had a series. David says he thinks it's on the seats; every time we turn around someone else is getting a cancer. I'm convinced we're all going to die of it.

I've been practicing hatha yoga. Yoga turns you more inward. My instructor puts a strong emphasis on God—whatever God you want to believe in. We start every session with a prayer; we end with a prayer. Recently it's been the prayer of Saint Francis. Then there's another prayer about peace, letting peace happen in the world and starting with individuals. It's all inward, trying to calm yourself, to free yourself of the anxieties and tension that we all carry, and be a better person physically and spiritually. I've given up red meat, caffeine. I'm trying to get my children to eat differently, trying to produce a less stressful environment all the way around, from what you eat to the way you look at things.

Jesus is God. I don't differentiate. I have no special affiliation to any saint. I think they uncanonized a whole bunch of them, didn't they? I don't know who is and isn't anymore. I think Mary and Joseph are still up there but I'm not sure about anybody else. My friend Kathy has a special devotion to Mary; I can't connect with that at all.

I pray when I need help! It's a conversation. When I have prayed about Bonnie I have literally gone down on my knees. I don't know why, but somehow I felt that on my knees was what I needed to do for her. I don't believe she'll get better. But I ask God to keep giving her the strength to keep getting through it. I do a lot of visualization with her, particularly in yoga class. I don't know whether you can send vibes to people or not, but I picture her a lot in my mind and think very positive and good things about her. It makes *me* feel better. As a matter of fact Bonnie was taught visualization when she got cancer. When our friend Paul got so ill with cancer his wife, who is a practicing Catholic, was convinced that he recouped so well from the first operation because so many people were thinking of him and praying for him and concerned and sending good vibes.

When I pray there's no image at all. It's like, "Here I am God, now this is what I've got to say today." I've thought several times about going to a church to pray, but then I've thought to myself, "No, that's not you, it's not necessary for you to do that." My friend Kathy's been praying for me for years. She figures that one of these days I'm going to come back to the Church. And that was one of the reasons my father went [on pilgrimage] to Yugoslavia, to bring his children back to the Church: None of us are practicing Catholics. I figure I have enough people praying for me that I'm a shoe-in, somehow or another.

Kathy and I have long talks and lots of laughs about it. She and my friend Maureen are both practicing Catholics who have a lot of questions and don't accept things on blind faith. As a matter of fact, Maureen and I were talking about the homosexual issue within the Church. It infuriates me what the Church is doing, and I was surprised that it really upset her, to the point where she has not been going to church. I was just reading in the *Times* on Sunday about the church group Dignity. It's obscene! You can be a murderer and go to confession and everything's all right and you can still be in the Church, but you can't be homosexual. It just does not make sense to me. If a person is a good person what the hell difference does their sexuality make? I have a couple of friends who are gay, they have been quote-unquote "married" for about twelve years. I've met friends of theirs who have been together nineteen years; these are monogamous men who are in a relationship which is not what you would call natural, but they love each other, they care about each other, and why should they be denied the solace of a church if that's what they want? I don't understand the reasoning.

The pope looks like such a jolly fellow, and his public relations have been wonderful. But at the same time he comes down so hard on too many issues, maybe on the basis that if he didn't the Church would completely fall apart—although it doesn't seem to be doing a whole hell of a lot of enormous recruitment; even with priests and nuns, they don't seem to be getting anybody anymore.

Catholics always feel they're *right* about everything. Always! As a kid I always felt sorry for people who weren't Catholics because they wouldn't get to heaven—I mean, it was just such a shame, if you could just bring them into the Church they'd be saved. A lot of my very good friends are Jewish. I've often wondered why. Probably because we're all brought up with the same type of guilt. I think there are many paths to God. It doesn't matter how you get there. You could be a good Buddhist, a good Episcopalian, a good Catholic, who cares?

I have so many friends, Catholic and non-Catholic, practicing and nonpracticing, who have had their tubes tied, I said we ought to start an association. I had my tubes tied and my mother was appalled. I said, "Look, I'm forty years old, with my second child, and I'm not going to have any other kids." I just don't see anything wrong about it, and I know practicing Catholics who have done the same thing. I don't think many people seriously hold to what the Church teaches about birth control. I do think that when you bring up the abortion issue it's very volatile. I mean, it's not something you want to bring up at a dinner party. It's a very emotional issue and we have friends who are wonderful people who are on both sides of the fence—friends who think abortion is murder and other friends who feel like I do— and there doesn't seem to be any changing of the minds on that issue. I think it must somehow come from your own life, what has happened or not happened to you. Well, maybe religion plays a part in it. But I have a devout practicing Catholic friend who had an abortion. It was a very traumatic thing for her but she went to confession about it and she said she felt a weight had been lifted from her. I was amazed that she could confess it and feel, "Okay, that's over and done with now." She feels pro-choice but she doesn't talk about it much [though personally she had trouble with having an abortion].*

That bishops' letter on women ought to be a humdinger. It's just like a group of male gynecologists getting together and deciding what women's bodies should look and respond like. Not that the whole letter would be on the sexual aspects, but it just strikes me as a little ludicrous that these men are going to get together when they don't allow women diddly squat within the Church anyhow, and now they're going to give us another letter telling us how better to keep our places. It's absurd.

I would certainly like to see the Church's position on women within the Church changed. The guys are always in charge. It's the same system that happens in the business world—[but] you expect more out of the Church for some reason.

When I started my business there was an awful lot of prejudice. A few of us in D.C. who were business owners had come up with slaps in the faces by various banking institutions and men in business and we were all tired, and we thought we could do an Old Girl Network that would provide us with some clout. We started [the Association of Women Business Owners] about '73 and now it's quite a big organization. I'm definitely a feminist. Yet when I decided to have a child I decided to stay at home. But I had made my success and done what I wanted to do and financially I could stay at home and have a child and still be paid for my business.

---

*In an update interview two and a half years later, Kathi told me she had marched at the large pro-choice demonstration in Washington the previous spring with a group of women in their forties and their teenage daughters, "from all different backgrounds and religious beliefs." "I [hadn't] marched in a long time, not since the Vietnam War," she added. "No one wants to have an abortion but you should be able to decide the issue for yourself."

Not that it wasn't difficult. That first year was very difficult for me; not being around adults, that was hard. My son Gavin only really knows me as a traditional mother. When I went back to work it was very concerning to him: He wanted to know what time I was leaving, what time I would be home, what I was doing during the day, because he had never known that I had another life. I took him upstairs once and showed him pictures and articles and awards; I was on one of my days where I felt he was assured I was a moron. He just couldn't quite understand that I had ever worked, that when we got married his father *didn't* have a job and *I* had the job. He doesn't connect.

Myself and another woman are the only women at home on this whole block; everyone else works. And I think, why not? My concern is women who believe that they can have it all. I don't think you can. I don't think you can have a real high-powered career *and* kids *and* a relationship with your husband and all the super-ness that women are supposed to be able to control. I've seen too many women burn out with it. I don't know what the answer is.

Feminism to me means options, primarily. That a woman has the same education [as a man] and has the options to do what she wants to do with her life and shouldn't be discriminated against because she's a woman. I think discrimination still continues. I think it always will. I don't ever think the day will come [when it doesn't], because women bear the children. The day will never come when we have the same maneuverability in business that men do. When you talk to women who have a little age on them, they find that out after a while. And if you *don't* burn out, something else short-circuits in your life.

[David] is an eighties father—or a seventies father. We have help, as you can see, but we spend time with the kids at night reading together, or David will put one in the bath when he comes home; he's always been like that. I've always told my friend I married a younger man because there were no set standards on how I had to be and how I had to act and what was expected of me, and I always found that older men had a preconceived notion of how a woman should be, and David's never been like that. If I came home and one side of my head was blue and one was orange he'd say, "Well! That's interesting." It's wonderful. He's happy with whatever I do.

We *talk* to the kids a lot. It's a lot more open than in my day; I think it was partly the era we grew up in, and the fact that when you have a big family you don't spend a whole lot of time talking and explaining and answering questions. There isn't a question Gavin couldn't ask me. Nothing would bother me. I want that kind of communication always. And I did not grow up with that.

I have a friend who's married with six kids and is seeking an annulment. She'll probably get it; it's just a matter of writing enough letters and being connected in the right places. It's ridiculous for her to be seeking an annulment. She's going to say he was nutsy or something before she married him; well, everybody told her that. She wants to remarry and it's important to her to remarry within the Church. I say what difference does it make? You want to get married again, get married, rather than not being able to get married in the Church or receive the sacraments because you're divorced. My friend Maureen whom I mentioned before is divorced; she has been going to church, she *has* been receiving the sacraments. Her theory is, the first marriage didn't work out, she's happy, she's a good person, she's remarried, she has a child, and nobody's going to keep her away from the Church. [She and her second husband] got married by a [Protestant] minister. Why shouldn't she be able to go into church and receive the sacraments? I think probably more Catholics are doing that. They're making those decisions on their own. I think they have to, because the Church's stand on it is absolutely ridiculous. It's as if the Church is making Catholics go back to that era I was brought up in where you didn't think, you didn't question, you just accepted everything on blind faith. Well, that's not the world we live in anymore. People don't do that.

Overall it's the inflexibility of the Church that I would want to change. If they had more flexibility within the Church they would not have as many people falling away. That seems very simplistic but it's what I see. I have heard over the years about priests within local parishes where parishioners will go for help, and they get someone who doesn't know about life and counsels them in a very rigid, narrow, confining way, and doesn't help them, who if anything turns them back into another quagmire of problems. Maybe in little parishes all across the world there are gifted priests who are able to counsel and deal with people, give them the right sense of direction, but I think that is unique.

I have tended to vote Republican, although I have a Democratic heart on a lot of things, because I have always felt Republicans were good for business. [In our update interview, Kathi was much more critical of the Republicans.] When I was in business I was particularly concerned about that, selfishly. I'm very concerned about the nuclear arms race. I don't know where we're heading. SANE, any of those things that come to the house, I usually give money to; if they were going to march someplace I'd go and march. I feel helpless about it. I feel that it's been taken out of our hands and there's not a whole hell of a lot we can do about it, which makes it even scarier. The marching and the protesting about Vietnam accomplished something. But this is so enormous and out of control. People are raising their voices but even that . . . I feel very, very discouraged about it.

Somebody asked me not too long ago whether Gavin was concerned about that. I said no, nothing that's ever been mentioned, although he's heard us talking about it. What has struck Gavin more than anything is the *Challenger* blowing up. He had wanted to be an astronaut. Not too long ago I got him a book from the library about astronauts and I said, "Wouldn't you like to go up in that?" He said, "Un-UNH." I said, "Why not?" He said, "It can blow up!" I said, "Yeah, but Gavin, it just hardly ever happens, it's so minuscule." He said, "I'm not taking that chance." I was surprised that it had made that much of an impression on him.

I do believe in capitalism. I think it's the only system that works. It unfortunately leaves a lot of "have-nots" in a very precarious situation. The gross national debt seems to be another horrifying thing. I don't pay much attention to that because I figure, what the hell, it's only going to get bigger and God knows what'll happen. I would like to see something done about the whole welfare system. [One of] the few things I have liked that Reagan has done is the theory that people need to pull for themselves and do for themselves. I believe that's absolutely true, whether it's raising money for the opera guild or learning to work to get your welfare check; there has to be a sense of accomplishment and pride. D.C. certainly has its share of homeless and down-and-outs and welfare recipients and people who for generations have not had a chance. What can be done with them long term, I don't know, when generation after generation has been on welfare. But the theory that you've got to give people their dignity and their pride before they can accomplish anything is the only thing that makes sense to me. People *have* to have something to strive for.

I don't think success is money, although that is what most of the world calls success. Success is contentment with yourself; being at ease with who you are and what you are and what you have in life; to be able to laugh easily and have good friends; to love people and have people love you—God, it sounds like a greeting card!

I believe that when someone dies, a part of that person lives on generationally, certainly in looks and attitudes but also in a certain spirit. Heaven must be being reunited with the people you love. It's hard for me to put God into that picture. I just envision peacefulness and serenity. I do believe there's something afterward. My husband doesn't. Kathy and I call each other up and talk about "the weekly travail." She has an Irish background also, so we talk about "the travails" and laugh about the fact that it's got to be better somewhere else, it's got to be better when we go home. We laugh about it, but maybe subconsciously what we're saying is, well, we do believe it.

Kathi Bowers Wallis went back to work two years after our interview as vice-president of a consulting firm. She had also begun "investigating the Quaker religion," she said. Her friend Bonnie, who had recently died, was a Quaker.

SIXTEEN

WHY THEY LEAVE AND
WHY THEY STAY

The only thing that makes the Church endurable is that it is somehow the Body of Christ and that on this we are fed.
—Flannery O'Connor

"Nobody leaves the Catholic Church," Jimmy Breslin once said.[1] Is this true of women? Over the course of several years, I met a growing number of women who, like Kathi, were no longer active Catholics; a few had joined other religious bodies. I also interviewed converts, women who had chosen, often as young adults, to embrace the Catholic faith and become members of the Church. The majority of the women I encountered, born and raised in the Catholic church, continued to define themselves as Catholics. But they often did so on their own terms rather than those articulated by church leaders or by the Catholic church of their youth.[2]

After months of sifting through the interviews, I began to notice the frequency of the language of feeding and nourishment in women's accounts of leaving and staying in the Church. Then the same words started to crop up in other places. "The Catholic church is not feeding them," a woman explained in a televised interview about new forms of worship and community among Catholic feminists.[3] This language might come naturally to any group of women, since women have traditionally devoted much of their lives to feeding others. All the more reason for women whose central religious ritual is a meal to speak of spiritual and communal fulfillment in terms of food.

"I go to church to feed my soul and that's why I'm having such a hard time," said Susan Johnson, who was shaken by some of the changes of Vatican II. "I was getting no feed for myself," said "Serena Townsend," speaking of the exhaustion and depression she had experienced as a young mother married to a corporate executive. Women who had left the Church or stopped going to Mass spoke of hungering, starving, lacking nourishment. "I attended Masses where I just felt angry," Pamela Montagno said, "and I felt not fed, just not fed in any way." "It just wasn't any spiritual food at all," Karen Doherty said of her experience at Dignity. Angela Rodriguez described her private prayer life in this way: "I meditate, I sit and try to become quiet and to listen. The very action of sitting and taking some time to be quiet, that in itself feeds me."

Pastoral care was one of the most basic forms of nourishment women mentioned in their comments about the Church. It had often made a critical difference in their lives in periods of crisis and transition. Birth, puberty, marriage, illness, change in employment, economic difficulty, divorce, death: Women's stories of love and loss of Church revolved around these times.

Iris Palmer, raised a Protestant, came to a Catholic church in Raleigh, North Carolina, in time of deep distress. She found both material and spiritual help at that parish, and stayed on as a member. "I have never known a Catholic church to turn anybody away who needed help," she said. "The Catholic church teaches you you have an obligation to your community, you don't live alone, you live in a world full of other people and you should look out for them as well as yourself." The two things she valued most in the Catholic church, she told me, were the forgiveness she heard preached and saw practiced, and the discretion of priests. "If you go tell a priest something, he's not likely to get up in the pulpit on Sunday morning and discuss what you told him. Some of these other churches you go and talk to a minister in confidence and all your business is in the street. I think a lot of people turn to the Catholic church just for the confidentiality between the priest and the person. And they don't pass judgment on you. I've sent people to a priest and the priest automatically made them feel relaxed by saying, 'Don't be afraid to say anything, I swear there's nothing I have never heard before.' "

Of all the life transitions requiring pastoral care, death and divorce affected women's sense of belonging most decisively. When Sheri Fedorchak's mother was killed in a car accident early in her college years, she found in the Church a place to grieve and be comforted. The priest and sister who served as Catholic chaplains and the community of students with whom Sheri had recently gone on retreat surrounded her with love and made themselves available to her when she needed to talk and weep. "All these people became a real support group for me," she said. "And then I became more active in the Church." For other women, the decisive influence was negative. Pastoral and liturgical concerns often merged in women's stories. "When my grandmother died," said "Rose Mazurkiewicz," "the priest would not bring her into the church because she had married out of her religion. And the day before she died Grandpa had consented to be married by a priest so she could receive the sacraments! Father V. said that after all those years of Grandma not practicing the faith—she went to church but she didn't receive communion—he would not allow her into the church, but would bury her from the vestibule. Well, my mother said, 'Forget it, I'll bury her Lutheran.' *Then* he accepted her into the church, because my mother threatened to bury her Lutheran. These were the kinds of things that never set with me."

Like death, divorce is a wrenching experience, full of desolate grief. Of all the issues that came up in conversations about pastoral care, it was by far the most painful and alienating. Jackie Haber of Hessel, Michigan, the mother of a young divorced woman, commented: "Divorce is a time when the church should be rallying around you rather than kicking you out or making you feel like an outsider." In divorce as in death, the issues of pastoral care and liturgical involvement meet: Personal support and welcome at the Eucharistic table were always linked, in practice and in women's minds. "My sister was married fifteen years to an alcoholic," said one young woman. "[She has been told] that if she is divorced she's not allowed to receive the sacraments; she's not divorced yet but she's been told this by the local priest. Her husband would not let her go to church, he did not want to go to church, and he ridiculed her for her faith. It's ridiculous that because she's trying to change this very destructive relationship she is technically banned from the Church. She is still going to church but not as often, and she's not likely to want to go. Her son just made his First Communion and she got a letter a week later from the church saying, 'You haven't been a regular participant so we are going to drop you from our information letters and mailings and we'll just send you a collection envelope at Christmas and Easter.' She's just so appalled. She threw it away. I think the Church should really be more understanding. This is a person whose life is falling apart and they're saying things like, 'You can't participate with us.' You're an outcast; it's like you're a leper. I don't think these stories are uncommon," the woman concluded. Her sister, she said, was thinking of attending a Protestant church.

Kathy Kasza began to weep when she spoke about the difficulties she had experienced in her home parish after her divorce. When she went to offer her services as a reader at Mass, Kathy's parish priest told her "that it was really nice that I wanted to do that, but if I would get up and be a lector I would be flaunting my situation and that he did not think it was appropriate for me to do it, and that perhaps if I waited several years I could. [Then]," Kathy continued, "our church initiated a plan by which they wanted you to pledge so much money to the church. I was not working at the time, I was living on sixty-five dollars a week, I couldn't pledge. They said, 'No, you can't be a member of the church.' " Kathy was ready to leave the parish when a new priest joined the staff; he asked Kathy to give the parish another chance and invited her to become one of the leaders in the Renew program.

"It's hard to be rejected and then to be rejected by your church," Kathy said after telling me about her husband's desertion, "until some day you wake up and you realize it's people that are rejecting you, not God. Divorce is a reality, a very painful reality that you don't always have a choice in," she said with tears in her voice. "Just because we are divorced, we are not dirty unclean people with no feelings. We are not people who did something wrong and deserve to be punished or excommunicated. We are very real, very good people who have a lot of good left in us, who want to do something not just for ourselves but for other people too." Kathy convened a group of divorced and separated parishioners in the context of the Renew program. In time, her parish began to change. "Thanks to me," she said, "they are much more aware of the fact that there are single parents out there who are hurting."

Several women spoke of a nourishment even more basic than pastoral care. The Church, they felt, should be a safe place that builds up the human person, a place where a woman can learn basic trust and develop self-esteem. Their experiences were very mixed. Janet Kanitz, a convert to Catholicism, found Catholic churches and their parishioners "warmer and just more caring" than other Christian communities. Raised a Catholic, "Sylvia Presti" found the Church to be "the one constant that has never changed" and "the one place I will always be accepted: There's no question, there's no criticism," she said. "I am a total person. I'm accepted there with all my faults, my failings, my good things, my bad things. It's home. I'm all there."

Gaye Lott's feelings contrasted sharply with Janet's and "Sylvia"'s. When Gaye was growing up, her mother, who was divorced and remarried, felt exiled from her church but raised her children as Catholics. Gaye remembers regular requests from the nuns at her school: " 'Gaye,' Sister would say, 'run across the street and pray for your mother, who we know is condemned.'" The Church, she felt, placed impossible demands on her and her peers during their youth in the pre–Vatican II era. "It's a very hard job to be a saint and I thought I probably would never be one," she recalled. Now close to fifty years old, Gaye had finally come to believe that she was good. "I no longer want to feel, 'Oh, Lord, I am not worthy,'" she said. "I had enough of that. I would rather have been told I was a little bit of God." It was the women's movement, Gaye said, that finally gave her a sense of worthiness, pride, and self-respect.

Several women felt the Church was especially delinquent in nurturing self-esteem in women. "I know God loves me as much as God loves any man," said Ann Richards Anderson. "I know that the Church loves me less. What worries me," she added, "is that by staying [in the Church], I collaborate in maintaining the low self-image of women too indoctrinated not to believe churchmen who tell them they are lesser people. This is a sin on the part of the Church. When does my participation also become a sin?"

Over a decade earlier, Ann had returned to the Church after an absence of several years. What drew her back, and kept her in, was the spiritual nourishment she received. "Church gave me a formalized time for spiritual reflection," she said. "Mothers of young children don't have time for anything, never mind a spiritual life. You don't have uninterrupted time. The liturgy gave me that, and the family religious education program did too. That was one of the best things: The kids go upstairs to their classes after Mass, the parents go downstairs to their own time of study and discussion."

Women around the country, hungry like Ann for a deeper relationship with God, complained about the quality of preaching in the parish. "I have great problems with the Sunday liturgy," said Abigail McCarthy. "But all my life I just blocked it out if I didn't like it. The homilies are so terrible. It's so important, it's the one chance at really instructing people and deepening their spiritual life. But these homilies are so ill-constructed. I wouldn't insult a class by giving such a poorly organized rambling presentation; the priests have rather good ideas but they don't take time to prepare well enough so that it holds together. And I really dislike their taking examples from the Donahue show," she added. "I told somebody I was going to get up and walk out the next time somebody started a homily with Donahue. The opportunities to hear really good homilists here in Washington are great," she continued. "So many of the Catholic University and Georgetown priests are helping in the parish; I guess it's some of the pastors and assistant pastors that upset me." "I don't get what I need," said "Cara Marini," who rarely goes to Mass anymore. "I need a message at church—or I just want to go for the service without the sermon. I get real tired of what's being said because it's too general, it's just too love and peace, it's not relevant to what I'm doing. I would want to hear more social-action type sermons, or sermons about how religion touches people in daily lives."

Barbara Kern of Indianapolis was a churchgoer raising her children as Catholics when we met. She liked the ritual and ceremony, she said, but deplored the homilies as "put-downs" and "negative." "It totally frustrates me that the hierarchy of the Church can continue to preach to people on such a meaningless level," she told me. "I don't think the Catholic church looks at who they're dealing with anymore. They're missing out on recognizing a large body of people that do want to have some religious force in their life. If not for the children, I'm not real sure that my participation would be any different than it was in my twenties [when I didn't go]. It's amazing to me to sit in a church where you know people have pretty intelligent thoughts about things and you're not being talked to like you have a mind."

People stay in church because in some way it mediates the divine to them. For many women, the Church failed in this basic mission. "Anne Marie Quinn" now goes to church only sporadically. "When I go to Mass," she said, "I like to feel that it's a real spiritual experience. I like to really get into it a hundred percent. If I find myself sitting in church looking at everybody walking up and down the aisle, I say to myself, 'I'm wasting my time. I'm not getting anything and I'm not giving anything. Why am I bothering? Why am I here?' "

"I would make it more a personal religion," Betty Anne Nogan answered when I asked how she might like to change the Church. "There would be no separation between what is said in a building called church and what you do when you leave the church. It would really be a life-style you carry with you. The church, the people, would be your support group. You wouldn't meet them in a building on Sunday for an hour, not know their name and go home. They would be there with you, you would feel connected with them. The help I need," she said, "is getting the courage together to do things I think are good, not commit those sins that are acts of omission. That's what I want a church to be for me."

When the deeds of the Church did not match its creed, women became frustrated, angry, and disaffected. When deeds and creed were one, women remained attached to the Church—and gave of themselves generously. "To me," said Beatrice Cortez, "the heart of the Catholic church is that it puts a lot of emphasis on social teachings; they have stood up for the unions because they believe in people that have their dignity and self-worth, they did that with education, they do that in terms of protecting the family. They put a lot of emphasis on that, more so than any other [church]." "There are institutional problems that really hold me back from embracing the Church," said "Elsa Colón," a Catholic Charities employee. "My commitment comes from the work that I do daily. . . . I love the work that's being done by the Church around the country, whether it's housing the homeless or community organizing or standing up against the administration's policy in Central America. A lot of that work comes from such a deep base and deep belief in God."

"The greatest threat to the world is not political or economic or military," Richard John Neuhaus writes at the end of *The Catholic Moment.* "The greatest problem in the Church is not institutional decline or disarray. *The* crisis of this time and every time is the crisis of unbelief."[4] Neuhaus must be listening to another part of the population. If the remarkably diverse group I interviewed is any reflection of the roughly thirty million people it represents, there is little crisis of unbelief among American Catholic women. The message of the Gospel, the person of Jesus, the power of the Holy Spirit, the presence of God in the world: These are rarely factors in disaffection from the Catholic church. For many it is the contradiction between the message of Jesus and the lived experience of the institutional Church that has become too much to bear. "If Jesus Christ walked in[to church] tomorrow," Ginny Peck said to me, "he would see all these guys in their robes and say, 'You know, you missed the boat. You really didn't get what I meant. How could you have seen who I was and how I lived my life [and not understood]?' "

I asked Sarah Hofheinz why she went to church. "I think habit is one reason," she answered. "Hope is another. Hope for a lot of things. Hope that the Church will be better, that it will be a more personal experience for me than it has been in a long time. [And]," she added, "it is something that we do for the children."

Women often left the Church or stopped going to church during their adolescent and young adult years. For many of them, this was part of the developmental task of becoming adults, discovering a sense of self distinct from their family of origin and determining whether to reappropriate the values and beliefs they had been taught as children. But Ann Richards Anderson, Sarah Hofheinz, and many others found motherhood a crucial turning point, as women of other faiths often do. They returned to church in search of religious values and structure for their children. Some were moved by the presence of their children to deepen their faith and resume the interrupted task of adult religious development. Others sought support for the difficult work of raising a family. "There's nothing like having children ask religious questions to make you realize there's something missing in your life," Ann Richards Anderson said. Ann returned to church during a period of great stress. The Boston school desegregation crisis was at its height and Ann and her husband, who were in favor of busing at the time and whose oldest child had just started school, were working to make peace in their unsettled Boston neighborhood. Their second child had been born with a cleft lip and palate and required intensive medical care. "I think that was the beginning of my reawakening of the need for some sort of religious or spiritual center to my life," Ann remembered, "because [our oldest son] Michael kept saying, 'Why did this happen? Why is David's face broken?' I said to him, 'Well, I think it's God's way of reminding us that it's not how people look that's important, and it's not how smart people are, it's what their heart is like and if they're loving people.' But in my own heart, I think, was the question, 'Why did it happen to us?' Six or seven people, including our closest friends, said to us, 'If it had to happen to anybody, it's good it happened to you two, because you'll be able to handle it.' Which was meant to be nice, but it was not." The Church did not provide all the answers for Ann, but gave her a safe and welcoming place to ask her questions, one where "what was in the heart" was the highest priority.

"I don't go to church," "Elena Martinez Wise" said to me. "But it's always with me. I feel very blessed." When her daughter was born, "Elena" said, "I truly believed if she was not baptized somehow I was neglecting her. I felt that she would have a communion with God by doing this, even though she was a small child. I felt God would be pleased if I did this."

Other women told me they had stopped going to church when they became mothers, overwhelmed by the demands and pressures of their daily life. "I stopped going," said Judy McDonough, who spent several years in the Philippines as the wife of a United States Information Agency official. "It was too much of an effort. It was enough to take care of my everyday life at that point and religion really took a back seat for a while." After Helen Doggett's divorce, there was no time for church. Economic survival and the care of her family were Helen's first priorities. "I was living in such turmoil," she remembered, "trying to keep everybody together. I was working two jobs. I didn't have time."

Ellen Reuter, in our second interview, spoke of her growing discontent with the place of women in the Church and of her continued commitment to raising her children as Catholics. "Both my husband and I believe kids need a tradition," she said. "It's a good vehicle for teaching values. We want them to know God and to know they're loved by some other being than their parents. I especially want them to know they can screw up and still be lovable to somebody, and they can make mistakes and that's okay, and the Catholic tradition of reconciliation gives them that. Our family rule is that you have to participate in church all the way up to confirmation preparation, which in our diocese is around tenth or eleventh grade, and then you can choose to be confirmed or not. I see it as a developmental thing," she added. "They need to leave the Church as they need to leave home. As they come back home as grownups, I hope they come back to the Church as grownups. What's hard," Ellen concluded, "is knowing I'm putting my stepdaughter and daughter into a system that's not particularly kind to women. But the perverse person in me says, 'Yes, but my baby bishops are going to make a difference.' "

Receiving spiritual and pastoral nourishment from the Church was one of women's greatest concerns when they discussed their church affiliation. Another, though less frequently mentioned, was their agreement and disagreement with church teaching. "I don't believe the pope is infallible. Does that mean I'm not Catholic?" "Cara Marini" asked. "I feel I have to accept it all or leave," said a young woman with whom I struck up a conversation at a professional meeting. Can one, in fact, not accept it all and remain a faithful Catholic?[5] If one disagrees with official church teaching—on infallibility, war and peace, racism, sexuality, economics—is one still a good Catholic, or, some will ask, still a Catholic?[6]

For many women, the answer to the question lay in their relationship to authority and in the way they defined their membership in the Church and the Church itself.

"The Roman Catholic church," Ruth Pakaluk said at the end of our interview, "has an identity and teaching that is completely independent of what any collection of members of that church think, believe, and do. It has to be acknowledged that the Roman Catholic church has a certain definition of itself and rules and expectations that all have an internal consistency. In America we're so used to sampling public opinion to find out what's true. What the individual members say, that's fine, but that doesn't mean that's what the Catholic church teaches or should teach. I think American society has a tough time comprehending that." I asked Ruth whether she equated "Church" with the teachings of the hierarchy. "I wouldn't say I equate it," she answered, "but if you want to know what is the Church and what does it teach that's where you look."

Ruth, a convert to Catholicism, found attractive and reassuring "this idea that you belonged to something larger than you to which you conformed your life and other people also had relationships to this larger thing; you were not responsible for dictating to other people what they ought to do, but there was a competent authority that would help each person. To me it seemed like a liberating idea because in Protestantism I was always plagued by this idea that you had to figure it all out for yourself and you were obliged and compelled to question each individual item of your life and faith." The practice of Catholicism, for Ruth, implied a fundamental and willing conformity with official teaching on all theological and moral questions; for her and her husband, she said, this assent was a sign of "becoming more conformed to what God's will is for you, and that was so different from this kind of mushy, aimless, relativistic quagmire we were in when we were in this Protestant church."

Other women shifted back and forth in their relationship to church authority. "Being a woman has affected me more than being a Catholic," said Betty Darko, whose children attend Catholic schools. "I practice my religion but not in an organized way. I'm not going to church constantly; I'm not involved that much, and most of the people my age [forty] that I know who are Catholic [aren't very involved either], if truth were known." Betty gave spirited and independent answers to my questions on women, family, and church. "I do consider myself Catholic," she said to me. "I feel I have Catholic values and am giving them to my children. Probably I have taken the things that I think are right and discarded some of the others. Which is wrong," she added. "If you are really and truly a Catholic you have to buy everything they want to give you." "Do you?" I asked. "No, I don't," Betty answered, "so I think my definition of being a Catholic is not what the Church would consider being a Catholic." "The Church?" I asked. "The Catholic church," Betty answered, "the Roman Catholic church, the pope. They are the ones who set the rules and make the decisions."

A few women were even more conflicted. RoseMary Fuss had disagreed for a long time with church teaching on birth control. "I see one's sexuality as an issue quite distinct from having children," she said. She stopped going to church "somewhere in the mid-seventies," she remembered. "I felt so compromised. I was a single woman and I felt there really wasn't a place for single people and their life-styles." Nevertheless, she continued to identify herself as a Catholic. Two years before we met, RoseMary and her husband, a divorced Catholic, were married by a Methodist minister. "I felt that whoever married us, the marriage was blessed by God," she said. "I felt an annulment would be hypocritical." A year or two later, when the couple decided to have a family, RoseMary's husband applied for an annulment from his first marriage. She explained: "It became important that the Church play more of a role in our lives than it had and I felt strongly that the only way that could happen was if the Church recognized the marriage." RoseMary was eight and a half months pregnant when we met; her husband had not yet received a determination about the annulment. "The big conflict for me is that it's difficult to baptize this child in a church that doesn't recognize the marriage of this child's parents," she said. "The Church not recognizing divorce is very unrealistic and appears to me cruel and un-Christian." RoseMary had again stopped going to church. "I just find it too difficult and too upsetting," she said. "I find it very difficult to deal with a church that does not recognize my marriage.

"Today," RoseMary said, "I feel there's a degree of hypocrisy on my part if [I disagree with certain positions and stay in], whereas I didn't feel that fifteen years ago. My husband says that in church today there is latitude for personal conviction and good conscience." When they went to church together in the early days of their marriage, he went to communion; she did not. "I felt you don't pick and choose among sacraments. If the Church was not going to marry me, then how could I really participate? There was conflict there. Maybe it's giving too much weight and credence to the Church as an institution; on the other hand maybe it isn't that important. To this day I still don't know."

But a majority of the women—all of whom had some point of disagreement with formal church teaching—identified themselves as Catholics with little sense of conflict. "I think I'm a Catholic, period," said "Cara Marini," answering the question she had asked herself earlier. "I don't consider myself fallen away, I don't consider myself nonpracticing. Although I don't go to church every Sunday and I don't believe everything they tell me and I don't hang on every word the Church says, I'm still basically a Catholic." Some women looked to the Gospel as the authority on what it means to belong: "Jesus was a very strong leader," said Ann Richards Anderson. "But I don't think he ever said, 'You, you, and you, jump out of the boat, because you're not doing exactly what I said.'" Often women looked to internal rather than external definitions of church membership: They were Catholic, they felt, because they knew themselves to be Catholic. "I suspect I feel like I'm a Catholic in the same sense that my husband feels he's a Jew," said Caryl Rivers. "It really doesn't make any whit of difference whether he's been in a synagogue in the past five years. His identity was formed by this culture. That's very much how I feel about Catholicism, that I am Catholic by *my* definition, which is the only one that really matters."

These women, many of them regular churchgoers like Ann, were unwilling to let others, lay or clergy, define them in or out of the Catholic church. "I get very angry about a lot of things in the Church, particularly [issues related to] women," Ann said. "But it's *my* church. They can't take that from me."

Pauline Jones felt the same way about the presence of racism in the Church as Ann did about the position of women: She stayed a Catholic and worked for change. In the 1950s and 1960s, Pauline recalled, she and her companions from the Catholic Interracial League "went all through Maryland in interracial groups, demonstrating by going to church and going to communion together. In one church the black people were all up in the balcony, and by the time they got down, all the other people had been to communion and back, notwithstanding that those [black] people had helped to build those churches with their own money. To educate people on racism and advocate the voices of black people in the church structure, that's always been my interest. I've been in front of that all my life," she added.

Pauline has been a member of the same parish all her life. Feminist theologian Mary Hunt, a generation younger, has left traditional parishes behind, but, she said to me, "I consider myself a terribly committed Catholic insofar as I love the Church enough to want to transform it. All of my work is about living out that faith perspective in ways that I am certain are as Catholic as my mother's belonging to the Legion of Mary, but they simply take a different configuration in my generation."

Catholic women (and Catholic men) continue to define themselves as Catholic because they believe that they, no less than the hierarchy, are the Church. If the Church is a "we" rather than a "they," there is no reason to abandon it; it would be like leaving part of oneself behind. What I heard from many women, despite their struggles to implement this belief in the local parish, was a strong sense of ownership: They belonged to the Church, but the Church also belonged to them. "It's my home," many said. "It's my family," said others. "It's just a part of you," "Clara Taylor" said to me, "even though you may not agree on all the beliefs of the religion." Asked why she and other women stayed in the Church despite their disagreements, Ellen Reuter reminisced about her family reunions. "The women really put them on," she said. "The women put on the food and painted the house; the guys parked the cars and played softball. The women made sure everybody was invited even though they didn't like them very much. That's why women can stay with the Church, because it's like family. Everybody has an Aunt Martha they don't like but still invite."

Culture was another frequent reason women gave for retaining their Catholic identity. For many, Catholicism was a visceral comfort, an affiliation so deeply lodged in their bodies and communal identities that they could not imagine themselves without it. "This Irish face is not going to go anyplace [else]," said Mary Hunt. "For cradle Catholics like me who were brought up in the tradition—for better, for worse—and in an Irish Catholic environment, it is more ethnic than dogmatic. There's a certain way in which the sights and sounds and tastes and smells of the tradition are much, much more compelling than anything about the dogma. [Being a Catholic] is consistent with my native ethnicity." Angela Rodriguez has taken classes on Zen Buddhism and Indian spirituality and exhibited great curiosity and sympathy toward other religions. But she was, she said, "not attracted to be in other churches. I am most at home when I go in a Catholic church. I don't want to be anything else. It's in my blood," she said, touching her lower abdomen, then her heart. "When I go in a Protestant church there's something missing for me. I like the smells in the Catholic church," she concluded.

"I like ceremony," Judy McDonough said cheerfully. "It's good for the spirit." Catholic women's stubborn sense of belonging often seemed linked to their sacramental experience. Bill Thompson, an organizer for Call to Action (a Chicago-based independent Catholic organization advocating church renewal) once observed that this identification with Catholicism "is not rooted in some common creedal expression. Creeds have functioned for people more like a mantra. Learning to say them was like the words to the song. The belonging has more to do with this: 'I get baptized into this. I eat at this table.' "

The Church, women's home, is where they meet God—or hope to meet God—in the breaking of the bread. "That's why I like the Church," said Pauline Jones. "We do have the sacraments and that to me is vital; that's one of the reasons I could never belong to any other church. Being anything else would be against my grain. Even though there is this racism [in the Church]," she said, "it still is better as far as I'm concerned than other faiths; we do have the unity of the sacraments and that sort of pulls us together." "I really struggle with why do I stay Catholic," said Ellen Reuter, "because the Catholic church in so many ways is so abusive to women. There's a lot about the Church that's offensive, but I think I stay because of the liturgy, because of Mass, the Eucharist. I believe real firmly in the reenactment of the Last Supper and that experience of closeness with Jesus. Sacraments, that's what the Catholic church has that no other church has." Three years later, Ellen said: "For me the sacraments are still untarnished by the antics of the clergy and that gives me sustenance, but it's just barely enough."

All religion is local: The local faith community may well be the single most important factor in a woman's decision to leave or stay in the Church, to define herself as in or out. The women I met joined the Church, stayed in the Church, or returned to it because somewhere within commuting distance, like Ellen and Pauline, they had found a congregation to call home. Usually this local church had leaders, both clergy and lay, who were sympathetic, helpful, and inspiring. Women spoke of it as a place of learning, where they could explore and deepen their faith with a group of peers and where the message of the Gospel was preached, taught, and prayed with conviction. They responded to the local church when it was a place of "care and feeding," where staff and parishioners were attentive to each other's grief, joy, and significant life transitions. Finally, women found most enlivening those congregations that recognized their gifts and gave them an opportunity for service, a way to translate their values into action both within and outside the faith community.

Two women I met during my visit to Cincinnati had found this constellation of qualities in their local church. Each woman swore that if she did not belong to this particular parish, she would have a great deal of difficulty remaining involved in the Church.

Roberta Tenbrink, a woman of Dutch and Alsatian ancestry, spoke to me in her apartment, the upper floor of an old farmhouse in a quiet, almost suburban neighborhood. Roberta is a member of the Community of the New Jerusalem, which began as a lay community within another parish and was granted canonical status as a separate parish some years later. Its prayer is in the Charismatic style and spirit, though it did not define itself as Charismatic at the onset. The congregation broke with the national Charismatic movement over the issue of the submissiveness of women, on which the national movement had taken a more traditional position. Women are involved at every level of the Community of the New Jerusalem and the congregation's ministerial team includes priests, laywomen, and laymen, all of whom take an active part in the leadership of the Sunday liturgy and the administration of the parish. The congregation has approximately 250 adults and an equal number of children. Roberta, a full-time social worker, served for a time as a member of the pastoral leadership team. A former Sister of Mercy, she left her order after discovering that a lively parish community could satisfy her desire to live an intense commitment to God better than life as a vowed celibate. "Here was a group of laypeople as excited about the Church as I was, wanting to commit their lives to God, to live the Gospel, still able to raise families, fall in love, live a holy life as married people," Roberta said.

Later the same day, I spoke with Myra Spivey, an African-American woman in her mid-thirties, in the office of Sister Joan, the associate pastor of Mother of Christ Church. Only a few minutes' drive from Roberta's neighborhood, the church stood on the same street as a public housing development of low brick buildings. Myra was single and the mother of two children; she had been divorced for nine years. Mother of Christ is a parish of women and children. Most of the adults are single parents; the great majority of them are black; the staff is white. The liturgy at Mother of Christ is a Gospel Mass with tambourines and hand-clapping, at once unmistakably Catholic and a lively experience of worship in the Afro-American religious tradition. At other parishes, especially those populated by two-parent families, Myra felt she would not be welcome, or at least not able to become active and grow into a leadership role as she had in this church.

Six years before our interview, Myra participated in a training program for what the local diocese calls Ministers of Service, laypeople prepared to take an active role in the volunteer leadership of their parishes. She entered the program after her church's pastor and associate pastor asked her to become involved and arranged for child care so she could attend the training sessions. Myra thrived on the study of Scripture and church history, which made her hungry for more learning. "The program really made my faith grow up," she said. "It made me want to grasp for more." Myra sings in the choir, trains and coordinates the parish's Eucharistic ministers, prepares children for First Communion and chairs the summer festival, Mother of Christ's major fund-raising event.

For several of the women I met, parish life changed with the advent of the Renew program, which deepened both their spiritual lives and their commitment to the Church. "Renew brought it all together," said Brigette Rouson. "At our church's workshops for [potential group] leaders in Renew, what came out was that while Saint Augustine's had this great reputation for being active politically and in the community, we were really lacking that spiritual base. We were losing people to the Fundamentalist Christian churches and we were beginning to feel that something was wrong, because there were people attracted to the parish who weren't at all interested in religion; they just wanted to be involved in the activities. So that's when we started to rethink things. I had gotten out of church for about a year [at that time], and Renew brought me back in."

For over half of the women affiliated with a local congregation, this community was the neighborhood parish; but for others it was a local monastery that welcomed lay guests for common prayer, a mothers' Bible study group, a "base community," a campus ministry center, a prison chaplaincy. Many women spoke of their involvement in small communities of faith. Like a growing number of Americans, they are beginning to choose a living-room-sized group as a primary congregation. This trend has crossed religious and denominational lines in the past two decades, encompassing the *havurah* movement in the Jewish community, Christian base communities, house churches, prayer groups, and the healing circles of *wicca* practitioners. For most, small groups are a way to deepen religious involvement and bring it closer to home.* Many women I met belonged to Bible study groups, prayer groups, and social service groups. While most were subdivisions of local churches rather than alternatives to them, these gatherings

---

*Fewer women had satisfying "cathedral experiences." Often conferences—youth meetings, women's conventions, Charismatic assemblies—provided this kind of large, varied congregation more than the local cathedral or parish church. But a few women praised the diversity and vitality of their city's cathedral. "When you go to a service at the cathedral," said Mary Esther Bernal, "you see the people come from all over town to worship. It is such a spiritual uplift. It just keeps you right in touch with the pulse of the people."

frequently seemed to provide more spiritual nourishment than the parish itself. Often women were affiliated with both a small faith community and a parish. For Christine Beckley, both her parish and her Charismatic prayer group are "church." Rafaela Canelo, a member of St. Peter's Church in San Francisco's Mission District, belongs to a base community similar to those in Latin America, in which a cluster of Christians gather to read the Bible and reflect on the relationship of Biblical faith to their daily lives and to the social problems of their community. These affiliations enrich one another; they are not mutually exclusive.

When "Serena Townsend" was raising young children, she became involved in three ecumenical groups of women meeting at different churches. She joked: "I was a Congregationalist on Monday, an Episcopalian on Wednesday, and a Roman Catholic the rest of the week." All three groups broke down the isolation of suburban life for their members. In one, a book discussion served as a springboard for the sharing of spiritual journeys and family stories. "Our group had a mix of ages," "Serena" remembered. "We had grandmothers and young mothers and all in between. The uniting thread was that we were all fairly traditional women, all raising families. We developed over the course of two years a wonderful community which shared experience and prayer life. We met every week and it became in effect a support group; it was a religious group, it was a prayer group, but it was feeding in a much broader sense." Some years later, "Serena" went camping on a "wilderness retreat" with a group of women in their forties. "All had kids in the teenage years and were all dealing with the same problems and issues, spiritually, physically, emotionally." Though each woman had a daily meeting with the retreat leader and the weekend allowed for plenty of solitude, the companionship of group members is what "Serena" remembers most fondly. "The wonderful thing [on this kind of retreat] is that everybody takes care of everybody else," she said.

A fraction of the women I met were involved in small communities identified with the loosely knit movement known as Women-Church; they conducted their own liturgical celebrations, blessing and sharing bread and wine in memory of Jesus or using other forms of ritual and prayer. But they were not the only ones who found church with other women. Many more women, like "Serena," belonged to groups in which their spiritual companions were female. The way women analyzed what this meant for their experience of church was not always the same; indeed, many women did not analyze the experience at all. Women in Susan Johnson's Bible study group in Corpus Christi, Texas, may well define what they are doing differently from the Washington, D.C., base community gathering in Diann Neu and Mary Hunt's house for worship and a potluck supper, but they have much in common. Everywhere Catholic women are gathering together for prayer, study, service, and celebration. Most of these groups tend, like the Women-Church base communities, to be egalitarian and without visible hierarchy. (Whether they name themselves "women's communities" is another question.) While priests are still pivotal figures in the religious lives of American Catholic women, there is, I found, an equally influential group of people in their spiritual development: other women.

In the Catholic women's movement, more focused in the 1970s on the issue of ordination, there has been a shift toward the issue of the religious self-determination of women. The women who meet in the small worship groups and large conferences of Women-Church have chosen this stance over that of church reform—though for some, religious self-determination and work to change existing church structures are not mutually exclusive. Rather than asking to be "let into the Church," these women have decided to go about "being Church." Unwilling to wait for the broader institution to change, they gather, worship, study, provide pastoral care, and work for social justice on their own terms. They have stopped waiting for permission. "What are they going to do to punish us," Mary Hunt joked. "Not ordain us?"

These are not women who have lost faith. On the contrary: It is because they wish to continue acknowledging the divine presence and the reality of the moral life that they have embraced the Women-Church movement, neither a new church nor, by the traditional definition, a schismatic group.[7] Some of these women remain members of parishes, moving back and forth between them and small base communities, living "both/and" rather than "either/or." For others, Women-Church is now the only place to call church. In praying together in small groups, these women are no different from the earliest Christian communities. In taking responsibility for their own religious expression by conducting their own liturgical celebrations, they are breaking a taboo. But in breaking the bread, reclaiming a simple gesture laden with centuries of religious meaning, they do not intend to desecrate, but to deepen and hallow the meaning of the sacrament. They mean to connect in a fresh way the gifts of the earth, the presence of God, and their daily lives.

With its informal, lay-led rituals, Women-Church says a determined no to hierarchy and a stubborn yes to sacramental worship. Are its liturgical celebrations valid? Some of the women I interviewed, who worship in these celebrations, say yes; many more of the women I met, and most church leaders, would say no. For some of the women I encountered, a more fundamental issue than validity or legitimacy was that of religious adulthood. "Women realize," one participant said to me, "that they have the power to celebrate and the power to heal."

What about the men? "Women-Church" (a term originally coined as "the *ekklesia* of women" by biblical scholar Elisabeth Schüssler Fiorenza[8]) is necessary, its participants say, as long as "Church" does not fully include women. Women-Church holds up as an ideal a "discipleship of equals" (another phrase contributed by Schüssler Fiorenza[9]) that includes both women and men. Self-determination does not mean secession. But a majority of Women-Church communities at this time are made up only of women; only a few include children and men. For this reason, most American Catholic women will probably not find in them a satisfying or at least a long-term alternative to the parish. Neither, from what they have told me, are many Catholic women satisfied with their parish churches, which fall short of honoring their presence, experience, and talent.

At the time of our original interview, "Serena Townsend" attended her local parish faithfully, if sometimes critically. The sacraments, she said, held her and fed her. Three years later, she told me of a visit to her city's cathedral. The liturgy that day "turned out to be a High Mass," she said. "It must have been Pentecost. There were sixteen or eighteen people on the altar and all of them were male. I sat in the pew and looked at this and the Church died. It disintegrated. Every psychic structure that was built around religion left. The image I had was of sitting in the sand, or ashes, or dust, after the holocaust, and I was trying to find even a small twig among the ashes, and I couldn't. The cathedral is in an area where within one square mile you would find every ethnic and racial group possible, and here are all these fat white middle-class males sitting there; there were two faces of color among them, [both] Asian," said "Serena," who is white. "I just sat there weeping through the whole thing. It was grief; it was loss. It was more painful even than when my father died. It was grief because it should be so beautiful, that's what the core of it is, and it had been so debased and destroyed by how it's lived.

"Then this young man came up to the microphone and said

the bishop had given him permission to say a few words. He had been brought into the Church at Easter; he was starry-eyed. I thought, 'Aren't you an incredibly articulate white, blond, middle-class man and they put the stamp of confirmation on you.' Didn't they have any women or Asians or blacks in the group? I almost walked up to the microphone and said, 'The archbishop didn't give me permission to speak, and I wish you well, but today the Church died for me.' But I didn't, of course, because you don't rain on someone else's parade."

Women like "Serena," I suspect, are the tip of a massive iceberg—or perhaps Claire McGowan, O.P.'s image of women as "the volcano within" is more apt.[10] These traditional mothers from the suburbs are even finding their way to Women-Church conferences, telling stories much like "Serena"'s in small groups or at the open microphone. They are women who, for years, have eaten at the Eucharistic table and fed the people around them through church-based service, teaching, and pastoral care. No longer the "loyal opposition," their experience is one of loss and disintegration, accompanied not only by anger but, even more, by intense grieving. For these Catholic women, the sacramental glue no longer sticks. There is no more food at the table.

Where do Catholic women go when they leave?

The hunger for God and the desire for community did not leave any of the women who, like "Serena Townsend," had decided they could no longer find a home in the Catholic church. "Serena" continued to seek spiritual nourishment after her day of mourning at the cathedral. She went on meditation retreats, started practicing Tai Ch'i, and began studying psychology and holistic health. Several women I met still identified as Catholics, but consciously avoided going to church. "I'm tired of it," Helen Doggett said. "I'll live my own life and be good and help people out and I just think that's the best I can do right now. And I don't have to be in church to pray, either." After commenting that parish liturgies had ceased to nourish her spirit, Pamela Montagno said, "Eventually I just thought, 'This doesn't make sense for me.' I am getting more out of my own prayer time or time alone, and also through my friends. We'd have some fine talks and sharings that I thought were really sacramental. Those times were more significant to me than when I went to Mass." "My husband and I sit on occasion and talk and pray together; we used to do it daily," said Ginny Peck, who, after raising her children as Catholics and years of involvement in the Cursillo movement, had grown disenchanted with women's place in the Church.

"I don't go anywhere [to church]. I miss having a community tremendously. It was incredibly important. I haven't lost faith," she added. "I've just lost the community."

For some women, politics or participation in voluntary associations aimed at social change function as substitutes for the Church. In organizations dealing with health care, peace, the environment, equal rights, child welfare, AIDS, poverty, racial justice, everywhere there are Catholic women. Many of them are alienated Catholics (lapsed, some would say; one called herself a "dormant Catholic"). They rarely darken the door of a church; they will probably never appear at any of the bishops' "listening sessions" on women or any other topic since they do not, and will not, interact with any formally Catholic entity; the only exceptions they make are relatives' and friends' rites of passage—baptisms, weddings, funerals. I met some of these women during my research. As Gail Benjamin had, they retained the Catholic emphasis on the communitarian dimension of morality. They believed in working within institutional structures, but they held out little hope for change in religious institutions and limited their activities to the secular realm. They brought care and fervor to their concern for community work and public life. Their language was loaded with references to the dignity of the human person. They also missed the mystery and mysticism of the Catholic church; they claimed the Church as their roots, but felt it was lost to them; they had nowhere to go with their spiritual hunger. These women were not Women-Church participants bent on religious self-determination nor activists working for change in the Church. Those two groups, though critical, have an active relationship to the *ecclesia,* the assembly of the Church, but for these women there was no *ecclesia,* no connecting community.

At another point of the constellation were women who, like "Serena," in some way embraced New Age practices, some in a highly disciplined and careful manner, others as eclectic tourists. Their paths also retained a kinship with Catholicism in their all-embracing approach to religious life, their focus on direct spiritual experience, and their determination to provide a vision of the cosmos, not just a view of the neighborhood.

"Jeanne Dupont," wounded by the harsh approach of her Franco-American Catholic upbringing in northern New England, experimented with various forms of worship and meditation, some involving trance states, others spiritual practices from non-Western cultures. Over time

"Jeanne" became increasingly involved in self-described pagan groups. Her God is a woman God, her religious practice "earth-honoring," she said. An avid reader with a sharp mind, "Jeanne" had first looked to feminist theology for guidance. But "the more I read of feminist authors who remained within the Church, the more impatient I got and the less use I had for it." When she discovered writings on the revival of Goddess-worship, she said, "that's when I felt I'd come home." Pagan spirituality suited "Jeanne" well, she said, because "I really don't have much patience with hierarchies of authority, especially those that tell me not to think or try to do my thinking for me. There isn't a clergy in the pagan form, it's a direct experience; it's very democratic and pluralistic."

Though some New Age movements appear to lack historical sensibility and social vision, "Jeanne" said social responsibility had become more important to her rather than less. "Spirituality," she said, "requires responsibility to living in the world. [Spirituality and politics] are the very same thing." "Jeanne" expected to go to Midnight Mass during her next visit to her parents' home at Christmas. Why? I asked. "Because I love it," she answered. Why? "The cultural tradition," she said. "I used to think of myself as an intellectual," she told me after our second interview. "I am coming to know myself more as an artist, and that distinction means that I am more interested in mysteries than in dogmas. I am more interested in things that belong to our dreams than to our laws."

"Alice Schwab," a regular churchgoer in a midwestern town, was described to me by a friend from her parish as a middle-of-the-road, active Catholic and traditional mother. Once we had met and I had offered her the option of speaking under a pseudonym, "Alice" told me that she went to church only for the sake of her husband and children. Unbeknownst to our mutual friend and to other parishioners, "Alice"'s belief system had entirely changed over the past few years and Catholicism had ceased to have much meaning for her.

"About a year and a half ago," "Alice" said, "I felt like it was time to go inward. I had spent my whole life looking for answers outside myself. On the surface," she said, "the Catholic church seemed to give me all the answers," but it did not strengthen or draw upon her inner life. At the time of our conversation, she was deeply immersed in the writings of Ruth Montgomery and Shirley MacLaine, but continued to go to Mass with her husband out of commitment to their marriage. "When I go there now I try to center inwardly," she said. "One of the things [at Mass] is to say we are not worthy—I don't believe in saying that."* "Alice" told me she experienced a conflict between educating her children and pleasing her husband on the one hand, and her own spiritual quest on the other. "If I were alone I would be doing something entirely different," she said.

"Why did the Catholic cross the road?" a recent article asked of the influx of Catholics into Evangelical Protestant churches.[11] Besides the dearth of good preaching and attention to spiritual experience, the lack of good pastoral care and warm fellowship in Catholic parishes account for many of their departures. So too does an unambiguous message of salvation. "The Catholic Church, often accused of being too dogmatic . . . actually leaves an extraordinary amount of room for mystery and ambiguity," the same article asserts.[12] Some Catholic women I met found less certainty in mainstream Protestant churches but were drawn to them for many of the same reasons: welcome and warmth, greater lay participation, and a more congenial message than in the church of their origins.

Gaye Lott's search was often a restless one. In pastoral preparation sessions for her first marriage, she said, she did not encounter much respect for her experience and feelings. "When Bill comes home with lipstick on his collar," the priest said to her, "you don't pay any attention to it, I don't want you to say anything, you just trust this man." When her first daughter was born in the early 1960s, Gaye said, "I knew this child was not going to be Catholic." She and her husband joined a Methodist church in Duluth, Minnesota. Some years later, they moved to Houston, Texas, and became Unitarians. "It was wonderful," Gaye remembered. "Music was very important in the church, there wasn't a dress-up-and-go-to-church [mentality], it was a comfortable, intellectual congregation. Your heart pounded in every service and they did innovative wonderful things that made you feel good." She enrolled her daughters in the Unitarian Sunday school. One day, driving home from church, Gaye heard her oldest daughter say from the back seat, "I don't care where babies come from anymore, I want to hear about Jesus." The child was about seven years old. "I thought to myself, 'I have come full circle,'" Gaye said. "No one ever told me where babies come from and here I have loaded her

---

*Women who reacted most strongly to statements about lack of worthiness and who took comfort in the view that they were "part of God" were often, like "Jeanne" and "Alice," survivors of early trauma such as incest or other abuse. Many of these women were drawn to New Age practices because of their emphasis on healing and wholeness.

with it and, 'I don't care anymore,' she says. I thought, 'Oh, no! How am I going to tell her about Jesus?' She knew her friends were getting something that she wasn't. And here I had gone all the way [in the opposite direction]. I'd had so much Jesus." Gaye's youngest daughter joined the Episcopal Church on her own as a teenager. After her second marriage, Gaye attended a small, independent "spiritual church" with an eclectic style of worship: "It was a nice place to go on Sunday, everything was nice, it felt good to go." Now, she said, "I'm religious but I don't go to church. I did go to Easter Sunday service with my daughter and they had a trumpet and I would still be sitting there if they hadn't put an end to the ceremony." She added, "I don't think we really ever took care of Jesus."

The Catholic women I met who had joined the Episcopal Church cited the presence of women in sacramental leadership as a factor in their decision. "That did it for me," said an advertising executive I know in Boston, "when I saw that woman priest up there." "It feels so comfortable," another woman said to me. "I feel at home, I don't have to strain and twist myself." On the other hand, Sandra Mondykowski Temple said she did not have "terribly strong feelings about women's ordination—I can take it or leave it—but it's nice it's there in the Episcopal Church." The granddaughter of Polish immigrants, Sandra became an Episcopalian for other reasons. "I guess it's come down to the *via media*, or as [the rector of my church] refers to it, the 'enlightened muddle' of the Episcopal Church," she told me. "There is a certain vagueness and gray area that the Episcopal Church is comfortable in. There's more of a sense of being able to follow your conscience on certain issues, not being dictated to." In the course of the reading and study Sandra undertook in the process of making her decision, she made "a very interesting discovery: that the Anglican Church is in communion with the Old Catholic churches in Europe, the ones that never accepted the infallibility of the pope doctrine that came in the nineteenth century, and the Episcopal Church in this country is in communion with the Polish National Catholic Church, which also never accepted the infallibility of the pope. My family is Polish National Catholic! I was baptized Roman Catholic as part of my father's campaign for us to be 'more American.' But our whole family were born, raised, baptized, confirmed [in] the Polish National Catholic Church. It was like a thunderbolt: 'There is a historical connection here!'

"Then I found out I was pregnant. That's when I decided to formally join the Episcopal Church. I knew I wanted to give the baby a religious education. And the more I thought about it the more I thought, well now what do I do? If I have her baptized Catholic I can't even receive the sacraments," said Sandra, who is divorced and remarried. "The Church changed so much [after Vatican II]," Sandra added, "but it didn't change a lot of the things that drove people out: birth control, divorce, clerical celibacy, abortion. [My daughter] is going to come home with the same kinds of questions I did because the Church has not changed in those basic ways, and the thought of looking a whole new generation in the eyes and saying, 'Well, I know that's what the Church teaches, dear, but . . . ' [does not sit well with me].

"I just gave it such a good college try for so many years," Sandra said. "If you're raised in the Catholic church and you're lucky enough to marry once and stay married, or to have a vocation and stick with it, in other words if you're fortunate enough in your life circumstances that you never have to come into open conflict in a basic way with the teachings of Church, then the Catholic church is for you. That was not my life experience, and rather than continue to try and turn myself into a mental and theological pretzel, I opted for what I clearly and comfortably admit is a compromise. I don't feel I've compromised myself theologically at all; but in terms of certain moral and social beliefs I am much more comfortable in the Episcopal Church. I wouldn't be comfortable in a non-Trinitarian atmosphere and I really do believe in the communion of saints. I just don't believe in the infallibility of the pope. I have terrible trouble with abortion, but I would prefer to have my own conflicts and terrible trouble with it, but be able to support women's freedom, than be dictated to and informed that that opinion puts me in a state of mortal sin. On the issue of divorce and remarriage, there are just so many circumstances that go into a decision to divorce and a decision to remarry; I don't feel it's black and white. The Episcopal Church takes marriage very seriously, but they take more into account the frailty of human nature and make more allowances for that." When Sandra's father died in 1985, "we couldn't have a funeral Mass for him because he was divorced and remarried. I remember not even being upset at that point, just saying, 'Well, that figures.' We had to have the ceremony out of the funeral home. A local priest did come to the funeral home to say a few words over the body before we took him to the cemetery and that's all we could have. I think that did it. My final decision came when I got pregnant, but I think the final emotional break came [before], at my father's funeral.

"I have valued being raised Catholic," Sandra added. "Although

I am no longer an active member of the Catholic church, it is not out of bitterness. I value what I received. I have a lot of respect for it. And I also had a lot of fun, as well as a lot of pain. I would have missed not being born Catholic and raised that way. I wouldn't have been me."

I often joke these days that of the Catholic women who were my classmates in divinity school or seminary, almost all, fifteen years later, have become Protestants or psychotherapists or both. Behind the jesting is the painful exodus from Catholicism of a wave of theologically educated Catholic women with a deep and generous commitment to ministry. The most appropriate name for it is the ecclesiastical brain drain. It is largely unacknowledged in Catholic circles. In the past two decades, Catholic women have flocked to Protestant divinity schools and to Catholic seminaries run by religious orders such as the Jesuits, Franciscans, and Dominicans. Then, after a few years of pastoral work in Catholic parishes, schools, or other institutions, many decide that there is no room in the Roman Catholic Church for what they have to offer. There is no mention of the ecclesiastical brain drain in the current round of research about the "priest shortage" in the Roman Catholic Church. Educated, intelligent, soulful leaders are leaving. No one in official circles talks about this departure because the existence of these women who were, in the words of the Catholic ordination rite, "ready and willing," was never institutionally acknowledged to begin with.

Maureen Dallison Kemeza, whom I met during my graduate studies in theology over fifteen years ago, shared with me during a brief interview her vivid memories of growing up Catholic in a working-class Irish-American family. A married woman with two children, she had worked as a youth minister in a suburban Catholic parish and was studying for a Ph.D. in ethics when I began the research for this book. A year or so later, she called to let me know of her decision to enter the Episcopal Church and prepare for ordination there. It was not simply her vocation to the priesthood, Maureen said, which led her to the Episcopal Church, but her desire to continue to grow and live with integrity in her faith. "In order to remain Catholic," she said to me, "I have to become an Anglican."

Later, Maureen gave me the letter she had sent to her many friends and colleagues, a thoughtful, moving statement reflecting a long process of prayer and study. "The sacramental sense of reality," she wrote, "is what I love and affirm; patriarchal authoritarianism seems only oppressive to me. I think my faith in Jesus Christ will be distorted by bitterness of heart unless I am part of a Church where there is equality and mutuality at every level, including the participation of women in sacramental leadership. . . . There is a dimension of loss in leaving the Church of my origins," she continued. "I owe more to the Roman Catholic Church than I could ever contain in a letter. That debt of love includes my gratitude to you, my friends, who have revealed so much to me of grace and of character at the heart of Christian life. I mean to hold on to what is good; in everything essential to hearing the Gospel and celebrating God's gracious love I hope to grow."

SEVENTEEN

JEANNETTE NORMANDIN

"Who will roll back the stone for us?"

Jeannette Normandin, a Sister of St. Anne in her late fifties, is not unusual among American nuns ("women religious") in her level of education and accomplishment. Her professional changes reflect a trend among American sisters toward a broader range of occupations and a renewed focus on the church's mission to the poor.

There was a time when faith was an assent to truth. I see my faith in a different light now: more as a willingness to let go of preconceived ideas of God. [Or as] letting God reveal in whatever way that happens to be, recognizing the movement or the breath of God in what's going on. God is in the suffering, just as God is in the joy. It's not that God dumps suffering [on you] and stands by and watches. God is in the moment. God feels close, God feels like friend.

I wanted to become a missionary. I had a strong desire to work with lepers. I was fifteen or sixteen. I made up my mind in senior year that I would definitely go. But one of the sisters said, "Why don't you consider the Sisters of St. Anne because we have all kinds of work. We have mission, we have teaching, we have nursing." She convinced me that if I really wanted to do God's will I should enter an "open-ended community." When I retell all this and see where I am now it really makes me laugh—how I swallowed so much.

My mother and father were deeply religious people and very gentle. It was a home filled with a lot of love and I really didn't understand the concept of sin until I went to school and the sisters were preparing us for First Communion and confession and I had to dredge up all sorts of things. I didn't have any of those hang-ups about a judging God. It was always a concept of a loving God.

My father worked for a shipping firm for textiles as the main shipper; earlier on I think he was a truck driver. My mother was a fancy stitcher in a shoe factory. I had two brothers and a half sister who is twelve years older than I. This was my mother's second marriage; she had a divorce from her first husband. We had children's Mass, so parents went upstairs, children went downstairs, and we never knew anything about our parents not going to communion. It was very easy for them to keep that very quiet—[Even First Communion] was separate [because in those days they didn't have family-based religious education.]

My half sister was married when I was eight years old. It never connected [that she was just my half sister]. I didn't really know of this divorce and remarriage until I was ready to enter [the Sisters of St. Anne]. This would have been an impediment to entering because, strictly speaking, I was illegitimate* and there would have to be a dispensation. So that's when my mother and father told me. It was devastating. I was filled with anger at my mother and father, that they would do such a horrible thing. Later I realized what loving people they were and how close to God they were. They just let me vent my anger. There were seven women in my [high school] graduating class who applied for entrance and I waited and waited; I was the last one to get an acceptance.

There was so much suffering for my parents. No priest would even look at [the possibility of an] annulment [with them]. Then they went to see a priest who said, "The only way you could ever receive communion is that you live as brother and sister." After all those years of married life, they consented to do that; no one had ever suggested that before. They spoke to me about it, nearly ten years after I entered the community. I certainly wouldn't have suggested that! Within a year [of their decision], my mother's first husband died and my parents' marriage was blessed by the Church. They became daily communicants right up until the time of my father's death.

In their struggle to be reconciled with the Church I think my parents developed a tolerance. My mother is eighty-seven now and she still says her Rosary and her Way of the Cross and watches Mass on TV. But she'll say things like: "I am so glad that the Church's teaching on marriage is changing, that it's easier to get annulments and that people don't have to suffer what we suffered." And she's open to people living together before marriage. Every family has nieces and nephews who are doing that and my mother would be the person in our family

---

*Today these children of non-Catholic second marriages are in no way considered illegitimate, but in Jeannette's day canon law required that they receive a special dispensation to enter a religious order.

that would never make a judgment. I remember that tolerance all our growing up. One of my first cousins eloped and was married outside the Church and his mother, my mother's sister, disowned him. He was in the Second World War and my mother wrote to him and sent him parcels every holiday. I think her tolerance came out of her pain and suffering.

I had a very happy novitiate. It was not very extraordinary. [We were in] Lachine, a little suburb just outside of Montreal where our mother house is located. Immediately after my profession* in '48 I was sent to British Columbia, in Western Canada, and I spent twenty-one years there. In a way I think that was my salvation. I wonder if I would have survived in the community if I had stayed East. It was all English-speaking in British Columbia. And there weren't the deep-rooted traditions, hence it was much more liberal.

I taught during most of my life there. Meanwhile, I was studying summers at Seattle University—that's the Jesuit University there. I got my degree in mathematics. In those days we would go to school a couple of summers and then we'd hold the fort at home a couple of summers and let other people go, and then we'd go back. So it took a long time. Later I got my master's in theology from St. Mary's College in California.

[In the early sixties I had changed] my direction from being a teacher to being involved with training of novices. Our formation was very structured, particularly in the vow of obedience, where the voice of authority was a direct voice from God. If a superior told you this was what you should do, then this was what you should do. I was comfortable with that for a while but gradually I started seeing some discrepancies between some of the things that were being asked and the feelings that I was having. I would look at the rule and look at what was happening to me developmentally, and in many ways I saw [the two realities] as contradictory. For instance, mealtime: It should be a time of sharing and a time of getting together; it was silence. Recreation: It's there to re-create one's spirit; it was a time when you were never idle; you always did something to keep yourself busy. Those were the kinds of things that went against the grain.

I [also understood] very clearly that "holiness" was "wholeness." When people were asked to do things that were counter to their personal development, it seemed to me that was not from God. Sometimes rules went before human needs and I really had problems with that.

---

*Formal vows as a member of a religious order.

At that time we were either teachers or nurses, [and I felt] if a woman was going to be able to respond [to her students] in the classroom as full human beings, she had to develop as a full human being. A lot of the formation did not respect that. I was also beginning to understand religious life* much more realistically as a way to live the Gospel more radically. And I was experiencing that liv[ing] the Gospel more radically *and* follow[ing] this rule was impossible.

I resigned as assistant directress of novices in '63 and was appointed a principal in Kamloops, British Columbia. It was a wonderful place, very unspoiled, with a bishop who had fourteen priests and ten thousand square miles and who loved to preach, who drove the school bus if the janitor was sick, who did the cleaning in the school.

I studied spiritual direction, and then came back East in the U.S. and worked as directress of formation in our province. I was very interested in spirituality and retreat work and spiritual direction, but I was beginning to see more and more that it was a luxury for the rich and for nuns. And I really had in my heart the great desire to make all things available to the poor. I was realizing how much we women were exposed to and able to get and looking at folk who couldn't afford to go make a retreat or didn't ever hear of spiritual direction. So I requested of my community the permission to look into that: I could remain as director of formation but I would like to move the center of action away from the big provincial house to an urban setting. At this time the number of novices was beginning to decrease too. I opened a house in Worcester [,Massachusetts,] called Esther House for Spiritual Renewal. It was a drop-in center for prayer for the poor, located on the boundaries of a low-income project.

Esther House was a wonderful community experience. There were three sisters and a candidate [novice] supporting the work of the house. We lived very frugally. We didn't put a price on anything that went on: If people wanted to leave a donation, they could; we devised a method so that we never knew who left what and how much. During that time we were never in want and all kinds of people came. It really flourished, and I was extremely happy.

Then I was in Washington, D.C., from '75 to '79. For two years I was both associate director of the Religious Formation Conference[†]

*In Catholic parlance, *religious life* means life in a vowed religious community or religious order. In recent years some have objected to the Catholic use of *religious life* to describe only a small fraction of the people who live the Christian life.
[†]National office dealing with the spiritual and communal formation of members of Catholic religious orders.

and Spiritual Director at the Paulist seminary. The next two years I did full-time spiritual direction at the Paulists. I guess my gift at the seminary was to put some heart into the head stuff that was going on. For the most part the Paulists are very creative men and very bright. My role in spiritual direction was to try to help them get in touch with what was going on in the heart and the feelings, and how God was revealing Herself-Himself to them in their life at that time.

This was not a closed seminary, so women were in classes with [the Paulist students] and they were recognizing the high caliber of women who were studying theology and would get to graduation and not be able to go on to priesthood. The men saw this and questioned their own movement toward priesthood and what it meant for them. I think every man who made a choice to go on to priesthood, having had his consciousness raised about what women were doing in the Church, had to do this with a certain amount of courage. I sensed that there was a desire to try to change: They wouldn't become priests who were going to canonize the status quo.

I have a gift of being able to address issues and not come on like a bulldozer. I feel very strongly about the role of women in the Church and woman's right for decision-making in the Church. On the other hand, I think I could hear the struggle of the men at St. Paul's trying to come to grips with that, and it was making me a little more tolerant. I was trying to hear that pain and struggle and still confront the injustice.

[When I came back from Washington] I started to look around at where I might do some volunteer work with the poor and it came to my attention that I had grown up in Framingham [,Massachusetts,] but had never set foot in the women's prison there, so in early '80 I started working there as a volunteer. It took me five months to get an appointment. I understood why after I got in there, because a lot of people go in as volunteers and then after a month they get tired, because the women don't give you a lot of adulation. The very first day I went, the priest who was there, John O'Connor, took me up to maximum security and left me alone without any orientation. He said, "I'll be back in an hour." The women I met that day won my heart and I knew I was going to continue doing that work. They have become my lasting friends.

[The women at the prison] asked me if I would do Bible study. I started doing a Bible study up there once a week; then gradually I was increasing my volunteer time [at the prison] and decreasing my retreat and spiritual direction time. Father O'Connor said, "I would really like to have you replace me as chaplain." So he proceeded to talk to Cardinal Medeiros and of course, the answer was no. But Father O'Connor had to leave because of state law (when you work in a "position of peril" you have to retire at sixty-five) and he spoke to the prison superintendent. The superintendent called me in and said, "I will create a position where you'll get paid on a consultant basis. You'll be called 'consultant for religious affairs' but in reality, you'll be the chaplain."

I initiated a dialogue with the auxiliary bishops and then in '84 right after Cardinal Law came in, I started asking for an appointment with him. Because as far as the archdiocese was concerned the position of chaplain wasn't empty. Even though John O'Connor wasn't on the payroll of the state, even though he would come just twice a month for Mass and that was the extent of his involvement, in the archdiocesan directory his name was listed as chaplain. After long fighting and many tears his name was removed [but the space] was [empty]: You would look on page 217 in the archdiocesan directory and find all the chaplains of the prisons listed and Framingham would be blank; there was no name there. I addressed that with the cardinal, with the publisher of the directory, with everybody. At an open meeting, too: The cardinal had four sessions with fifteen religious women and we were sharing wonderful things about community and ministry and our concerns. I was looking at the caliber of the women in that room, the expertise and the dedication, and I said, "My big concern is that our ministries are not taken seriously." And I said: "A case in point, and I tell this personal anecdote simply to make my point, is that after working in my ministry over five years, I open the Catholic directory to the section on the chaplains in prisons and find it blank. Now what would that say to you about the meaning of the ministry?" I said, "I know what it says to me." And he said, "That's going to be changed," and it was.

When it became clear to me that I had been at the prison long enough I said to the cardinal that I wanted to make a strong recommendation that whoever took my place should be a woman because I felt that a woman could understand the pain and the oppression of the women there. I also suggested that it might be a good idea to appoint a part-time priest to take away some of the burden of having to find priests all the time for Mass. I did communion services* and

---

*At a communion service, as opposed to a Mass, the Scriptures are read, and hosts or bread consecrated at a previously celebrated Mass are distributed. These services may be led by a

all kinds of other services, but we always had to find priests for Mass.

The cardinal said, "I want you to know I wouldn't even consider having a priest replace you, it has to be a woman. However there's an ecclesiastical technicality. It cannot be a 'chaplain,' so she will be 'pastoral minister.'" You know, prisoners don't understand that term. "Minister" means "Protestant" to them. Anyway, my door in the prison said "Catholic Chaplain, Sister Jeannette Normandin." In the archdiocese it was "pastoral minister."

I went to the prison after having been in the seminary, where you hear people speaking in theological terms all the time. I kept using jargon. And the wonderful gift that the women would have is they'd scrunch up their nose and say, "Whaaat?" And I'd laugh with them and say, "You're right on. You don't know what I'm talking about. I'm going to have to struggle to say what's in my heart and you tell me if you understand." They helped me so much to articulate my faith and my journey in simple terms.

I remember asking one woman what her image of God was. And of course she said, "Whaaat?" I said, "Well, how do you see God?" And she said, "See God, I don't see God. I think I feel God." Then I said to her, "Just tell me, when you pray, how do you pray?" She said, "I sometimes say 'Our Father,' that prayer, because I know that, but I just kind of talk to God." Then she started telling me how she would talk: "Like last night, I was saying to God, 'It's a damn good thing you got me in here because it made me stop and get off those drugs. Otherwise I'd probably be dead on the street. That's how I know you love me.'" So she wasn't blaming God for putting her in prison. God was very much in her struggle and she came to prison and stopped to reflect on her life. There was the image of a loving God in the midst of all that pain and all that suffering, where I would have expected that people would be angry. Though I've met some who are angry at God.

Often when they're talking about their experience of God they may use some of the foulest language. They'd say, "Excuse me, Sister, I didn't mean that," but then they'd go right on. When I was first there, there was a lot of talk in my religious community about the simplicity of life-style and all that. Of course, the women in the prison were asking me, what does that mean, to take a vow of poverty, and especially, what does it mean to live a celibate life? It doesn't have any

---

layperson and have increased in frequency since the number of priests has begun to diminish in the U.S.

meaning in their life: "You mean you haven't got a man yet? You have to have somebody out there."

I would say, "There's a practical dimension of celibacy which I think you could understand; if I had a family, I would not be able to be with you the way that I am; I would have other concerns. But there's also another dimension: My relationship with God is really a love relationship, and as that grows and deepens, I can hear you when you're talking to me at another level. The closer I grow in my relationship with God, the less judgmental my hearing becomes. I'm not hearing you in a way of 'She's a prostitute' or 'She's a crook' or 'She's a murderer.' We're sisters together. We're walking together with the same God."

In the prison, liturgy was wonderful. Not that it was very creative. Often it was simply a communion service where we would read the Scriptures and talk about them and then break bread. Even when a priest would come for Mass, there was always that moment after sharing the Word, no matter how formally it was done, where the women cut through the formality and said exactly what was going on in their life. You'd have the most formal priest reading the Gospel and then someone would say, "Wow, that's great," or "Man, was that ever neat," and then something from their life. They were very rich moments.

Success is not always making it to the top. Sometimes the external looks as though you haven't made it, but what goes on inside is a real success because you come to grips with things that you wouldn't have come to grips with. I've really had to look at what success is since the prison. One can work very closely with a woman and help her get all the pieces in place, and she goes out and she's out two months and she's back in prison. I've tried to get pockets of religious groups, like the sisters, who would take in a woman coming out of prison and be a support system for her. She may stay two months and leave and get back on drugs. There's another one who'd been on the street since she was nine years old, lived with the sisters for two and a half months after she came out of a drug program, and has been drug-free almost a year, and has her own apartment, a car, a job, and is preparing for confirmation now, growing in her relationship with God. They're all successes. To be accepted into a living situation and realize that they're loved in a way that's not exploitive and manipulative, but loved for who they are, gives them a greater sense of themselves. And then each teensy weensy bit of a sense of self makes one more whole, and therefore on the road to success. What looks like disaster often is success. The Crucifixion is a perfect example.

Now I'm working in Boston, at Social Justice for Women, a non-profit organization. [One of their programs] is the Women's Health and Learning Center; they address every possible aspect of women's health for prisoners. They're going to open a home for women who are pregnant and have to do time, so that they won't have to go to Framingham and they can have their babies. They work on the issues of the mentally ill in prison. I was called to spearhead a program of alternative sentencing that would have a two-fold focus, restitution and rehabilitation. We would be based primarily in the Boston Municipal Court, but we would take cases from other courts if it seemed appropriate. I am now the director of the program; it's called Community Services for Women in Alternative Sentencing Program. I have an attorney working with me ten hours a week and I am working thirty hours a week. We presented our first case in Suffolk Superior Court on December 15, and we won the case.

That woman had serious charges—arson, assault and battery with a deadly weapon—she could have gotten up to forty-one years. She had been in prison twenty years ago but had no convictions since then. But the judge wanted to give the program a chance, so this woman, who has had a long psychiatric history, is not in prison. She's doing community service; she has ongoing therapy; she's going to do some monetary restitution; she's in a supervised housing situation and attending a transition club for socialization skills; and we're working very closely with the Department of Mental Health. I'm in contact with her every week and with probation once a month. It's a real well-rounded package.

What we want to do is take women who have not been to prison yet, but who run the risk of going because of numerous charges, mostly prostitution, and try to help the woman address the real causes of the direction her life has taken. If indeed she would like to move in some other direction we work out a plan together. I will just say, "These are all the things available," not, "Here's a program for you." We work it out together.

As a sister I've experienced a lot of stereotyping. The "good little nun," for instance, especially in legal circles, in courts, or in circles where you're dealing with serious social ills: "You're just a nun; you don't really know life." And I want to say, "How do you know I don't?" I get very angry. It's stereotyped what a sister is. You don't know about anything. Sex, oh my God, you know nothing about that—you don't know anything because you're a nun. And what pains me a lot—and this used to happen at the seminary as well as prison—is that people will put on me what their experience of "Sister" or "Catholic church" has been. That's why I think taking off the habit has helped a lot, because sometimes people would see someone in a habit and all the hang-ups about the Catholic Church and about sisters came to the fore and were projected.

I had to make a decision about business cards in my new work, which is not church-oriented at all, and we talked about should I be "Sister Jeannette" or should I be "Jeannette"? I'm the only sister and one of the few Catholics in the group I'm working with, and we all decided to use "Sister," because I'm not ashamed of who I am, and part of who I am is "Sister." And it may be an opportunity to break down some stereotypes, because I can come to a session of the court or to an attorney or judge and say, "I've been inside [the prison] for six years, so I do know what's happening." [Of course] the title ["Sister"] can be helpful and it can be annoying [too].

I put the name "Spirit" on what I feel: that I have always been led in my life. I always know exactly where to move next because things fall into place for me. It's always been clear. I very rarely find myself in the dark without seeing light somewhere. When I left the prison, people were saying to me, "What are you going to do?" I would say, "I don't know" and I really didn't. I remember going to a counselor and saying, "I really feel at this point I want to leave the prison, it's been six years and I think I've done what I can do there. I don't think I want to be with that system anymore, I would like to be outside doing something for the women, but I don't know what, and I want to know if it's okay to let go of that job in this state of mind." And my order was just great. They said, "Jeannette, leave, and take as much time as you need. Take plenty of time to rest and understand where you should be moving and don't worry about the money." I was overwhelmed. I wept at that graciousness. Because not many people can let go without a lifeline out there.

To get back to the Spirit, for me, that was the Spirit speaking: "Push out, launch out into the deep and move and I'll show you." And almost out of nowhere, I'm looking around, I have in my mind I want to open a house for women coming out of prison and all of a sudden I get a call from this office in Boston to come and have lunch with women I knew through Aid to Incarcerated Mothers.* I knew them from inside the prison. They asked me if I would ever consider doing

---

*A nonprofit organization in Boston that helps incarcerated women maintain their relationships with their children.

something in alternative sentencing. And everything happened.

I was raised that human beings are basically good. I tend to be a little bit Pollyanna in that I just believe people are basically good and I've never changed through all that I've seen and experienced. The prison just deepened that understanding.

I think the desire of God for the world is that we re-create the world to its initial wholeness. And we each have a role to play in that. Some are called [to be faithful] through the Muslim faith and some through the Catholic faith and so on. God doesn't love me better than you, or you better than me. God loves me where I am today in this moment, in my quest for truth. We have to be faithful to what we're hearing, that's what faith is. I was taught that you don't set foot in a Protestant church. But I never learned that at home. At home I was raised that other paths are okay.

I really think we have to accept birth control. It doesn't make any sense to me that the direct fruit of all intercourse has to be a child. Conjugal union is a union of love and that's the meaning of it. I often look at the women at the prison, some who use abortion as birth control, and also some who just have many children because that's the only creative thing that they can do, and it's so hard for the children. This is all very emotional. It's wrong to take life, life is sacred, so I think one has to be careful about creating life. But in the reality of every day, among the poor especially, and the oppressed, sometimes people just find themselves [finally] being accepted by someone, which leads to intercourse, which leads to the creation of life, and then what? I would never sit down with a woman and say, "You should have an abortion." I will sit with a woman and help her to grapple and support her in her decision, whatever decision she makes, and help her to grapple with that decision before God. If a woman chooses to have an abortion and she hasn't got the money to do it, she should be allowed to follow her choice. But it's been my experience working with women who have had abortions that the psychological damage is tremendous and there has to be another way to deal with this. It's not simple, not simple.

I wish we could talk about abortion more openly in Catholic forums without being ostracized as heretics, turn it over, share light with each other, share experiences, and have a forum where that can happen. We have a forum in our feminist groups but that excludes a whole sector [of the population].

I remember the superintendent at the prison saying to me, "How do you stay in [the Church]?" She's a Catholic. I said to her: "How do you stay in the Department of Corrections?" I said, "I stay in because I have a tremendous support group, and I believe that anything can change." And, in essence, she said the same thing.

I went from rejecting Mary to seeing her as a tremendously strong woman who played a very important part in the history of the world by being faithful and bringing about Jesus' coming, which turned the world upside down. I think I put her on hold around Vatican II. That woman with her hands folded and her eyes raised was not anything I could follow. My own image of holiness was changing. Then I realized I just couldn't keep her on hold forever. I had to look at this woman in the Scriptures and the documents of Vatican II and in my own imagining of what she was like. I guess every time I see women in the Gospel, I always put Mary in there too, so I've been able to develop a composite picture of her. I see her as a strong woman, not as a saccharine, pietistic person who never said a word and who always took everything. It's so clear in the Scriptures how she pondered things and made them part of her being and worked out of them. I'm sorry there isn't more about her in the Scriptures but I certainly see her as a woman of strength and character. I think she's a model for women today in the Church, by her decision-making and by her active presence in the ministry. The little we know of her from the Scriptures, she's always been an active participant in the ministry.

I love the image of the women going to the tomb on Easter Sunday morning—you know, they were the first—and on the way, as they're running, they're saying, "Who will roll back the stone for us?" They're fully aware that when they get there, there are going to be armed guards, but they're not standing back asking the questions. They're asking as they're running. I think that's what women religious are doing.

EIGHTEEN

"YOU'RE A WHAT?" CATHOLIC WOMEN AS MINISTERS

Jesus was at Bethany in the house of Simon the leper; he was at dinner when a woman came in with an alabaster jar of very costly ointment, pure nard. She broke the jar and poured the ointment on his head. Some who were there said to one another indignantly, "Why this waste of ointment? Ointment like this could have been sold for three hundred denarii and the money given to the poor." And they were angry with her. But Jesus said, "Leave her alone. Why are you upsetting her? What she has done for me is one of the good works. You have the poor with you always, and you can be kind to them whenever you wish, but you will not always have me. She has done what was in her power to do; she has anointed my body beforehand for its burial. I tell you solemnly, wherever throughout the world the Good News is proclaimed, what she has done will be told also, in memory of her."

—The Gospel According to Mark

Jeannette Normandin's story about the blank space in the archdiocesan directory brought back this memory: Madison, Wisconsin, the late nineteen seventies; I am working as a chaplain at St. Paul's University Catholic Center, the parish serving the university community. I am the first woman chaplain, but not the first female staff member, Saint Paul's has ever had. Priests make up less than half the staff; they and I are the only ones with the title and job description of chaplain. I am in my mid-twenties, a couple of years out of divinity school, with one other chaplaincy position behind me, also at a large state university.

It is a weekend night and I am attending a party populated by graduate students and young professionals. We grip our beer bottle or glass of cider and ask each other the inevitable, "What do you do?" "I'm a chaplain," I say to the woman who has just asked me this question, "at Saint Paul's Catholic Center." "You're a *what?*" the woman responds. "Chaplain. You know," I say. "A minister in an institution. A religious leader." "What religion are you?" the woman asks. "I'm Catholic," I answer, trying to act casual.

The woman looks puzzled—more than puzzled: as if she is beginning to question my sanity. "Catholics don't have women chaplains," she answers. I sigh and go into the explanation I have given so many times before at so many parties: A chaplain means someone who ministers in an institution, like a university, a school, a prison, or a hospital, as opposed to a person who ministers in a parish. (In this case I happen to be both a parish minister and a university chaplain, which complicates the explanation.) The title *chaplain* is descriptive of a type of ministry and does not indicate either ordained or lay status, though traditionally chaplains have been ordained clergy. In addition to priests, there are now large numbers of theologically educated Catholic laypeople, nuns, and religious brothers, who are working in ministerial positions in the Catholic church. (Later, I learned to answer in shorthand: "They don't ordain us, but they hire us.") I take a deep breath after the explanatory paragraph and wait for a reaction.

"But you can't be," the woman says. "I *know*. I'm Catholic. And I tell you, there's no such thing."

Being the first woman chaplain at St. Paul's was a challenge in itself. Though not everyone I met outside St. Paul's denied my professional existence, explaining to strangers how it could be possible became an additional—and inevitable—component of the job.

A decade later, an article in Boston's archdiocesan newspaper, pleading for support for "religious vocations," painted a bleak picture: closed churches, people unable to practice their faith, and "no one to minister to the needs of the people"—a look into the future, the article suggested, if current trends in vocations continued in the Catholic church. The article was misleading in its implication that clergy are the only people functioning as pastoral ministers in Catholic institutions. Professional ministers in today's American Catholic church—in parishes, schools, hospitals, chanceries, and agencies—also include laypeople, many of them theologically trained at the graduate level, and in some cases, more extensively schooled in biblical studies, liturgy, and church history than their ordained colleagues. There is no shortage of religious vocations in the American Catholic church. There is only a shortage of vocations to the priesthood as it is currently structured from men willing to take a vow of celibacy. Hundreds of theologically educated laymen, laywomen, and nonordained members of religious orders (sisters and brothers) experience a call to exercise religious leadership and have in fact been called to serve as hospital, university, and prison chaplains, teachers of theology in Catholic schools, seminary professors, parish associates or associate pastors, spiritual directors at retreat centers, and church-based social justice workers.[1] The most common position is probably that of director of religious education (the equivalent of the minister of education in a Protestant parish or the temple educator in a synagogue), a position that in Protestant traditions was often women's first entrance into full-time parish ministry. In the dioceses most affected by the current shortage of priests, nuns and on rare occasions laypersons serve as parish administrators, filling most of the administrative duties and pastoral responsibilities of a parish pastor.[2]

Some Catholics have begun to view the new professional class of theologically trained laypeople as an elitist group or a new clerical class separate from the body of the laity. Laypeople in ministry—many of them women—do in fact have a mixed identity, neither fish nor fowl. They are professional church leaders who nevertheless remain part of the laity. Few of the ones I know see themselves as separate from the rest of the Church. There seems to be confusion among their critics between elitism and professionalism. For the most part, professional lay ministers' work is enhanced by their sometimes awkward bridge status: Catholic women, especially laywomen, will always know what it is to be an "ordinary" church member. When Marty Woodward, leaving paid professional church work for a time, served on her parish council during her pregnancy and her son's infancy, she was able to bring to the council the expertise she had built up in her professional ministry; her tenure on the parish council also enriched her awareness of parish life, an understanding she brought back with her when she returned to a paid leadership position.

Women in full-time professional church ministries have career paths less traditional and linear than men's, though their level of education is in most cases equal or higher. This also tends to be true of women leaders in other religious traditions. Maureen Dallison Kemeza, the friend who recently joined the Episcopal Church, once remarked to me that in the time it took her to begin and complete her doctorate, stretched out over a full decade while she worked and raised her children, an ethics scholar of our acquaintance who is a Roman Catholic priest had built an entire career, moving from a junior faculty post to an endowed chair. Both are impeccable scholars and thoughtful theologians—in fact, they are cordial colleagues—but their lives and work look very different. You took longer to earn your Ph.D., I said to Maureen, but he will never have your perspective on relationships, commitment, and community, and that viewpoint is a vital part of your theological contribution.

Economic factors present Catholic women with additional burdens during their years of theological training. Many of the women work, study, and raise children; some study part-time because they cannot afford full-time study and their seminaries cannot provide enough financial aid. Most have accumulated massive educational debts. "When I went to seminary," said Mary Hunt, "I had to take out a student loan to pay my tuition and my Jesuit classmates not only had their tuition, room, and board paid, but their spending money, their books, and their vacations taken care of. I had to take on a second job." Salaries in church jobs are low and benefits often minimal, a source of strain for both sisters and laywomen. Nuns today must pay rent for themselves and contribute to the financial support of their retired sisters. As for laypeople, my colleagues in campus ministry used to speak of the "thirty and out" syndrome, in which laywomen and men, willing to work during their twenties for minimal salaries,[3] tended to change careers in their thirties because they were beginning families, or could no longer make ends meet even as single people committed to a simple life-style.

Self-censorship was another recurring issue in conversations with Catholic women in ministry. During a two-year stint as a reporter and photographer on a diocesan newspaper, Pamela Montagno found it hard "writing not from an objective journalist's perspective but from the perspective of the Church. What I was writing was always supposed to conform with the doctrine. Whenever I would write that little censor was in the back of my mind." Many church-employed women disagreed with official teaching on sexual matters; often they gave hesitant answers to my questions about contraception and abortion; several gave resolute answers and asked not to be quoted by name. When I asked for her position on abortion, one of these women answered: "I feel strongly that women need to have the choice, and that the Church ought to do something so that women don't have to make that choice. The Church is being a hypocrite when it says women may not have abortions but does absolutely nothing to alleviate the problems women have by addressing sexism and racism, supporting women who are single parents, helping women who have ten kids by helping them financially and by being as politically active in supporting better welfare benefits as they are in supporting antiabortion things. I realize there are a lot of Catholic people out there trying to do the right thing," she added, "but the official stance is hypocrisy." She asked for anonymity, saying, "My bishop would kill me; I would lose my job."

Many women in campus ministry and a smaller number of those who work in parishes preach during Sunday Mass, a function technically disallowed by the official Church.[4] The price of this preaching ministry is a kind of conspiracy of silence, a duplicity that allows the preaching to take place but forbids any public comment on the fact that it is occurring. In one of the dioceses where I worked, the bishop knew quite well that I was preaching regularly at Sunday Eucharist— my church and his chancery were no more than a mile from one another—to a congregation of several hundred people. We took care never to speak about it, and he knew that I knew he knew. "Don't tell me about it, and I won't have to tell you to stop," was the unspoken agreement. Our situation was not unusual; I know of many such cases, including some of the women I interviewed. "The bishop knows but doesn't want to know publicly," one woman said to me. In two of the dioceses where I worked, the press stayed silent about the fact that women staff members were preaching at the local church or college chaplaincy, though they knew it would have made a good news story: They collaborated in our duplicity, not wanting to jeopardize a ministry they knew would be eliminated if they reported on it. Only when controversy arose and the preaching stopped did the local newspapers mention that liturgical "irregularities" had been taking place.*

---

*Both events occurred after I had left my position. One of the women affected by these decisions

Despite the limits on the roles of women in the Church, Catholic women work in a remarkable variety of ministries. Religious vocations are not only coming from a new part of the population: They are also taking on new forms. Marty Woodward is the Catholic chaplain at Hollins College, a small women's school in the hills of Virginia. Raised a Presbyterian, Marty became involved in the civil rights movement in her teens; she spent a period of time in India during college, an experience, she said, that "turned me upside down." An accomplished musician, she worked as a youth director for the YWCA in her hometown after her graduation, studied at the Presbyterian School of Christian Education in New York, and moved to Lafayette, Louisiana, to work as a youth minister. She opened an ecumenical, interracial coffeehouse. "In Lafayette in 1968 that was not an easy thing to do," Marty remembered, but seventy teenagers became involved. "The Klan," Marty said, "raised its nose quite quickly." At a midnight meeting of the church session [governing board] she was given twenty-four hours to get out of town. She went into hiding for several weeks with some French Dominican nuns who had come to Louisiana to work with the poor, and, from her hiding-place, encouraged the youths to continue the coffeehouse without her.

During this period of retreat, Marty spent most of her time in prayer. Her dialogue with God eventually led her into the Catholic church. Although she had close Catholic friends and had been studying the differences between the Reformed and Catholic traditions, Marty said, "I had never thought that the route would be to change traditions; it was my commitment to ecumenism that was important. And I found myself really horrified because I knew what it would do to my family. [But] from the moment I decided on that Christmas Eve day, there's never a moment I doubted that God had led me to this point."

Marty went to work in Washington, D.C., at the U.S. bishops' Office of Ecumenical Affairs after she left Louisiana in the late 1960s, "a very positive experience," she said. She then served as associate chaplain at Chicago's Loyola University, and as director of religious education in a Montclair, New Jersey, parish whose members numbered in the thousands. In addition to her master's in theology and religious

is now a chaplain at a Catholic women's college; another has left the Catholic church. In one case the church staff itself decided to limit the woman's liturgical involvement following a complaint in the small but influential, highly conservative *Wanderer,* a national publication; in the other case, the bishop intervened directly after receiving complaints from visitors to the church, which already had a long history of tension with the diocese on issues pertaining to liturgy and sacraments.

education, Marty holds an advanced degree in guidance and a doctor of ministry degree. Her two children were born after she and her husband moved to Virginia, where he is director of Legal Services of Roanoke Valley. While her children were young, she interrupted her professional work; she became president of the parish council when she was pregnant with her second child. She had been at Hollins for several years and was completing a term on the Advisory Council to the National Conference of Catholic Bishops when we met.

At Hollins, Marty told me, she tries to help young women "to grow in the inner and outer journey, to look at what they had planned to do with their lives and what the Gospel values are calling them to." She presides and preaches every Sunday at a communion service which she says "is 'the' Catholic service at our campus.' " "There is no priest at Hollins," she explained. "I am it. We are a mission diocese; we do not have enough priests to meet the needs of all sixty-three college campuses. The priests in my region themselves made the decision that I should do a continual Sunday-obligation communion service,* the bishop concurred, and that's what I have been doing for four years." Every fall, at the Hollins orientation and parents' weekend, Marty explains the workings of her chaplaincy to familiarize students and their families with her ministry and increase their comfort level and participation. This orientation includes her explanation of the difference between a communion service (where no consecration takes place and previously consecrated hosts are distributed), and a Mass (where the prayer of consecration takes place). I asked Marty whether she felt limited in any way by not being ordained. "I don't dwell on what I don't have," she said. "I pray and I work with those folks."

While most of the women who work on parish staffs are religious educators, I also interviewed parish-based outreach workers and community organizers and the former associate pastor of an inner-city church. Some women had helped to create their parish jobs, like Ellen Reuter, who works as a counselor at Sacred Hearts of Jesus and Mary Church in Sun Prairie, Wisconsin. She holds two master's degrees, in early childhood development and social work, and worked as a home trainer and a social worker before coming to Sacred Hearts. "It's something I'd always been interested in doing," she said, "because I think that churches need to be community centers more. People always go to their priest when they have problems and often their priest doesn't

---

*Meaning that students' "Sunday obligation" to attend Mass could be fulfilled by attendance at the communion service.

know what to do. Priests are not trained as therapists and they certainly don't have the time to see somebody once a week for six months. And at health maintenance organizations, you wait two or three months to get in to see a therapist who is not even the therapist of your choice. I thought, 'People deserve better than that.' " Ellen approached the pastor of Sacred Hearts, whom she had known for many years, and negotiated a contract allowing her to work part-time and devote herself to the care of her infant son. She offers family, couples, and individual therapy on a low sliding scale. Three priests, a deacon, several nuns, and two laymen serve on the staff of Sacred Hearts, which holds seven masses each weekend and has four hundred children in the parish school. Ellen is the only laywoman on the staff.

"It's exciting but lonely," Ellen said of her work. "There's nobody else doing it. The confidentiality the people who see me deserve and get means I can't go to the other people on the staff and say, 'Oh God, this last session was just a killer, you're never going to believe what these people did'—because those people may well be cup ministers, religious ed teachers, and other people in the community; [so there is even greater confidentiality than at a mental health center]. There's no one to share the hour-by-hour day with, which was available at the mental health center I worked at before. At the same time it feels real good to be doing something I've always wanted to do, something I really believe in very strongly.

"I'm real clear," Ellen said, "that I'm not a 'Christian therapist.' I'm a therapist who's a Christian. I don't open the session with a prayer or quote Scripture a great deal. I offer people the same kind of therapy they get at a mental health center, but in their church, with somebody they know has the same tradition they have and respects their tradition—and it's affordable. When I tell people what I do, I think I'm often looked at as one of those do-gooders who works in a church, and I'm working hard to make it clear that I'm as much of a professional as any other social worker."

Diane Williams was preparing for parish ministry when we met. A student in the master of divinity program at the Washington Theological Union, she was twenty-nine years old, born and raised in Baltimore, the oldest of three children. She attended Catholic schools from parish elementary school through her college years at Georgetown University. She initially planned to be a high-school religion teacher, but after becoming involved in a vibrant urban church, decided to move toward parish work. Diane had worked as community outreach director at St. Augustine's Church in Washington, where she was still a parishioner, and was a staff member at the Children's Defense Fund at the time of our interview; she was working there twenty hours a week, studying full time, and serving an internship at the campus ministry of the University of Maryland.

"I plan to develop the gifts that I have and use them in the best way that I can in the Church," Diane said, "listening to people, being open to sharing their experiences and challenging them to be in touch with God working in their lives. People generally don't talk about God with their co-workers or their spouse, or their children, or their neighbors or their family or friends. I think we all hunger to do that and we need an environment that says it's okay to do that. I do have a gift to invite that out of people. And I have a gift for listening. What I'm preparing myself for is parish ministry in the area of adult religious education," Diane continued. Traditional Catholic religious education that stops at confirmation, she said, "isn't always enough to carry you through adulthood and the challenges of life. So I'm excited to see a new trend in the Church toward religious education for a lifetime, and I want to be a part of developing that kind of a process in a parish."

"Elsa Colón," an urban community organizer working with parish members and their neighbors, came from a "very activist" family of Puerto Rican and Irish ancestry. "I grew up feeling a sense that my life and calling were to do service in the world, to work to change the world so that it would be a more human and loving place, more equal and more just." Her family was not formally religious, but her parents "embraced the Gospel and lived it and talked about it." A few years into adulthood, "Elsa" realized, "I had worked in politics long enough to know that there was something very vital missing. There was no faith, there was a real lack of spiritual content to the work. And it began to feel to me that the whole viewpoint was to win power, and I always felt, 'To win power for what? For whom? To do what in the world?' There was a vacuum of spiritual and humanistic content in a lot of the political world I had been involved with. I wasn't consciously looking," "Elsa" continued, "but I began to open up to the idea that maybe political organizations were not the way I needed to express who I am in the world." She went to work for the local Catholic Charities office, which was sponsoring parish-based community organizing in poor neighborhoods of the city. This work, she said, led her back to Mass. "I love the work that I do," "Elsa" said, "empowering other people." She works ecumenically, bringing together people from various traditions and backgrounds around the issue of tenants' rights. "It's really important that we not just work as Catholics," she said, "but bring out the base in our faith as Christians."

Beatrice Cortez and Carmen Badillo work in south Texas parishes as consultants sent by the Office of Parish Development of the San Antonio archdiocese. When I asked Beatrice to explain her ministry as a parish consultant, she summed it up in one short sentence: "I'm teaching people to think!" The priest who had helped found COPS also began the Office of Parish Development for the archdiocese, using the COPS organizing model to enhance parish life. "The bottom line" of the office, Beatrice said, "is to equip people, empower people so that they can act out their Christian values in the community around them. You're constantly about building the Body of Christ." The parish consultants work in three ways, Beatrice said. "We do Scripture reflection. We do relationship-building. And then we put faith into action: You look at the needs of the community and act out your faith. It is because we are Church that we get involved. Because these persons that we may not even know are our brothers, then we are responsible for them."

Social change and change in the life of the parish go hand in hand in Beatrice's work. In one small town near the Mexican border, she remembered, people said to her, " 'Well, we like what you do in San Antonio but don't bring politics in here.' So I said, 'Okay, fine. You want to be poor the rest of your life, you want your kids to be uneducated, you want your kids to be on drugs, you want your kids to have no hope, okay, we'll just pray, we'll just go to church on Sunday.' Well, they saw in the paper that the state of Texas wanted to build this nuclear waste dump [in their community] and they called me up frantically: 'Please come out, we know you know how to organize, we need to stop this. The state wants to build a nuclear waste dump two miles from our high school!' I said, 'I'm sorry, but I can't help you.' 'Why not?' 'Because you'll have to get involved in politics,' I said, 'you have to fight the governor, you have to fight your senator, you have to fight your state representative, everybody and anybody, you have to get them on board and confront them.' So," Beatrice said with satisfaction, "they got involved.

"The parish leadership," Beatrice said, "is challenged in every sort of way" by the work of the parish consultants. "The pastor is king of the hill and we recognize that. The pastor is the most powerful position there is in the Church—next to motherhood," she added. "What we do is go in there and acknowledge his power. But we also begin to raise questions with him about strengths and weaknesses. The more secure the pastor is, the better the results. The more insecure, the minimal result, because he hangs on to his power." Shared power in the parish, Beatrice said, was one of the most satisfying results of her work. "I would like there to be more empowerment of the lay people," she told me. "Because in the end it's the people at the parish that give the strength to what is Church. I don't like to quit," Beatrice said. "We're not going to change anything by complaining. There's two kinds of people in this world, actors and spectators. The spectators are the ones that complain, but I want to deal with actors."

Marie de Porres Taylor directs both the Office of Black Catholics of the Diocese of Oakland and the National Black Sisters' Conference. The walls of her office are lined with awards: the Martin Luther King Award for Outstanding Community Service of the United East Oakland Clergy, the Rose Lasanave Service Award "in recognition of devoted and valuable services rendered to the apostolate of the Church in the black community." A photo of black Catholic church leaders, some priests in albs and stoles and some women wearing albs, also hangs in her office. African statues and masks and books by theologian Avery Dulles, W.E.B. DuBois, Gandhi, and Maria Montessori line her shelves.

Marie de Porres (her middle name is taken from Saint Martin de Porres, one of the Catholic church's black saints) became a Catholic at the age of twelve. "I always wanted to be a sister," she said. The first African-American member of her religious order, the Sisters of the Holy Names of Jesus and Mary, Marie de Porres suffered from intense prejudice on the part of her sisters when she entered the community. Sent into the heart of Oakland by her community during the racial unrest of the late 1960s "to calm the black students," she said with a smile, she found that the experience "made me militant rather than quiet." She became involved in the black Catholic movement nationally and in the founding of the National Black Sisters' Conference. For five years she worked as associate pastor at Saint Benedict's Church in Oakland; her responsibilities ranged from visiting the sick and sacramental preparation to youth ministry and involvement in the civic community of Oakland. She served as president of the United East Oakland Clergy, the first woman to lead the city's black ministerial organization. Her current responsibility in the diocese of Oakland, whose population is a mix of Asian, black, Latino, and white, is to address programmatically the spiritual and communal needs of black Catholics. She lives with another black sister in the heart of East Oakland, the poorest area of the city. "I wanted to find a home where my own people would feel comfortable and would feel that I was a part of them," she said, adding that during her years of work at the parish in East Oakland, she had lived in the more affluent, primarily white neighborhood in the hills above the city. When she decided to move into the city, she said, "some of the young people said to me that my moving to East Oakland gave to them the indication that someone cared, that someone really felt that where they lived was important, because all they had experienced was sisters moving out of convents and abandoning the people."

Across the San Francisco Bay, Mary Bridget Flaherty, a Religious of the Sacred Heart, works as chancellor of the Archdiocese of San Francisco, the first woman in this position. The daughter of a surgeon, she considered a career in medicine, worked as a teacher, financial officer, assistant provincial of her religious order, nurse's aide, and parish associate. When the chancery offered her the job, Mary B., as she is known, wondered at first "if this was a token position," as Jeannette Normandin did when she received the invitation to work at the Paulist seminary.

Chancellors' job descriptions vary widely throughout the country. Canon law requires only that they oversee the diocesan archives and serve as civic and canonical notaries. Mary B.'s predecessor, a priest with a background in banking, oversaw the financial operation of the archdiocese. Mary B.'s responsibilities are broader and more pastoral: She is charged with the oversight of day-to-day operations of the chancery, whose 130 employees work in 32 departments and offices. She serves on the archbishop's administrative team and supervises the personnel office and the office of priestly formation. Mary B. spends much of her day listening; her work, she said, is "basically enabling." She spoke warmly of Archbishop Quinn—"a giant among his peers," she wrote to me a few years after our interview, "in the vanguard in his quiet, holy, scholarly, and strongly humanitarian way. How blessed we are!"

Some Catholic women have chosen to minister outside of church structures. Mary Hunt and Diann Neu founded the Women's Alliance for Theology, Ethics, and Ritual (WATER) in 1983 in Silver Spring, Maryland, after extensive studies in theology, ethics, and liturgy and several years of experience as chaplains, teachers, social activists, and leaders in Catholic feminist groups. "What I wanted to do didn't exist," Mary Hunt remembered. "If it was going to work, I'd have to create it." Today, WATER is an educational center, think tank, resource center, and meeting place for women. WATER hosts a monthly breakfast for women in ministry in the greater Washington area as well as workshops on psychology, ethics, and spirituality and seasonal liturgical celebrations. Its services and programs draw both women involved in established religious groups and women who have left them behind. In addition to teaching, writing, leading worship, and running retreats in the Washington, D.C., area, Mary and Diann and their associates travel around the country and to Latin America and Europe to share their liturgical and theological resources with and learn from other religious feminists, including Protestant and Jewish women. They began their work at WATER, Mary said, "at considerable financial risk and sacrifice," but, she added, they have traded the security of an institutional affiliation for independence and creativity.

Mary Hunt studied theology and has spent all her years of ministry as a laywoman. Diann Neu entered the Sisters of Providence immediately after Vatican II and left the order a decade later. At the age of eight, she had experienced, she said laughing, "a classic call. In a May procession, in my parish church, Holy Name in Beech Grove, Indiana, wearing a peach dress, in front of the statue of the Blessed Virgin Mary, I heard that I was being called to something special in life. I have gone back to that moment and renamed it time and time again. Early on I named it as a call to be in religious community." By the time Diann began her graduate studies in theology, she had reinterpreted this event as a call to ordination. "Liturgy has always been a constant in my life," said Diann, who is nationally known for her creativity in designing and leading services of worship. These liturgies celebrate the religious seasons of the year—Christmas, Lent, Easter—but also the seasons and transitions of life: blessing a new home, celebrating a coming of age, mourning a loss. Some involve the blessing of bread and wine; many do not. Ordination is no longer an immediate goal for Diann; instead she has chosen to function in a ministry she names as sacramental.

Other women have left the church in which they grew up to seek ordination in other communions. After graduating from a Catholic college with a triple major in music, philosophy, and drama and being involved for years as a leader in church youth activities, Mary Olivanti became a full-time liturgy and music coordinator at a Catholic parish serving a large state university. "I had no real role models," she said, "and the expectations were never real clear. But it was a good experience and I felt very much a part of the life of the Church." In her second year on the job, she experienced "a strong call to word and sacrament ministry" and a "denominational crisis" prompted, she said, by questions about the definition of the sacraments and their relationship to the witness of Scripture and the teaching authority of the Church. She took a part-time job as music director at the university Lutheran parish and began to study and explore both the Episcopal and the Lutheran churches. "By that time," she said, "I had become quite aware that God was calling me to some form of full-time ministry, and I had an inkling that it was ordained ministry. I was beginning to feel very marginal in the Catholic church, on the outside looking in. I had a sense of not belonging there, that it wasn't home anymore."

During this time, Mary became seriously involved with the man who would become her husband. They met with a Lutheran pastor, a woman serving as one of the university chaplains, for a combination of premarital counseling and introduction to Lutheranism, "working through [all the] issues [together]," Mary said, "helping us identify both our commitment to our relationship and our commitment to ministry, and finding a church in which we could be at home." Mary's husband, who had been a Catholic priest for over two decades, was the son of a Catholic mother and a Lutheran father. They were received into the Lutheran church and married in a Lutheran ceremony; the homilist at their wedding was Mary's maid of honor, one of her former colleagues from the Catholic university parish staff.

At the time of our interview, Mary and her husband were serving as co-pastors of two small congregations in Michigan's Upper Peninsula. Their partnership in marriage and their partnership in ministry were "very much intertwined," Mary said, "because that's for us the way God is calling us to serve His church and His kingdom. That may not be true for other couples but it is true for us. [Working together] is fun," she said, adding, "The discipline we need that keeps our marriage going is to make sure we have time alone together on a regular basis; and we have a child so there's also a need for family time for the three of us."

I asked Mary whether being a mother and a wife had an effect on her ministry. "Absolutely," she said. "It gives me some ways of understanding and a commonality with parishioners. There are times when there is conflict between my duties as the pastor and my role as wife and mother. They are mostly time conflicts. But because Jim and I share one full-time position I feel comfortable saying no when I find my hours are getting over what I'm being paid for and it's not an emergency or a crisis, saying, 'This is family time' or, 'I'm sorry, but that's our day off.' It's fun watching my daughter. When we first came here she started hearing people calling us Pastor Mary and Pastor Jim so she started calling us Pastor Mama and Pastor Daddy. It was hard that first year for her to learn that she had to sit in the pew even though

Mommy or Daddy was up in front leading the worship. I'm sensitive to the kinds of pressures that a parish or a society will put on a preacher's kid and Jim and I work not to add to those pressures—to be good and the best student and well behaved at all times. We want her to be a kid as much as possible."

While both male and female parishioners may be initially resistant to women ministers, most of them, either immediately or in the course of time, welcome them and value their work. After Mary Bridget Flaherty's appointment as chancellor was announced, she said, "I was overwhelmed by the positive response, people I didn't know, women who worked in a bank and had seen it in the paper and would call me up and say 'Yea!' I had letters from our senators, representatives, city officials, religious congregations, the little woman in the pew— and the priests were wonderfully warm and accepting. At one point I said to the archbishop, 'If there's been any flack, you've gotten it, because I haven't.' He said, 'I haven't either.' Either they're keeping it to themselves or people were ready for it in the Archdiocese of San Francisco."

What ultimately matters to church members is whether women ministers are competent, caring, and reverent. May Kast, a woman in her sixties, is an active volunteer at St. Bernard's parish in Madison, Wisconsin, and a member of the National Council of Catholic Women, a mainstream Catholic women's organization with chapters around the country. She spoke to me about one of the nuns serving on her church's ministerial team. "Sister Vera Bittel is on the staff and she's the pastoral assistant and she does so much for the elderly," May said. "She's the one who runs the coffees and the dinners for senior citizens, and she visits people in their rooms. She's a very important part of church life. The priests never had the time; there were so few priests. Sister Vera is so gentle, she is very well organized, she keeps a lot of people together."

"Regina White" served a sentence at the prison where Jeannette Normandin was a chaplain. She spoke of Jeannette's ministry with warmth and gratitude. "Jeannette was after me," she said. "I was locked up in maximum security for hitting someone and she came bouncing through, so I'm saying to myself, 'Who the hell's this lady?' She told me after, 'I just took a liking to you,' and she kept coming up and giving me books and writing paper and we struck up a friendship. I felt like she was somebody that I could really talk to. She's probably the first person I really trusted with a lot of garbage that I had inside. Then she kept coming after me to go to church.

"I can't say that jail was a bad experience," "Regina" added, "because I got a lot of good out of it—Jeannette, number one. She helped me feel a little bit better about myself so I could accomplish a few things. There's a lot of good people in there that didn't go for my defenses, Jeannette and a couple of the officers. They'd see right through them. I'd try to push people away. They'd say, 'We don't buy that about you, "Regina," it's just a front and you're a good person.' And it would make me think: 'Well, am I? Am I?' Jeannette kept coming after me. I felt like a piece of shit. I remember telling her one time, 'I don't know why you're wasting your breath on me, I'm no good or I wouldn't be in here.' She kept saying stuff to me and I'd go in my room and think about it and I'd deny it and then I'd avoid her but she just kept coming after me, she kept haunting me. I'm glad she did, I really am. She didn't give up on me. I don't know why. I didn't feel like I was worth saving. I think she gave me a lot of hope. I feel so much better now."

The term *ministry* is broadly and widely used these days in Catholic circles, a direct consequence of the Second Vatican Council's focus on the Christian vocation inherent in baptism and in what the Council documents call "the universal call to holiness." One hears a lot in parishes and church conferences these days about "the ministry of all the baptized" (a term American Catholics prefer to the "priesthood of all believers"). While many women and men have left religious orders and the ordained ministry in the past two decades, a far greater number of American Catholic laypeople are now involved in church leadership and service. They teach children and adults about their faith, comfort the sick, feed the hungry, and help others to pray. Just as the ordained clergy are no longer the only ministers, membership in a religious order is no longer the only or primary option for dedicated service. Vocations to Christian service have increased; the forms they take on have changed. "I think it's great to have vows, but I don't think everybody has to," said Pamela Montagno. "There's a whole new mold of laypeople who are religious and spiritual. They're religious but they don't fit into that mold of taking those three vows." As Catholic women now ascribe a broader meaning to the term *ministry,* so too they are beginning to question the use of the terms *religious women* to describe nuns, and *religious life* to describe membership in a religious order. "*Religious women* as a term is disastrous," Pamela said. "Hell, I'm a religious woman."

Everywhere, Catholic women pour out their time and talents in response to the needs around them, some in public life and in the workplace, others in the internal life of the local church. Mar Londo of Green Bay, Wisconsin, sees her counseling job "as a way of healing and mending. I'm sure that one of the reasons my work is so meaningful to me is that it's a way to live out the spirituality in my life." Ann Valdez, a full-time public health administrator, has been a volunteer hospital minister for three years, bringing communion to Catholic patients and visiting people in the intensive care and oncology units. "I seem to have kind of a gift," she said, "for dealing with people who are critically ill and dying and for dealing with their families." Rafaela Canelo's chief concerns in the life of her neighborhood are housing problems and the needs of undocumented immigrants. Her inspiration, motivation, and support come from the small base community to which she belongs. "The ecclesial base community is part of the living church of Christ," she said. "We gather together once a week. We join together to pray, to reflect on the Gospel, and to discover how we can live the Gospel in the reality in which we live. Seeing the problems under the light of the Gospel, we see, we analyze, and we look for ways of acting." There is no single model or set expectation of what group members will do to live out their faith commitment "At the moment of taking action we have different callings, different gifts," Rafaela said. "So not all of us are engaged in one thing. For example, I have my social vocation, but others prefer the liturgy or social service, so each of us does it in a different way."

The most hidden of the unpaid ministries is probably that of prayer. While almost all of the women I met prayed, one had made prayer the center of her life and ministry. "I didn't grow up wanting to be a nun," said "Genevieve O'Rourke," a member of a cloistered contemplative order. "It came on me later in life, at the age people decide to be married or have a career. It was just a deep attraction; it was nothing dramatic, nothing sensational. In my twenties I just re-alized that life is short and we only pass this way once and I wanted to use it in a very fruitful, productive way. It was a falling in love with God and wanting to give my life." By living in a community whose main work is prayer, "Genevieve" said, she was "witnessing by my life to the deepest dimension of our being, the dimension in which we are in relationship with God.

"Falling in love with God as revealed in Jesus brought me to live in a life apart," said "Genevieve," "but we are one with all the world: Our physical separation in no way separates us from the world and all its cares and concerns. Saint Thérèse of the Child Jesus is the patroness of the missions and yet she was a cloistered nun." As did all the women I met who were involved in some form of ministry, "Genevieve" sought to acknowledge and develop the gifts and talents of others. "When people come to us for prayer," she said, "I try to encourage them to pray themselves and say that I'm joining them, that their prayers are important too." She added: "World hunger clamors for our action, but contemplation brings us in touch with another hunger, and that's the hunger of the human spirit for God, whether we are aware of it or not. So our major social concern here is to awaken, foster, nourish this deepest hunger of our eternal spirits."

Other volunteer ministries offer the most basic of nourishment. I visited May Kast at her house on the edge of Madison, Wisconsin's East Side. A slight woman with an infectious laugh, she grows flowers outside her door, a riotous array of them, some taller than she. May grew up in Australia, converted to Catholicism, married a German-born man and emigrated to the U.S. as a young woman. She is the mother of eight children, all grown. May cooks for funerals, weddings, and marriage preparation days at St. Bernard's Parish. "When the kids got a little bit older," she said, "I realized so many people had been working in the church when I couldn't work—you had to bathe the babies and all, and by the time you got through you were too late to do anything [at church]. So I said well, soon as my kids get a bit older, I'm going to take over and work like I've seen other people." May had learned to cook in large quantities through her involvement with 4-H, helping to make the 4:00 A.M. breakfasts on the fairgrounds. "So I wouldn't be afraid if someone called up tomorrow and said they wanted lunch for one thousand," she laughed. Church members pay for the food and May plans the menu, shops, and supervises a crowd of other women volunteers. Every meal is a new creative project. "If I'm going to make something it has to be something special, something nice and not just thrown together. Whether you write or cook," she said, grinning at me, "you've got to make an art of it. You've got to do your best. You've got to do it nice.

"I've learned to love people so dearly working in church," May continued. "I think it's made me a better person. I told the bishop [who used to be pastor of our church], 'Do you know what? I used to think it was a barbaric custom, eating and drinking and being merry after a funeral. In Australia a funeral is a funeral; it was solemn.' And I said, 'People going to eat after the funeral? I could hardly bear it.' And then I learned that Americans come from far, from all over to the funeral, and if people don't feed them in church, they have to take them to a restaurant, which is most difficult, like sometimes you have a hundred people and it'll cost you a fortune. In the Bible," said May, "Jesus always enjoyed a meal or he invited people to eat. So finally I realized it is very important to do this for people because it saves them a lot of work and a lot of worry at a time when, how can you think of getting food? I've realized that this is an important part of the Church—that socializing and taking care of things, when people cannot do it themselves."

The women I interviewed who were active in parish life were frequently involved in liturgical ministries as Eucharistic ministers, lectors, musicians, and sacristans. As the sacristan for her parish in Carmel, Indiana, Charlotte Giddens prepares the altar and the priests' vestments for Mass, a responsibility she took on out of gratitude, she said, following a parish renewal program. "I was so moved by that I knew I had to do something for this parish," she said. Mary Esther Bernal was also motivated by gratitude to give her time and talents to the Church. Now the director of bilingual education for the San Antonio School District, she began her educational career as a teacher of music in the public schools. As a very young woman, she had received thirty dollars a month for playing the organ at the city's cathedral; the money paid for her college education. "Since I came back to the Catholic Church," she said, "I have volunteered my services, because I am very appreciative." In addition to directing the cathedral choir, Mary Esther has founded a children's choir. "These children come from poverty homes," she said, "they've never had voice lessons, and they don't have any opportunity to study. I have the richest people in San Antonio offering to pay me to teach their children music and I've rejected their offer. That children's choir has given me tremendous satisfaction musically. They are the little diamonds in the rough, my babies, ranging from age five to age thirteen, and the offshoot is that some of the parents have become active at the cathedral and joined the adult choirs."

Ann Richards Anderson has served as a Eucharistic minister on and off during her years of involvement in the Church. "Sharing the Eucharist, physically passing it out is a very profound experience," she said. "It really makes you look more deeply into yourself as made in God's image and having an obligation to act in God's image. It's like, if you're not really living this in your life, what are you doing up here?" "In some areas they [still] don't want women as Eucharistic ministers," Dorothy McFadden commented, referring to the fact that some parishes resist having women distribute the bread and wine of communion, a practice that is now widespread in most parts of the U.S. "A woman feels better being part of the Church," Dorothy added. "There are people who will not go to *communion* still [if a woman is giving it out]!" May Kast exclaimed. "They will not go unless it's a priest, and that's wrong, because there aren't very many priests, and one of these days people are going to have to accept the fact that laypeople will have to do a lot more in the Church." Because of the centrality of the Eucharist, many women equated "involvement in the Church" with "playing an active liturgical role" as Dorothy McFadden did in speaking of Eucharistic ministers and Teresita Bravo-Paredes did when she rejoiced in her daughters' opportunity to be altar girls.

All over the country, in about half the parishes I heard of including small rural congregations and large suburban churches, there are altar girls. In one Midwestern urban parish I visited, adults as well as children, both male and female, serve as acolytes, as people performing this ministry are also known. When the bishop comes to visit the parish, the actors in the liturgical drama change: The female altar servers vanish and the sister who serves on the staff no longer leads the closing prayer as she usually does at the end of Mass. "Ridiculous!" said the parish member who told me about this change of scene. "The women are running the churches. I don't think we should have to stand in the shadows when the big guys come in."

"I have no specific gripes," Jackie Haber said when I asked how she felt about the position of women in the Church. "I guess I would like to see some of the girls be able to be acolytes, altar girls," she added. In the suburb of Detroit where she used to live, Jackie said, "There was a period when we had altar girls and then the cardinal said it was against the Church, so the girls had to obey that, which I always thought was ridiculous. I'm glad to see that women are able to read the Scriptures and distribute Holy Communion. What puzzles me so much is, if women are able to distribute Holy Communion, why can't the girls be altar girls?"

From altar girls and Eucharistic ministers, our conversations moved to the subject of women's ordination. For over half the women I interviewed, the ordination of women was an emotional and highly charged topic, whether they opposed or supported it. But for several women, it was of no concern at all. "I've never given it a thought," said Joy Duffy, the executive secretary from San Francisco. "They probably would be qualified," she added, "and a woman is consoling to a lot of people." Some women said to me that they "could go either way." "It wouldn't bother me if the time came," said Jackie Haber. "I'd be open to it," said Dorothy Wodraska, the physical education teacher and pro-life activist from Indianapolis. "I'm not pro or con."

Familiarity with women in ministerial roles always seemed to influence women's position on ordination. The women from south Texas who did not know any married clergy were opposed to making priestly celibacy optional; yet they often favored the ordination of women (celibate women only, in keeping with their views on marriage and ministry). While they had never met an ordained woman, they often spoke admiringly of competent, dedicated women in positions of religious leadership, the nuns with whom they had prayed and worked throughout the years. From this positive experience of Catholic sisters to imagining women priests there was only a small step. Here again, experience shaped opinion.

"Well, of course I'm for women," said May Kast after praising Sister Vera, "and there's wonderful women whom I would accept as priests. A lot of Catholic women and Catholic men wouldn't, but I've met women who were so wonderful that I'm sure they could be priests if it was allowed, and I wouldn't hesitate to go to confession or anything to a woman." She added: "A woman like Mother Teresa, of course she gets the laurels that she truly deserves because there's not too many people that give their lives like she does. But do you think the Church would ever accept her as a priest, with all the good that she has done in this life? I suppose after thousands of years it is pretty hard to break down all those laws."

"A lot of us wish Sister Joan could be ordained," Myra Spivey said, speaking of the associate pastor of her church. "She knows everybody inside out. Sister Joan is white," Myra added, "but inside she's black. She has come to know this area, she has come to know the black people so well; she fits in so well. When she's not here everybody's lost. I would say she has more influence on us than our pastor because she's always here. She's here for us."

Of the minority who opposed women's ordination, only a few presented a historical or theological argument against it. Often, women simply felt uncomfortable with the thought of women clergy. Sometimes emotional discomfort and religious belief combined. "I don't see women priests," said Mary Callanan, who supervises a staff of 144 people. "I still see women's job as helping out. Christ had twelve apostles and they were all men."

A majority of the women I interviewed favored the ordination of women; a majority also wanted to see the celibacy rule change. But these two groups were not necessarily the same people, though there was plenty of overlap. Those women who supported both changes in the discipline of the Church usually made an explicit connection between the two. Often, they felt that priestly celibacy, women's exclusion from priesthood, and teachings on sexuality and reproduction were related to one another, and that the link among them was the fear of women and sex. In much of the Western world, Caryl Rivers observed, "a split evolved between nature and spirit, with woman representing nature and man striving for spirit and God. I think celibacy is rooted in this whole thing: that if nature is bad, woman is bad, and one must transcend and get higher and get above. Celibacy is mixed up with fear of sexuality." Like many women, Caryl felt the ban on ordination of women, at its root, had little to do with theological logic and far more to do with gut reaction and psychological process. "I have a hunch that the whole thing is about womb envy," she said. "Why is religion controlled by men? Very early on, men looked around and saw that women controlled the real mystery of life, and that was such a tremendous power. I think that male taking over of the institutions of religion was really based on finding a way to control a set of mysteries, and I think it operates to this day. Why in the name of God should anybody feel threatened by a ten-year-old girl going to the altar?" she added, in reference to a recent controversy about altar girls. Speaking of what she saw as related issues, priestly celibacy and women's or-dination, Caryl said, "It all has to do with this issue of controlling the mysteries and who does God belong to anyhow?"

"Many of the issues of sexuality," said "Joanne Grace," have been a cause of real suffering for women and just would not have happened if the male influence had not been so total [in the Church]. Like enduring a bad marriage because divorce was totally wrong and women owed total obedience to their husbands." She added, "The changes we need can only come about if we have women as priests and married clergy. I think as long as we have an all-male hierarchy women are going to continue to suffer and be treated as less than full human beings, full people of God." "If we recognize women as valuable," said Brigette Rouson, "then we *have* to ordain women! We have to. And if we recognize women as valuable and marriage as special and important, then at some point we've got to allow priests to marry."

Most of the women who favored women's ordination believed, like "Joanne Grace," that ordaining women and noncelibate men would help solve many of the Catholic church's problems. But an outspoken minority cautioned against viewing these changes as a panacea, stressing both the need to change the priesthood itself and their fear of women's co-optation into a structure they viewed as unhealthy. Clergy-lay di-visions and abuses of power, they pointed out, can be just as grave in churches with married and female clergy as they are in the Roman church.

Though "equal talents, equal rights" was not the sole factor in their support for women's ordination, to many women the issue evoked and represented the broader question of women's role, talents, and worth in the Church. "I'm in favor of it. I'm as good as any man," Judy McDonough said when I asked how she felt about the ordination of women. For women like Judy, a practicing Catholic and the mother of eight children (one of them an altar girl), there is a dissonance between opportunities opening to women in the secular world and restrictions placed upon them in the Church. Women's daughters digest the message in simpler form. I recently heard of a little Catholic girl who, when her religion class was asked how many sacraments there were, raised her hand and answered, "seven for the boys and six for the girls." The missing sacrament, of course, is ordination.

Women's ordination, many women felt, would be good for the Church. Most did not view it simply as a question of equal opportunity.* They believed that in keeping women out of the ordained ministry, the Church was depriving itself of its own gifts—those women had to offer—and thwarting in many women the gifts they could make of themselves. "Women have a lot to offer," said Brigette Rouson, "and the Church is just ignoring the opportunity; it is just not Christ-like. The way our society has conditioned us, women tend to be more willing to listen. You've seen the surveys that say men interrupt more, women listen more. That's a reality that may change down the road, but right now women tend to be more willing to understand, more able to identify with oppression, less concerned with power and control than with achieving good things and bringing good people together. I think that the same role many mothers have played in their families, women can play as priests. What a hell of a potential is there."

The women's ordination movement has never focused on what Mary Hunt calls the "add women and stir" formula. It has been concerned with church renewal and reexamination of the priesthood as much as with advocating the ordination of women. A good number of the women I interviewed—none of them involved in the women's ordination movement but all reflecting its current preoccupations—said that although they were in favor of ordaining women, their priorities

---

*The women's ordination movement in its early days (the first national conference on women's ordination was held in 1975 and led to the formation of the organization Women's Ordination Conference) stressed that women do not have a "right to be ordained" as much as a right to have their vocation to ordination tested and recognized as men do. "Do I have a vocation to the ordained ministry?" The difficulty of discerning a call one is not supposed to have has, for many women, blurred the answer to this question.

lay elsewhere. Structural change in church government, a stronger role for the laity, and the broader concerns of women in the life of the Church were their chief preoccupations.

"I'm always in the middle, it seems," Abigail McCarthy said. "I have a little problem with making ordination the be-all and end-all as some of the feminists in the Church do. As long as Mass has to be celebrated by a man, I'm willing to accept the Mass. I have friends who won't go to a liturgy performed by a man. To me that's almost cutting off your nose to spite your face, because I do believe in the [apostolic] succession and I do believe in the Eucharist as a living presence. It just seems to me too extreme. But I know it's offensive; I want women to be ordained too." Later, speaking of the bishops' pastoral on women, she said, "If this letter came out with a real emphasis on the equality of women spiritually, and an emphasis on the need for education, understanding of women, women's history, it could be useful; but I don't think that's the way it will be. And of course as long as women are denied ordination on the basis of the shape of their bodies, there's a basic problem. As long as you can subscribe to that notion, you can't really write about women." As other women did, Abigail McCarthy expressed hope that the priesthood would change. "I think the priest should be selected out of the people, that we are all priests," she said. As for church government or "jurisdiction," which in the Roman Catholic Church is combined with ordination, "there is no reason why priesthood should be coupled with government," she added.

Public discussion about the ordained ministry in the Catholic church has shifted its focus from the nature and abilities of women to the needs of the Church, and specifically the need for Eucharist. The question has changed from, "Can women serve as ministers?" to, "What sort of ministry does the Church need?" After reminding his readers of the shortage of priests (which often leads priests to pastor clusters of parishes, thus reducing the number of Eucharistic liturgies they are able to celebrate), a priest named William Shannon recently wrote in a Catholic magazine: "We Roman Catholics are in danger of losing the Eucharist. . . . This strikes at the very heart of our existence as church. There is a very old liturgical dictum: *Eucharistia facit Ecclesiam* ('The Eucharist makes the church'). Without the Eucharist we are not church. . . . Our problem is not vocations or campaigns for vocations. Our problem is that we are asking the wrong question. The question we need to put to ourselves is this: 'How can we continue to provide the Eucharist for future generations of Catholics?' . . . The question regarding the Eucharist is the one that is of primary importance. The question about the recruitment of celibate male candidates for the priesthood is of secondary importance. It is a way of answering the primary question. Is it the only way?"[5]

But some Catholic women—even those who favor the ordination of women in principle—have been asking whether the ordination of women would in fact be good for the Church—or for women. When they ask, "What kind of ministry does the Church need?" their answer is unlikely to be "sacramental priesthood as it is presently structured and understood." "I see a tremendous need in the Church for women ministers," said Sara Whalen of Madison, Wisconsin. "Whether they have to be priests or not is beside the point. I think we have to have women who minister to each other. I feel we do that every day," she added. "We don't need these ordained ministers particularly."

For these women, ministry in a broader sense was more important than ordination. "I think we all minister, men and women, whether you're ordained or not ordained," Anne Burke said to me. "I think there's a call. Some people feel called to minister in the traditional sense, on the altar. Women are called just the way men are, and I resent the fact that the Catholic church doesn't recognize that. But the other piece is I don't want women to participate in a system that I find to be very oppressive anyway."

Other women had equally mixed feelings. "I'm not really sure about a hierarchy," said college student Kathryn Schuler, "if it's necessary to run a church. But if I did find it was necessary, then of course [I'd have] both sexes represented." "Certainly women should be priests," said sixty-four-year-old "Kitty Riordan." "I never can believe when I read anybody that says why they can't. That's nonsense they're talking. 'Tradition,' all this stuff? They're scared to death. I never heard archbishops sound so afraid as when women started to [talk about that issue]." But, she said, "I wouldn't give five cents worth of energy now for women to become priests. I would not work for that. Do I want women to buy into that, that old cult? I do not."

"My position," said Mary Hunt, "is that I would like to forsake ordination in favor of ministry. By that I don't mean to back off from the justice demand of ordination. But I think the institutional Church will posture on this by ordaining women deacons. I think that is a recipe for disaster. I don't think they're going to get ordained for a while," Mary continued, "but when they are ordained they're going to be so co-opted it's going to make their heads spin; and it's going to divide women. It'll sap off the best and the brightest and they will be played off [against the other women]. The women who, with the best of intentions, will get ordained and be celibate and become women bishops and cardinals will retard any kind of real change in the Church. The difficulty in the church is not that we don't ordain women, it's that we have a hierarchical structure in which you have ordination into a clerical caste, whether it's a man or a woman. Just ordaining women is not going to solve the fundamental problem, which is that there are the religious doers and the religious receivers. I'm not interested in putting women into that. I feel women's ordination is counterrevolutionary.

"Forsaking ordination for the sake of ministry," for Mary and for others who identify with Women-Church, also implies a move toward religious self-determination and a change in the traditional understanding of the sacraments. The Church does have a right to and need for the Eucharist, these women argued, but Eucharist and ordination need not be coupled.* "I think women should be encouraged to function sacramentally," Mary Hunt said. "People have to understand the sacraments in a quite different way, that the priest is not the dispenser of the sacraments. Women want to be priests because they don't think they can function sacramentally. Well, I can function sacramentally without being ordained and I do. The most important thing at this point is to encourage people to understand that these sacraments are valid."

Marty Woodward and Jeannette Normandin lead communion services as part of their ministry, services during which they read the Bible and distribute previously consecrated hosts or bread. Because they do not consecrate the hosts, these women are not celebrating Mass; the service may, according to Church guidelines, be led by a layperson. Diann Neu and Mary Hunt, on the other hand, ignore official definitions and restrictions and name as sacramental the celebrations they hold in their home and at larger Women-Church gatherings. Both of these experiences raise questions about the definition and nature of sacrament and ordained ministry. Are either of them in any way sacramental? And if they are, what then is the meaning of ordination?

The ministering women I met are part of a new generation of church leaders (*generation* is a broad term since their ages ranged from twenty to seventy). They work inside and outside church structures,

---

*This perspective is no longer limited to people who identify with Women-Church; men and women gathered at the 1991 Call to Action conference, most of them white, suburban, and over fifty years old, also brought up the issue of celebrating the Eucharist without the leadership of ordained clergy—a notion which would have been unthinkable to this group of people only a few years ago.

both improvising and drawing on what usable past they find in the Catholic tradition. Most of the women who spoke to me of a call or vocation to ministry (ordained or not) made clear to me that the church community was always a part of this call. There was a dialogue in their lives between their inner sense of calling and the invitation by the community of faith to minister in its midst. God's voice, for these women, spoke in both places.

Three years after Maureen Dallison Kemeza told me she was joining the Episcopal Church, she and I were speaking on the telephone, catching up on a busy period in both our lives; I had just heard from an old seminary friend of ours, Catherine Mooney, who had entered the Religious of the Sacred Heart shortly after finishing her master's in theology and had gone to work in Argentina in the fields of religious education, health care, and human rights. She was back in the U.S., completing a doctorate in church history and continuing her involvement in human rights and service to the poor. Maureen and I spoke of our friendship and of the paths the three of us had taken in the ministry, each so different from the other. Our conversation evoked the women I had met on my travels: May Kast, tending her flower garden and cooking meals for times of grief and celebration; Carmen Badillo and Beatrice Cortez, helping church members in rural south Texas to move "from spectators to actors"; Diann Neu, creating rituals and prayers for ecumenical groups of women; Ellen Reuter, the patient healer, listening to wounded lives in the privacy of her office; Ann Valdez, sitting for three hours with a dying man, holding his hand.

"Remember," Maureen said to me, "fifteen or eighteen years ago in seminary, when we wondered: 'Where are the women? Where are the role models? Where are the women to show us the way?' " She paused and said: "We are the women we were looking for."

NINETEEN

SYLVIA PARK

"I thank God every day that I had my religion."

Sylvia Griffin Park was ninety-two years old at the time of our meeting in the summer of 1986. She spent most of her life in Idaho and Utah, both states with a large Mormon population. She looked at me steadily with sharp luminous blue eyes, her speech a little muffled, but her opinions firm and clear.

I wasn't supposed to have had the name Sylvia, I was supposed to have been Geraldine, but Father R. came down from Pocatello and he said, "I came to baptize the baby" and Mom said, "I'm taking her to Pocatello to be baptized," and he said, "I'm going to baptize her today." So she told him she was going to name me Geraldine; he said, "No, we're going to name her Sylvia Perpetua."

Mom was a widow; she had seven children; I was a year old in August and my father died in September and Mom raised us good, good Catholic Christians. All the relatives wanted to take us and she said, "No, I'm keeping them all together." And she did. She kept boarders, did housework, and raised us good Catholics. I tell you, she had a hard time putting us all through Catholic schools, but she made it, and God bless her for it. It's due to my dear, dear ancestors, my Irish ancestors, that we kept the faith. They were all born in Ireland except my mother. It was really hard with all the Mormons pulling against you and trying to convert you and everything.

When I got big enough to go out I went to dances. One night this young man asked me to go. He was a very nice, good-looking young man. He told me afterward that my folks were afraid—he'd borrowed the fifty cents from them to take me to the dance! Of course he wasn't Catholic when [we were] married and I had to be married at the rectory, I couldn't even put my foot inside the door [of the church]. Well, my husband was a prince of a fellow, and I tell you, he was a better Catholic a lot of times than I was. When I was sick or had babies, he always saw to it that the children got to Mass every day and said their prayers. [And he was] very patient. But he had emphysema, very badly, so he was really, really sick. I prayed and prayed that he'd come into the Church and one day Father M.—God help that boy that left [the priesthood]—asked Dad, "Wouldn't you like to be a Catholic?" and he said, "Sure, I would." So Father M. came the next day and baptized him, and Dad never got out of bed. He died maybe four or five months after and he died a good practicing Catholic. He was seventy-eight when he died. He had his mind and everything but he was a very sick man.

God was very, very good to us. Many days we didn't know whether we'd get enough to feed the children because my husband didn't earn enough money—he was a railroad man—but we always managed. His children *never*, never went hungry or wanted for anything, and that's why when I was keeping house I fed many, many transients, because I knew *my* children had never gone hungry and I didn't want anyone else to go hungry, and they didn't. And that's why I try to give money to the food bank at church, so that no one'll want for food.

God's sure been good. He gave me my two lovely daughters to take care of me. That's all I have left of the four I had. My youngest son Dick died of cancer and he and my one and only daughter that was left besides the twins died within five months of each other. I've had lots of crosses, but thank God He gave me the strength and faith to bear them. I tell you, it was hard. If I didn't have a good Christian husband, although he wasn't a baptized Catholic, I couldn't have done it.

I liked the Church as it was. I liked fasting from meat on Fridays and I liked Lent, and Wednesdays and Fridays keeping the Lenten fast; and I liked First Fridays and all of those practices, and the Sacred Heart devotions, because they gave me a good deal of comfort and a great deal of help how to take care of things. And the Church with all these practices was so good to me and took care of me in every way.

I wouldn't criticize my church, but I do think they're a little too lenient in lots and lots of ways [today] and they're not strict enough in lots of the teachings. Like, you get married, and you don't want to live with the guy. So you go and get the marriage annulled for no reason whatever and get married again. I don't like that! I like "When you're married, you're married, and stay married."

I wouldn't like women to ever be ordained priests and I'm not particularly fond of married men being priests. I think they've got enough responsibilities to take care of a family and all that. I don't think women have any place being ordained. Our dear God would have ordained women if he had intended them to be priests. *I* think. I think women should teach religion, and help all the others, but I don't think they should take the place of priests or do what is the duty of priests. I think they should just mind their business.

I think a woman's place, God made it to be in the home. I never worked a day in my life: I stayed home. I will have been married seventy-one years in September. A man came around [once] to take the census of my good Irish grandmother, and she said she'd be married fifty years, and he said, "To one man?" And she said, "Well, how many men would you want me to have?" I've been married to one man seventy-some odd years and thank God for that. I had a good marriage to a very kind, very Christian, good to my children, good to everybody [man]. I was really fortunate in having such a good man.

The Holy Family—I'm very devoted to them. They do so much for me. They keep me walking and safe from falling. Sometimes I use the rote prayers to them, sometimes I make up my own. I love the Blessed Mother. She's so wonderful: a real mother to me, takes care of me, asks her dear son to give me strength and help and grace, everything I need in this world.

[These days] I get up and have my breakfast, and I come in here and sit until I get kind of settled and I say my Rosary and some other prayers. And I always try to say my morning prayers before I get out of bed. Then later on I say another Rosary for all the poor souls, and all during the day, little ejaculations* and prayers, thank God for everything. I always say my blessing for my food, thanksgiving for my food.

I remember when my grandson told me he was going to be a priest. It was in the morning, and he was going up to the university and he came in about ten o'clock all dressed up and I thought, "What's happened?" and he talked a bit and I could see he was pretty nervous and pretty soon he said, "Grandma, I've got to tell you something." And I thought, "Mike's going to tell me he's going to get married." That's the first thing I thought of. And I said, "Well?" He said, "I'm going to go to the seminary." Oh, I almost dropped

---

*Brief prayers consisting of a single word or short phrase.

all of the dishes; and I thanked God right there and then for him; and he is such a good priest. [A good priest is] when they keep their vows, and keep to the purity of their—whatever you call it, and [a good priest is] one who takes an interest in getting people into the Church and telling them about the Church, and helping other people find their way in life.

I think it's none of the bishops' business [to write all these statements]; they're carrying things too far. They think they know more than what God intended the Church to be. I think they're usurping their authority, and I think they should follow what the Church teaches. The pope is supposed to be the supreme leader and they should kind of abide by what he teaches. [And] that Hans Küng.* I think he ought to have been thrown out of the Church a long long time ago.

I think the world is in a way very, very irreligious. I think people kind of throw God aside and think they can do their own without Him, but one of these days He's going to show them that they have to have God in their lives.

[If I could change the world I'd change] all this immorality in it. I'd teach them to be moral, decent people and to live up to God's rules. [And I'd] just put the Church back where it was. All the rules and regulations and commandments and all the different things we were supposed to do and live up to. I'd exhort people to live the Church as it was and it should be and as it was intended to be by God, and not go off on any wild ideas.

[I have a picture of God in my head when I pray,] oh *yes*. [I see God as a] very kind, understanding person. He looks just like— when I pray to the Holy Family, I picture the Blessed Infant and the Blessed Mother and Saint Joseph. Saint Joseph taking care of them, and leading them all safely. They've answered my prayers in many ways.

[The most important thing in my life] is my religion. My religion, my church, my God. What would I do without God? In all my trials and tribulations. Thank God I still got my religion, I never lost it or gave it up. I kind of wavered, not giving it up, just getting lax in it.

---

*The Swiss Catholic theologian whose recognition as a Catholic theologian was withdrawn by the Vatican's Sacred Congregation for the Faith in 1979. The Vatican criticized Küng for his writing on papal infallibility and on the person of Jesus Christ. Although Küng is no longer a member of the Catholic Theological Faculty of the University of Tübingen, Germany, he continues to teach at the university. His recent works examine the relationship between Christianity and other major world religions.

That didn't last, 'cause I saw I was getting nowhere. Oh, I thank God every day that I had my religion. I'll be ninety-three if I live till the end of August.

Sylvia Park died on March 19 of the following year at the age of ninety-four, on the feast of her favorite saint, Joseph, the great provider and protector.

TWENTY

THE FUTURE, IN THIS LIFE
AND THE NEXT

Do not smile and say
you are already with us.
Millions do not know you
and to us who do,
what is the difference?
What is the point of your presence
if our lives do not alter?
                    —*Dom Helder Camara*

There's life in this religion. Even in death
there's life.
                    —*"Elena Martinez Wise"*

"We all learned the dessert concept of heaven," Ellen Reuter said to me. "How you put yourself last, how nothing here really matters; how the reward will come later. But in the last twenty to thirty years we have decided it matters how you live here. The afterlife matters less. We assume there is an afterlife and we leave that up to God. But meanwhile we need to do something about the Kingdom here on earth.

"As women got into a more direct relationship with God," she continued, "we became more adamant about living a Christian life— and much more furious about injustice: injustice to us, injustice to our children, injustice to the earth. That has taken away the dessert part of heaven. We never talk about heaven except in terms of being reunited with loved ones. Which has to say something about the place of love in our lives."

With these words, Ellen Reuter unknowingly summarized over one hundred women's statements about death and the future—in this life and the next.

The theologian Rosemary Ruether expresses the sentiments of many of the Catholic women I met: "Our responsibility," she writes, "is to use our temporal life span to create a just and good community for our generation and for our children. It is in the hands of Holy Wisdom to forge out of our finite struggle truth and being for everlasting life. Our agnosticism about what this means is then the expression of our faith, our trust that Holy Wisdom will give transcendent meaning to our work, which is bounded by space and time."[1] Most of the Catholic women I met believed that there is a life after the one we know on this earth. But, with a few exceptions, they did not spend much time speculating about it. "Something is there, God knows, we don't," was the most common attitude I encountered. Catholic women have great faith in the presence of a continued or transformed existence, but have little inclination to speculate about what the nature of this existence is or will be.

Catholic women's views on death, the afterlife, and the end and goal of human history reflect elements of the Church's traditional belief about the resurrection of the dead, the survival of the whole person (bodily as well as spiritual), and the survival of the human self after death.[2] I heard more explicit talk about life after death than about resurrection, though I may have framed my questions in a way that led the conversation in that direction. There is confusion among Catholic women (but no more than in other quarters) between immortality and resurrection. "The whole world that comes to us through the Bible [, both the Hebrew Bible and the New Testament,] is not interested in the immortality of the soul," biblical scholar Krister Stendahl writes. "And if you think this, it is because you have read this into the material. . . . The question to which resurrection is the answer is not the question about what is going to happen to us when [we die]. The question is not: What is going to happen to little me? Am I to survive with my identity or not? The question is rather whether God's justice will win out. . . .[3]

"Resurrection," Stendahl says, "answers the question of theodicy, that is, the question of how God can win, the question of a moral universe. Does crime pay? Does evil win? Where is God's promise and power? Will God ultimately come through? Will the kingdom come somehow so that righteousness flows forth and justice is in the midst of us all? That is the matrix, that is the womb out of which the dream and thought and hope and prayer for the resurrection emerged out of the Jewish community in times of martydom and suppression."[4]

A few women seemed to hold two contradictory beliefs at once, both denying and affirming the possibility of bodily resurrection. This resurrection is a sign, according to Catholic theology, "not simply [of] the salvation of our soul but . . . [of] the salvation of our whole being."[5] "It's very hard to imagine that there isn't [an afterlife]," said Ruth Pakaluk. She found it easier to believe in immortality of the soul than in the classic Catholic belief in the resurrection of the body. "There's an immaterial aspect to a human being, it's obvious, it's undeniable. [So that survives] because death seems to be part of the material order, so it just doesn't seem to make sense that this immaterial thing should be bound by the laws that govern matter." As for the resurrection, Ruth said, "[That doctrine] takes the body very seriously. But it took me a long time to incorporate it into my picture of the world. A human soul on its own is really nothing: The soul and the body are a unit. When you understand this you understand better why death is such an abhorrent thing, because the separation of body and soul is a complete destruction of the human being."

A few women spoke of the Kingdom or the reign of God, the fullness of God's presence in all things and people which Catholic theology says is the outcome of history, a time when all creation will be transformed, "the product of divine initiative and human collaboration alike."[6] "Christians are called," the U.S. bishops write in their pastoral on war and peace, "to live the tension between the vision of the reign of God and its concrete realization in history." Women who made explicit reference to the reign of God defined it both as the world to come, given by God, and the world they themselves were trying to build. "That's the most important thing for me, to be about the reign of God," said Rafaela Canelo. "When I think of the Kingdom of God I think of Jesus. He came here to the world born of the Virgin Mary, right? In order to begin again to restore all, to unite all humanity, in a common work of peace, of justice, and of love: This is the Kingdom of God." God is in charge, this group of women said, and someday we will know what this all means; meanwhile, we try to do God's work.

Even if they are not sure what the afterlife will bring, the belief that there is a life of some kind after the one they know, and the trust that God is ultimately in charge, colors Catholic women's lives, gives them a long view. Their beliefs about death seem directly related to their belief in the existence of a moral life and a moral universe. For them, life has meaning and purpose—and so too death, as a part of life, cannot be meaningless. "I really do have a strong sense of something eternal, so much bigger than us and so much deeper than what I've ever tasted," said Marty Woodward, whose remarks showed the influence of her favorite theologian, Pierre Teilhard de Chardin, S.J. "What keeps me going is just this sense that the world is evolving, the world is becoming closer to that which it was intended and created to be, that there has been tremendous growth."

"A big part of [Catholic identity] is understanding the life cycle," "Elena Martinez Wise" answered when I asked what she thought was distinctive about Catholicism. "There is a continuation of life. Death is awful, it's a shock, but there is some comfort too in death. If it's ingrained in you, it can never be taken away whether you go to church or not. I know my husband [who is Jewish] fears death, and you cannot make someone understand it if it's not part of their belief. And the Catholic church gives you this wonderful security. For me personally it doesn't [have to do with resurrection]. It's just that I don't fear death in the sense of finality, since I always feel God will take care of us, that somehow He'll be involved.

"There's very few religions that offer that," "Elena" said. "There's life in this religion. Even in death there's life."

"Kitty Riordan" was in her sixties when we spoke. Her husband was ill with a degenerative disease and she was in failing health. "I really do believe that there's more to our lives than the everydayness," "Kitty" said, "but I also believe that the everydayness is very important. I have been thinking a lot about life after death. I really do believe what I say in the Creed. I believe in the resurrection of the body. I believe that we really are going to have a new kind of life. And in some way I believe that is connected very, very closely with our life here."

"I think death is like a short sleep and then you awaken to something else," said Karen Doherty. "And then you're joined with something bigger, something beyond my comprehension." "There is no such thing as death to me," Carmen Benavente de Orrego-Salas said. "There is only transformation. I cannot imagine nothingness. I only see 'allness.' " "Death," said Gaye Lott, "is going back to an energy force that is God."

Raised to believe in heaven and hell, the majority of the women tended not to think in those terms. They often mentioned what they had learned in catechism, then proceeded to modify, question, or discard these beliefs. When they did speak of heaven or hell, the vision of heaven prevailed. Only a few speculated about hell, wondering whether human beings did in some way suffer the consequences of evildoing. Margaret Slattery mused: "There are a lot of puzzles in my mind still about life and death. I guess there's a hell. I don't think there are too many people in it."

Only a handful of women envisioned heaven and hell in literal ways. Rosemary Klem of San Francisco had the most simple and graphic image of the hereafter: "I'm just crazy about angels," she said. "I can't wait to go to heaven. I think heaven is going to be marvelous. It's going to be full of angels and lots of little babies. We're going to meet some fine people there," she added. Most of the women were less precise and less certain. "I feel very deeply that God is going to be a tremendous surprise to me," "Joanne Grace" said. "I strongly believe in life after death," said Judy McDonough. "I'm not positive how it looks, but I know somehow or other I'm going to end up—hopefully!—in Jesus' presence. And that thought alone has gotten me back to church."

Several women, grappling for words to describe a mystery of which they could barely conceive, turned to literature and art, finding it easier to speak by analogy. "Did you see [the movie] *Fanny and Alexander?*" Bridget Palmer asked. "I love the idea of the father being able to come back and watch over [his children]." "I do believe in an afterlife, always have, never had any trouble with that," Sandra Mondykowski Temple said. "I see heaven as a reunion with the Holy Spirit that I really couldn't define. By the same token, if you've really botched it up in this particular life, I really do believe that what goes around comes around. You suffer in this life, no matter what the surface may be. And you get what you deserve when you die. I don't believe that's being licked by flames in a particular geographical place called hell. But I really like Charles Dickens's concept of Jacob Marley in *A Christmas Carol,* that Jacob Marley in chains and fetters was doomed to wander the earth and view the suffering of humankind and feel all the anguish and be absolutely helpless to do anything about it for all eternity. Perhaps that's a bit literalistic but that's the closest I can come, I think, to a definition of what I honestly believe some people merit. That's my definition of hell."

"Death is the depth of life in a double sense, the furthest extreme of human suffering and the final test of God's redemptive power," writes the theologian Leo O'Donovan, S.J.[7] Women shared not only their beliefs about the afterlife but their feelings about death, their own and that of others. "Twelve years ago," "Joanne Grace" remembered, "I had a mastectomy and was told if I were lucky I'd live another five or ten years." Over a decade later, "Joanne" was in excellent health but at the time, she said, "I had to adapt to the idea that I would probably have a very short life. So that was a real turnaround in my life. It changed my concerns: I became more involved with my family, with my friends. That was more important than the kind of work I did, the kind of clothes I wore, what people thought; I became aware that one should truly make the most of each moment—the classic kinds of things. But mostly I had this feeling of gratitude for all the good things that had come to me and for the things that still were with me. And certainly the feeling that God was looking out for me and it would be all right, and not to worry about the details and rules. Actually," "Joanne" said, "the structure of the Church became less important too. I just thought, let the church hierarchy say what they will in their ignorance or knowledge. That really isn't very important. The Church is the people of God. The Lord has looked out for us all these hundreds of thousands of years and He will [continue to do so]."

I asked "Joanne" whether her faith had either changed or made a difference in her life during her bout with cancer. "There was no crisis of faith," she answered. "But there certainly was a change in the intensity. Those early years when I was fighting the cancer I had a very intense feeling of closeness to God, and I must say I miss that. On the other hand perhaps it was at a level and a motivation that could not be sustained. It was certainly an instance where, as they say, your faith really helps you—as well as the faith of those around you." How did her faith help? "I guess the feeling that the Lord was with me, that if indeed my life was going to be a whole lot shorter than I had ever expected somehow He'd give me the strength to accept that. It was a freeing thing in a way, I think because I've gone through some of the work of dying and maybe I won't have quite as much work next time it comes around."

Though several women spoke of their fear of death, a far greater number told me that death did not frighten them. "I'm curious to see what it's going to be like," said college student Leticia Zamarripa. "I'm not afraid of death." "Death used to scare me," said Dolores Reuter, who was in her fifties when we spoke, "but it doesn't anymore. I think when I die my soul will go join with this light and go back to God and be part of the whole. And if I've lived a 'good life' the light will be brighter, and I'll add [to it]," she said with tears in her eyes. "I don't really believe in hell. And if there isn't a God, there's just nothingness, and I don't know it's nothingness, so what difference does it make?"

"I've thought a lot about death and afterlife," said "Cara Marini," a woman in her late thirties. "Growing up you were scared to death to die because what if you went to hell, what if you died with a mortal sin on your soul? So I went through a period of being afraid of death. When I let go of the whole mortal sin concept and got more flexible about what I thought about that, and became more sure of myself in believing in goodness and a good God, I became less afraid to die. I went through a period where I went to a funeral and I did not go up to the coffin because I did not want to see a dead person. It was real scary, final, negative. And then last July when my dad died I was with him. It was an incredible experience to watch someone die. So I'm not afraid of it anymore. I don't want to die because I don't want to lose life, that's what it boils down to; I want to live to be very old. But I'm not afraid to die. I don't know what's on the other side. I don't know if there's an afterlife. I want to believe there is."

One of Marlene Jones's close friends had just died of cancer the week before we met: "He was a musician personified," she said. "He turned choirs into choruses you couldn't believe. And now my Philip is conducting God's choir. He's gone to a place where there's no pain, there's no suffering, where there's no bad. I'm not afraid of death," Marlene continued, shifting the topic from her friend's death to her own. "I don't look forward to leaving my family, my friends, my son, but I do look forward in my own way to seeing that old man up there with that gray hair," she said, referring to her picture of God. "I want to see Jesus. I want to see Mary. I want to see my grandparents and Philip and my friends who've gone on. I guess in the forty-three years that I've lived I've done a little bit of suffering, and I know that when I go there, there will never be any suffering again. Not ever. 'No more weepin' and a' wailin' '—isn't that how it goes?"

Between our first and second interviews, one of Ellen Reuter's best friends became ill, first with breast cancer, then with leukemia. She died not long before our update interview. "Judy's death," Ellen said, "made me feel mortal in a way nothing else has before. At her funeral, I heard people say, 'If I died, would this many people come?' I remember when she first had cancer and the people in her husband's office arranged for food for six weeks and I lined up child care for their son and I remember thinking, I wonder if anybody would do this for me? What would happen if I got sick? What community do I belong to?"

When women mentioned Jesus in connection with death they often spoke, like Marlene, of meeting him, or meeting him again. "He's the Savior," "Madeleine Mitchell" said. "He's the father of the world. I want to see him one day." But, she added, "not too soon." "Jesus was a real person," said College of Saint Elizabeth student Nathalie Nepton. "Maybe he is here on this planet just waiting to show up."

"Since persons are the most vivid reality I know, I feel there must be a persistence of personality," Abigail McCarthy said. "I often have a sense of the presence of the people who have gone before me. I can't believe that they do not persist in some way. But I think it's a very changed existence, beyond what we can manage to imagine." Even more than the persistence of personality, it was the persistence of relationship that preoccupied the women. For them, as Ellen Reuter pointed out, the notions of heaven and of reunion with loved ones were inseparable. Suffering, death, sin, evil: All of those were made of broken connections. In heaven, as the women saw it, the breaches were healed, the separations mended. "I'm sure there is [an afterlife]," said Sarah Hofheinz. "And if there isn't I'm not going to worry about it, because it won't make any difference. But I'm very optimistic. I do believe in a heaven. I think that keeps me going, because I'll see all those people I care about in heaven."

Even before the final reunion in heaven, the connection remains. Some women had a vivid sense of the presence of their loved ones who had died—parents especially, but also spouses and friends. The communion of saints is no abstract doctrine in the lives of Catholic women. Everyone is or can be present: dead relatives, hungry children on the other side of the globe (or the other side of town), first-century martyrs, absent friends.

"I believe that there is existence after life," Margaret Slattery said, "and I do believe that the dead are very close to us. I often think that my parents are someplace very close." "If I really feel in need," said Nancy Vitti, "any one of them, my husband, my grand-mother, anybody, I can get some kind of reassuring feeling that they're with me; and no matter how tough things are, somehow they will help me find a way." "Serena Townsend" told me she had "had the sense of the presence of the people who are dead that is more than just remembering them or thinking nicely about them." This happened, she said, "not very often, a couple of times after my father's death. Maybe it happens at times when you need it," she added, "or it's a gift. But there's no question in my mind that he's still alive. He's not involved in worrying about us. He's not there hovering over the table watching whether you eat your cereal or not. I assume all the saints are that way."

Even as they lived in the perspective of an ongoing life with God, women expressed concern for the future of the world they knew in a language both precise and poignant. Their apprehension about the future inevitably revolved around their children and those of other people, and the double planetary threat of environmental damage and war.

"The most important thing within the U.S. now is the human spirit," said Rafaela Canelo. "How are the youth living spiritually, the youth who are the future of the U.S.? This is the most important. Are they being destroyed? Or are they being built up? Are they living a spirituality? And how are they being helped so that they may develop, so that they will be whole persons? *Person!* I don't say *plastic*, understand?"

Janet Kanitz was the mother of five children and was expecting twins when I interviewed her; several of her children crowded around us while we spoke. Janet's principal concern, she said, for now and for the future, was to "grow them up right." "As a mother I always worry about my family, their future," said Beatrice Gallego. "My young one is attending college and I always pray for her future. I worry about what the world will be for my grandchildren. What's in store for them? I don't know, and that's my fear." "I certainly am for arms control and destruction of some of our nuclear power," "Joanne Grace" said to me. "For myself, I guess I don't worry about the imminence of nuclear war. It's like a tornado, I suppose. It's a possibility and I don't see that I'm going to do myself any good by worrying about dying that way. On the other hand I am concerned about the legacy we're giving our children and our grandchildren because I think for them it is a strong possibility within their lifetimes."

In our century, Leo O'Donovan, S.J., writes, "an entirely unprecedented situation has emerged. Humanity stands face to face not simply with the grievous loss of its individual members but now with its own *extinction.*"[8]

While a majority of the women worried about nuclear war, the women under thirty, across geographical, class, and cultural boundaries, were unanimous: "Will I survive?" was their question, but even more so, "Will the earth survive?" "I don't find the same joy of life in the younger generation," Abigail McCarthy observed. "I really think they grew up with the shadow of the Bomb. I grew up in a period where you just thought things were going to get better, and of course they grew up hearing that we might end everything. And when you think of those drills when they had to go under desks, and we had all those ridiculous things during the Kennedy administration when my children were little. Everybody was supposed to fix a bomb shelter in his house. That certainly had something to do with the psyche of children."

"I worry," said college student "Inez Garcia," "because I don't want to die because two countries are at war. I want to go when my time is right, not before. It worries me a lot because I think sooner or later there's not going to be a world left with all the nuclear things that we have going on. It's probably a race to see who can get the most and I think it's wrong, because if there were ever to be a nuclear war it would kill so many people, especially so many innocent lives, just because of maybe two people in this world that made a difference and said, 'Yes, we're going to war.' Why should millions of people die on account of two people that disagree?"

"I don't think the world is in good shape," said twenty-eight-year-old "Caroline Wong." "A lot of places still have war going on and there is famine and natural disaster. The second thing that bugs me is nuclear war. It's really scary and disgusting. If there is ever a nuclear war, that's the end of the human race. And the third thing is that in developed countries like the U.S. or like the European countries, there's a lot of waste. I really hope that in the future our economy can recycle more, especially plastic. I hate plastic." "Humans have a brain and it's important that they use that to explore the universe and to learn," said Sheri Fedorchak, a park ranger in her twenties. "But also we shouldn't use it to our destruction. When I vote for people I look at how they feel about the environment because I feel that if we ruin our air and our water and cut all our trees down, that we're cutting our lives too, and I think that's part of what God gave us; and we've got to take care of it."

Other women spoke of the destruction and violence they witnessed every day on the street. Two years after our initial interview, Karen Doherty reported: "I've been having an experience [that is] almost indigenous to being a New Yorker. I am finding it hard to stay a liberal. [One day I was] in the subway at 50th Street, midtown, in the middle of the day. I was reading a book and I saw these kids run by me and a nightstick land at my feet and a cop running and yelling, 'Get out of the way! Get out of the way!' Six or seven cops were running after these kids and found they had just shot somebody; the police officer didn't know if they still had their gun on them; he was yelling at me to get out of the way in case one of them fired. Because of crack, terrible muggings, and crime all over the place, even in the day you've got to keep your eyes open every second. It just seems like a gigantic wave: You're getting drowned. You pay these horrendous taxes, every year they go up. I know I'm really going for a crisis: how to be empathetic or compassionate to people who have been dealt a bad hand in life, but on the other hand try to survive with your own boundaries and feelings of safety shrinking on a monthly basis without getting angry, without getting hard. I can feel myself getting harder and I don't like it and I don't know what to do.

"You can't go a day without five or six people approaching you asking you for money," Karen continued. "I give money to at least one person a day. People say, 'Don't even open your bag.' You're trying to figure [out whether you should] and by the time you figure, the person is gone. A young man asked me [a while ago]. I really felt he was hungry; that stayed with me. I still feel badly about that. My heart hasn't totally turned to stone. You don't know what to do anymore. I don't even know who to be mad at. I just get so mad that such things have to be."

"I am really worried about the way the world is going," said Abigail McCarthy. "I think we are declining as a productive country and I think we haven't really recovered from the 'me-ism' of the seventies. We have to recover some unifying principles other than our being a power in the world. And in the Church I'm worried about the divisions. I think they're very profound. I don't see any great church leaders at this time, and I just hope that the Lord who said He would be with us all days will produce some. They're probably there and we don't know it."

Though most of the women did not speak of resurrection in so many words in their reflections on the future in this life and the next, they did address the fundamental questions of change and human hope to which resurrection is the Christian answer. God is the final arbiter, they agreed. Life can be good, but the world is in terrible shape. Can things change? Can they change for the better? Who will change them? If we try to do so, will our labor be in vain? Is there hope for the future? Is there, in fact, life in the midst of death?

A few women were believers in fate. Some events, they said, were inevitable—in the world and in individual lives. "It's all predetermined," Helen Doggett said. "I believe in fate," said "Anne Marie Quinn." "Your destiny is marked from the time you're born and you're not going to change it." I asked her about free will. "You do have freedom but there are some things that are going to happen in your life and there are some of us that are going to suffer large tragedies or happinesses. We have freedom of choice but not everyone was born with just a blank. I think we're all born for a reason. We're all here for a purpose, we all have a mission to accomplish here. That's what I mean by fate."

Some wished for change but wondered whether it was possible. "That's my prayer all the time," said May Kast. "For the people in Africa, the terrible governments in South America. I say, it must be time for change soon. Those poor people are taken advantage of all the time. They haven't a chance to pick themselves up. Their climates are bad, they have rotten governments, there must be more for them. And then I think, well, God must be testing them. Look at Lebanon," she added. "There's just no way out, it seems. Nobody wants peace. They keep this up year after year. And governments in South America have total disregard for humanity. You wonder where their spirituality is."

Where change seemed impossible, women valued perseverance and fortitude. "I think the Catholic church recognizes in a way that I don't get the sense other religions do, that the point is to endure," Ann Richards Anderson said. "The triumph is in endurance. And the human condition is really sort of a mess."

"We can choose to live with great hope or with great despair," Mary Hunt said to me, "with great fear or with great trust. I generally tend to live with great hope and great trust. My experience has been that things get better as time goes on, and my faith is that death is a passage to some extended reality of this one, that's connected with this reality but beyond it. I have seen small changes and I feel part of a tradition and a history, I can see that justice does win out: The proud are put down and little people and little things do finally triumph. It doesn't mean every day I'm hopeful and I'm certainly not Pollyanna-ish but I think things do eventually come around." "I never lose hope," "Elizabeth Heilig" told me. "I have a pretty hot hope fire that keeps burning, no matter what."

A large proportion of the women I met dealt with suffering, evil, and death in their lives by addressing them actively and consciously, creating hope by committing acts of hope. " 'Blessed are the meek' used to [mean stay quiet]," said civics teacher and community activist Beatrice Gallego, a mother and grandmother. "It used to mean be seen and not heard." Now, Beatrice said, she and her peers understand as blessedness the knowledge that one is meek and the willingness to take action about "your faith and your rights. Meek," she said, "has been redefined." At the time of our interview, Beatrice's community organ-

izing group was fighting the siting of a toxic waste facility behind a
local park by the Kelly Air Force Base in San Antonio. In order to get
fifty-five drums of chemicals relocated, the group was taking on the
Texas Water Commission, the Air Control Board, and the Department
of Defense, and had brought the city's administration into the conversation.

Judy McDonough's son Jude died at the age of nine in an accidental
fire in Brazil, where she and her family lived for several years. "That
was the turning point of my religion," Judy said. "Something like that
makes your whole life stop. So I started going to church again. I made
a very definite commitment to my religion and it certainly was a great
help." Jude was one of six children. "We were back about a year," Judy
said, "when all the Cambodian stuff was going on and my husband
was working for the Cambodian section of Voice of America." Her
husband was asked to organize translators to meet a planeload of
children from Cambodia. "When the plane arrived," Judy said, "they
were older kids. We found out all the people the adoption agencies
had lined up expected babies, and they didn't want the older kids.
After Jude died we felt like there was this tremendous gap, like jumping
from six to one, even though we had the five around; it felt like there
was so much more room for more." Judy and her husband legally
adopted two Cambodian boys aged seven and ten from among the
children on the airplane.

Women who worked to create hope in the form of personal
and social change were under no illusion about the complexity of
the task. Often the means and results of their work were not what
they had planned. Ann Richards Anderson had vivid memories of
the time she and her family spent supporting school desegregation
in Boston during the busing crisis of the 1970s. "I can't explain what
it's like living in a society like that," she said. "The Justice Department,
after swearing that they would protect anybody who bused their kids,
wouldn't do anything. We were threatened with Molotov cocktails,
got our windows broken in the middle of the night, and had 'nigger-
lover' sprayed on our house. The police wouldn't do anything. It
was a horrendous time. In the midst of this, no wonder I thought
I needed the Church! Although I didn't connect it in my mind, at
the time."

Ann's oldest son, she said, was bused to "a wonderful school,"
but his bus was attacked every morning. "The poor kid was only
six years old. The bus would be stoned every day, and that went
on forever, not just the first year. [The kids would] hide under their

seats; they just took it for granted that that's how life was." Finally, Ann said, "we decided we couldn't live this way. It was not worth turning our life in an uproar." They moved to the suburbs.

"It was the hardest thing I ever did," Ann said. "Because I really feel your life and spiritual life and purpose in the world is all tied up with community. I felt like my whole meaning in life was gone. But like my mother's old saying, 'The Lord works in strange ways,' here we were in a huge house. There was a notice in the church bulletin that this girl needed a home, and I thought to myself, maybe *that's* why we moved [out here]; maybe our next life is to be a family for somebody, maybe that's the new purpose. She had just turned fourteen. She's from El Salvador. She's eighteen now. The thought was that she and her siblings would come here and go to school and learn English, and 'when things settle down they can go back home.' So they sent her up for supposedly a year or so. But things did not 'settle down' and she's been here ever since."

"Work is getting to be a lot more fun," Karen Doherty reported after sharing the news of the chronic illness she had developed since our first interview and her observations on crime and homelessness on the streets of New York. "[It does when] you don't think you're going to the top. Not that I wasn't a risk-taker before but now I am doubly so. We did a program on ethics in the workplace and foreign investment and a program on corporations and the environment; also a study on child care and on managing employee health care, how to be compassionate and give your employees the best you can. I volunteered with the approval of the CEO in a project to help displaced homemakers to get back in the workplace, and I'm one of two managers out of eighty to have someone from United Cerebral Palsy [in the office]. And," she added, "we're going to do a membership meeting on the issue of homelessness. So I have a reputation as the departmental conscience, but I can get away with it. I've never worked better or come up with better ideas."

"I feel bad when I see people not using their potential," said Sheri Fedorchak, "and that's what keeps me going: Gotta use it, gotta use it. Dying sometimes [makes me afraid] because I want to do a lot before I die. And I want to have myself in gear for what comes after. I know it's not something you earn, but it's something that you think about. I feel like it's just another dimension. I don't know what it will be like. But if you are a Christian you believe that you don't have to wait to get to heaven until you die, you can start experiencing parts of that on earth."

At opposite ends of the country, Rafaela Canelo, the urban activist, and "Genevieve O'Rourke," the cloistered contemplative, used different vocabularies to speak of the same reality. "The Kingdom of God," Rafaela said to me, "is that all of us with the entire, entire universe return again to live the Kingdom that is here on earth and also reaches toward the infinite.* [It does not mean] that when I die, I am going to save myself and go to heaven because there is the Kingdom of God. No, it's *here!*"

"Jesus as the Alpha and the Omega, the Way, the Truth, and the Life these are not just titles," "Genevieve" declared. "It's a life that's dynamic and vibrant. It's eternal life shared with us now. It's not something we're coming into some day down the road. We share it *now.*"

---

*Rafaela's language was far more poetic in the original Spanish: "*Ese reino que esta aqui en la tierra y que trasciende hasta lo infinito.*"

NOTES

Prologue.
Epigraph. Ursula K. Le Guin (from a commencement address at Bryn Mawr College) *Dancing at the Edge of the World* (New York: Grove Press, 1989).

CHAPTER 2. PLURALISTIC AMERICANS, POETIC ADULTS

Epigraph. Andrew Greeley *The Catholic Myth* (New York: Scribner's, 1990);
Vincent Harding "Toward a Darkly Radiant Vision of America's Truth" (Cross Currents XXXVII # 1, Spring 87);
Virginia Woolf *Three Guineas* (New York, Harvest/HBJ 1966) as quoted in Sarah Ruddick's *Maternal Thinking* (Boston: Beacon, 1989).

1. Carol Gilligan, *In a Different Voice: Psychological Theory and Women's Development* (Cambridge, MA: Harvard University Press, 1982).
2. At the time of this writing, two drafts of the pastoral letter had been published. During a visit to the Vatican in the spring of 1991, the bishops were urged to downgrade the proposed document from a pastoral letter to a statement "with a lesser value of authority." They decided to complete what they had begun, and planned to discuss a third draft in June of 1992 and to vote to approve a final version in November of the same year. The bishops had received criticism both from feminists (who urged them not to write a pastoral on women's concerns but instead to write about patriarchy and sexism) and from conservative women (who accused the bishops, as did the Vatican, of being unduly influenced by "secular" or "radical" feminism).
3. Jean Baker Miller, M.D., *Toward a New Psychology of Women,* 2nd ed. (Boston: Beacon Press, 1986) pp. xix–xx.
4. Vincent Harding, "Toward a darkly radiant vision of America's truth" (an open letter to the authors of *Habits of the Heart), Cross Currents,* Vol. XXXVII, (Spring 1987), pp. 1–16.
5. Catharine MacKinnon, "Desire and Power," in *Feminism Unmodified* (Cambridge, MA/London: Harvard University Press, 1987), pp. 46–63.
6. Henry Hampton, "The Camera Lens as Two-Edged Sword," *The New York Times,* January 15, 1989.
7. See Elisabeth Schüssler Fiorenza's *Bread Not Stone: The Challenge of Feminist Biblical Interpretation* (Boston: Beacon Press, 1984).
8. For a more detailed examination of this question, see Chapter Six, "How Many? Who Leaves? Who Stays?" of Andrew M. Greeley's *The Catholic Myth: The Behavior and Beliefs of American Catholics* (New York: Charles Scribner's Sons, 1990) and Section Three, "How to Count Catholics" of Joseph Claude Harris's excellent study, "The Catholic Population of the Diocese of Cleveland: The Present and the Future" (December 1990). Gallup surveys define as Catholic any person who says

he or she is a Catholic. Other institutions use different criteria: the National Catholic Directory uses estimates by parish clergy; the National Pastoral Planning Council (NPPC) uses sacramental participation as the basic criterion, calculating proportion of baptisms to births and Catholic funerals to deaths. The most commonly accepted percentage figure is Gallup's figure of Catholics at 28 percent of the adult population. The March 1991 National Survey of Religious Identification directed by Professor Barry Kosmin of the City University of New York puts the figure at 26.2 percent. Since many of the estimates do not include children or adolescents under eighteen, one must bear in mind that the data about "total number of American Catholics" are somewhat skewed; the Catholic population as a whole is a young one, especially in the rapidly growing Hispanic communities. According to George Gallup, Jr., and Jim Castelli's *The American Catholic People* (New York: Doubleday, 1987), 29 percent of American Catholics are under thirty, in contrast, for example, to 18 percent of Methodists, Presbyterians, and Episcopalians.

9. Greeley, *The Catholic Myth.*
10. Ibid., p. 73. See also Andrew M. Greeley's *The Irish Americans: The Rise to Money and Power* (New York: Warner Books, 1981).
11. George Gallup, Jr., and Jim Castelli, *The American Catholic People: Their Beliefs, Practices, and Values* (New York: Doubleday, 1987), p. 3.
12. For a fuller discussion of regional differences in American Catholicism, see Jay Dolan, *The American Catholic Experience: A History from Colonial Times to the Present* (Garden City, NY: Doubleday/Image, 1985, 1987) and Jay Dolan, ed., *The American Catholic Parish: A History from 1850 to the Present* (Vol. I: The Northeast, Southeast and South Central States; Vol. II: The Pacific, Intermountain West and Midwest States) (Mahwah, NJ: Paulist Press, 1987).
13. According to the National Survey of Religious Identification published in 1991 by Professor Barry A. Kosmin of the City University of New York (CUNY) Graduate Center, the percentage of persons answering "none" to a question asking for their religious affiliation was 17.2 percent for residents of Oregon, 14.0 for Washington State, and 11.9 for Idaho, in contrast to 1.6 percent for North Dakota, 5.6 for Minnesota, 2.6 for Mississippi, 5.5 for New Jersey, and 4.9 for Texas. In addition— this is harder to establish through this kind of statistical survey but easily verified by residents of the Northwestern states—actual *participation* is considerably lower than the percentage of those who *identify* with a particular tradition.
14. Lucien Richard, O.M.I., Daniel Harrington, S.J., and John O'Malley, S.J., eds., *Vatican II: The Unfinished Agenda: A Look to the Future* (Mahwah, NJ: Paulist Press, 1987), p. 105.
15. Karl Rahner, S.J., "Towards a Fundamental Theological Interpretation of Vatican II" (English text of an address delivered by Rahner on April 8, 1979, at the Weston School of Theology, Cambridge, Massachusetts) in Richard, Harrington, and O'Malley, *Vatican II: The Unfinished Agenda.*
16. Rembert Weakland, O.S.B., "Taking up a global church agenda: diversity of cultures, unity of faith require structural adjustments," *National Catholic Reporter,* 10/13/89.
17. Joel Garreau, *The Nine Nations of North America* (New York: Avon Books, 1981), p. 217.
18. Sally Cunneen, *Mother Church: What the Experience of Women Is Teaching Her* (Mahwah, NJ: Paulist Press, 1991), p. 43.
19. Greeley, *The Catholic Myth,* pp. 1 ff.

20. Ibid., p. 7.
21. David Toolan, S.J., "The Catholic Taboo Against Schism: Strained but Holding," *Religion and Intellectual Life,* Vol. VII (Fall 1989), pp. 36–37.
22. Greeley, *The Catholic Myth,* pp. 33 ff.
23. Elizabeth Dodson Gray, ed., *Sacred Dimensions of Women's Experience* (Wellesley, MA: Roundtable Press, 1988).
24. Sally Cunneen presents a thoughtful and inspiring discussion of matter and spirit, public and private life, and human interdependence in *Mother Church,* particularly in the chapters entitled "Reconnecting Love and Truth" and "Spirituality in This World."
25. Pastoral Constitution on the Church in the Modern World (*Gaudium et Spes*), 4., in Walter M. Abbott, S.J., ed., *The Documents of Vatican II* (New York: America Press/Angelus, 1966), pp. 201–202.
26. "Justice in the World," World Synod of Bishops, Rome, 1971. *Renewing the Faith: Catholic Documents on Peace, Justice and Liberation,* David J. O'Brien and Thomas A. Shannon, eds. (Garden City, NY: Doubleday/Image Books, 1977) p. 391.

CHAPTER 4. BECOMING A CATHOLIC WOMAN

Epigraph. St. Augustine *Confessions* 10,8.
1. The Sister Formation Conference was initiated in 1953, Sister Marie Augusta Neal, S.N.D., writes, to "develop a professionally adequate and spiritually grounded pre-apostolic education for new members.... The American leadership was emphasizing professional competency for the services provided and an updated theological training as well" (*From Nuns to Sisters,* Mystic, CT: Twenty-Third Publications, 1990, p. 30).
2. Mary Gordon, "Getting Here From There: A Writer's Reflections on a Religious Past," in William Zinsser, ed., *Spiritual Quests: The Art and Craft of Religious Writing* (Boston: Houghton Mifflin, 1988), p. 28.

CHAPTER 6. KNOWING GOD, NAMING GOD

Epigraph. Dogmatic Constitution on Revelation (*Dei Verbum*) I.6 Second Vatican Council November, 1965.
1. George Gallup, Jr., and Jim Castelli, *The American Catholic People: Their Beliefs, Practices, and Values* (New York: Doubleday, 1987), p. 24.
2. See Research Report, The National Survey of Religious Identification, 1989–90, the City University of New York study directed by Professor Barry Kosmin and published by CUNY in March 1991, p. 4.
3. Jay Dolan, *The American Catholic Experience: A History from Colonial Times to the Present* (Garden City, NY: Doubleday/Image, 1985, 1987), p. 230.
4. See Chapter 1, "Sainthood," in Catherine M. Mooney, R.S.C.J., *Philippine Duchesne: A Woman with the Poor* (New York/Mahwah, NJ: Paulist Press, 1990).

CHAPTER 8. THE COMMON GOOD

Epigraph. "Justice in the World" Statement of the World Synod of Bishops, 1971.

1. "Action on behalf of justice and participation in the transformation of the world fully appear to us as a constitutive dimension of the preaching of the Gospel," World Synod of Bishops, Rome, 1971, in *Renewing the Faith: Catholic Documents on Peace, Justice and Liberation,* David J. O'Brien and Thomas A. Shannon, eds. (Garden City, NY: Doubleday/Image, 1977), p. 391.
2. Peter J. Henriot, Edward P. DeBerri, and Michael J. Schultheis, *Catholic Social Teaching: Our Best Kept Secret* (Maryknoll, NY: Orbis/Collins Dove, 1988).
3. Joseph Cunneen, panel presentation at the Symposium "Good News to the Poor: A Hundred Years of Catholic Social Teaching," celebrating the 100th anniversary of Pope Leo XIII's encyclical *Rerum Novarum,* Emmanuel College, Boston, April 5, 1991.
4. "Economic Justice for All: Catholic Social Teaching and the U.S. Economy," National Conference of Catholic Bishops, 1986.
5. One example of this awareness among women of various countries and traditions is the confession prepared by the Rev. Lena Malgren for a service during a Women's Fair in Uppsala, Sweden, in 1987 and titled "A Confession for the Timid:"

O God, I confess before you that I have not believed in my own possibilities, but by thoughts, words and deeds I have belittled myself and my capacities

I have not loved myself as much as others. I have not loved my body, my looks, my gifts, my own way of being.

I have let others govern my life; I have allowed myself to be disregarded and abused.

I have believed the judgments of others more than my own.

I have allowed people to be disrespectful and spiteful toward me without daring to tell them to stop and desist.

I confess that I have not dared to aim at my full potential. Cowardly, I have avoided the fight even when my case was just. I have bowed out in order to avoid trouble.

I confess that I have not dared to show that I can, not dared to be as capable as I can be.

O God, father and creator, O Jesus, our brother and savior, O Spirit, our mother and comforter, forgive me for despising myself. Restore me, make me trust myself, give me the true love of self.

6. "Economic Justice for All: Catholic Social Teaching and the U.S. Economy," paragraph 179.
7. These documents include Pope Leo XIII's 1891 encyclical *Rerum Novarum,* Pope John Paul II's *Laborem Exercens* in 1981, and the Latin American bishops' Medellin and Puebla statements in the second half of this century. Some of these can be found in David J. O'Brien and Thomas A. Shannon, eds., *Renewing the Earth: Catholic Documents on Peace, Justice and Liberation* (Garden City, NY: Doubleday/Image Books, 1977). For a quick overview of Catholic social teaching, see the special November/December 1991 issue of *Salt* entitled "The Busy Christian's Guide to Catholic Social Teaching," vol. II, No. 10.

8. Globally, women are half the world's population, perform two-thirds of the world's work in terms of hours, earn one tenth of what men earn, and own one percent of the property. (Source: "State of the World's Women, 1985," *New Internationalist* (published for the United Nations, Oxford, U.K., 1985, p.1.)

9. George Gallup, Jr., and Jim Castelli, *The American Catholic People: Their Beliefs, Practices, and Values* (Garden City, NY: Doubleday, 1987), p. 79.

10. Ibid., p. 82.

11. "The Challenge of Peace: God's Promise and Our Response, A Pastoral Letter on War and Peace." National Conference of Catholic Bishops, May 3, 1983.

12. Gallup and Castelli, *The American Catholic People,* p. 85. They also write, "There are a number of American Catholic missionaries in Central America, and they are a new kind of post–Vatican II missionary, emphasizing social justice and community development, as well as preaching the Gospel and carrying out traditional works of charity. At the same time, bishops in the region have been outspoken champions of the poor and vocal critics of violence from both the Left and the Right. . . . For American Catholics," the authors continue, "El Salvador conjures up two main images. The first is the assassination, in 1979, of Archbishop Oscar Romero, who was gunned down while saying Mass in the cathedral at San Salvador. The second is the grave containing the bodies of four American church women— Sisters Ita Ford, Maura Clark, and Dorothy Kazel and lay worker Jean Donovan— who were murdered by right-wing death squads. All five deaths were the result of the Church's identification with the poor and their demands for social justice. Further militarization in the conflict with El Salvador is perceived among American Catholics as a threat to their fellow Catholics" (pp. 85–86).

13. Robert N. Bellah, Richard Madsen, William M. Sullivan, Ann Swidler, and Steven M. Tipton, *Habits of the Heart: Individualism and Commitment in American Life* (Berkeley, CA: University of California Press, 1985).

14. Robert Bellah and his colleagues make a useful distinction between organization and institution in their sequel to *Habits of the Heart, The Good Society* (New York: Alfred A. Knopf, 1991). Or see the excerpt of their material in *Commonweal,* July 12, 1991, Vol. CXVIII, No. 13 titled "The Good Society: Shaping the Institutions That Shape Us," pp. 425–429.

CHAPTER 10. A WOMAN'S WORK

Epigraph. Marge Piercy "For Strong Women" in *Circles on the Water: Selected Poems of Marge Piercy* (New York: Alfred A. Knopf, Inc./Borzoi, 1982), p. 257. This poem was originally published in her collection *The Moon Is Always Female;*
Louisa May Alcott, *Little Women* (as quoted in *The Quotable Woman,* Elaine Partnow, ed. (Garden City, NY: Anchor Books, Anchor Press/Doubleday, 1978, p. 65.).

1. Sally Cunneen, *Sex: Female; Religion: Catholic* (New York: Holt, Rinehart, 1968), p. 5.

2. Mary Jo Weaver gives a lively and well-documented account of Catholic feminist movements, groups, and theologies in *New Catholic Women: A Contemporary Challenge to Traditional Religious Authority* (San Francisco: Harper & Row, 1985).

3. First spoken at the second national conference on the ordination of women in

the Catholic church, "New Women, New Church, New Priestly Ministry" in Baltimore in 1978.

4. I am indebted to Mary E. Hunt for the analysis of contemporary feminism contained in her article, "Packaging Feminism for the Abortion Debate," *Conscience,* Vol. XII (July–August 1991) and especially for her distinction between "women replacing men, female thinking replacing male" and "an active search for justice for all."

5. Jean Baker Miller, M.D., *Toward a New Psychology of Women,* 2nd ed. (Boston: Beacon Press, 1980). Judith V. Jordan, Alexandra G. Kaplan, Jean Baker Miller, Irene P. Stiver, and Janet L. Surrey, *Women's Growth in Connection: Writings from the Stone Center* (New York: The Guilford Press, 1991).

6. Jordan, Kaplan, et al., *Women's Growth in Connection,* p. 5.

7. "Few words have the power to stop strong women in the pursuit of justice for women as does the word lesbian," writes pastoral psychotherapist Lorna Hochstein, a Catholic woman. "The label lesbian is used as an insult and perceived to be an insult. . . . Whether we are primarily heterosexual or primarily lesbian, we have all been taught to fear, to hate and to distance ourselves from that lesbian part of ourselves which is drawn in love and passion to other women." Hochstein continues, "Loving women is not about hating men. Loving women is about loving ourselves—all of ourselves, that part of our heart that is erotically attracted to women in addition to that part of our hearts attracted to men." (Lorna M. Hochstein, Ph.D., "The Usefulness of Lesbian Hating," paper delivered at the Women-Church forum "Unwrapping the Silences," Episcopal Divinity School, Cambridge, Massachusetts, October 13, 1990).

8. See John Deedy, "Church and Labor: Can This Marriage Be Saved?" in *Salt,* (March 1991), Vol. II, No. 3, pp 6–11.

9. Elena Stone, "Honoring the Everyday: Invisible Labor in the Life of a Community Day Care Center," paper delivered at the Annual Convention of the American Sociological Association, August 1991.

10. Mary Catherine Bateson, *Composing a Life* (New York: Atlantic Monthly Press, 1989), pp. 178, 179.

11. Bateson, *Composing a Life,* p. 166.

12. Ibid., p. 186.

CHAPTER 12. LOVING WELL

Epigraph. Elizabeth Dodson Gray *Sacred Dimensions of Women's Experience* (Wellesley, MA: Roundtable Press, 1988).

1. Articles in Catholic periodicals continue to argue the respective merits of marriage and vowed celibacy, often as they pertain to ordained ministry, and continue to ignore the experience of those who have not chosen either of these life-styles. See, for instance, in the July 12, 1991, issue of *Commonweal,* "Enabled for the Kingdom: A Reflection on Celibacy" by Lucretia B. Yaghjian.

2. Mary E. Hunt develops this idea and others in her book *Fierce Tenderness: A Feminist Theology of Friendship* (New York: Crossroad, 1991).

3. National Coalition Against Domestic Violence, as quoted in Stan Grossfeld, "Women Suffer War on the Home Front," *The Boston Globe* (September 1, 1991).

CHAPTER 14. WE ARE CHURCH (OR ARE WE?)

Epigraph. Marty Haugen, "Gather Us In" © 1982 GIA Publications Inc.; L. Camatari, S.J., "Rex Regum in Splendore," translation by Ronald A. Knox; refrain by Richard B. Curtin in *The Catholic Hymnal* and service book © 1966 Benziger Editions, Inc. NY.

1. I used this expression sometimes during the interviews, borrowing from the title and subject of theologian Rosemary Haughton's book *The Catholic Thing* (Springfield, IL: Templegate Publishers, 1979).

2. Saint Augustine, Sermon 272: To the Newly Baptized, on the Blessed Sacrament. Latin Text, *Patrologica Latina,* Tomus XXXVIII (J. P. Migne, ed. Paris: 1865 1246–48).

3. Again, the women I interviewed seemed to echo their Christian predecessors of centuries ago. The historian Caroline Bynum, in her study of women mystics and Eucharistic devotion in thirteenth-century Europe, writes that women in all stations of life "were inspired, compelled, comforted and troubled by the eucharist to an extent found in only a few male writers of the period" (p. 122). "The eucharist was . . . more than an occasion for ecstasy. It was also a moment of encounter with the *humanitas Christi* [the humanity of Christ] which was such a prominent theme of women's spirituality. . . . This humanity was, above all, Christ's physicality, his corporality, his being-in-the-body-ness" (p. 129). "Women's devotion to the body and blood of Christ was . . . an affirmation of the religious significance of physicality and emotionality. The eucharist was, to medieval women, a moment at which they were released into ecstatic union; it was also a moment at which the God with whom they joined was supremely human because supremely vulnerable and fleshly."

   Bynum argues that women's ecstasy upon receiving the eucharist served as an alternative to the authority of priestly office, endowing their role as "nonpriests," quintessential recipients, with new spiritual significance. In addition, Bynum writes, "Concern with the literal following of Jesus, with the problem and the opportunity of physicality, was a basic theme in thirteenth-century religiosity. But it was reflected and espoused especially intensely in women's lives and in women's writings. . . . Their writing is full of reference to being created in God's image and likeness" (p. 146).

   Citations are taken from Chapter Four, "Women Mystics and Eucharistic Devotion in the Thirteenth Century" of Caroline Walker Bynum's *Fragmentation and Redemption: Essays on Gender and the Human Body in Medieval Religion* (New York: Zone Books, 1991).

4. William Reiser, "Inculturation and Doctrinal Development," *Heythrop Journal* 22 (1981), p. 135, as quoted in Lucien Richard, O.M.I., Daniel Harrington, S.J., and John W. O'Malley, S.J., eds., *Vatican II: The Unfinished Agenda* (Mahwah, NJ: Paulist Press, 1987).

5. Archbishop Raymond Hunthausen was disciplined by the Vatican in 1985 for his stands on church doctrine and practice. In a rare intervention in local episcopal governance, the Holy See named the Reverend Donald Wuerl as auxiliary bishop of the Seattle Archdiocese without consulting Hunthausen, and ordered Hunthausen to relinquish final authority in areas of church life, including liturgy,

priestly education, biomedical moral issues, diocesan relations with former priests, and ministry to homosexuals. This arrangement was widely criticized by U.S. Catholics, including church leaders, but the U.S. bishops took a public stance supporting the actions against Hunthausen after their Fall 1985 meeting in Washington. Several bishops indicated privately [source: Religious News Service] that they would work behind the scenes to have Archbishop Hunthausen's authority restored. The Holy See subsequently appointed a commission of three American bishops to resolve the crisis; following their recommendation, full authority was restored to Hunthausen in May 1987 and Auxiliary Bishop Wuerl was transferred; however, Bishop Thomas Murphy of Great Falls/Billings, Montana, was simultaneously named Coadjutor Archbishop of Seattle, Hunthausen's heir apparent.

6. George Gallup, Jr., and Jim Castelli, *The American Catholic People: Their Beliefs, Practices, and Values* (Garden City, NY: Doubleday, 1987), Chapter Five, "A Tolerant People," pp. 59 ff.

7. Margery Eagan, "Reincarnation of Latin Mass may be answer to prayers," *The Boston Herald,* March 13, 1990.

8. The Notre Dame Study of Catholic Parish Life, begun in the early 1980s, consists of a regional history of parish life from 1850 to the present and an interdisciplinary examination of contemporary parish life. The University of Notre Dame's Cushwa Center is also conducting a study examining the history and experience of Hispanic Catholics in the U.S. Hispanic parishes were not included in the original Notre Dame Study. Among the many books published as a result of the study are Joseph Gremillion and Jim Castelli's *The Emerging Parish: The Notre Dame Study of Catholic Life Since Vatican II* (San Francisco: Harper & Row, 1988) and Jay Dolan, ed., *The American Catholic Parish: A History from 1850 to the Present,* 2 vols. (New York: Paulist Press, 1987).

9. "The American Catholic Parish of the 1980s," transcript of talk by David C. Leege, Ph.D., in *The Parish in Transition* (Proceedings of a Conference on the American Catholic Parish, May 1985, sponsored by FADICA—Foundations and Donors Interested in Catholic Activities, Inc.), David Byers, ed. (Washington, D.C.: National Conference of Catholic Bishops, 1986), p.15.

10. Sally Cunneen, *Sex: Female; Religion: Catholic* (New York: Holt, Rinehart and Winston, 1968). Chapter Four, pp. 41 ff., is entitled "The Proof Is in the Parish." It is interesting to note that already, in the mid- and late 1960s, women were clamoring for smaller, more intimate communities of faith and complaining about the size of their parishes—and about poor working relationships with their pastors.

11. The subject of women's intimate involvements with Roman Catholic priests merits far more space than I am able to allot to it in this book. Some thoughtful and serious studies of this topic are under way, notably the cross-denominational and cross-cultural work by Rev. Elizabeth Rice Smith, Th.M., Psy.D., on religioerotic attachment (a concept she has coined) and the research by Kathleen Sands, Ph.D., on the effect of mandatory vows of celibacy on priests and the women with whom they are involved. See, by Kathleen Sands, "Secret Heartaches: Priestly Celibacy and the Women It Touches," in *Miriam's Song II* (West Hyattsville, MD: Priests for Equality, [n.d.]) and presentation at Unwrapping the Silences forum, Episcopal Divinity School, Cambridge, Massachusetts, October 13, 1990. Elizabeth Rice Smith's forthcoming book is entitled *Holy Seductions: Unspoken Tales of Sexual Desire, Attachment, and Danger in American Religious Life.* See also my brief opinion

piece, "Sex, Power, and the Sacred: It's Time to Talk," in *Harvard Divinity Bulletin* XX:3 (1990–1991), first published by the *Los Angeles Times* in abridged version as "What Constitutes a Whole Person?" (September 7, 1990).

12. Second Draft of the U.S. Bishops' Pastoral on Women, "One in Christ Jesus: A Pastoral Response to the Concerns of Women for Church and Society," #123. National Conference of Catholic Bishops, April 3, 1990.

13. Sally Cunneen in her recent *Mother Church: What the Experience of Women Is Teaching Her* (Mahwah, NJ: Paulist Press, 1991, p. 19) looks back on her study of American Roman Catholic women in the mid-1960s, *Sex: Female; Religion: Catholic:* "American ideas of equality were helping these women criticize their unequal place in the church, while their faith in God and strong belief in justice, stimulated by church teaching, had sharpened their ability to criticize American individualism."

14. See the Notre Dame Study of Catholic Parish Life for confirmation and further details. One may refer, for instance, to Gremillion and Castelli, *The Emerging Parish,* pp. 68–69.

15. "I was really surprised how few women came," said Sarah Hofheinz, who participated in the hearings held in her city of Indianapolis in preparation for the drafting of the pastoral. "And it was very interesting what kind of women came. There were not very many of me; I made one of my friends come because I anticipated there being very churchy people there. [And that's who was there:] very churchy people whose whole life revolves around church. I'm not criticizing those people [but] for sure, it did not reflect the composition of our parish." Women at the Indianapolis hearings, Sarah said, stressed two points: "that there should be a pride in family and they did not feel that there was a pride in family anymore. [And] more responsible roles for women in the church. That they are not just the cookie bakers and that there should be recognition of the value of women and what they do in the Church."

CHAPTER 16. WHY THEY LEAVE AND WHY THEY STAY

Epigraph. The Gospel according to Luke 13:10–13; Flannery O'Connor *The Habit of Being* (Sally Fitzgerald, ed.).

1. Interview, in Peter Occhiogrosso, *Once a Catholic* (Boston: Houghton Mifflin, 1987), p. 176.

2. The author and psychologist Eugene Kennedy, in his book *Tomorrow's Catholics, Yesterday's Church: The Two Cultures of American Catholicism* (San Francisco: Harper & Row, 1988), distinguishes two Catholic cultures, separate but interrelated. They are, Kennedy says, the main division in the American Catholic church, more so than the "progressive/conservative" split. "First culture" Catholics are preoccupied with the Church's institutional life and structure; "second culture" Catholics bypass rather than confront structured church authority. "Progressives" and "conservatives" are, in fact, both in the "first culture." "When a great American newspaper or magazine assigns its religion editor to do a story 'on the Catholic Church,'" Kennedy writes, "they invariably mean the first or the institutional culture. That is 'the church' reported on, analyzed, speculated about almost endlessly, frequently

with an emphasis on the challenge to established authority that is implicit in some recent occurrence" (pp. 7–8).

"The institution," Kennedy writes, "is a temporal, phenomenally fixed medium for realities that transcend its structures as the sun does a solar battery or a magnifying glass. The church is, in fact, essentially a mystery, in whose proclamation and service the institution finds its sole justification. This insight is the source of tension between the two cultures of American Catholicism. Culture One is intrinsically dependent on the church *as institution* for its existence. Culture Two is intrinsically dependent on the Church *as mystery* and only extrinsically dependent on it as institution. Second culture Catholicism is given little media coverage because first, it is hard to report on a mystery, and, second, because it would be too much like reporting on ordinary life" (pp. 8–9).

Second culture Catholics, Kennedy said in a newspaper interview, are not just "Catholics-in-name only. Their lives are often deeply attuned both spiritually and emotionally to the church as a sacramental source of teaching, pastoral interpretation and consolation." But as Catholicism has taught them, "they believe and think for themselves," Kennedy says. "They form their own consciences as they confront moral choices and they do this without necessarily perceiving themselves as rebels against institutional order. To act independently and responsibly is not revolt against authority. Most people regard it as growing up." (*Valley News*, White River Junction, VT, September 4, 1987).

3. WBZ-TV, Boston, *7:30 Report*, October 14, 1991.
4. Richard John Neuhaus, *The Catholic Moment: The Paradox of the Church in the Postmodern World* (San Francisco: Harper & Row, 1987), p. 284.
5. For a thoughtful discussion of this question and of the nature of infallibility, particularly as it pertains to the issues of birth control, divorce, and democracy in the Church, see Philip S. Kaufman, O.S.B., *Why You Can Disagree . . . and Remain a Faithful Catholic* (Bloomington, IN: Meyer-Stone Books, 1989).
6. Both lay Catholics and members of the hierarchy have tended to focus this question selectively on moral teaching about sexuality and issues pertaining to the nature of authority in the Church. Catholic teaching against nuclear war and in favor of the rights of workers is clearly articulated, yet few bishops publicly condemn Catholic politicians for an antilabor stance, and not many Catholics feel that their working in the nuclear weapons industry places their church membership in jeopardy.
7. For a discussion of Women-Church in relation to traditional definitions of schism, see Mary E. Hunt, "Spiral Not Schism: Women-Church as Church," *Religion and Intellectual Life*, Vol. VII (Fall 1989), p. 83.
8. See Elisabeth Schüssler Fiorenza: *In Memory of Her* (New York: Crossroad, 1983), pp. 343 ff. "Epilogue: Toward a Feminist Biblical Spirituality: The *Ekklesia* of Women."
9. Fiorenza, *In Memory of Her,* p. 350.
10. Lecture given at the Paulist Center, Boston, MA, winter 1992.
11. Robert J. McClory, "Why Did the Catholic Cross the Road?" in *U.S. Catholic* (vol. 56, No. 1) (January 1991), pp. 6 ff.
12. Ibid., p. 10.

CHAPTER 18. "YOU'RE A WHAT?" CATHOLIC WOMEN AS MINISTERS

Epigraph. The Gospel according to Mark 14:3–9.
1. These comments appeared in another form in an opinion piece I wrote in Boston's archdiocesan newspaper, *The Pilot* (December 11, 1987) titled " 'Vocation shortage?' Nonsense."
2. See *They Call Her Pastor: A New Role for Catholic Women* (Albany, NY: SUNY Press, 1992) by George Washington University professor of sociology Ruth A. Wallace, Ph.D., a sociological study of twenty Catholic parishes throughout the United States headed by women, half of whom are married and half of whom are nuns. All were appointed by their bishops to be primarily responsible for the care of their parishes. These appointments are on the rise around the United States, but still tend to be in poor, isolated, rural parishes.
3. My annual salary in Madison in 1977, the year I began, after three years of graduate study and one other job, was $10,000.
4. Some canonists argue that the new Code of Canon Law may allow for exceptions to this rule, and also point to the fact that since Vatican II, "the legal basis for preaching has shifted from jurisdiction to baptism" (p. 151, and see pp. 134 ff., James H. Provost, "Lay Preaching and Canon Law in a Time of Transition," in Nadine Foley, O.P., ed., *Preaching and the Non-Ordained: An Interdisciplinary Study* (Collegeville, MN: The Liturgical Press, 1983).
5. William H. Shannon, "Are There Any More Priests Out There?" *America* (October 21, 1991), vol. 165, No. 10, pp. 240–242.

CHAPTER 20. THE FUTURE, IN THIS LIFE AND THE NEXT

Epigraph. Dom Helder Camara *The Desert Is Fertile* (Maryknoll, NY: Orbis, 1976).
1. Rosemary Radford Ruether, *Sexism and God-Talk: Toward a Feminist Theology* (Boston: Beacon Press, 1983), p. 258.
2. See Richard McBrien, *Catholicism,* 2 vols. (Minneapolis: Winston Press, 1980), p. 1137 and the Church documents he quotes, the Vatican II *Dogmatic Constitution on the Church* (n. 51) and *Pastoral Constitution on the Church in the Modern World* (n. 39) and the Vatican Congregation for the Doctrine of the Faith's 1979 "Letter on Certain Questions Concerning Eschatology."
3. Krister Stendahl, "Immortality Is Too Much and Too Little," in his *Meanings: The Bible as Document and as Guide* (Philadelphia: Fortress Press, 1984), p. 296.
4. Ibid., p. 197.
5. McBrien, *Catholicism,* p. 1162.
6. Ibid., p. 1159.
7. Leo J. O'Donovan, S.J., "Death as the Depth of Life: A Rereading of Eschatology in *Gaudium et Spes*" in Lucien Richard, O.M.I., Daniel Harrington, S.J., and John W. O'Malley, S.J., eds., *Vatican II: The Unfinished Agenda* (Mahwah, NJ: Paulist Press, 1987), p. 217.
8. Ibid., p. 203.

BIBLIOGRAPHY

Abbot, Walter M., S.J., and Very Rev. Msgr. Joseph Gallagher. *The Documents of Vatican II*. New York: Guild Press, America Press, Association Press, 1966.

Barciauskas, Rosemary Curran, and Debra Beery Hull. *Loving and Working: Reweaving Women's Public and Private Lives*. Bloomington, IN: Meyer-Stone Books, 1989.

Baruch, Grace, Rosalind Barnett, and Caryl Rivers. *Lifeprints: New Patterns of Love and Work for Today's Women*. New York: New American Library, 1985.

Belenky, Mary Field, Blythe McVicker Clincy, Nancy Rule Goldberger, and Jill Mattuck Tarule. *Women's Ways of Knowing: The Development of Self, Voice, and Mind*. New York: Basic Books, 1986.

Bellah, Robert N., Richard Madsen, William M. Sullivan, Ann Swidler, and Steven M. Tipton. *Habits of the Heart: Individualism and Commitment in American Life*. Berkeley, CA: University of California Press, 1985.

————, eds. *Individualism and Commitment in American Life: Readings on the Themes of Habits of the Heart*. New York: Harper & Row, 1987.

Brown, Alden V. *The Grail Movement and American Catholicism 1940–1975*. Notre Dame, IN: Notre Dame Press, 1989.

Brown, Joanne Carlson, and Carole R. Bohn, eds. *Christianity, Patriarchy, and Abuse: A Feminist Critique*. New York: The Pilgrim Press, 1989.

Camara, Dom Helder. *The Desert Is Fertile*. Maryknoll, NY: Orbis Books, 1976.

Cateura, Linda Brandi. *Catholics USA: Makers of a Modern Church*. New York: William Morrow, 1989.

Corn, Alfred, ed. *Contemporary Writers on the New Testament: Incarnation*. New York: Viking Press, 1990.

Cox, Harvey. *The Silencing of Leonardo Boff: The Vatican and the Future of World Christianity*. Oak Park, IL: Meyer-Stone Books, 1988.

Cunneen, Sally. *Mother Church: What the Experience of Women Is Teaching Her*. Mahwah, NJ: Paulist Press, 1991.

————. *Sex: Female; Religion: Catholic*. New York: Holt, Rinehart and Winston, 1968.

Curb, Rosemary, and Nancy Manahan, eds. *Lesbian Nuns: Breaking Silence*. [no city given] The Naiad Press, 1985.

DeMott, Benjamin. *The Imperial Middle: Why Americans Can't Think Straight About Class*. William Morrow, 1990.

Dodson Gray, Elizabeth, ed. *Sacred Dimensions of Women's Experience*. Wellesley, MA: Roundtable Press, 1988.

Dolan, Jay P. *The American Catholic Experience: A History from Colonial Times to the Present.* Garden City, NY: Doubleday/Image Books, 1985, 1987.

———, ed. *The American Catholic Parish. Volume I, The Northeast, Southeast and South Central States: A History from 1850 to the Present.* Mahwah, NJ: Paulist Press, 1987.

———, ed. *The American Catholic Parish. Volume II, The Pacific, Intermountain West and Midwest States.* Mahwah, NJ: Paulist Press, 1987.

Eck, Diana L., and Devaki Jain. *Speaking of Faith: Global Perspectives on Women, Religion and Social Change.* Philadelphia, PA: New Society Publishers, 1987.

Farley, Margaret A. *Personal Commitments: Beginning, Keeping, Changing.* San Francisco, CA: Harper & Row, 1990.

Feraro, Barbara, Patricia Hussey, with Jane O'Reilly. *No Turning Back: Two Nuns' Battle with the Vatican over Women's Right to Choose.* New York: Poseidon Press, 1990.

Fischer, Kathleen. *Women at the Well: Feminist Perspectives on Spiritual Direction.* Mahwah, NJ: Paulist Press, 1988.

Foley, Nadine, O.P. *Preaching and the Non-Ordained: An Interdisciplinary Study.* Collegeville, MN: The Liturgical Press, 1983.

Fowler, James W. *Stages of Faith: The Psychology of Human Development and the Quest for Meaning.* San Francisco, CA: Harper & Row, 1981.

Gallup, George, Jr., and Jim Castelli. *The American Catholic People: Their Beliefs, Practices, and Values.* Garden City, NY: Doubleday, 1987.

Garreau, Joel. *The Nine Nations of North America.* New York: Avon, 1982.

Giddings, Paula. *When and Where I Enter: The Impact of Black Women on Race and Sex in America.* New York: William Morrow, 1984.

Gilligan, Carol. *In a Different Voice: Psychological Theory and Women's Development.* Cambridge, MA: Harvard University Press, 1982.

Glazier, Michael, ed. *Where We Are: American Catholics in the 1980's. A Celebration for Philip Scharper.* Wilmington, DE: Michael Glazier, 1985.

Greeley, Andrew M. *The Irish Americans: The Rise to Money and Power.* New York: Warner Books, 1981.

———. *The Catholic Myth: The Behavior and Beliefs of American Catholics.* New York: Charles Scribner's Sons, 1990.

——— and Mary Greeley Durkin. *How To Save the Catholic Church.* New York: Elizabeth Sifton Books, Viking, 1984.

Gremillion, Joseph, and Jim Castelli. *The Emerging Parish: The Notre Dame Study of Catholic Life Since Vatican II.* San Francisco, CA: Harper & Row, 1987.

Haughton, Rosemary. *The Catholic Thing.* Springfield, IL: Templegate, 1979.

Heilbrun, Carolyn. *Writing a Woman's Life.* New York: W.W. Norton, 1988.

Hellwig, Monika K. *Jesus: The Compassion of God*. Wilmington, DE: Michael Glazier, 1983.

———. *Understanding Catholicism*. Ramsey, NJ: Paulist Press, 1981.

Henriot, Peter J., Edward P. DeBerri, and Michael J. Schultheis. *Catholic Social Teaching: Our Best Kept Secret*. Maryknoll, NY: Orbis/Collins Dove, 1990.

Hoge, Dean. *Future of Catholic Leadership: Responses to the Priest Shortage*. Kansas City, MO: Sheed & Ward, 1987.

Holland, Joe, and Ann Barsanti, eds. *American and Catholic: The New Debate*. South Orange, NJ: Pillar Books, 1988.

Hunt, Mary E. *Fierce Tenderness: A Feminist Theology of Friendship*. New York: Crossroad, 1991.

Isasi-Diaz, Ada Maria and Yolanda Tarango. *Hispanic Women: Prophetic Voice in the Church*. San Francisco: Harper & Row, 1988.

Kaufman, Philip S. *Why You Can Disagree—And Remain a Faithful Catholic*. Bloomington, IN: Meyer-Stone Books, 1989.

Kavanaugh, John F., photos by Mev Puleo. *Faces of Poverty, Faces of Christ*. Maryknoll, NY: Orbis Books, 1991.

Kenneally, James K. *The History of American Catholic Women*. New York: Crossroad, 1990.

Kennedy, Eugene. *Re-Imagining American Catholicism: The American Bishops and Their Pastoral Letters*. New York: Vintage Books, 1985.

———. *Tomorrow's Catholics, Yesterday's Church*. San Francisco: Harper & Row, 1990.

Kilcourse, George, ed. *Catholic Theology in North American Context: Essays on the Theme and with an Introduction by Monika K. Hellwig*. The Catholic Theological Society of America, 1987.

Kolbenschlag, Madonna. *Lost in the Land of Oz: The Search for Identity and Community in American Life*. San Francisco: Harper & Row, 1988.

Le Guin, Ursula K. *Dancing at the Edge of the World: Thoughts on Words, Women, Places*. New York: Grove Press, 1989

Lernoux, Penny. *People of God: The Struggle for World Catholicism*. London: Penguin Books, 1989.

Lorde, Audre. *Sister Outsider: Essays and Speeches by Audre Lorde*. Freedom, CA: The Crossing Press, 1984.

Lukas, J. Anthony. *Common Ground*. New York: Vintage Books, 1986.

Luker, Kristin. *Abortion and the Politics of Motherhood*. Berkeley, CA: University of California Press, 1984.

McCarthy, Abigail. *Private Faces, Public Places*. Garden City, NY: Doubleday, 1972.

McGoldrick, Monica, John K. Pearce, and Joseph Giordano, eds. *Ethnicity and Family Therapy*. New York: The Guilford Press, 1982.

McGrath, Sr. A. M. *Women and the Church*. Garden City, NY: Image Books, 1976.

Meehan, Francis X. *A Contemporary Social Spirituality*. Maryknoll, NY: Orbis Books, 1983.

Milhaven, Annie Lally, ed. *The Inside Stories: 13 Valiant Women Challenging the Church*. Mystic, CT: Twenty-Third Publications, 1987.

Miller, Jean Baker. *Toward a New Psychology of Women,* 2nd ed. Boston: Beacon Press, 1980.

Mooney, Catherine M., RSCJ. *Philippine Duchesne: A Woman with the Poor*. Mahwah, NJ: Paulist Press, 1990.

Murphy, Margaret. *How Catholic Women Have Changed*. Kansas City, MO: Sheed & Ward, 1987.

Neal, Marie Augusta, SND de Namur. *Catholic Sisters in Transition: From the 1960s to the 1980s*. Wilmington, DE: Michael Glazier, 1984.

———. *From Nuns to Sisters: An Expanding Vocation*. Mystic, CT: Twenty-Third Publications, 1990.

———. *The Just Demands of the Poor: Essays in Socio-Theology*. Mahwah, NJ: Paulist Press, 1987.

Neuhaus, Richard John. *The Catholic Moment: The Paradox of the Church in the Post-modern World*. San Francisco, CA: Harper & Row, 1987.

O'Brien, David J., and Thomas A. Shannon. *Renewing the Earth: Catholic Documents on Peace, Justice and Liberation*. Garden City, NY: Doubleday/Image Books, 1977.

Occhiogrosso, Peter. *Once a Catholic: Prominent Catholics and Ex-Catholics Discuss the Influence of the Church on Their Lives and Work*. Boston, MA: Houghton Mifflin, 1987.

O'Keefe, Mark, OSB. *What Are They Saying About Social Sin?* Mahwah, NJ: Paulist Press, 1990.

Osiek, Carolyn, RSCJ. *Beyond Anger: On Being a Feminist in the Church*. Mahwah, NJ: Paulist Press, 1986.

Plaskow, Judith, and Carol P. Christ, eds. *Weaving the Visions: New Patterns in Feminist Spirituality*. San Francisco, CA: Harper & Row, 1989.

Randour, Mary Lou. *Women's Psyche, Women's Spirit: The Reality of Relationships*. New York: Columbia University Press, 1987.

Ravitch, Diane, ed. *The American Reader: Words That Moved a Nation*. New York: Harper-Collins, 1990.

Richard, Lucien, OMI, Daniel Harrington, SJ, and John W. O'Malley, SJ., eds. *Vatican II, The Unfinished Agenda: A Look to the Future*. Mahwah, NJ: Paulist Press, 1987.

Rivers, Caryl. *Occasional Sins*. New York: Pocket Books, 1973.

Ruddick, Sara. *Maternal Thinking: Toward a Politics of Peace*. Boston, MA: Beacon Press, 1989.

Ruether, Rosemary Radford. *Contemporary Roman Catholicism: Crises and Challenges*. Kansas City, MO: Sheed & Ward, 1987.

———. *Sexism and God-Talk: Toward a Feminist Theology*. Boston: Beacon Press, 1983.

Schneiders, Sandra M. *Beyond Patching: Faith and Feminism in the Catholic Church*. Mahwah, NJ: Paulist Press, 1991.

Schüssler Fiorenza, Elisabeth, and Mary Collins. *Women: Invisible in Church and Theology. Concilium* Edinburgh, Scotland: T. & T. Clark, 1985.

Stendahl, Krister. *Meanings: The Bible as Document and as Guide*. Philadelphia, PA: Fortress Press, 1984.

Tannen, Deborah. *You Just Don't Understand: Women and Men in Conversation*. New York: William Morrow, 1990.

de Tocqueville, Alexis. *Democracy in America*. Specially edited and abridged for the modern reader by Richard D. Heffner. New York: New American Library, 1956.

Toolan, David. *Facing West from California's Shores: A Jesuit's Journey into New Age Consciousness*. New York: Crossroad, 1987.

Ware, Ann Patrick, ed. *Midwives of the Future: American Sisters Tell Their Story*. Kansas City, MO: Leaven Press, 1986.

Weaver, Mary Jo. *New Catholic Women: A Contemporary Challenge to Traditional Religious Authority*. San Francisco, CA: Harper & Row, 1985.

Zanotti, Barbara, ed. *A Faith of One's Own: Explorations by Catholic Lesbians*. Trumansburg, NY: The Crossing Press, 1986.

Zinsser, William, ed. *Spiritual Quests: The Art and Craft of Religious Writing*. Boston: Houghton Mifflin, 1988.

INDEX